ROANOKE COUNTY PUBLIC LIBRARY
HOLLINS BRANCH LIBRARY
ROANOKE, VA 24019

S0-BAI-508

Contents

ARISA

Chapter 31: Lost Time   ...4

Chapter 32: Memory's
Truth   ...43

Chapter 33: Betrayal   ...82

Chapter 34: False
Embrace   ...122

Secret King's Room

The story so far

Tsubasa and Arisa are twin sisters separated by their parents' divorce. They finally reunited after three years of being apart, but their happy time together came to a sudden end when Arisa jumped out her bedroom window right in front of Tsubasa, leaving behind a mysterious card...

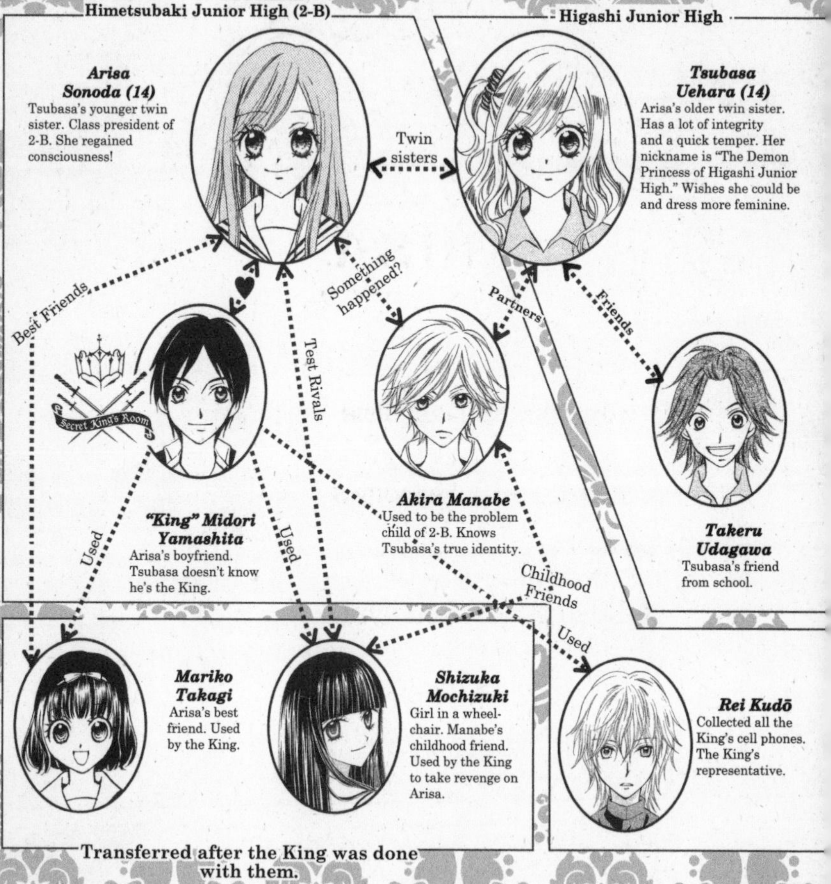
Himetsubaki Junior High (2-B)
Higashi Junior High
Arisa Sonoda (14)
Tsubasa's younger twin sister. Class president of 2-B. She regained consciousness!
Twin sisters
Tsubasa Uehara (14)
Arisa's older twin sister. Has a lot of integrity and a quick temper. Her nickname is "The Demon Princess of Higashi Junior High." Wishes she could be and dress more feminine.
Best Friends
Something happened?
Partners
Friends
Test Rivals
Secret King's Room
Akira Manabe
Used to be the problem child of 2-B. Knows Tsubasa's true identity.
Takeru Udagawa
Tsubasa's friend from school.
"King" Midori Yamashita
Arisa's boyfriend. Tsubasa doesn't know he's the King.
Used
Used
Childhood Friends
Used
Mariko Takagi
Arisa's best friend. Used by the King.
Shizuka Mochizuki
Girl in a wheelchair. Manabe's childhood friend. Used by the King to take revenge on Arisa.
Rei Kudō
Collected all the King's cell phones. The King's representative.
Transferred after the King was done with them.

In order to discover the secrets Arisa was hiding, Tsubasa pretended to be her and attended Himetsubaki Junior High. In Class 2-B, a mysterious internet presence called "The King" led to strange incidents and bullying.

The King's representative, Kudō, manipulated the class out of fear. He was trying to make them the best class in the world. Things got out of hand, and they ended up murdering someone. Midori suggested they hide the body. Tsubasa's true identity was revealed, enraging Class 2-B, who locked her in a basement. Tsubasa has no idea Midori was behind everything! She managed to escape and rushed to the hospital, where Arisa finally woke up from her coma!

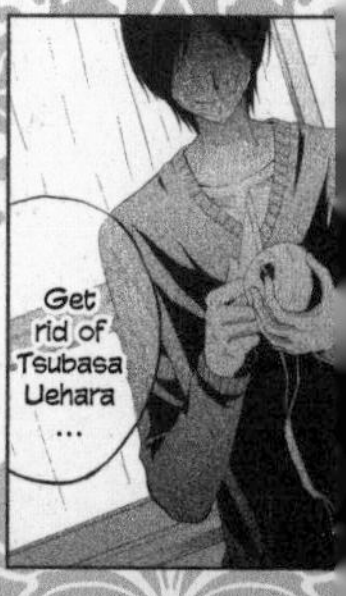
Get rid of Tsubasa Uehara ...

Chapter 31: Lost Time

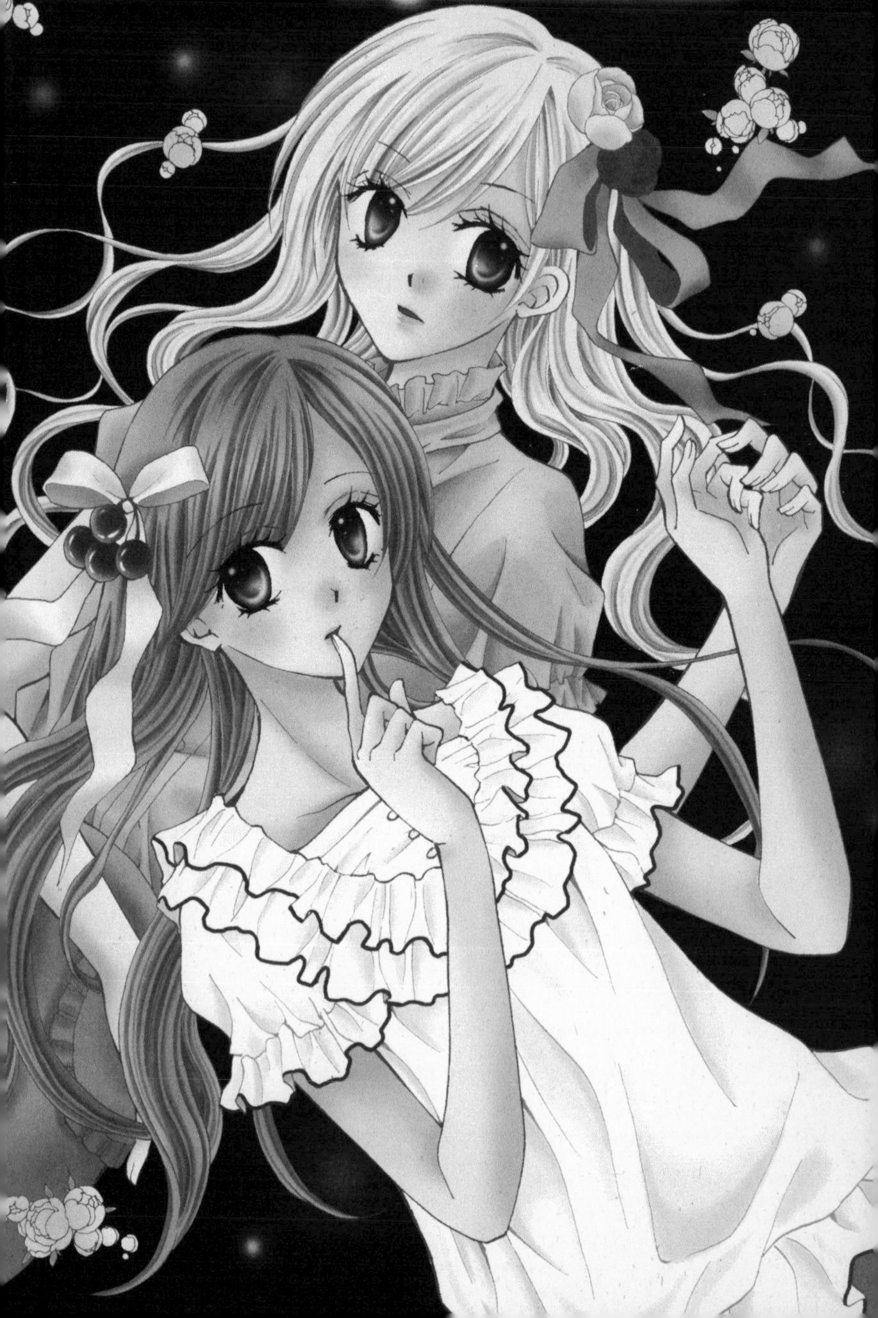

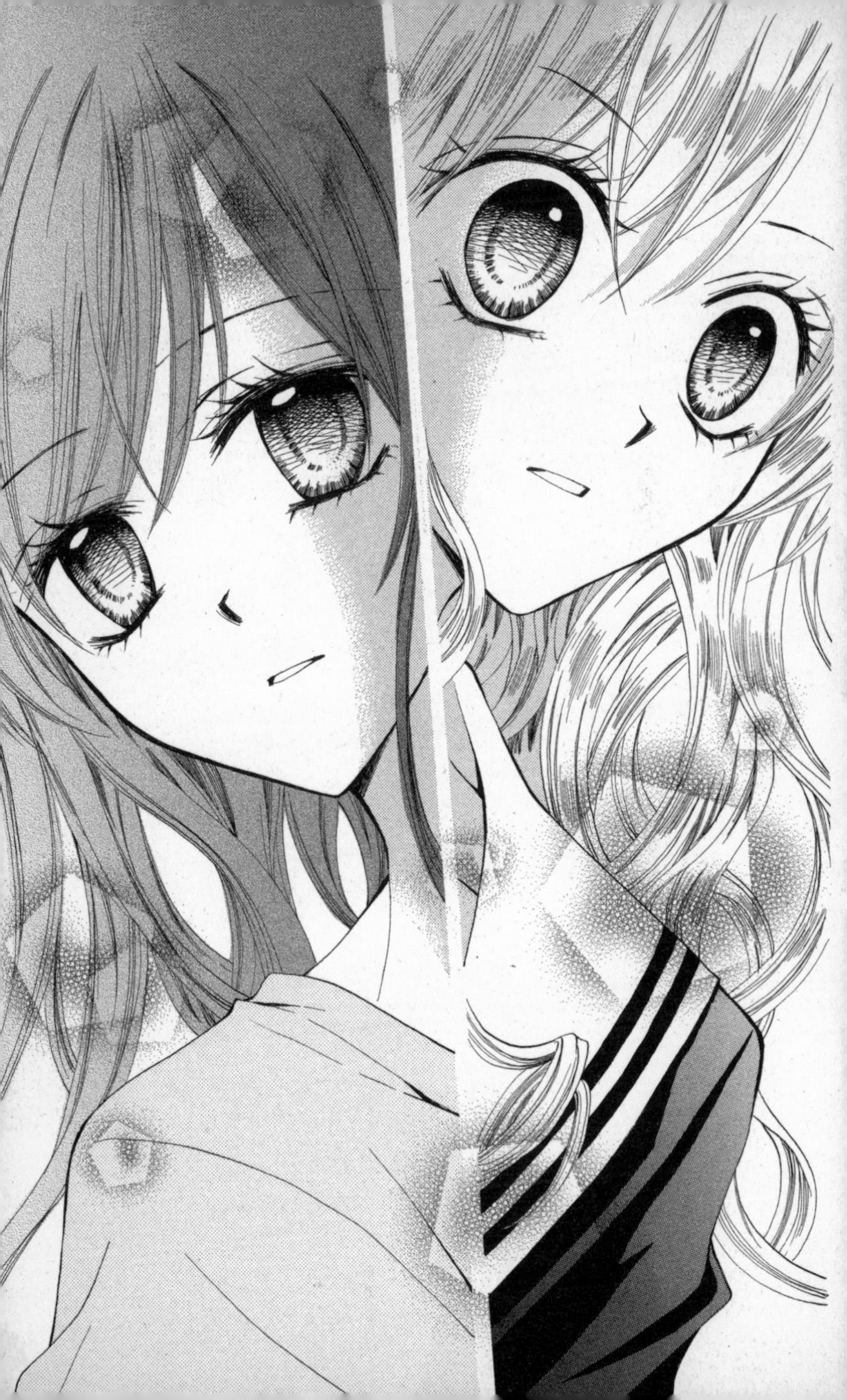

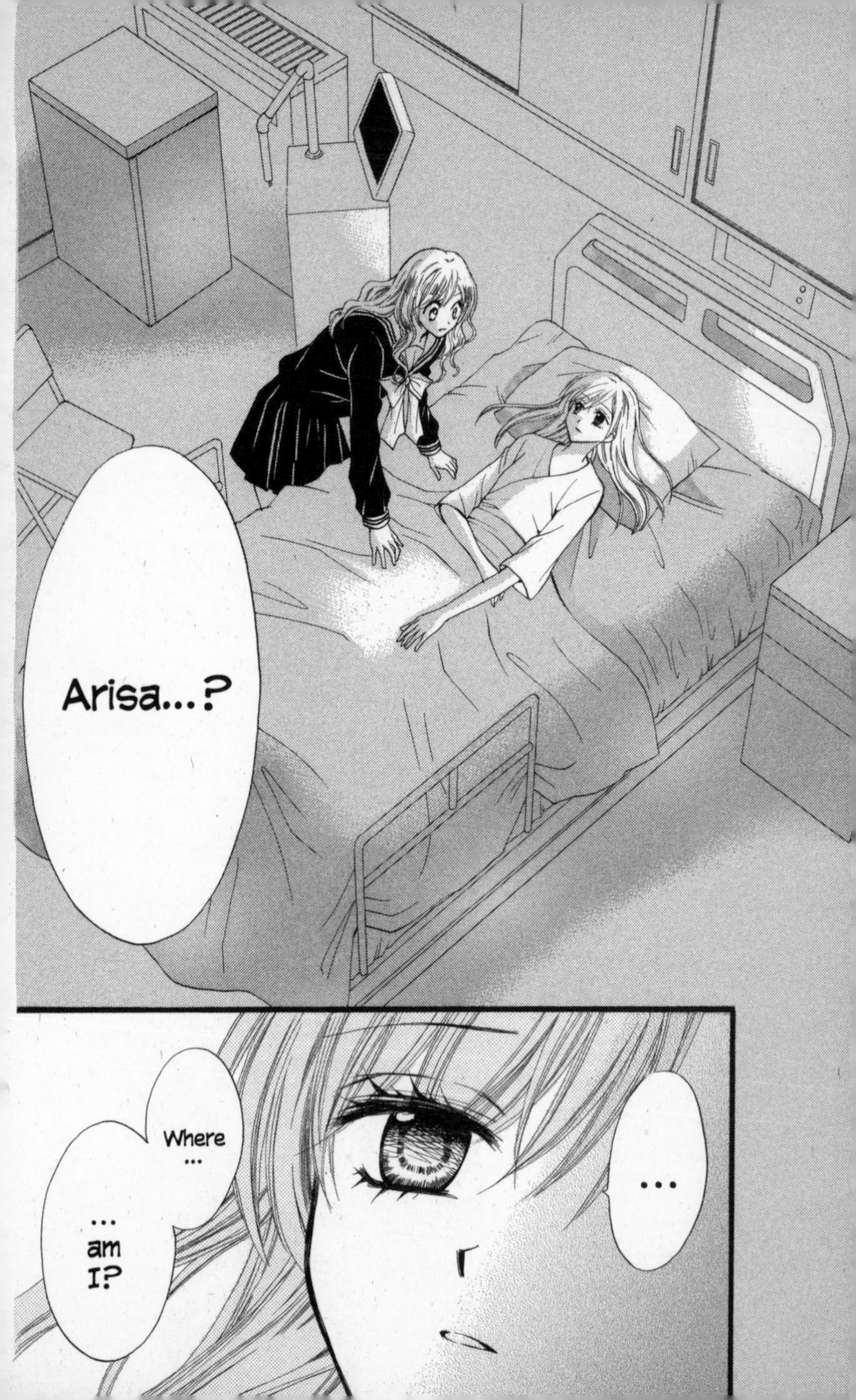
Arisa...?
...
Where ...
... am I?

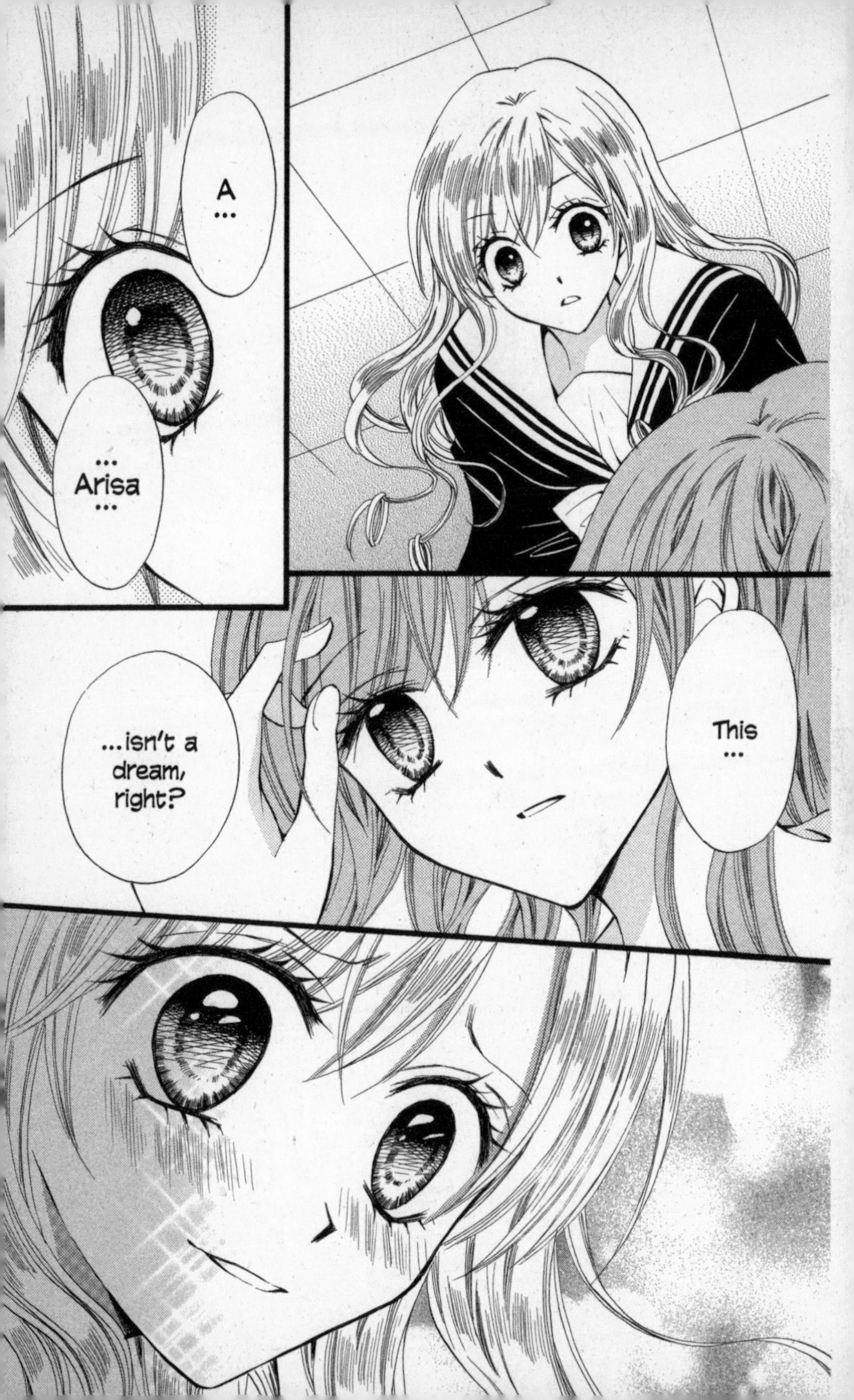
A...
...Arisa...
This...
...isn't a dream, right?

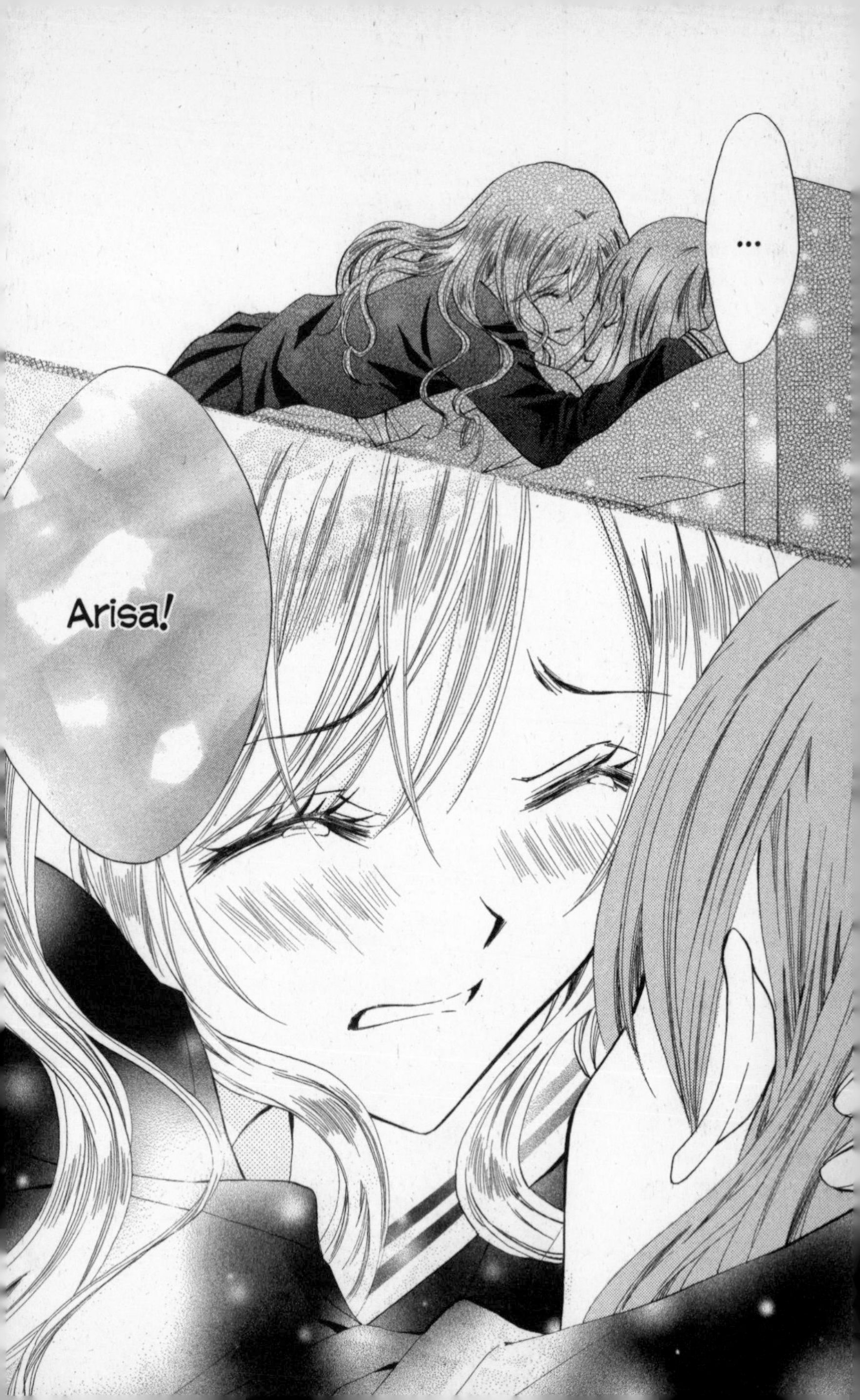
...
Arisa!

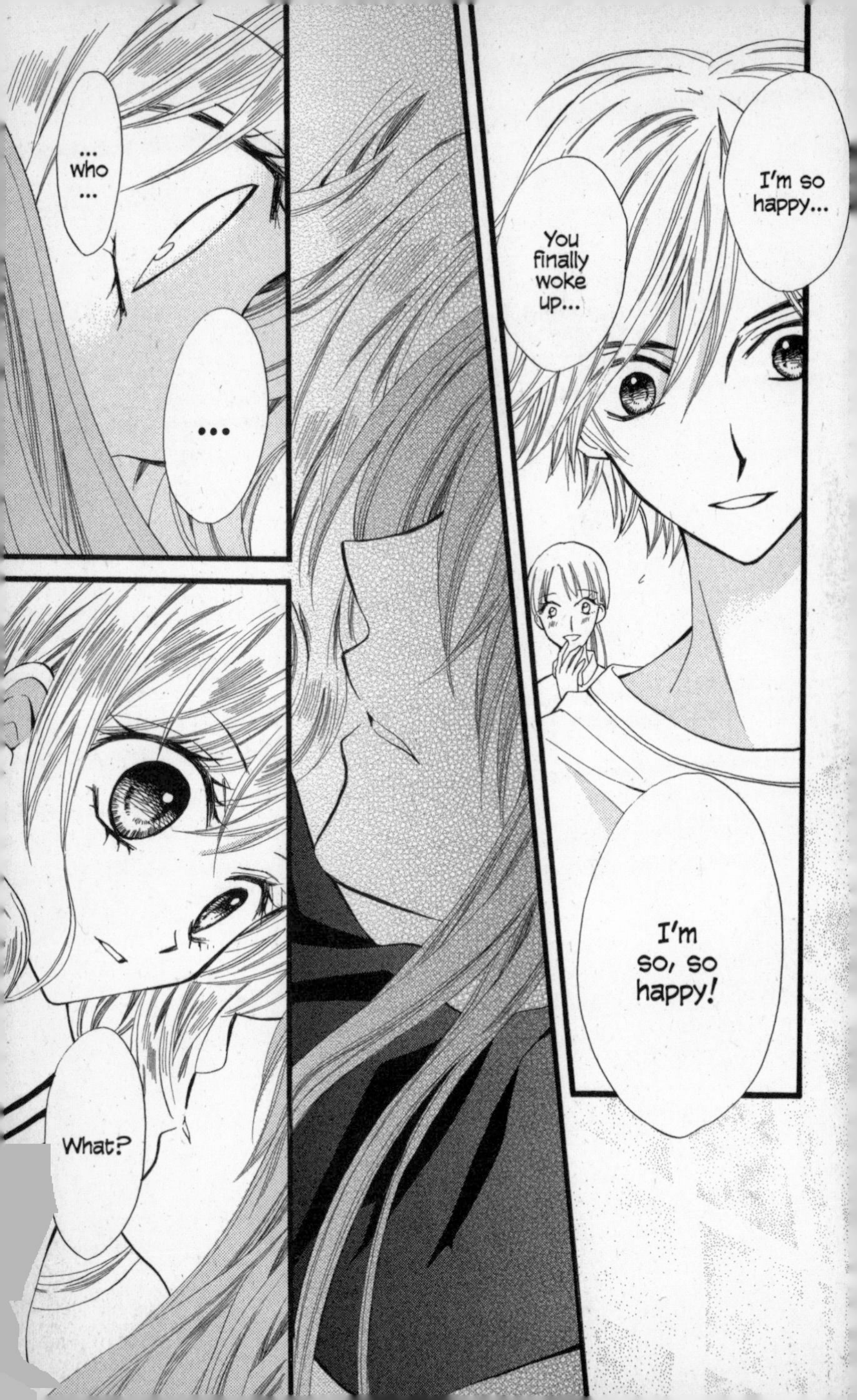
I'm so happy...
You finally woke up...
I'm so, so happy!
... who ...
...
What?

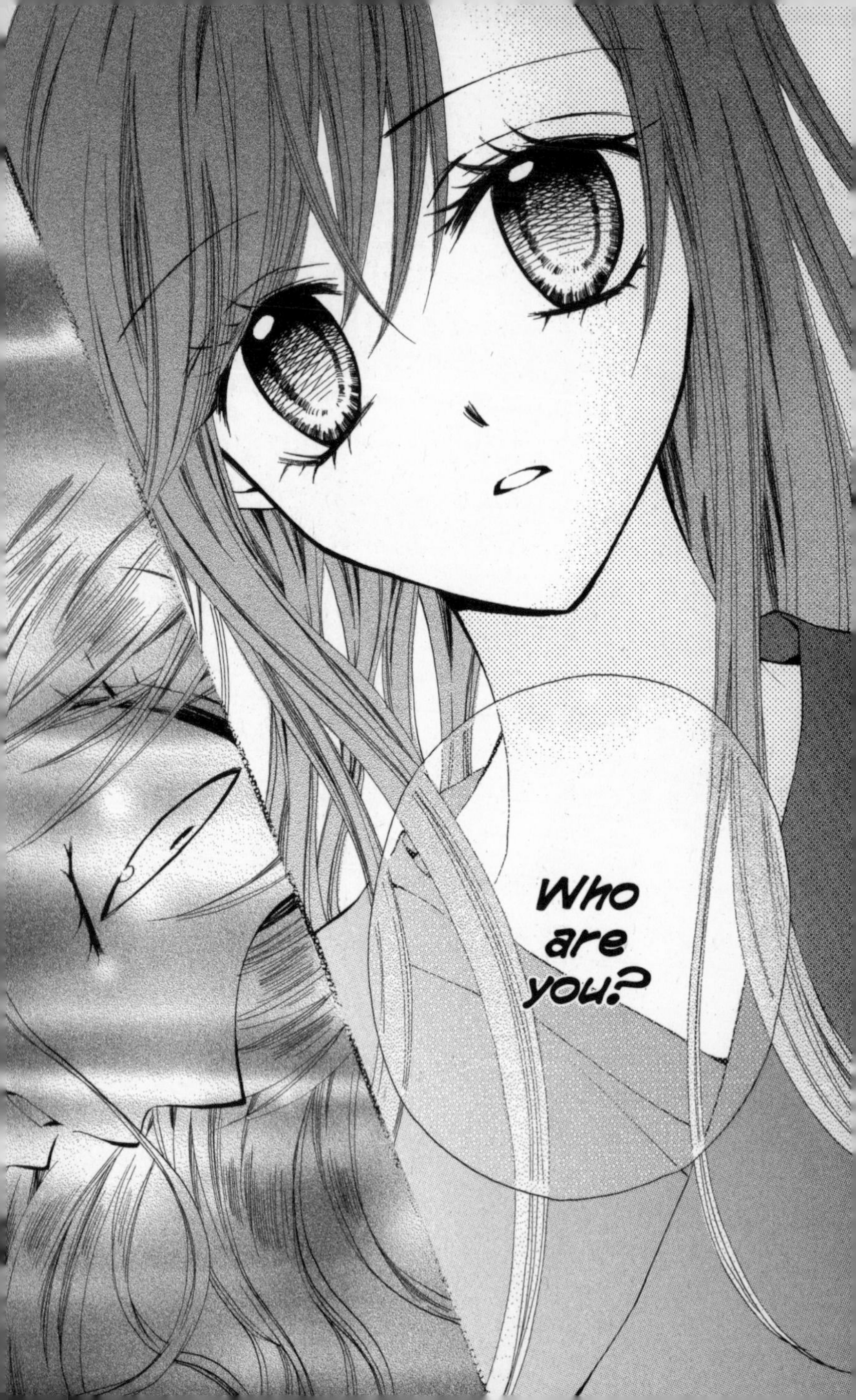
Who are you?

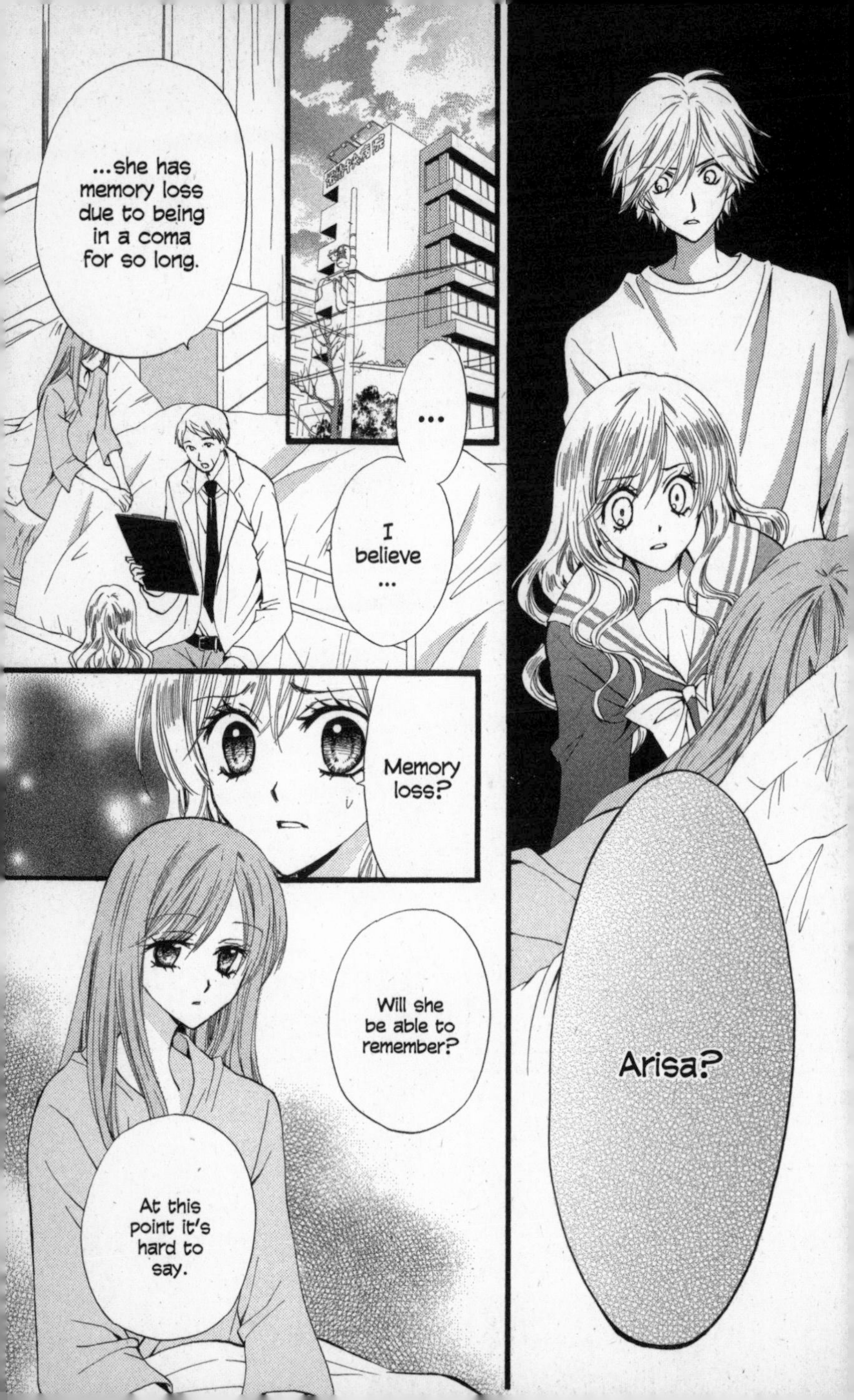
Arisa?
...
I believe ...
...she has memory loss due to being in a coma for so long.
Memory loss?
Will she be able to remember?
At this point it's hard to say.

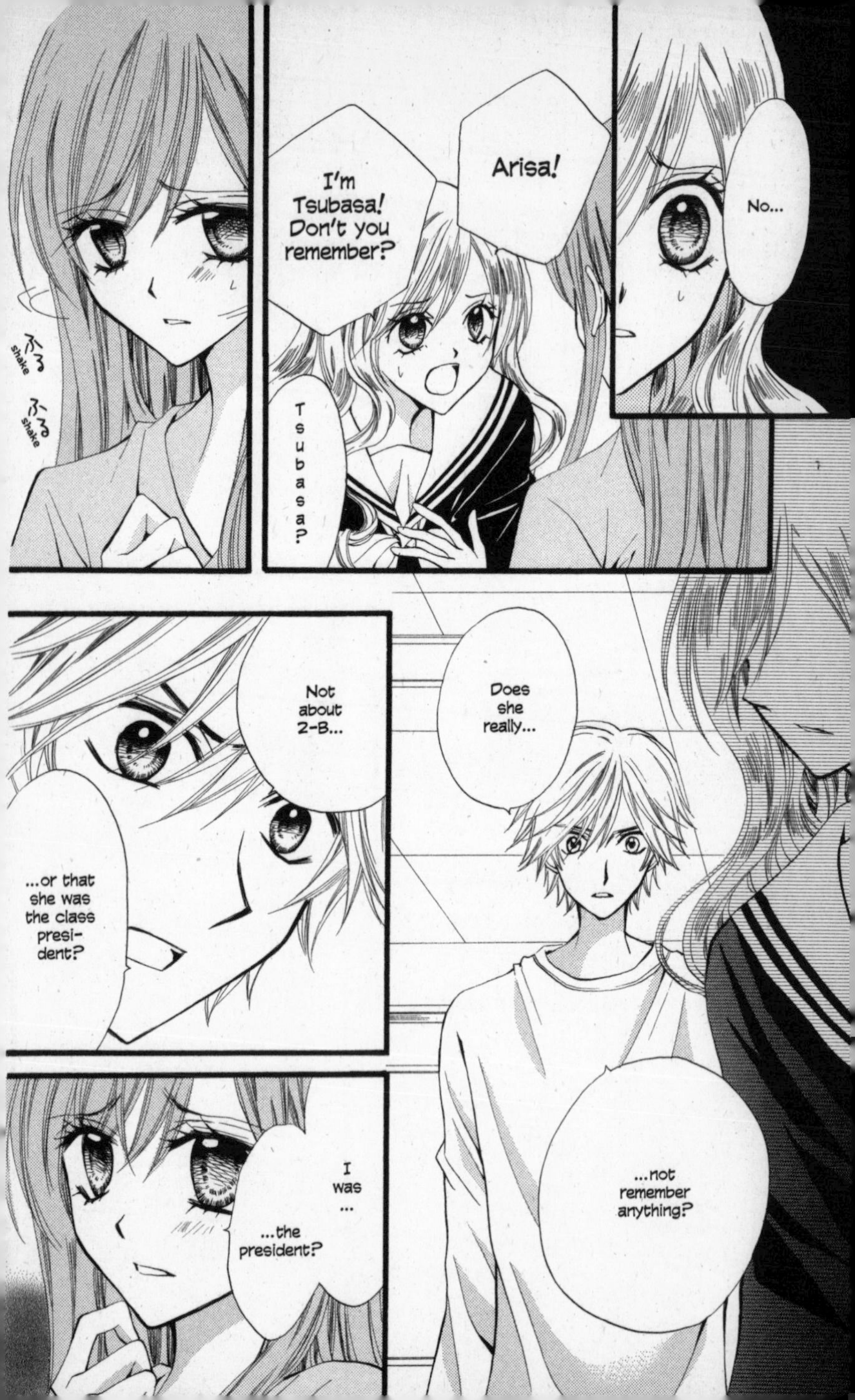
No...
Arisa!
I'm Tsubasa! Don't you remember?
Tsubasa?
ふる shake
ふる shake
Does she really...
...not remember anything?
Not about 2-B...
...or that she was the class presi-dent?
I was ...
...the president?

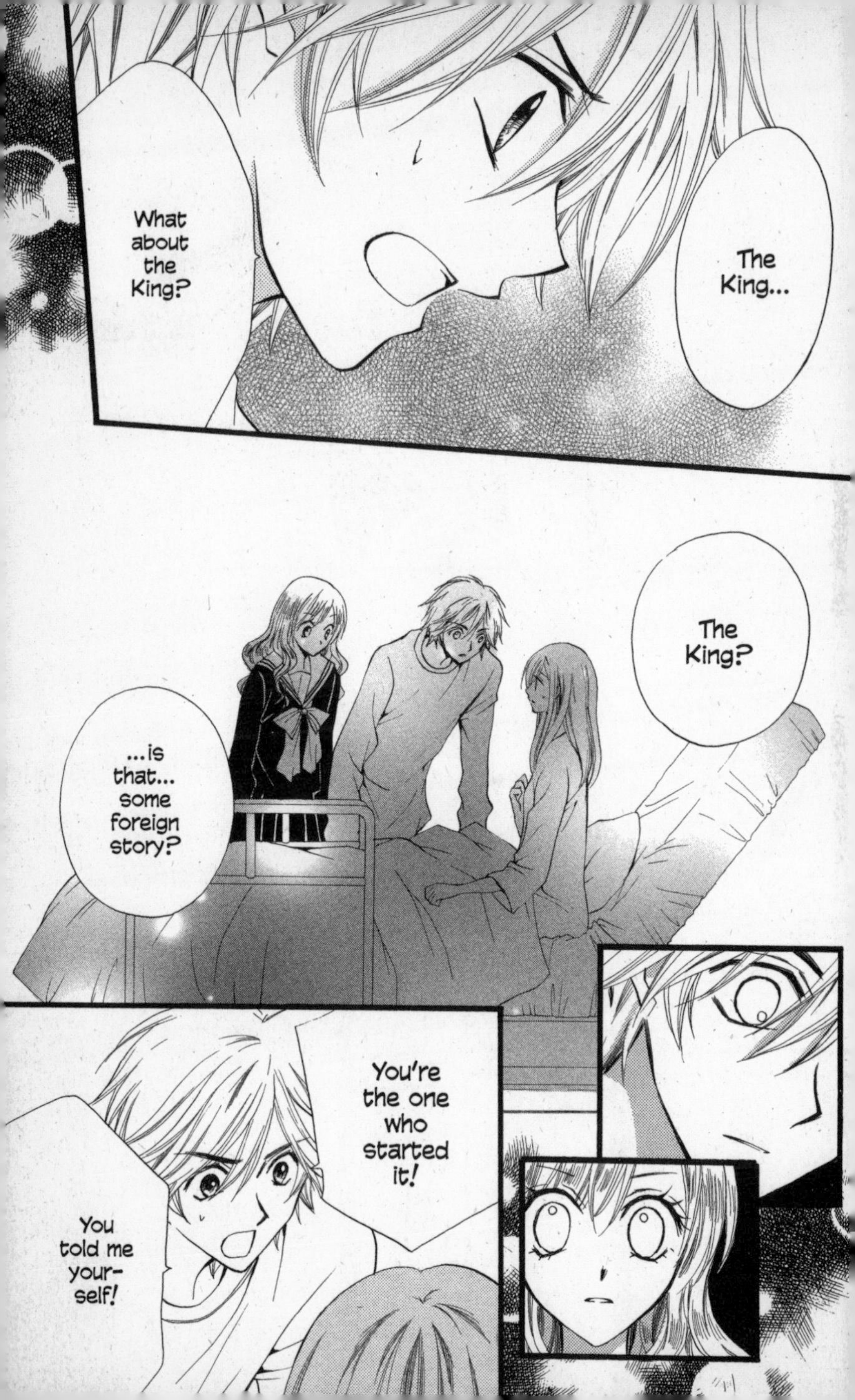
The King...
What about the King?
The King?
...is that... some foreign story?
You're the one who started it!
You told me your-self!

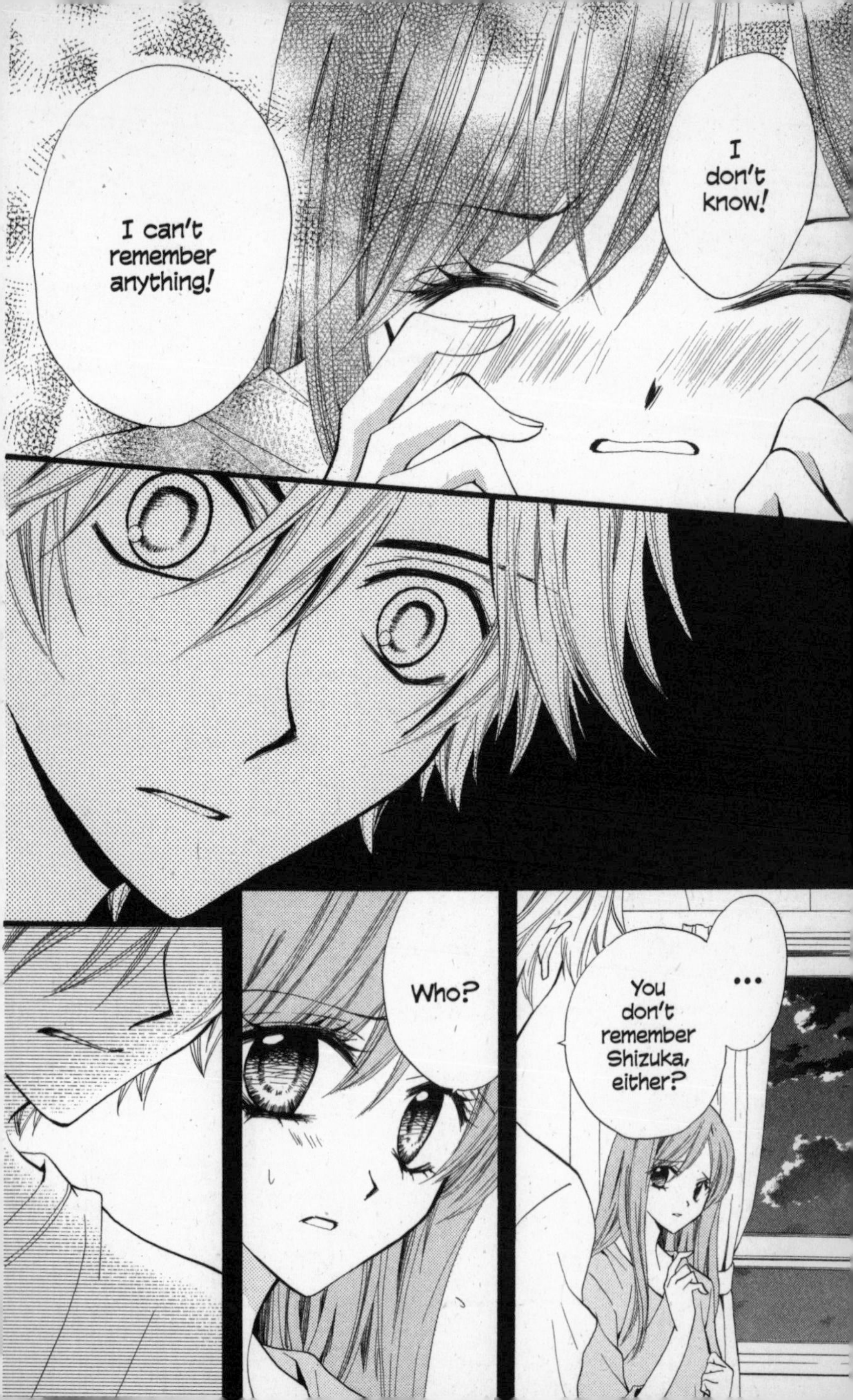
I don't know!
I can't remember anything!
...
You don't remember Shizuka, either?
Who?

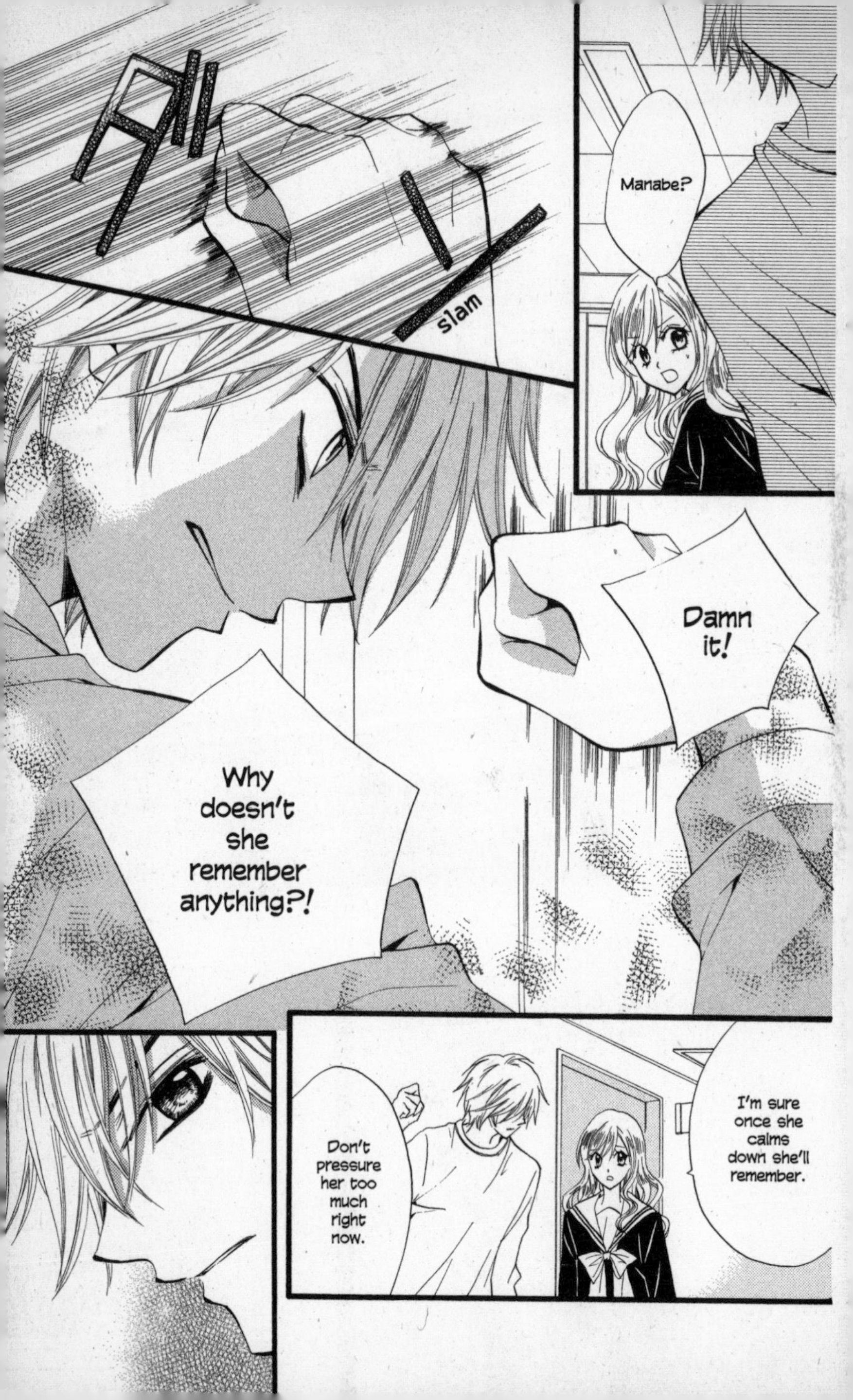
Manabe?
slam
Damn it!
Why doesn't she remember anything?!
I'm sure once she calms down she'll remember.
Don't pressure her too much right now.

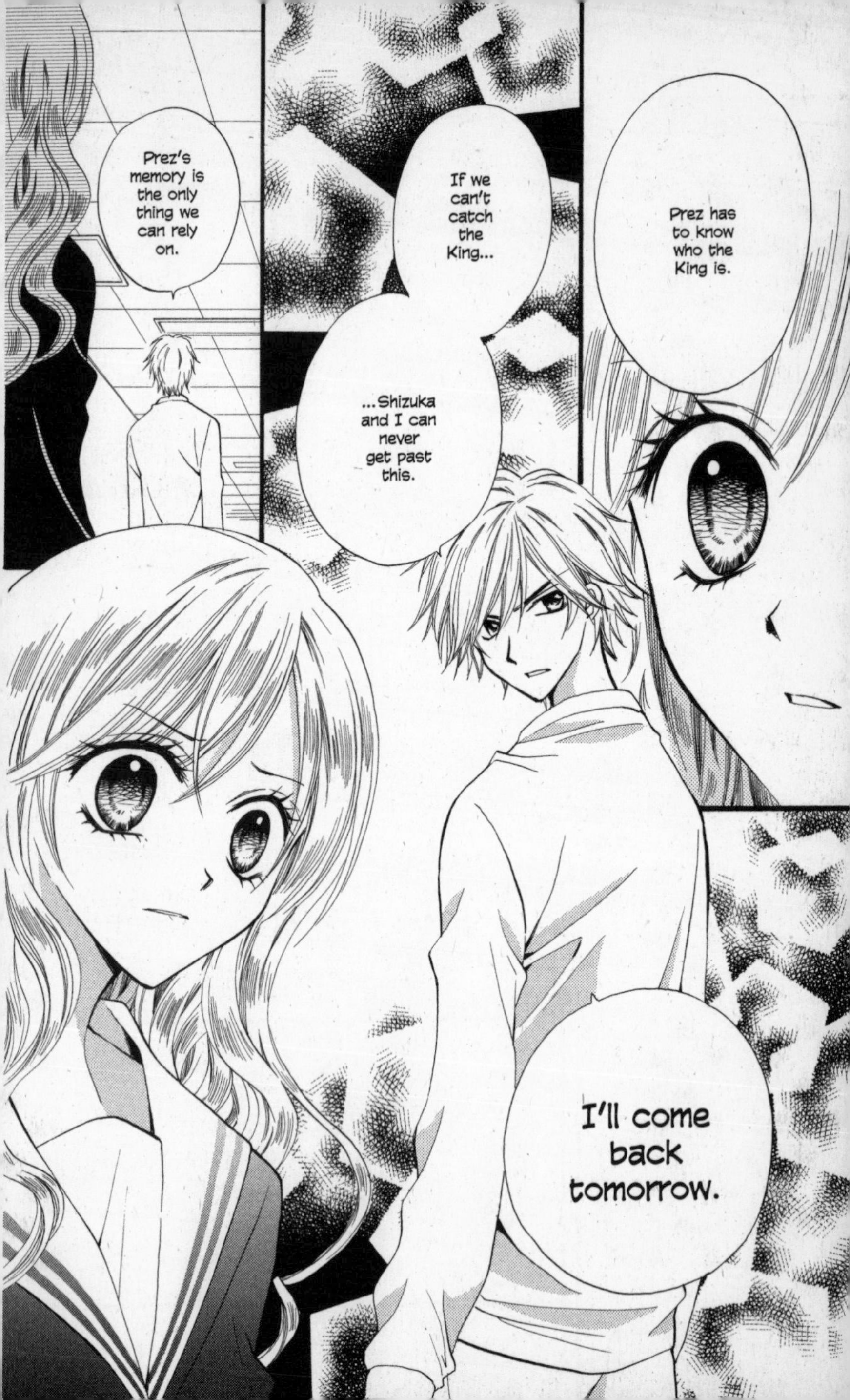
Prez has to know who the King is.
If we can't catch the King...
...Shizuka and I can never get past this.
Prez's memory is the only thing we can rely on.
I'll come back tomorrow.

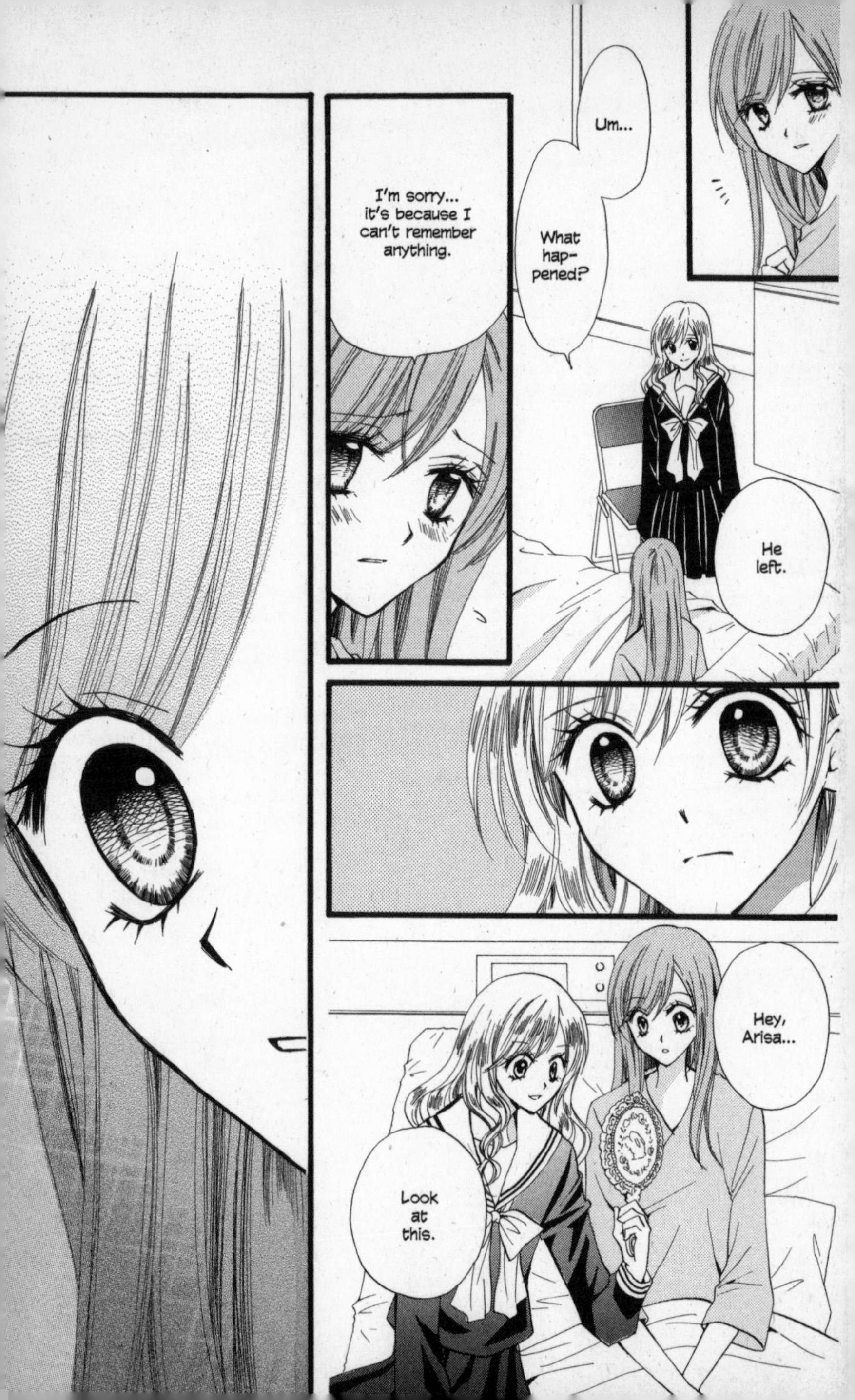

Um...
What happened?
He left.
I'm sorry... it's because I can't remember anything.
Hey, Arisa...
Look at this.

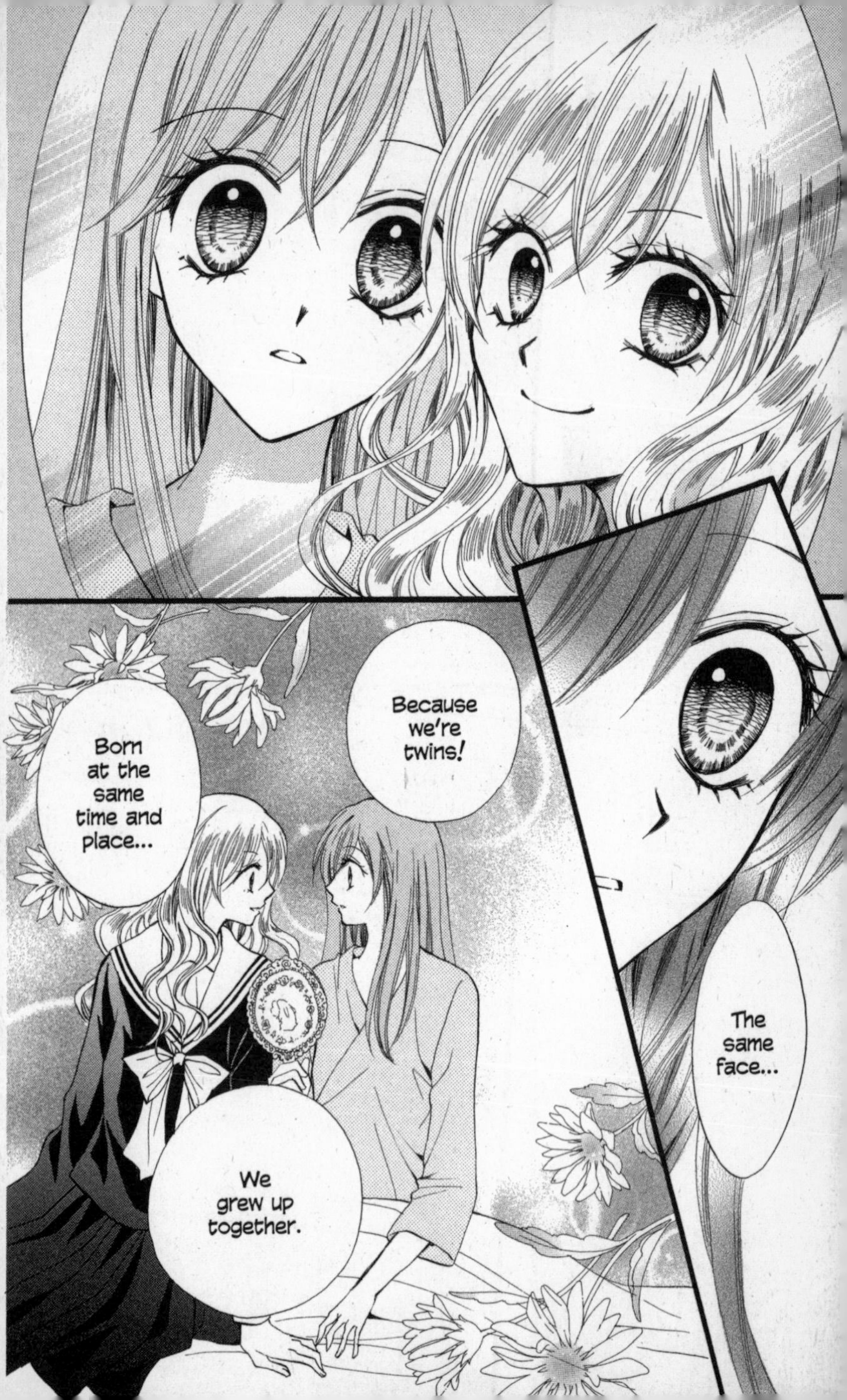
The same face...
Because we're twins!
Born at the same time and place...
We grew up together.

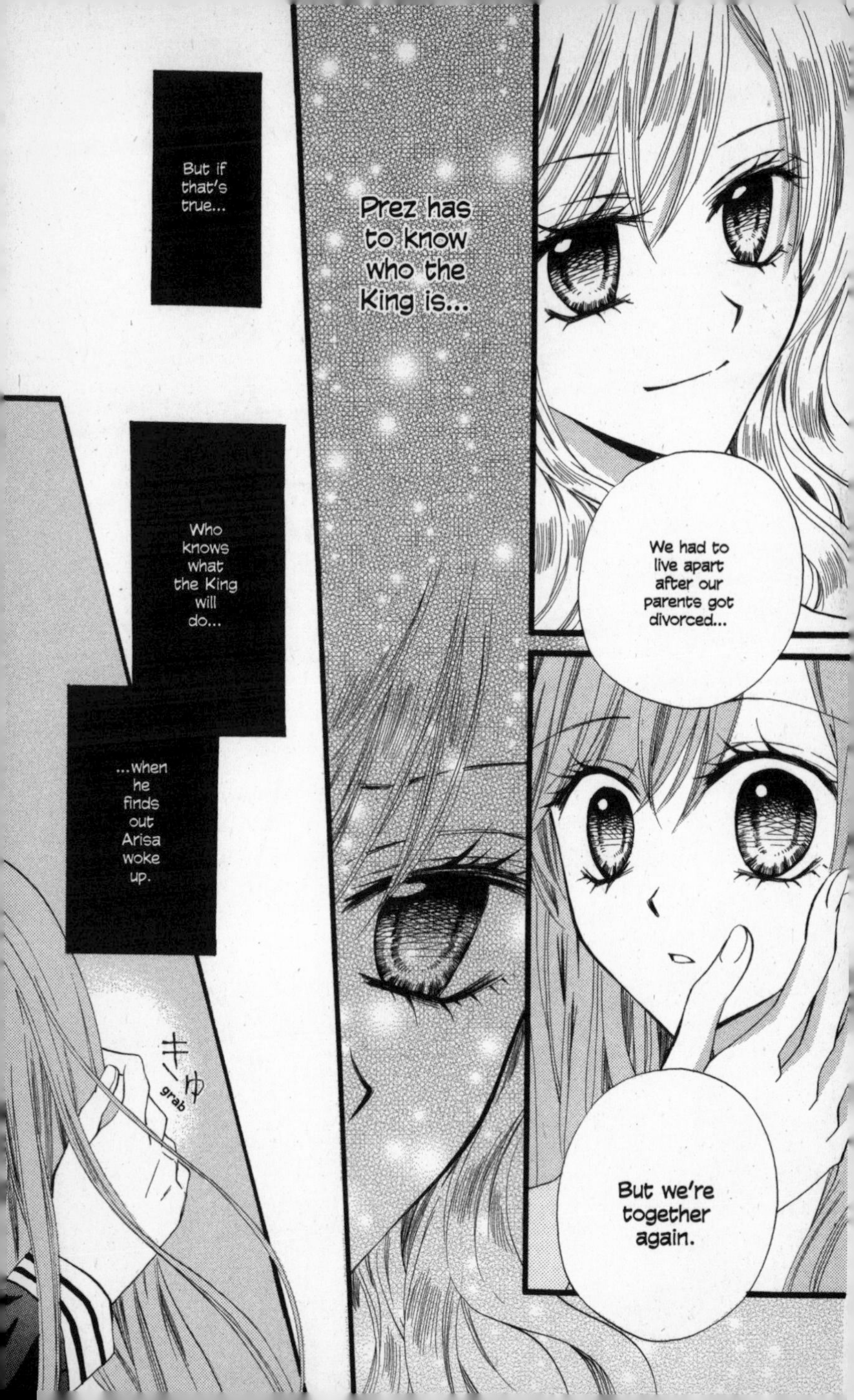
We had to live apart after our parents got divorced...
But we're together again.
Prez has to know who the King is...
But if that's true...
Who knows what the King will do...
...when he finds out Arisa woke up.
キュ
grab

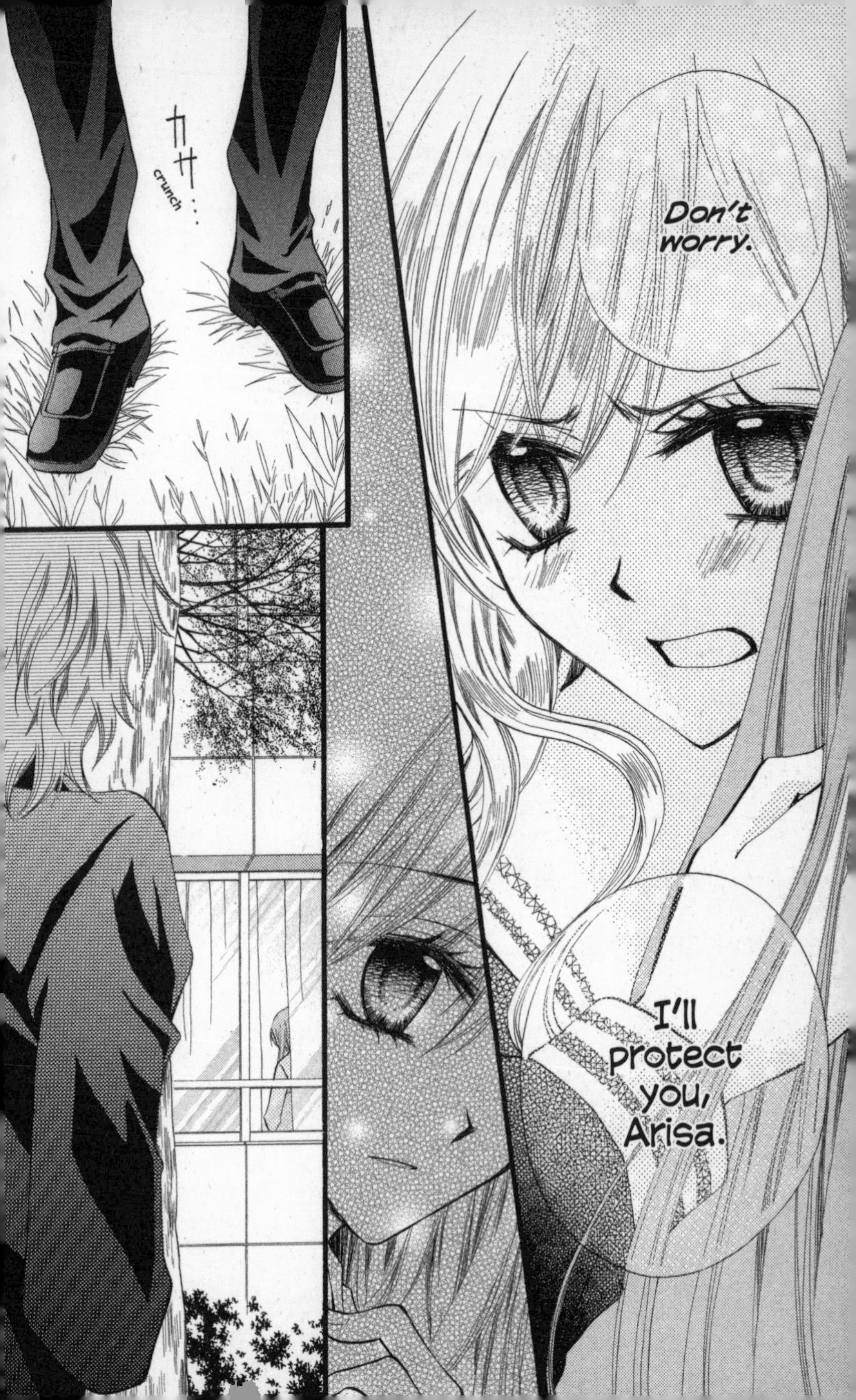
Don't worry.
I'll protect you, Arisa.
カサ…
crunch

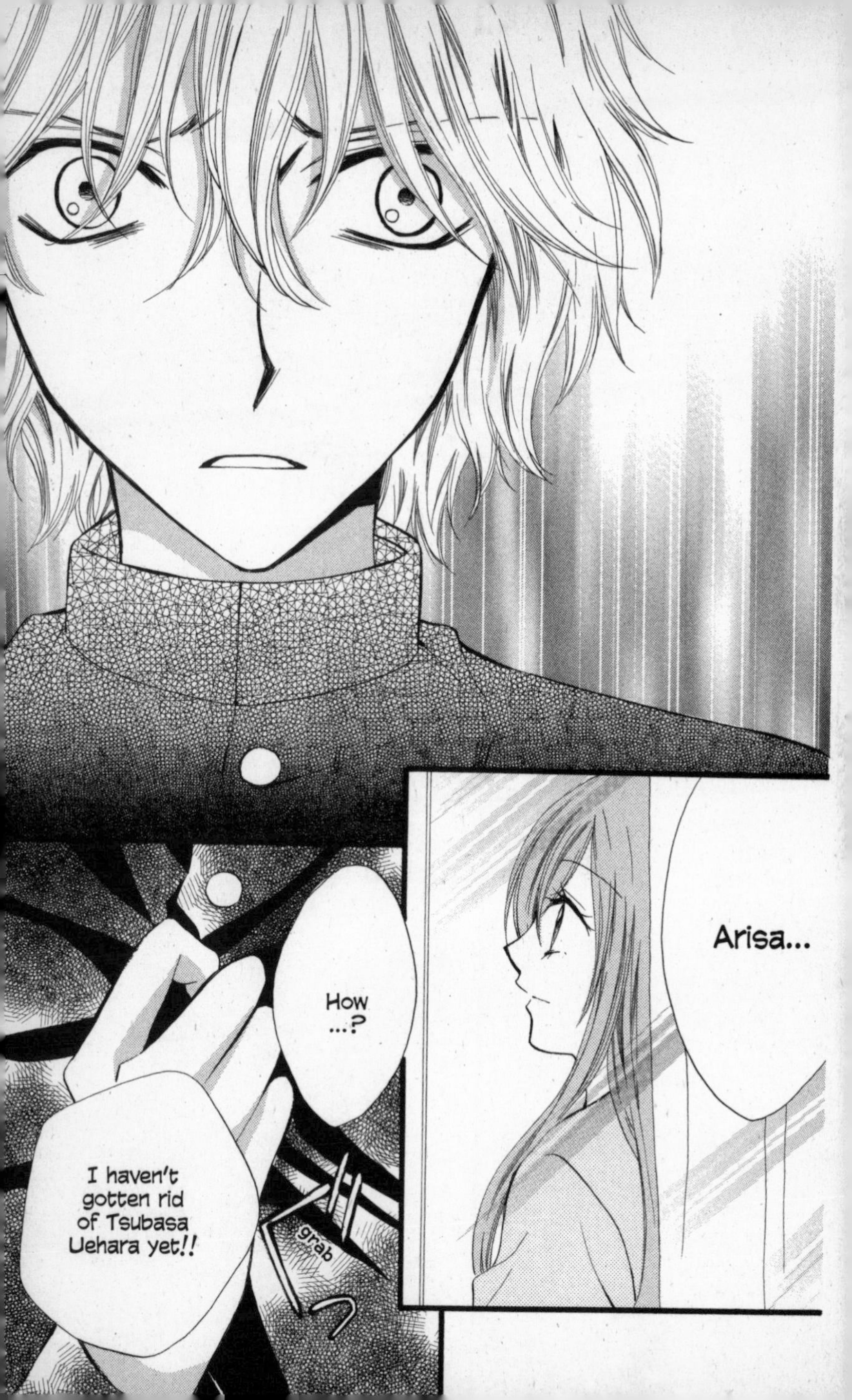
Arisa...
How ...?
I haven't gotten rid of Tsubasa Uehara yet!!
grab

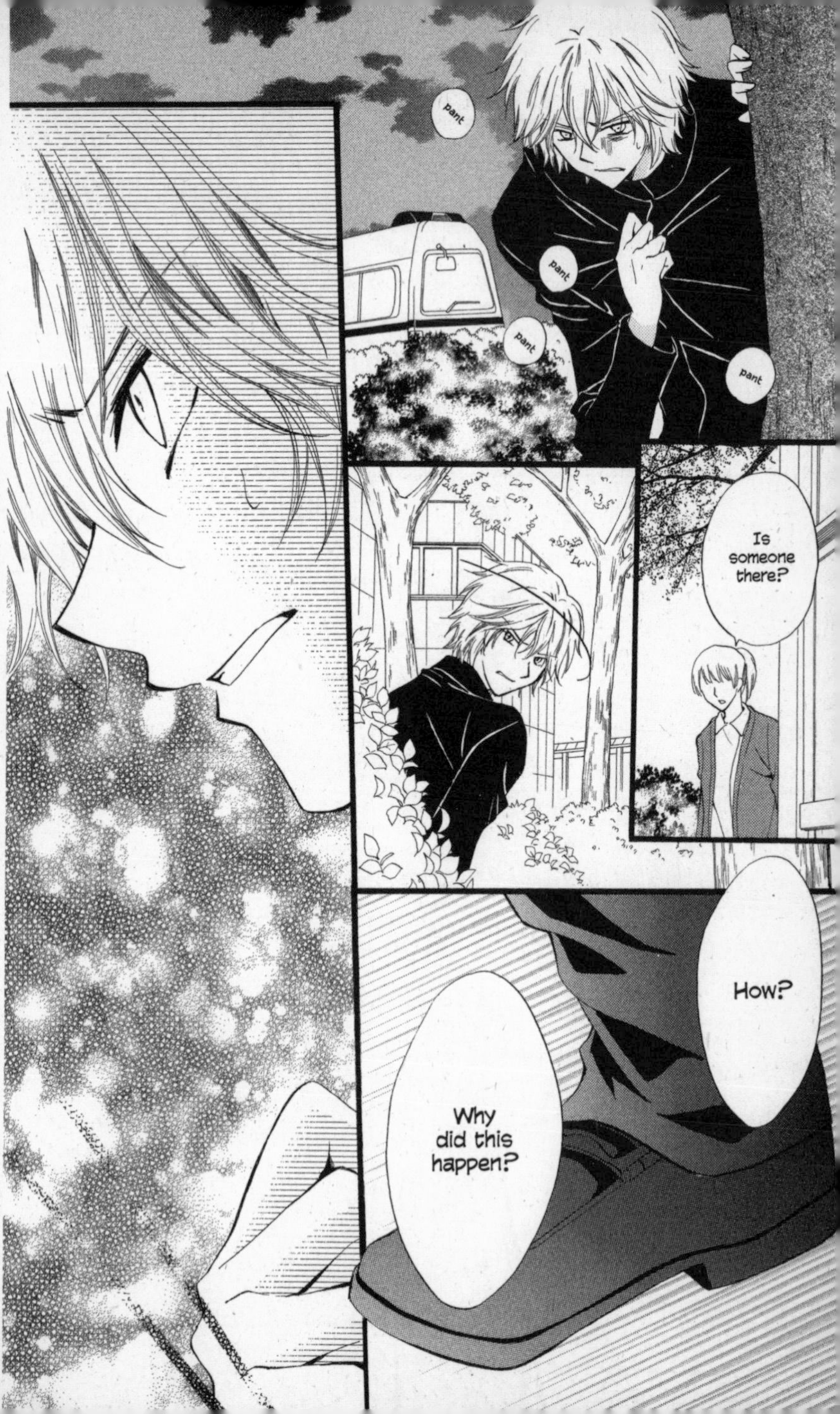
pant
pant
pant
pant
Is someone there?
How?
Why did this happen?

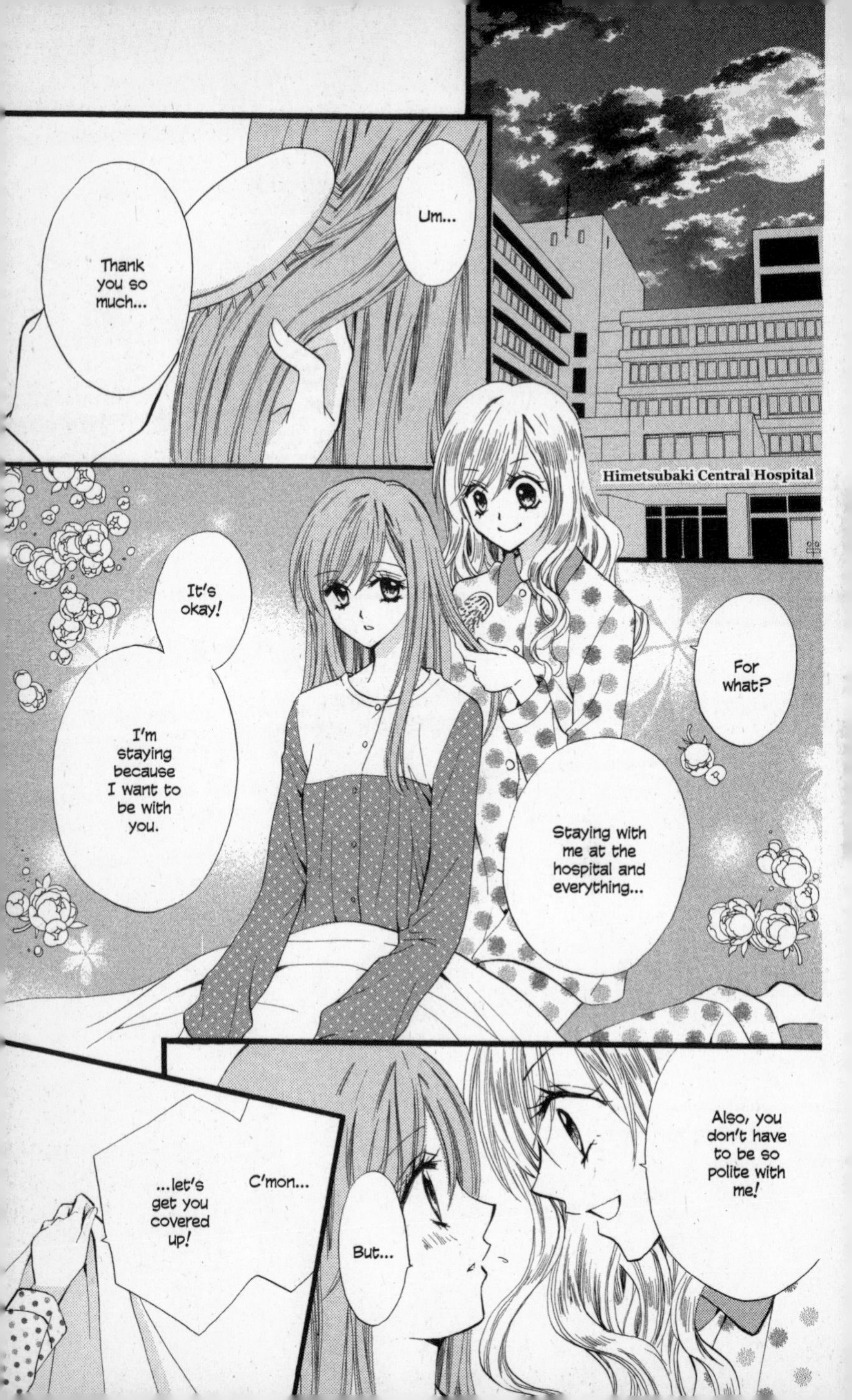
Himetsubaki Central Hospital
Um...
Thank you so much...
For what?
Staying with me at the hospital and everything...
It's okay!
I'm staying because I want to be with you.
Also, you don't have to be so polite with me!
But...
C'mon...
...let's get you covered up!

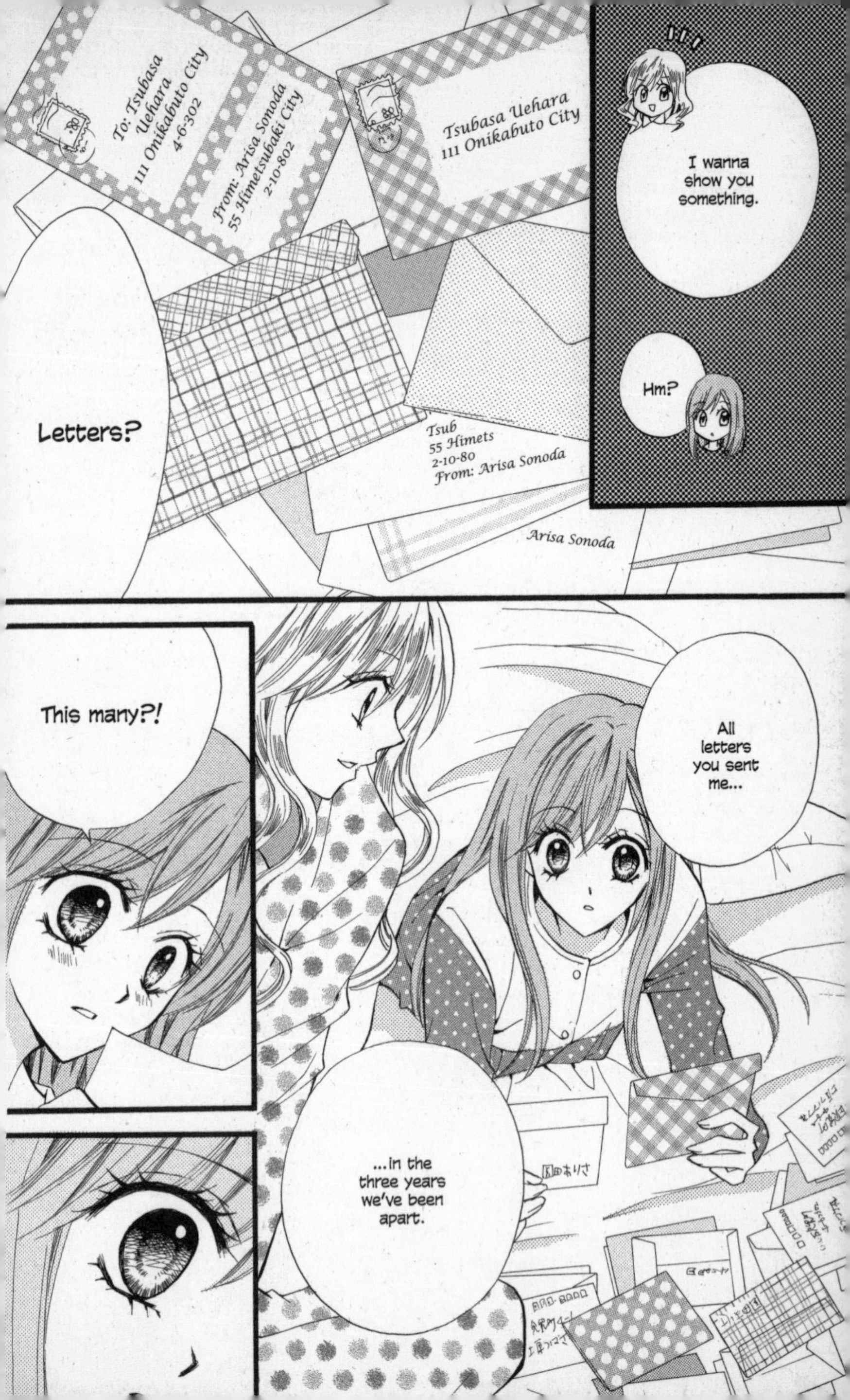
I wanna show you something.
Hm?
Tsubasa Uehara
111 Onikabuto City
To: Tsubasa Uehara
111 Onikabuto City
4-6-302
From: Arisa Sonoda
55 Himetsubaki City
2-10-802
Tsub
55 Himets
2-10-80
From: Arisa Sonoda
Arisa Sonoda
Letters?
All letters you sent me...
...in the three years we've been apart.
This many?!

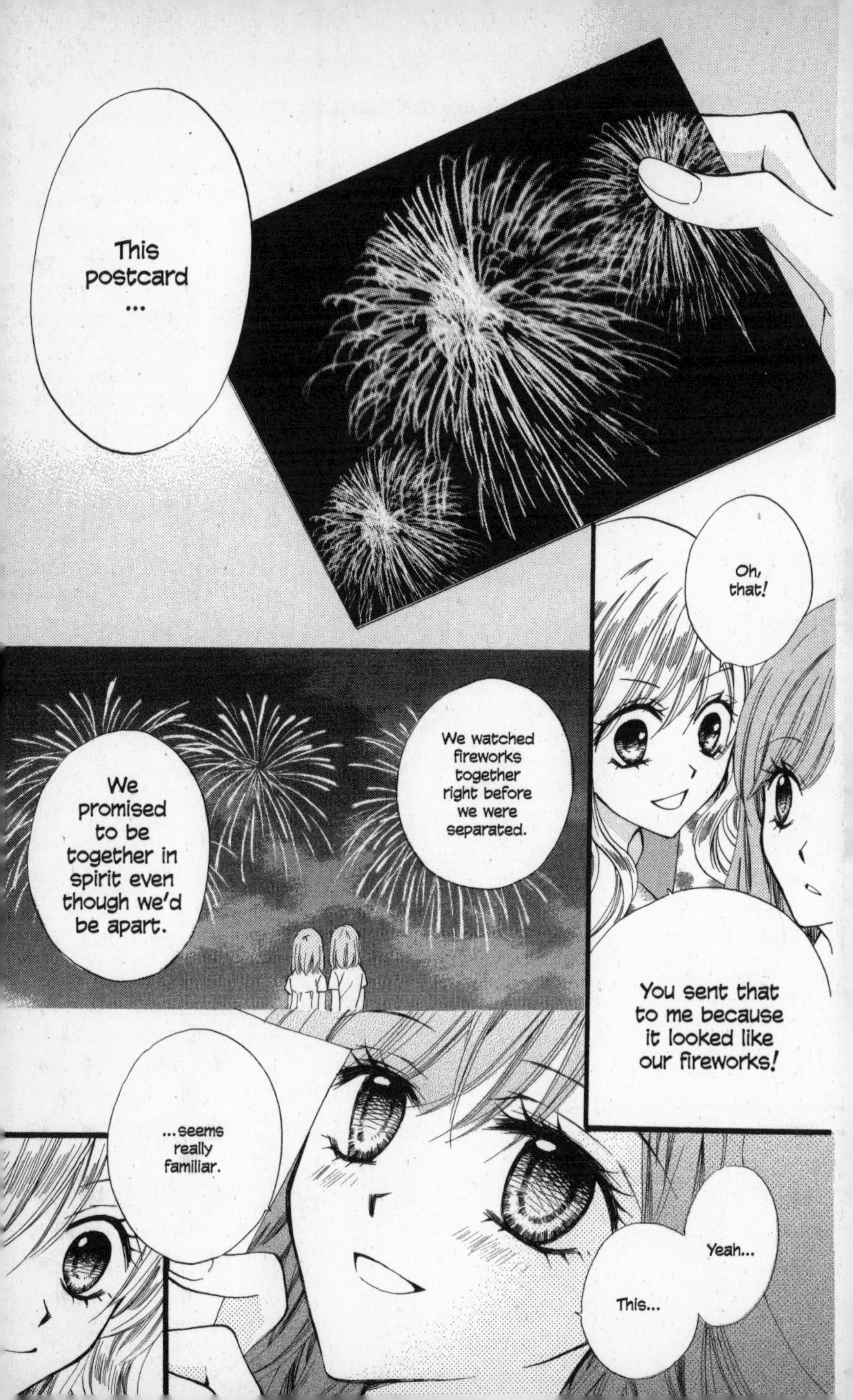
This postcard ...
Oh, that!
You sent that to me because it looked like our fireworks!
We watched fireworks together right before we were separated.
We promised to be together in spirit even though we'd be apart.
Yeah...
This...
...seems really familiar.

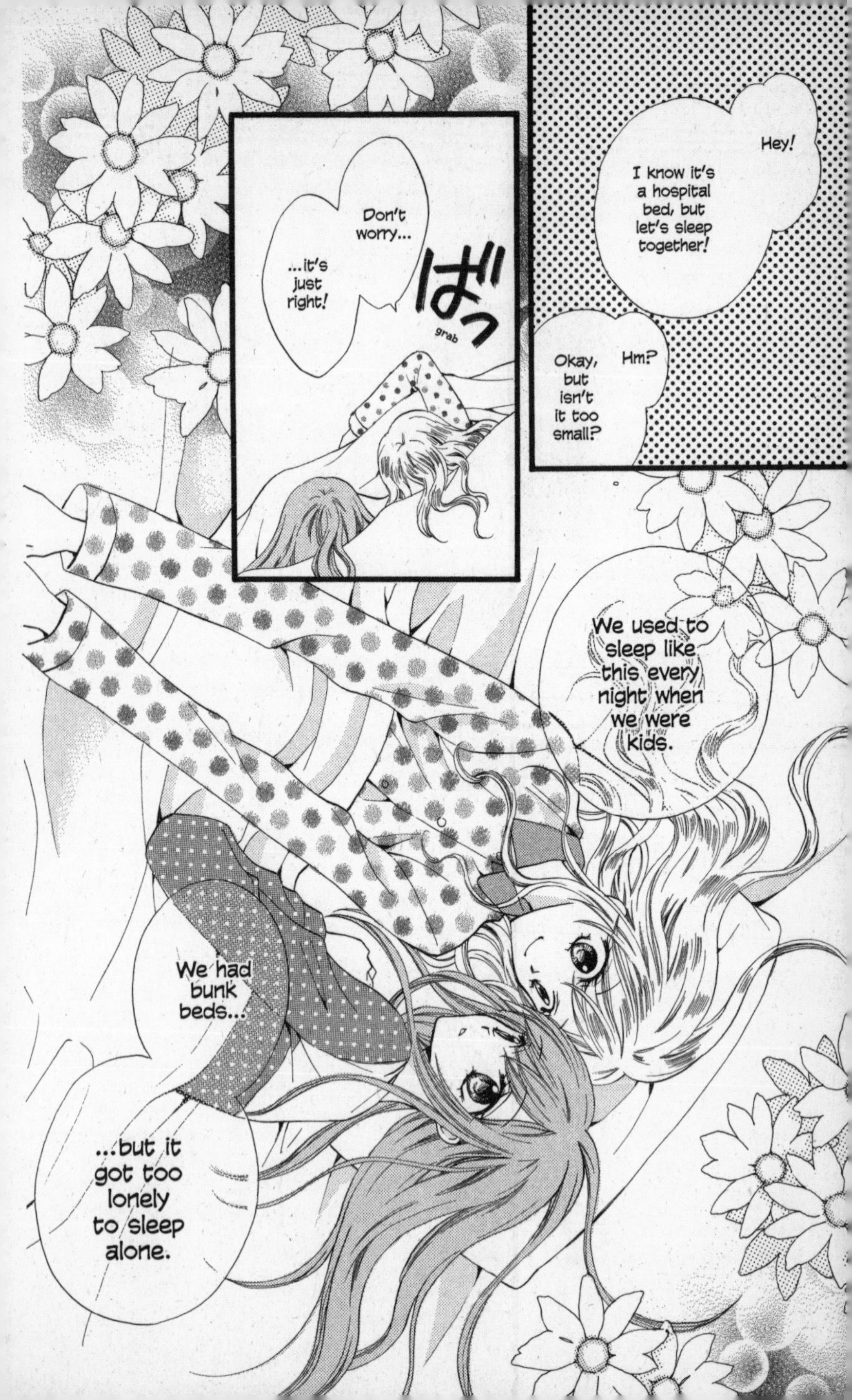
Hey!
I know it's a hospital bed, but let's sleep together!
Hm?
Okay, but isn't it too small?
Don't worry...
...it's just right!
ぱっ
grab
We used to sleep like this every night when we were kids.
We had bunk beds...
...but it got too lonely to sleep alone.

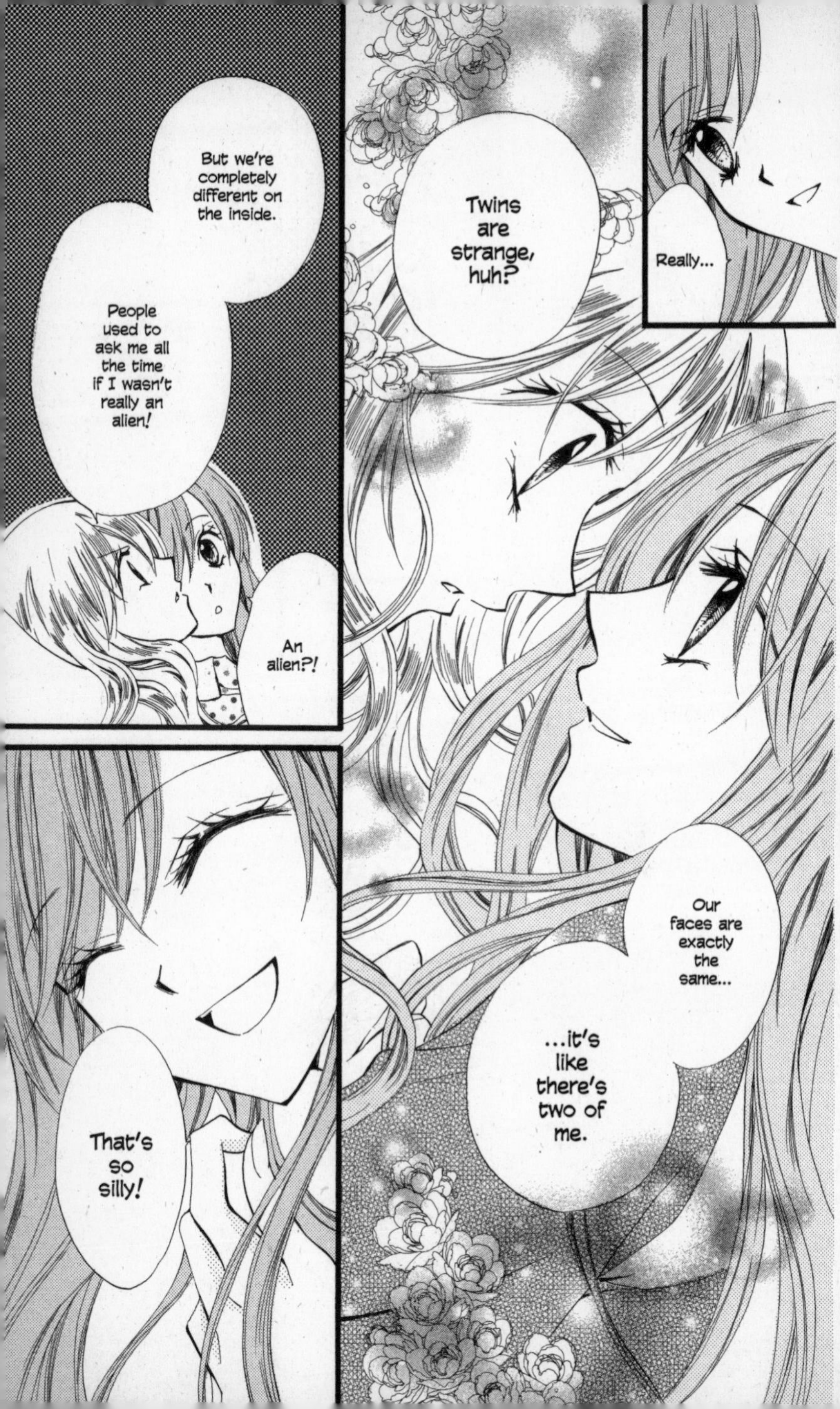

Really...
Twins are strange, huh?
Our faces are exactly the same...
...it's like there's two of me.
But we're completely different on the inside.
People used to ask me all the time if I wasn't really an alien!
An alien?!
That's so silly!

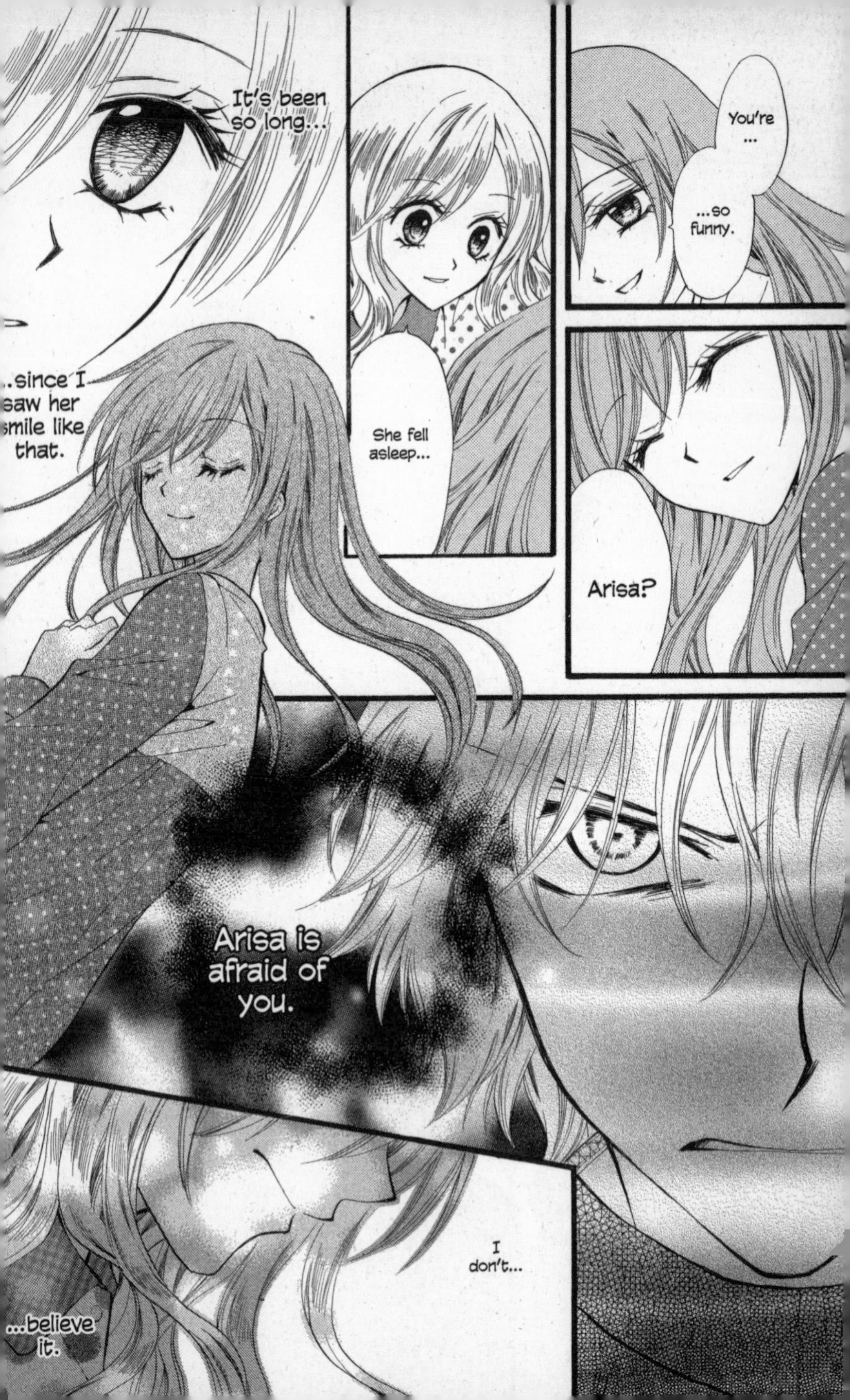
You're ...
...so funny.
Arisa?
She fell asleep...
It's been so long...
..since I saw her smile like that.
Arisa is afraid of you.
I don't...
...believe it.

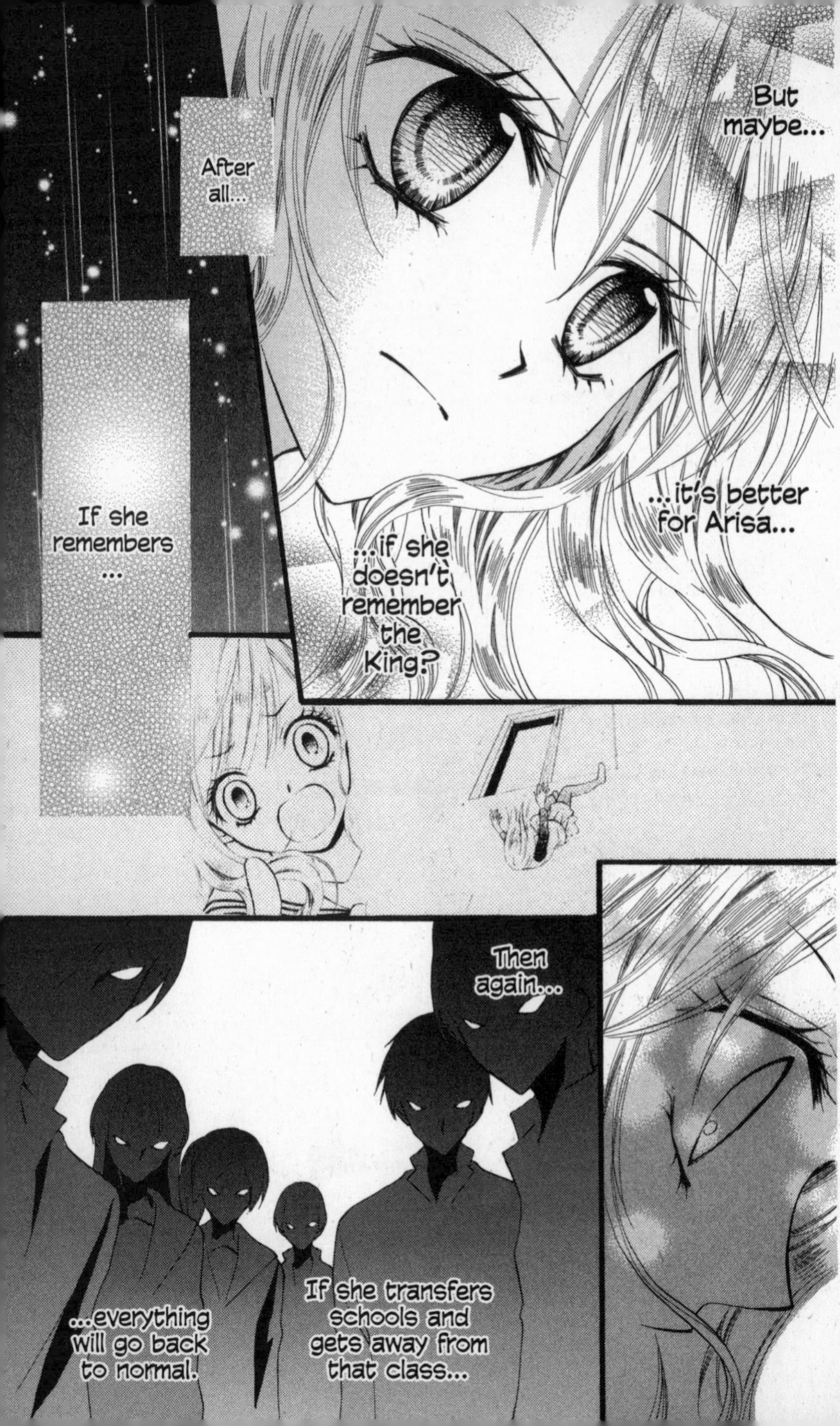
But maybe...
...it's better for Arisa...
...if she doesn't remember the King?
After all...
If she remembers ...
Then again...
If she transfers schools and gets away from that class...
...everything will go back to normal.

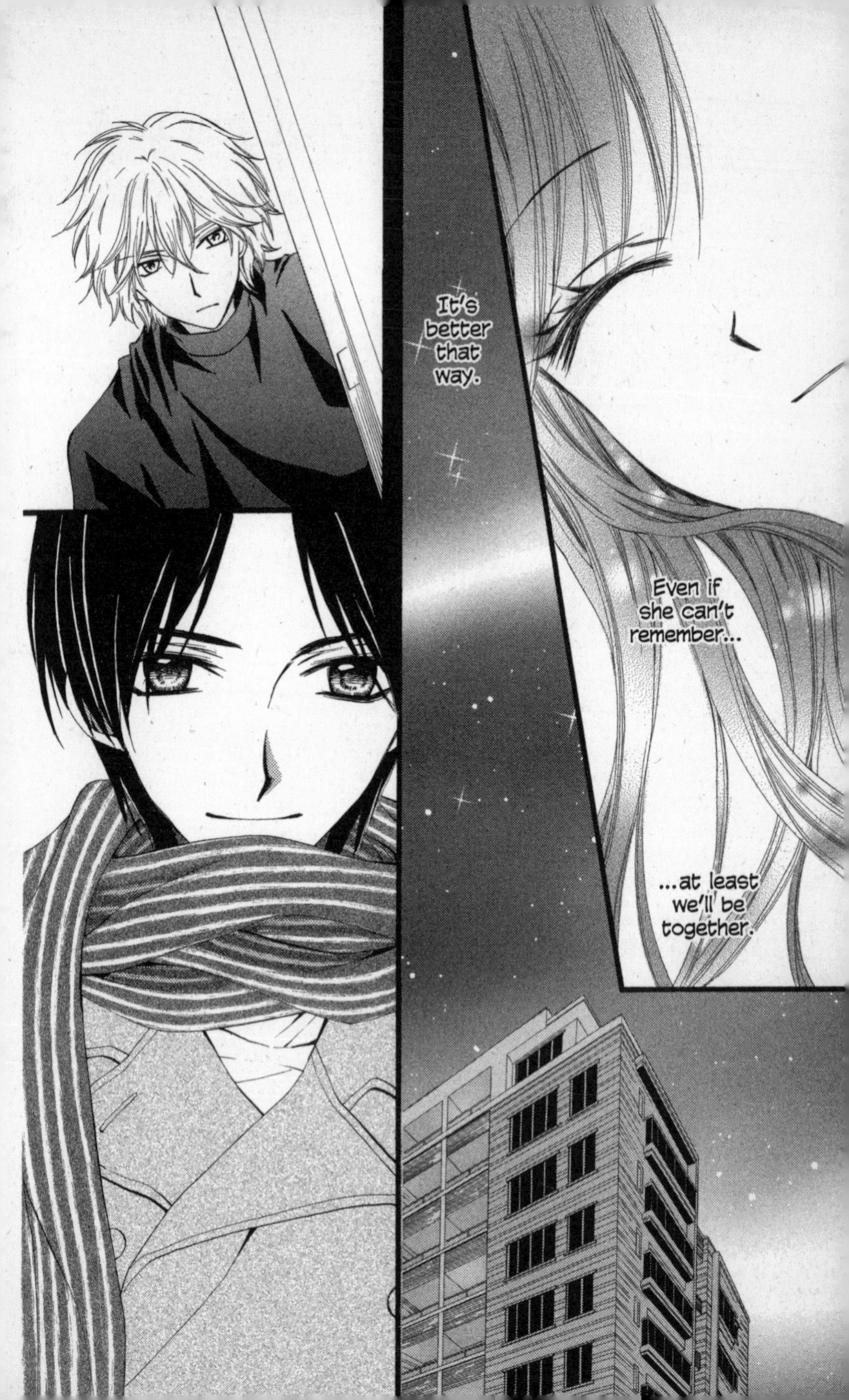
Even if she can't remember...
...at least we'll be together.
It's better that way.

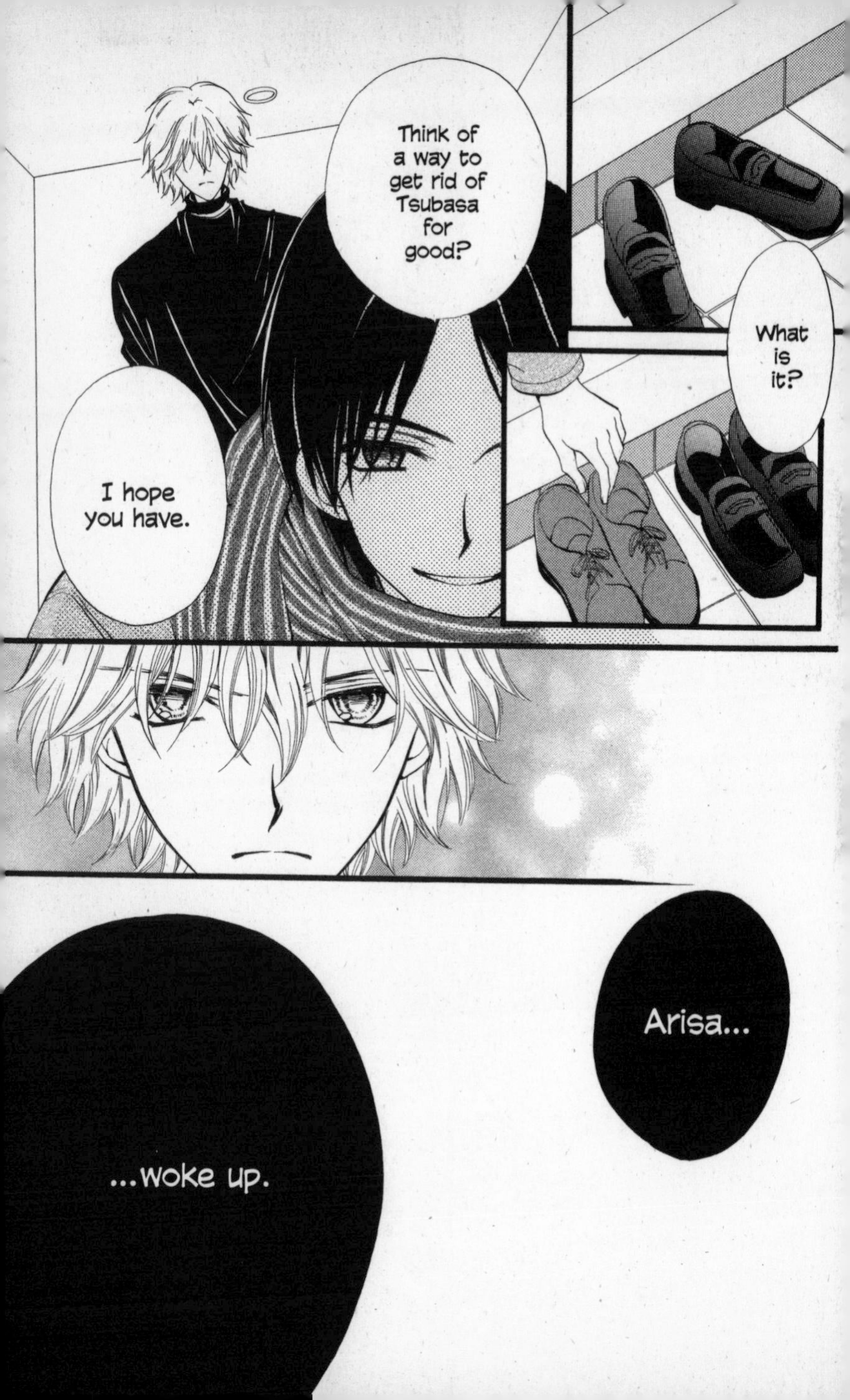
What is it?
Think of a way to get rid of Tsubasa for good?
I hope you have.
Arisa...
...woke up.

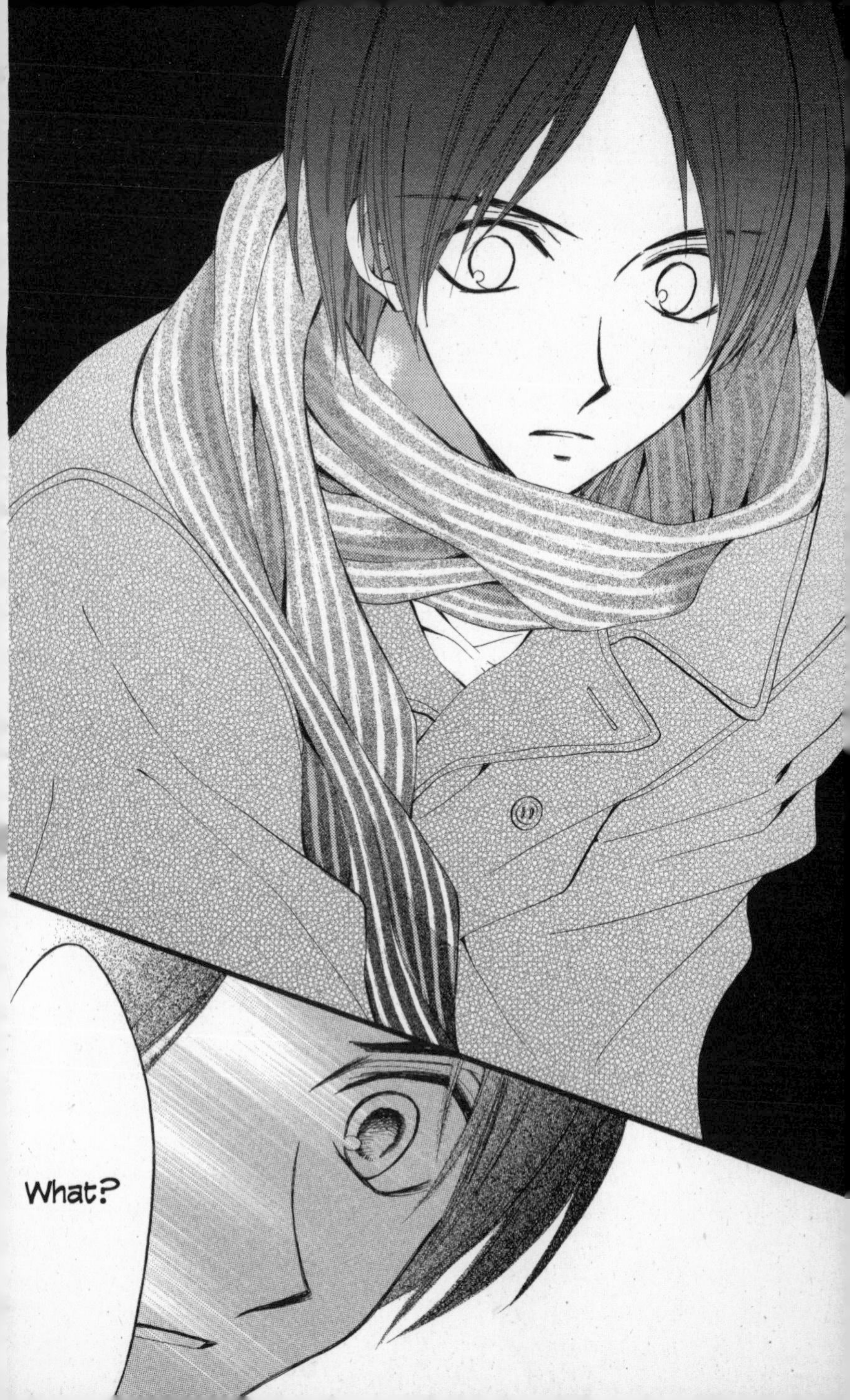
What?

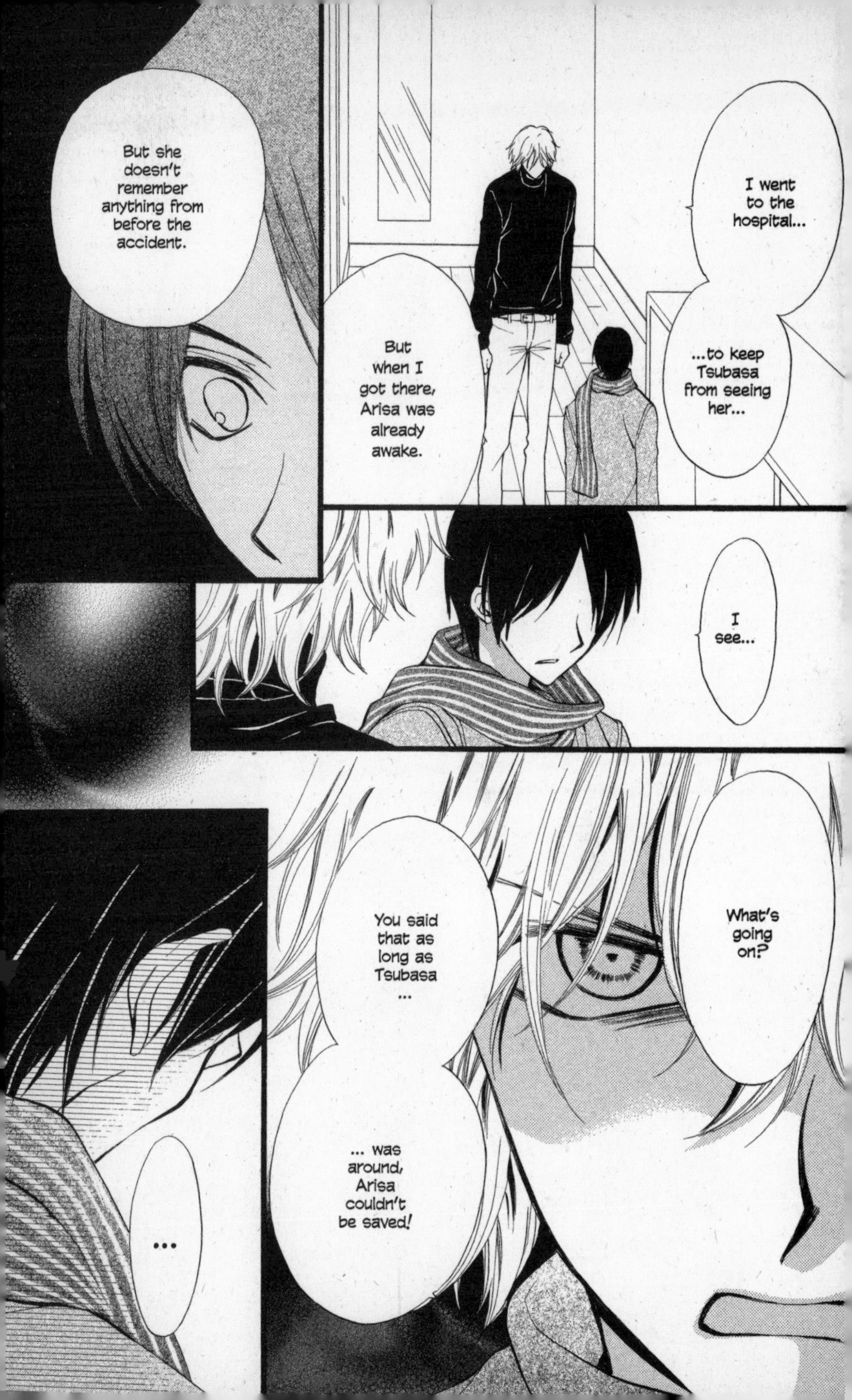

I went to the hospital...
...to keep Tsubasa from seeing her...
But when I got there, Arisa was already awake.
But she doesn't remember anything from before the accident.
I see...
What's going on?
You said that as long as Tsubasa ...
... was around, Arisa couldn't be saved!
...

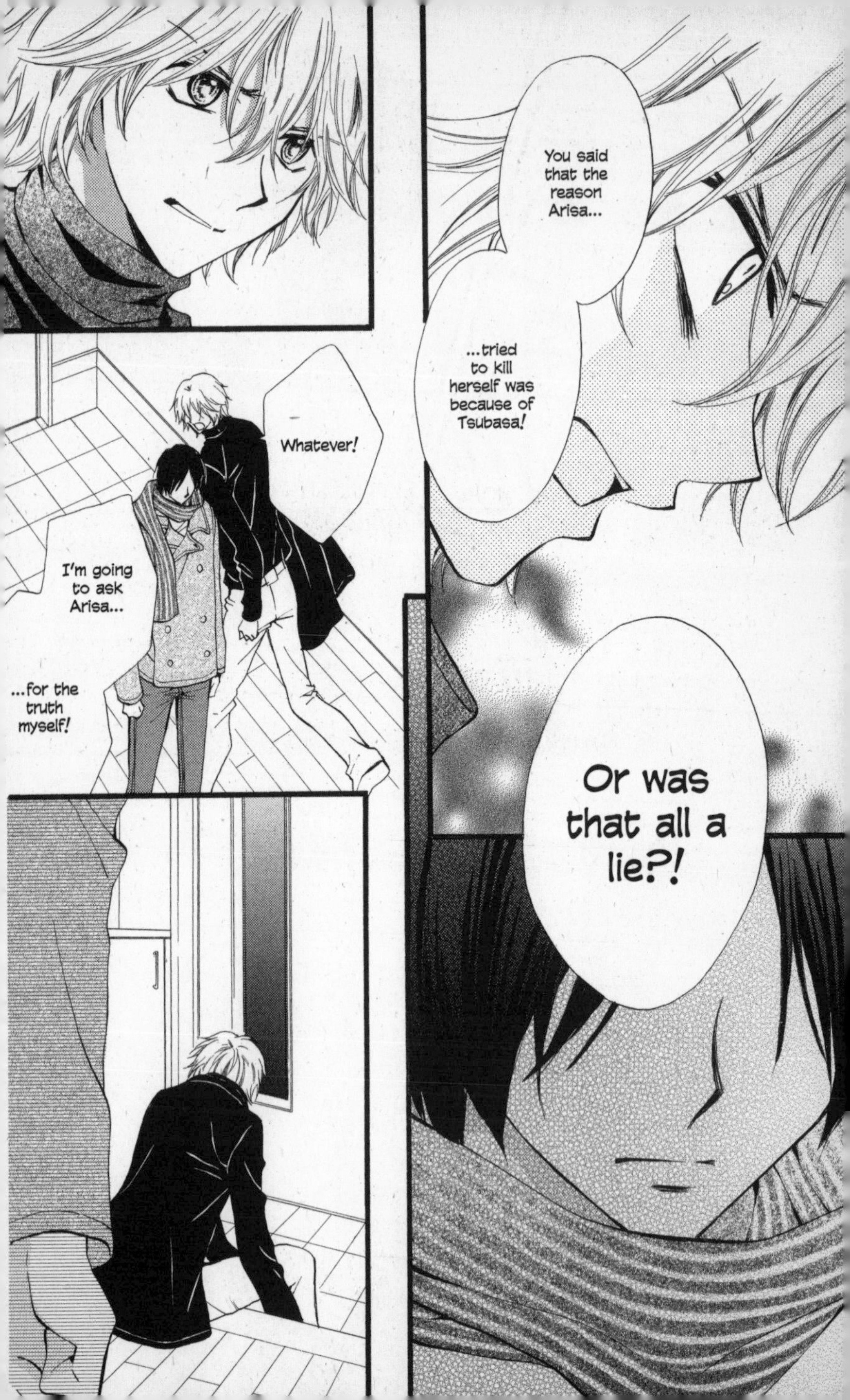
You said that the reason Arisa...
...tried to kill herself was because of Tsubasa!
Or was that all a lie?!
Whatever!
I'm going to ask Arisa...
...for the truth myself!

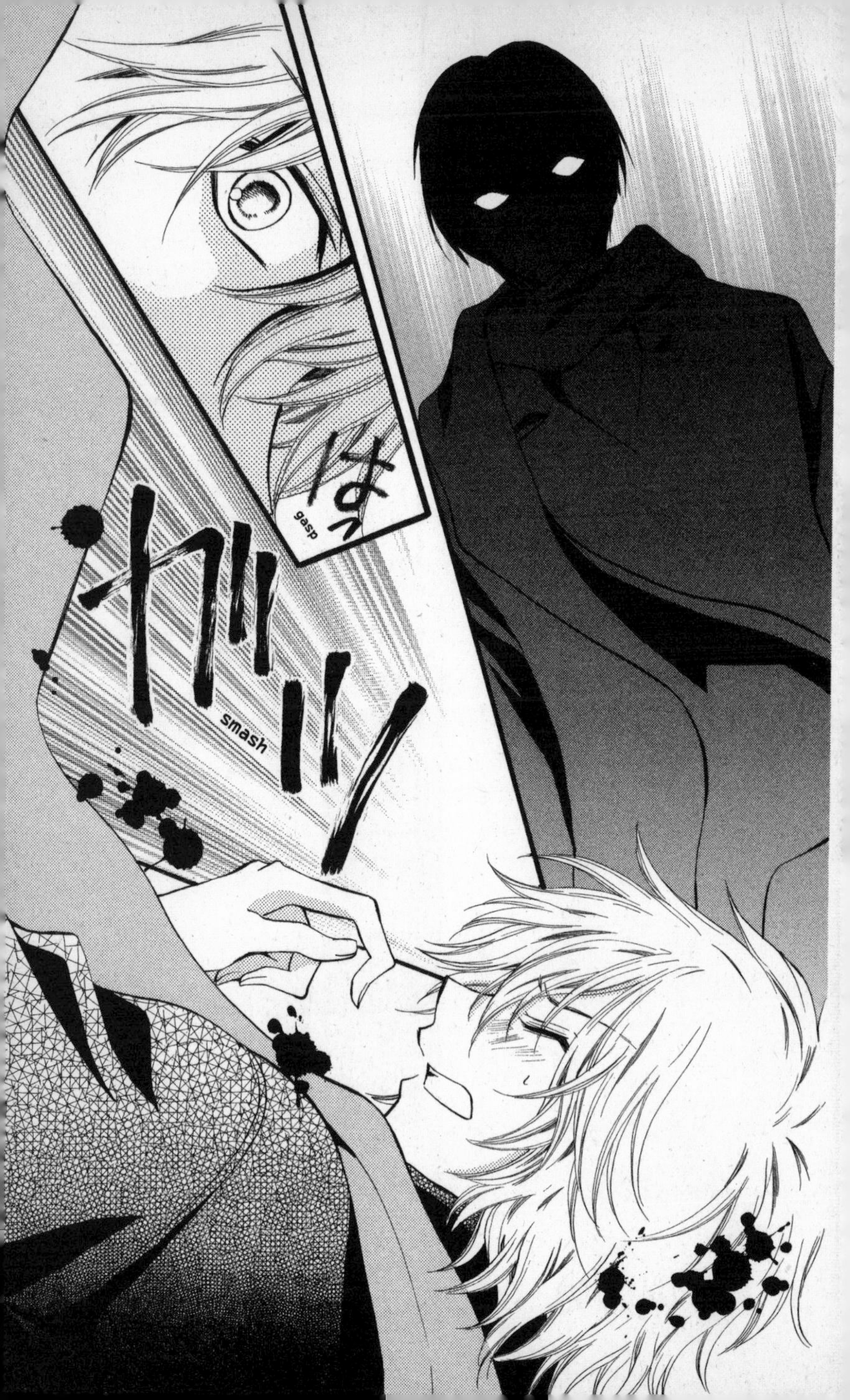
はっ
gasp
ガシャン
smash

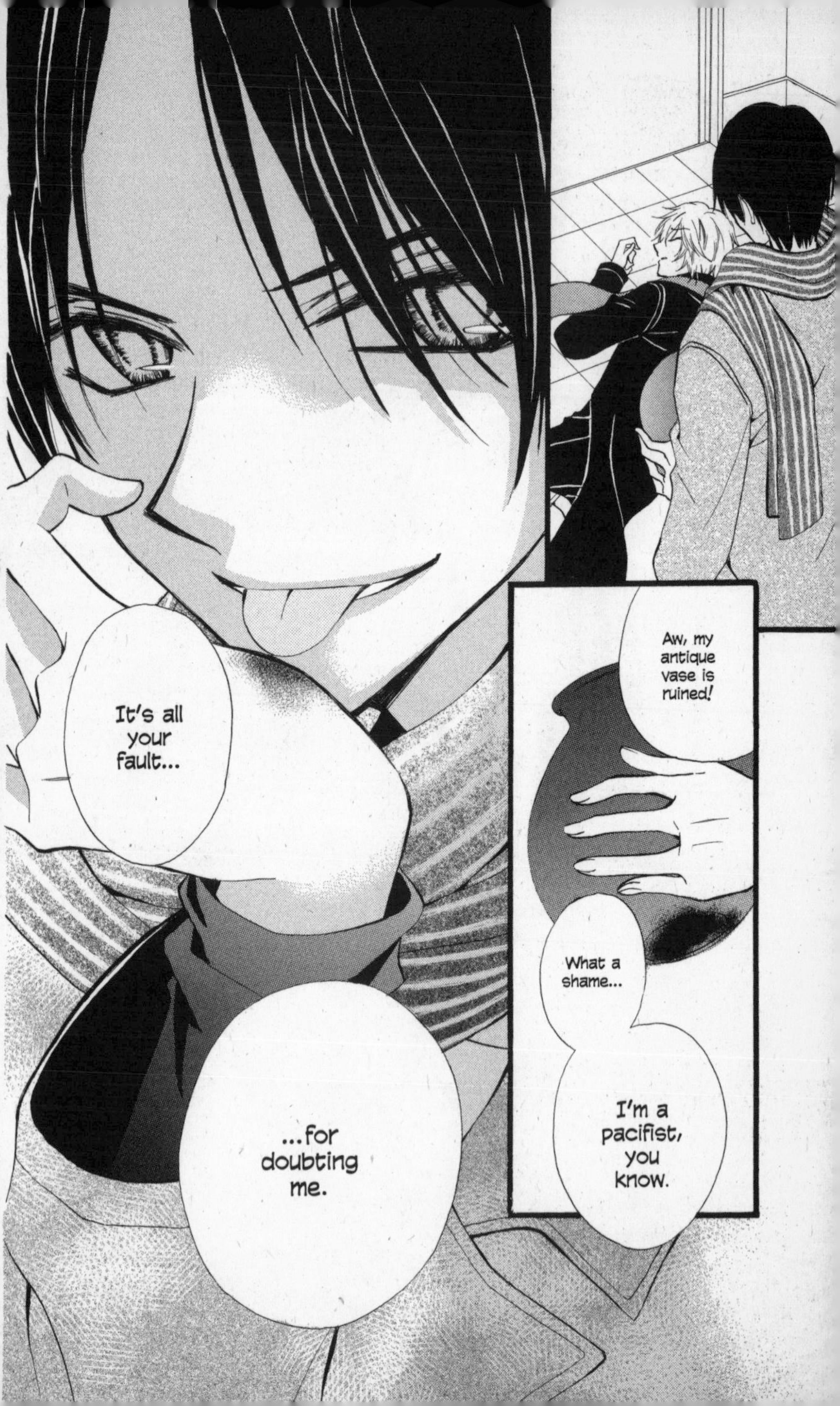
Aw, my antique vase is ruined!
What a shame...
I'm a pacifist, you know.
It's all your fault...
...for doubting me.

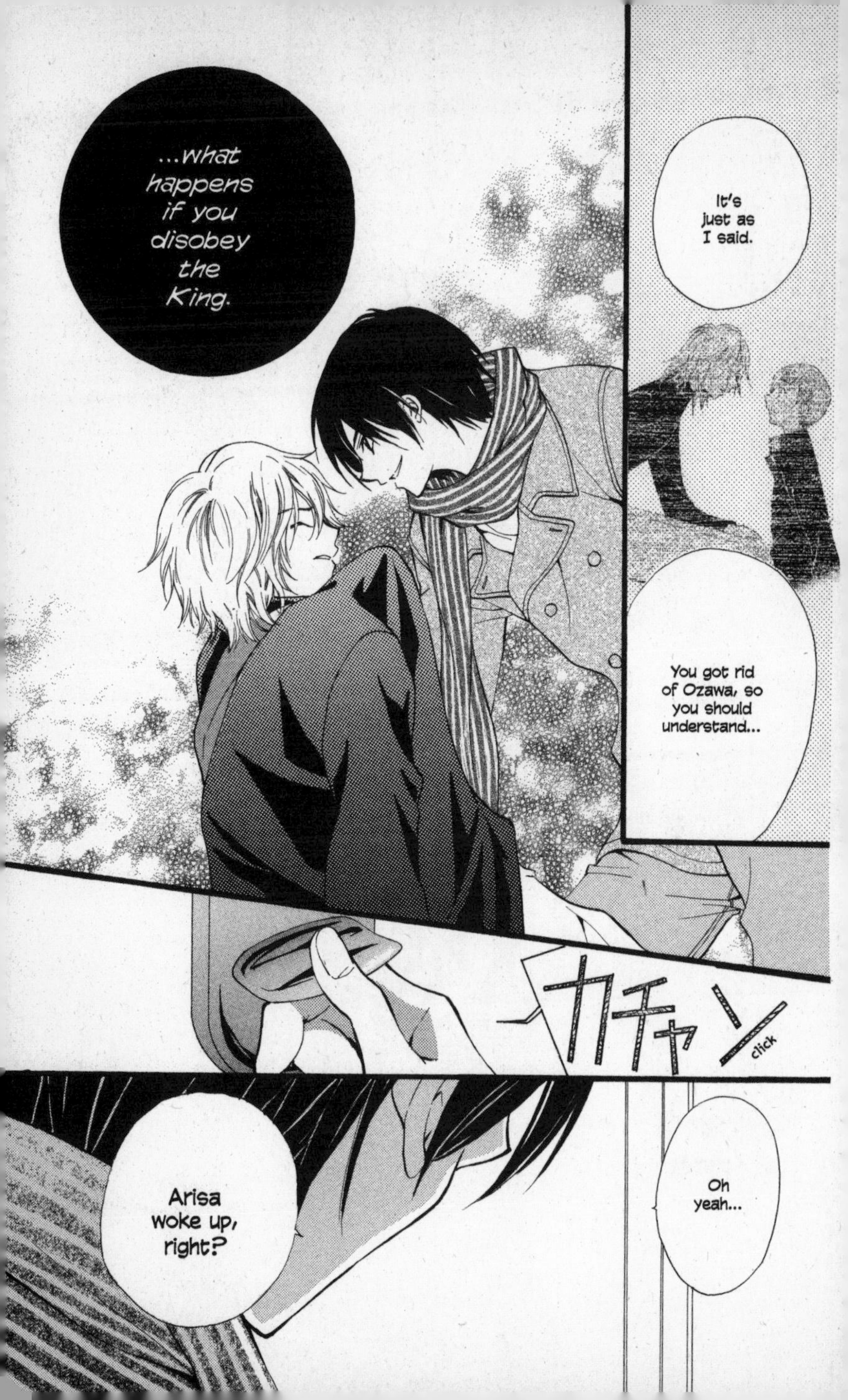
It's just as I said.
You got rid of Ozawa, so you should understand...
...what happens if you disobey the King.
カチャン
click
Oh yeah...
Arisa woke up, right?

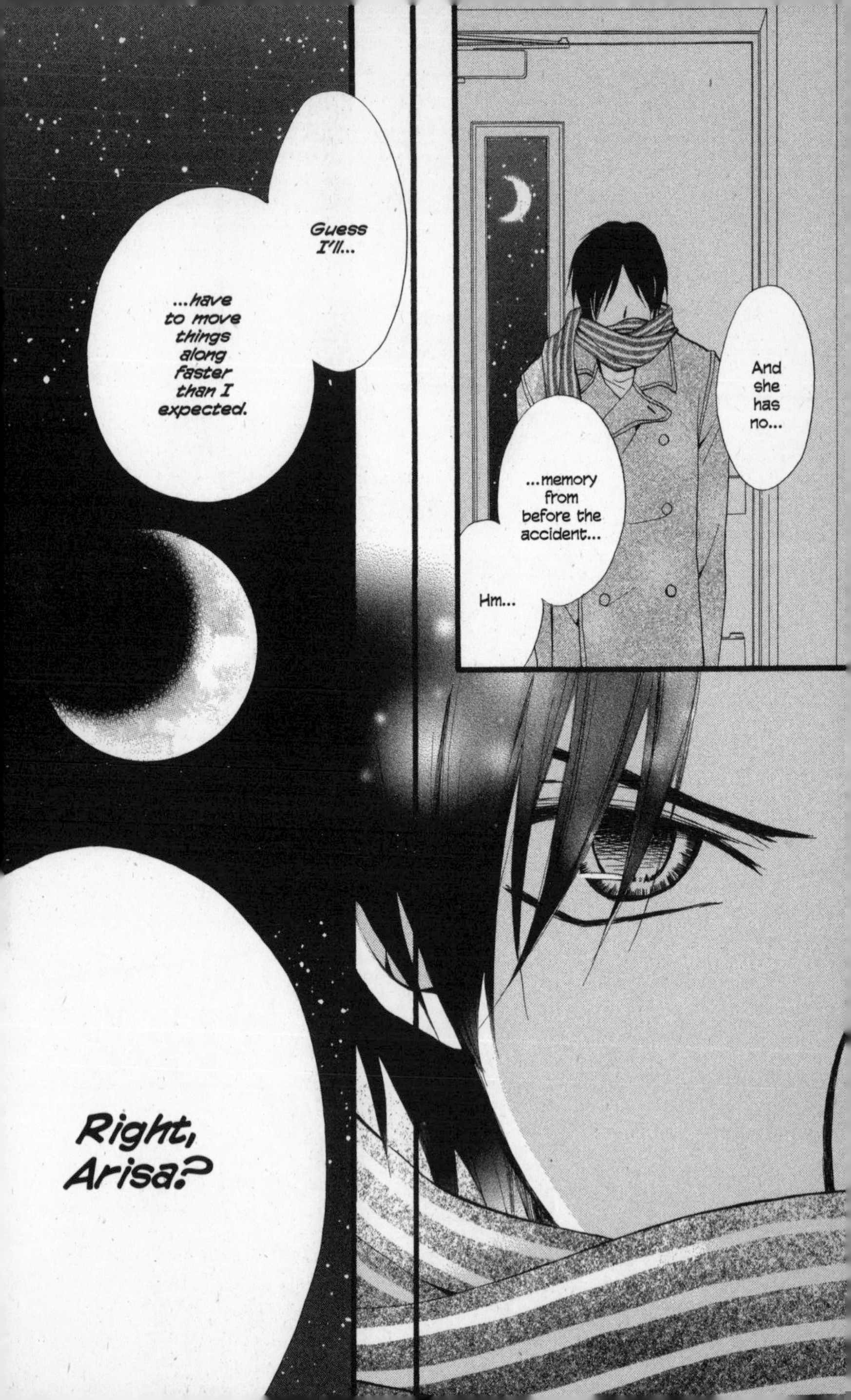
And she has no...
...memory from before the accident...
Hm...
Guess I'll...
...have to move things along faster than I expected.
Right, Arisa?

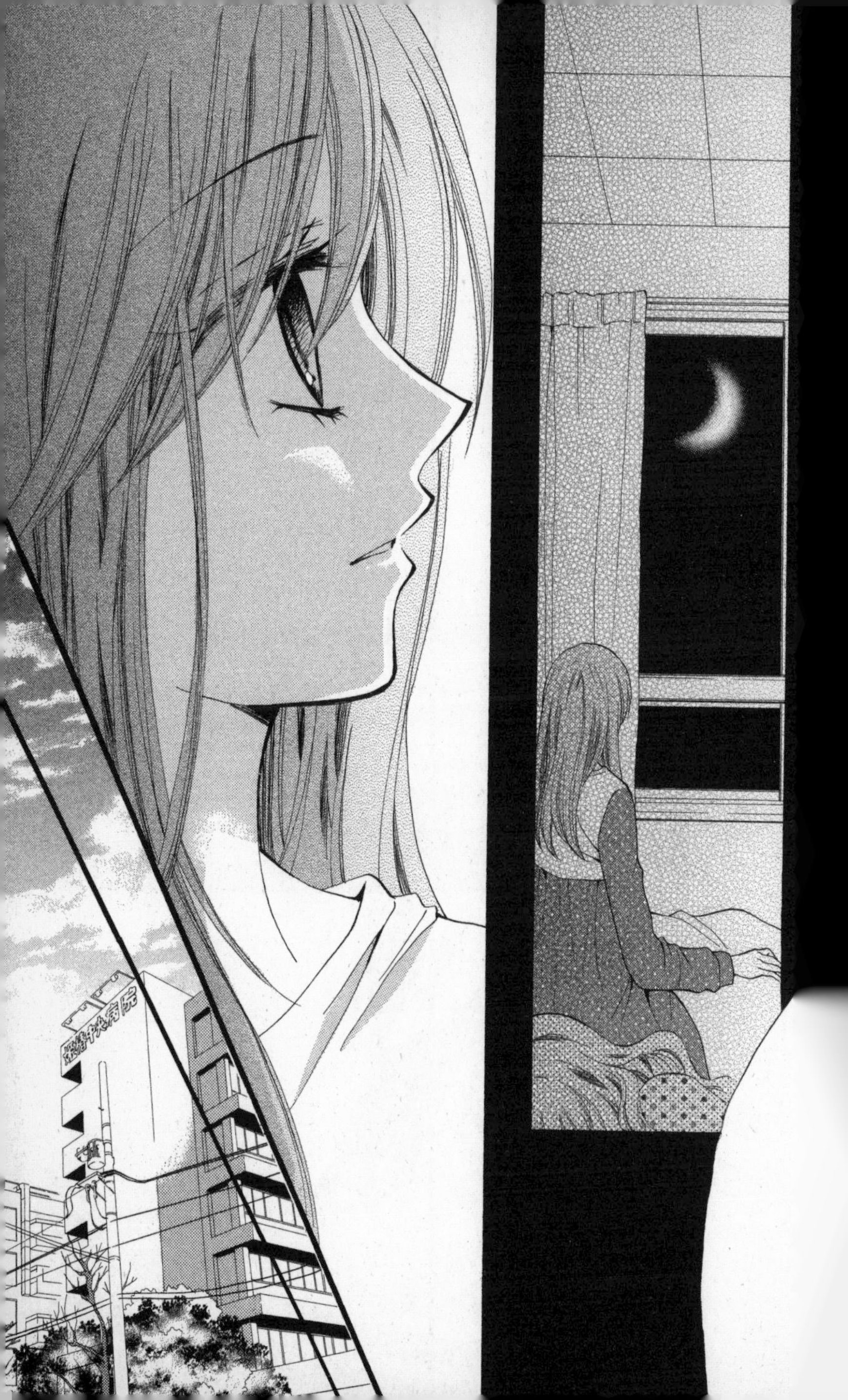
中央病院

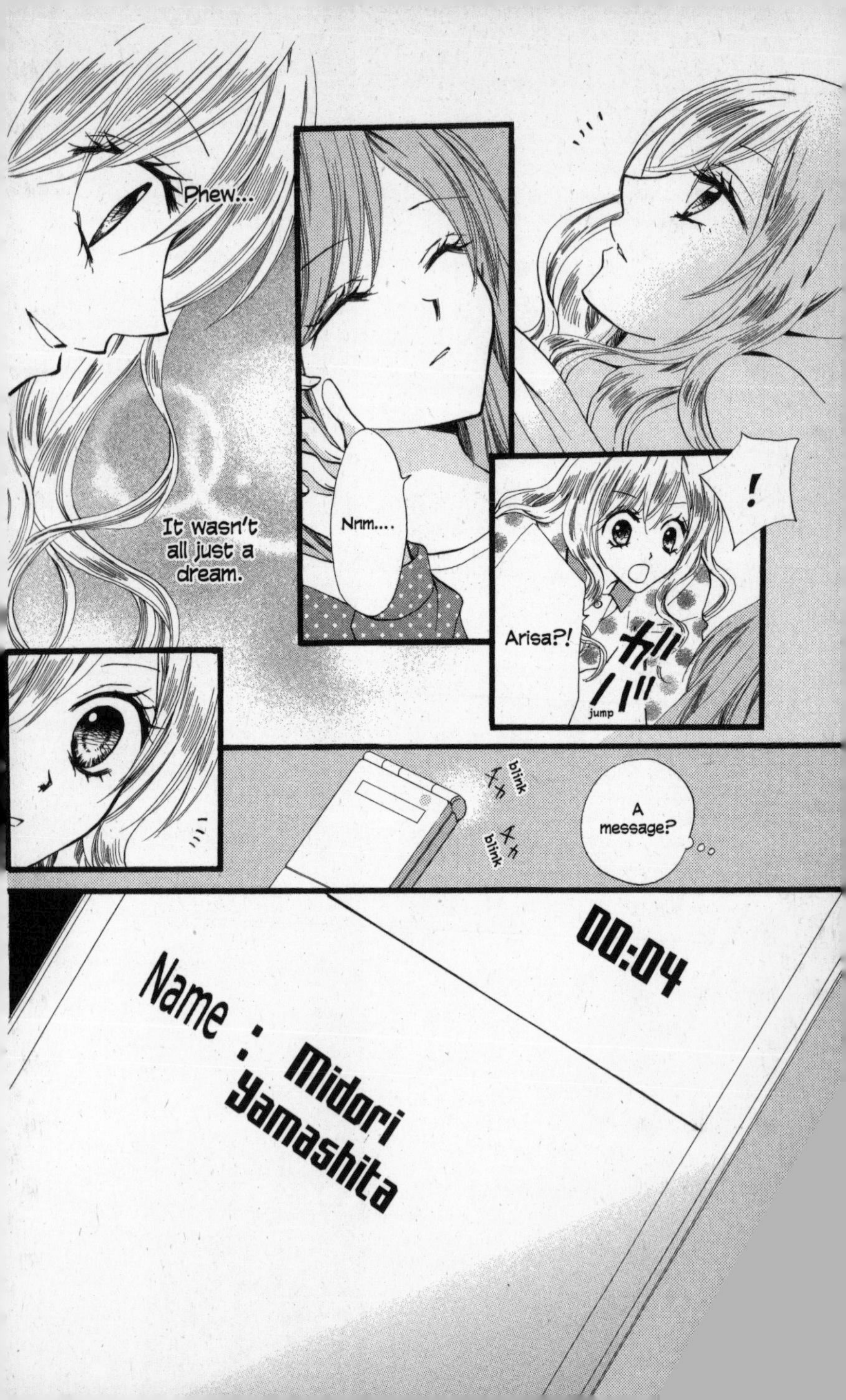
Phew...
It wasn't all just a dream.
Nnm....
!
Arisa?!
jump
blink
blink
A message?
00:04
Name : Midori Yamashita

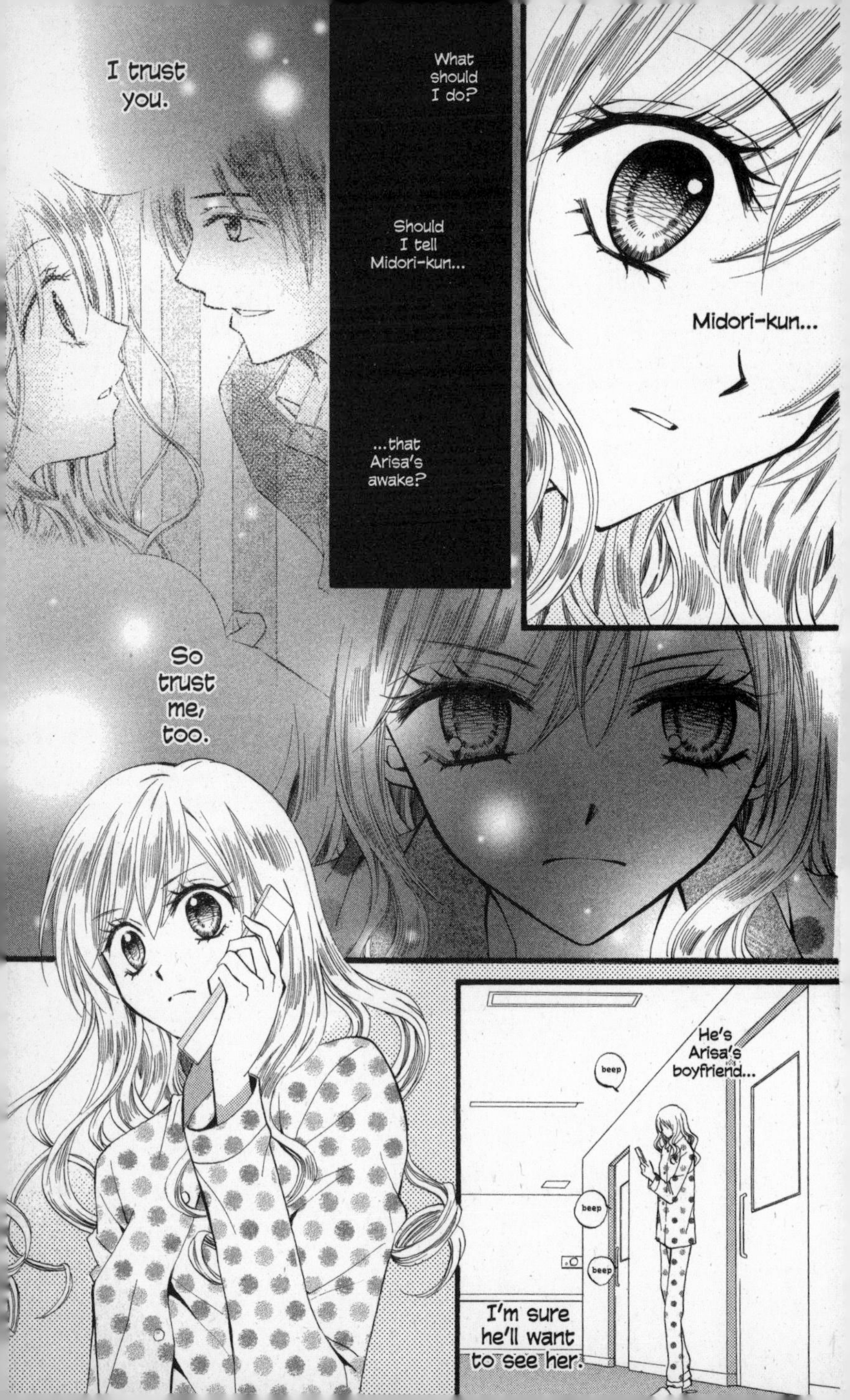

Midori-kun...
What should I do?
Should I tell Midori-kun...
...that Arisa's awake?
I trust you.
So trust me, too.
He's Arisa's boyfriend...
beep
beep
beep
I'm sure he'll want to see her.

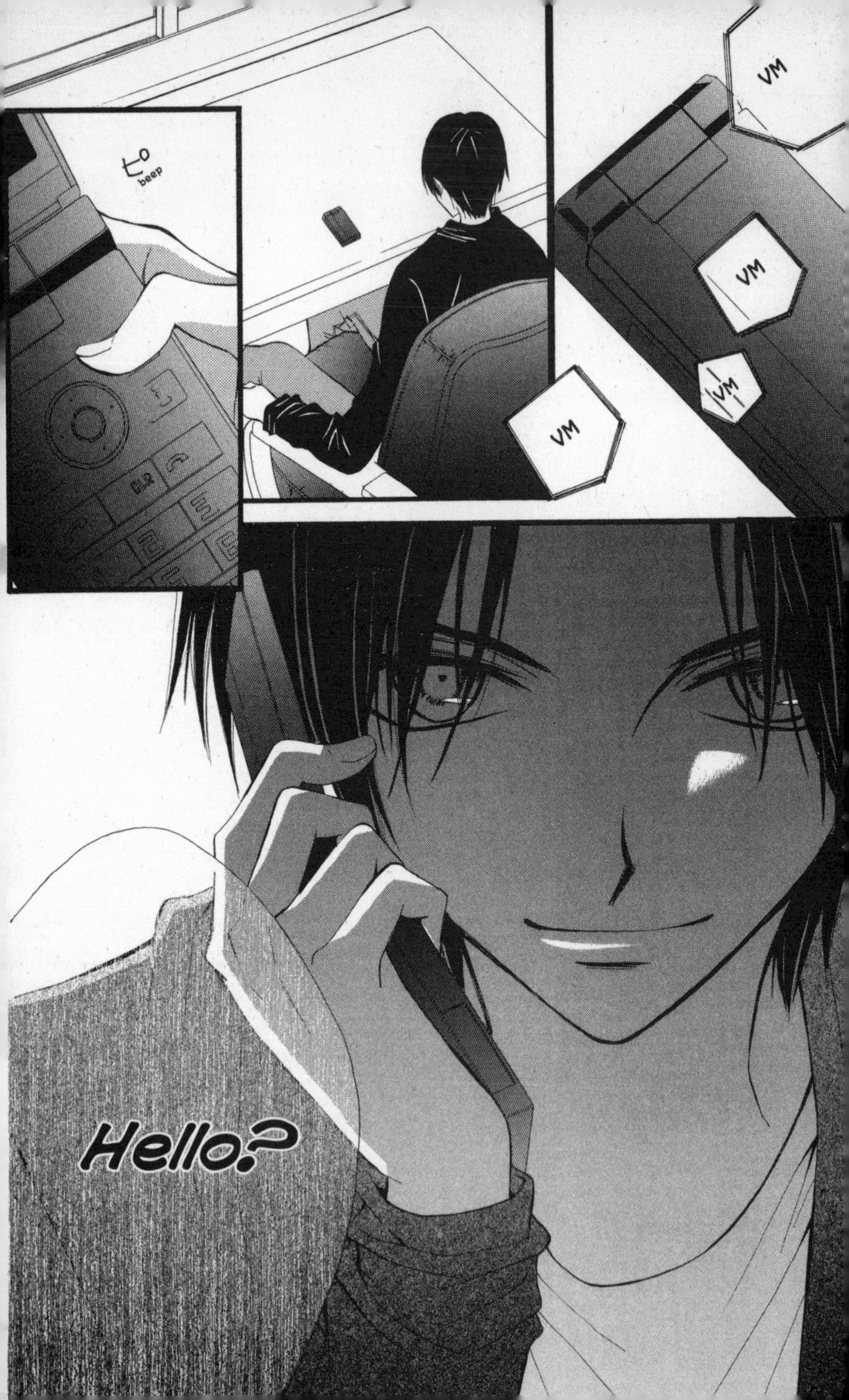
VM
VM
VM
VM
ピ
beep
Hello?

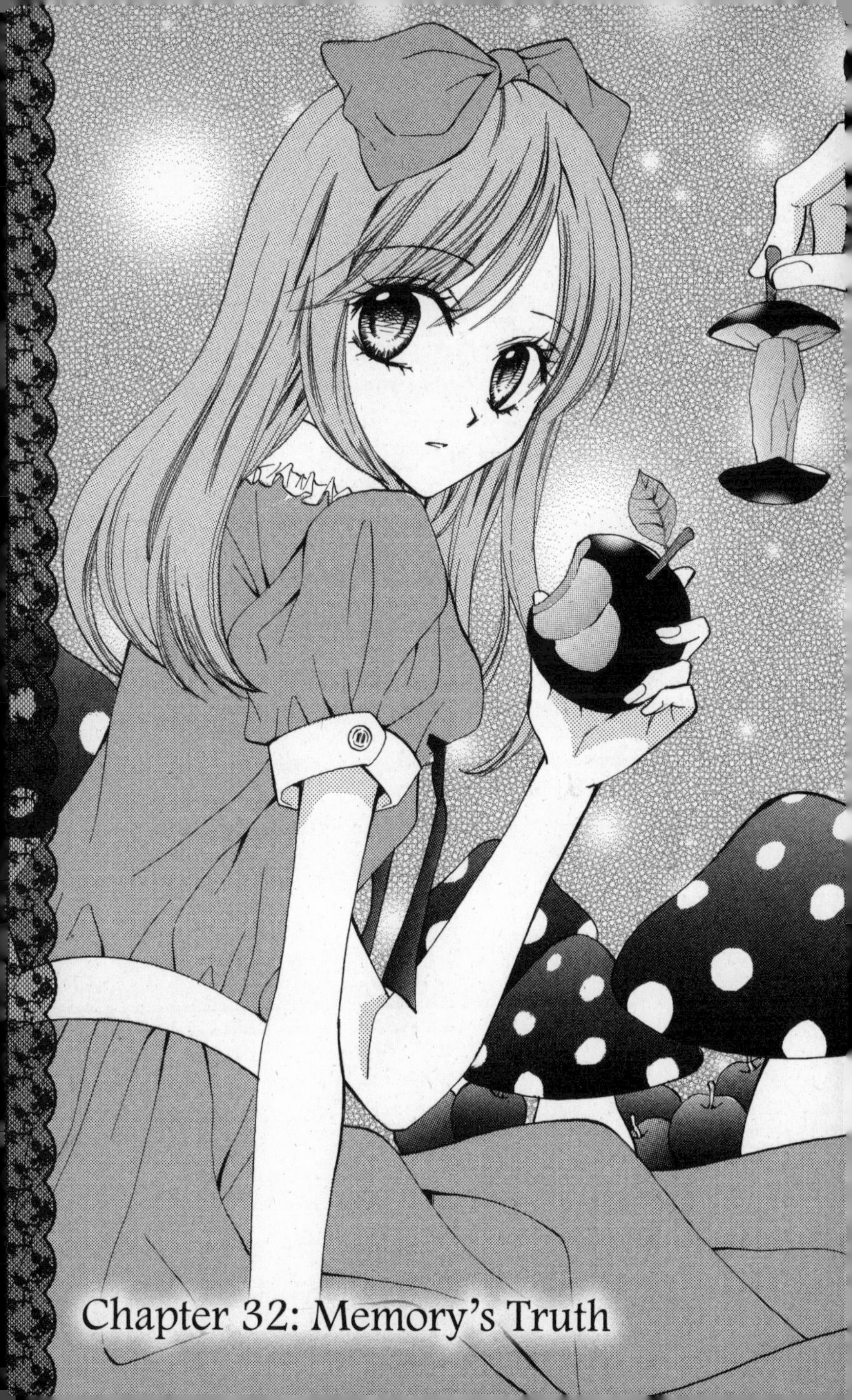

Chapter 32: Memory's Truth

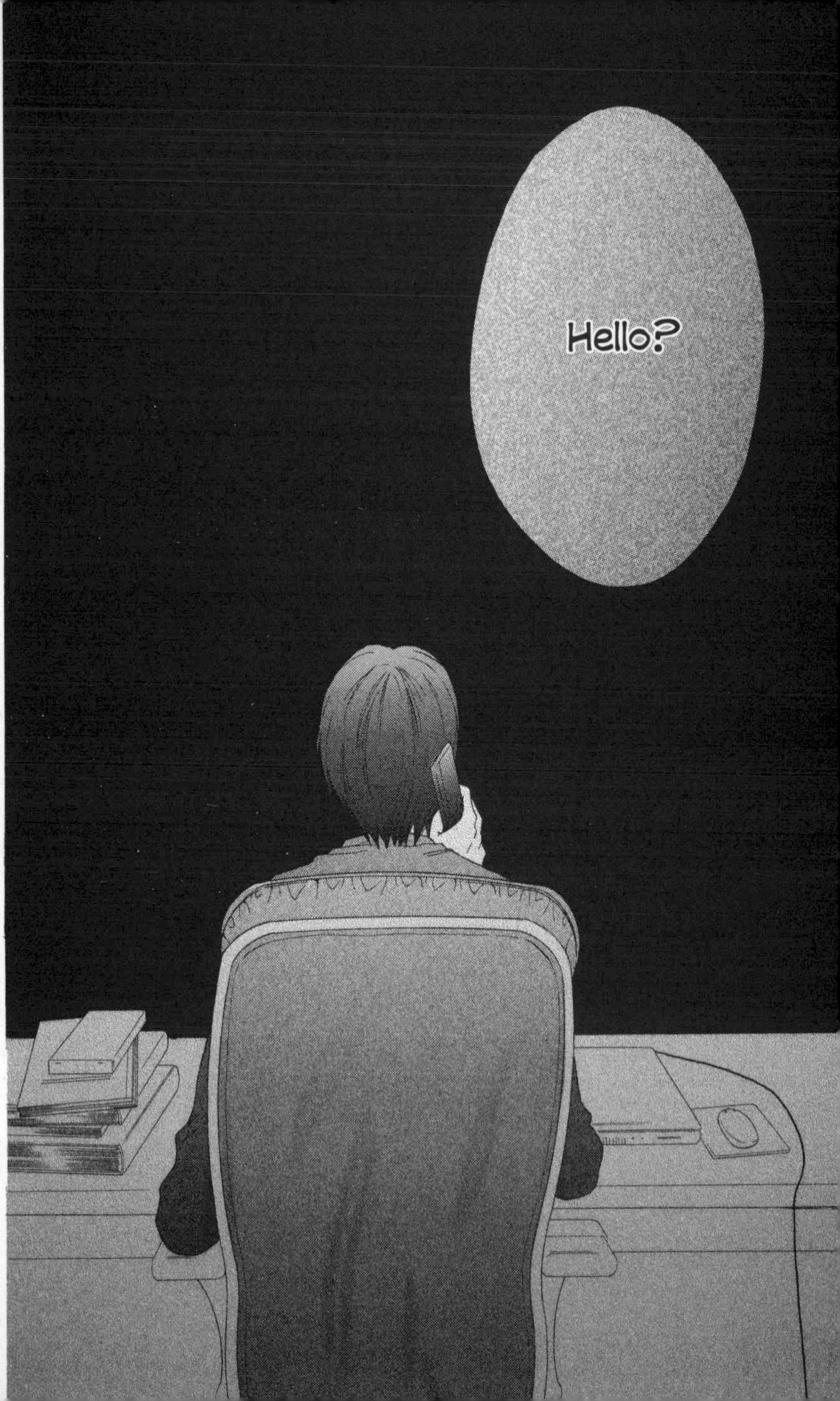
Hello?

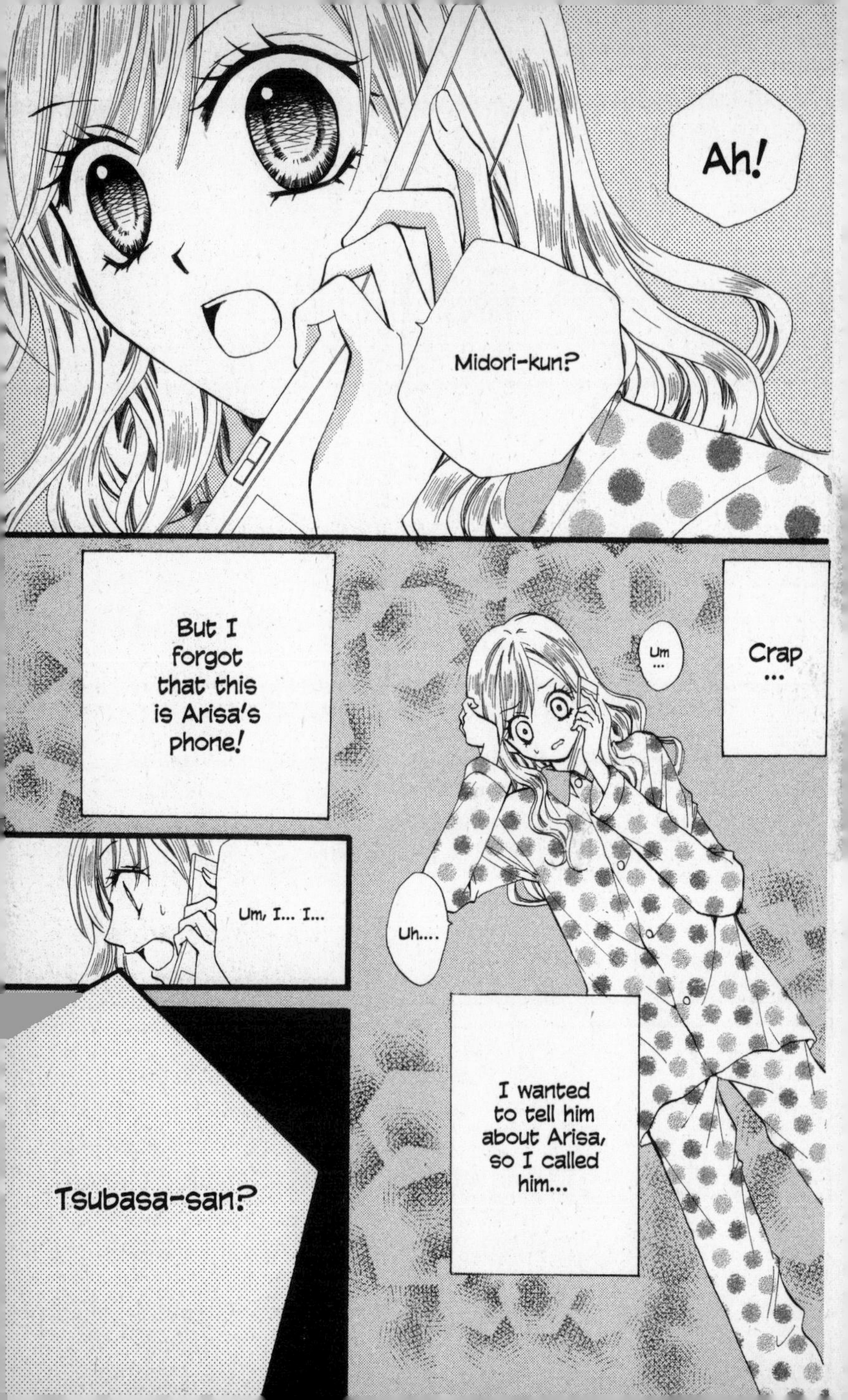
Ah!
Midori-kun?
Crap ...
Um ...
But I forgot that this is Arisa's phone!
Uh....
I wanted to tell him about Arisa, so I called him...
Um, I... I...
Tsubasa-san?

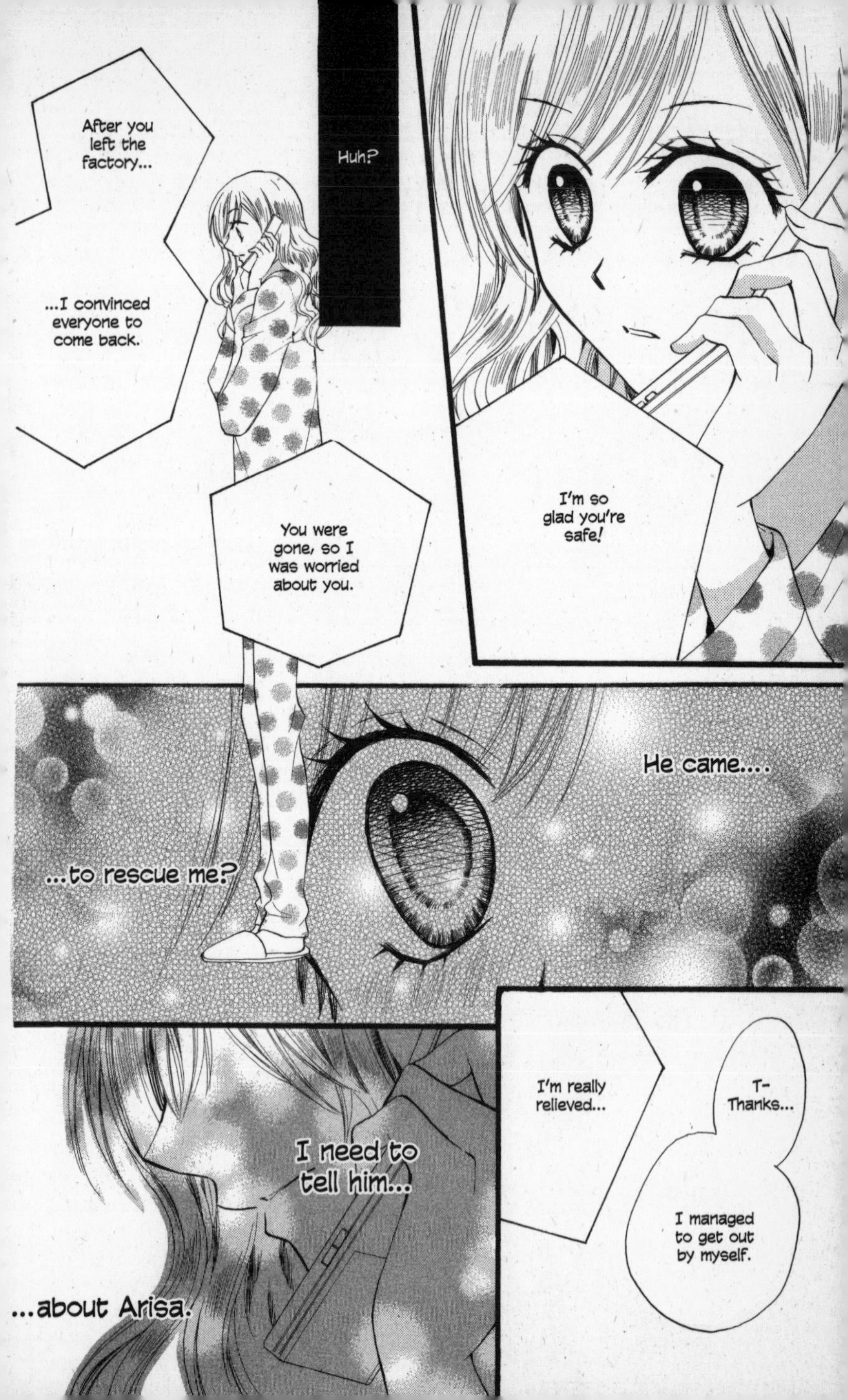
I'm so glad you're safe!
Huh?
After you left the factory...
...I convinced everyone to come back.
You were gone, so I was worried about you.
He came....
...to rescue me?
T-Thanks...
I'm really relieved...
I managed to get out by myself.
I need to tell him...
...about Arisa.

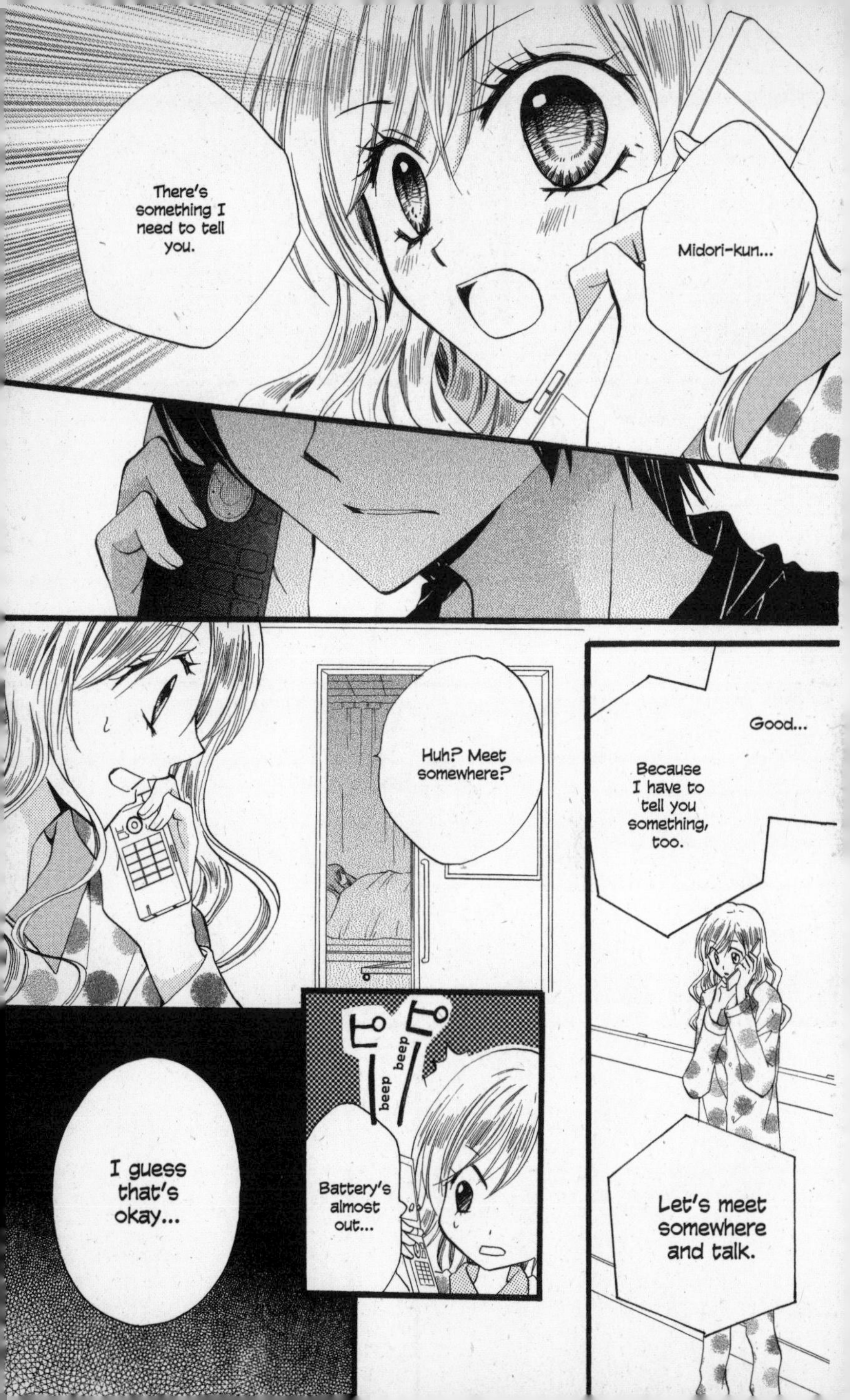

Midori-kun...
There's something I need to tell you.
Good...
Because I have to tell you something, too.
Let's meet somewhere and talk.
Huh? Meet somewhere?
beep beep
Battery's almost out...
I guess that's okay...

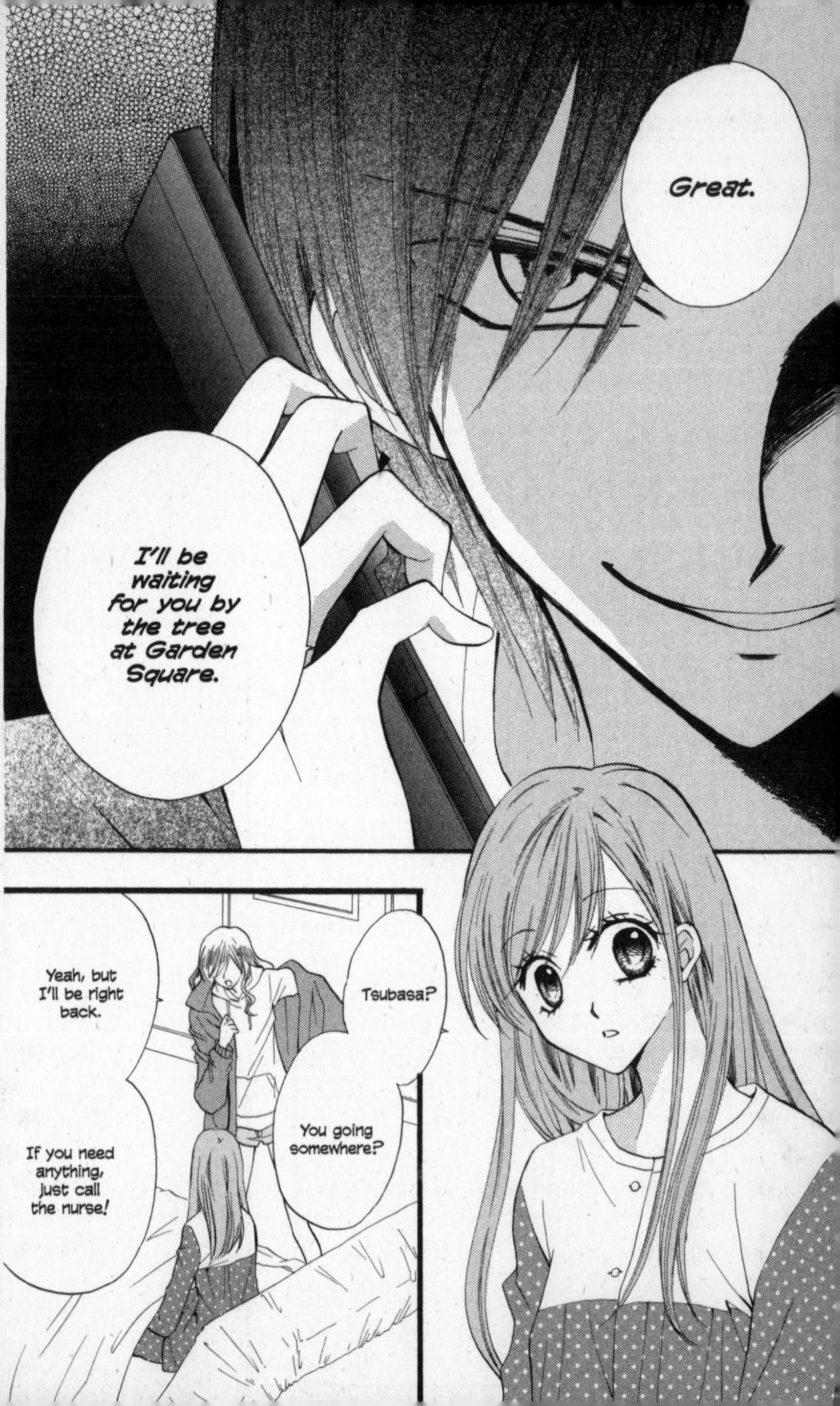
Great.
I'll be waiting for you by the tree at Garden Square.
Tsubasa?
You going somewhere?
Yeah, but I'll be right back.
If you need anything, just call the nurse!

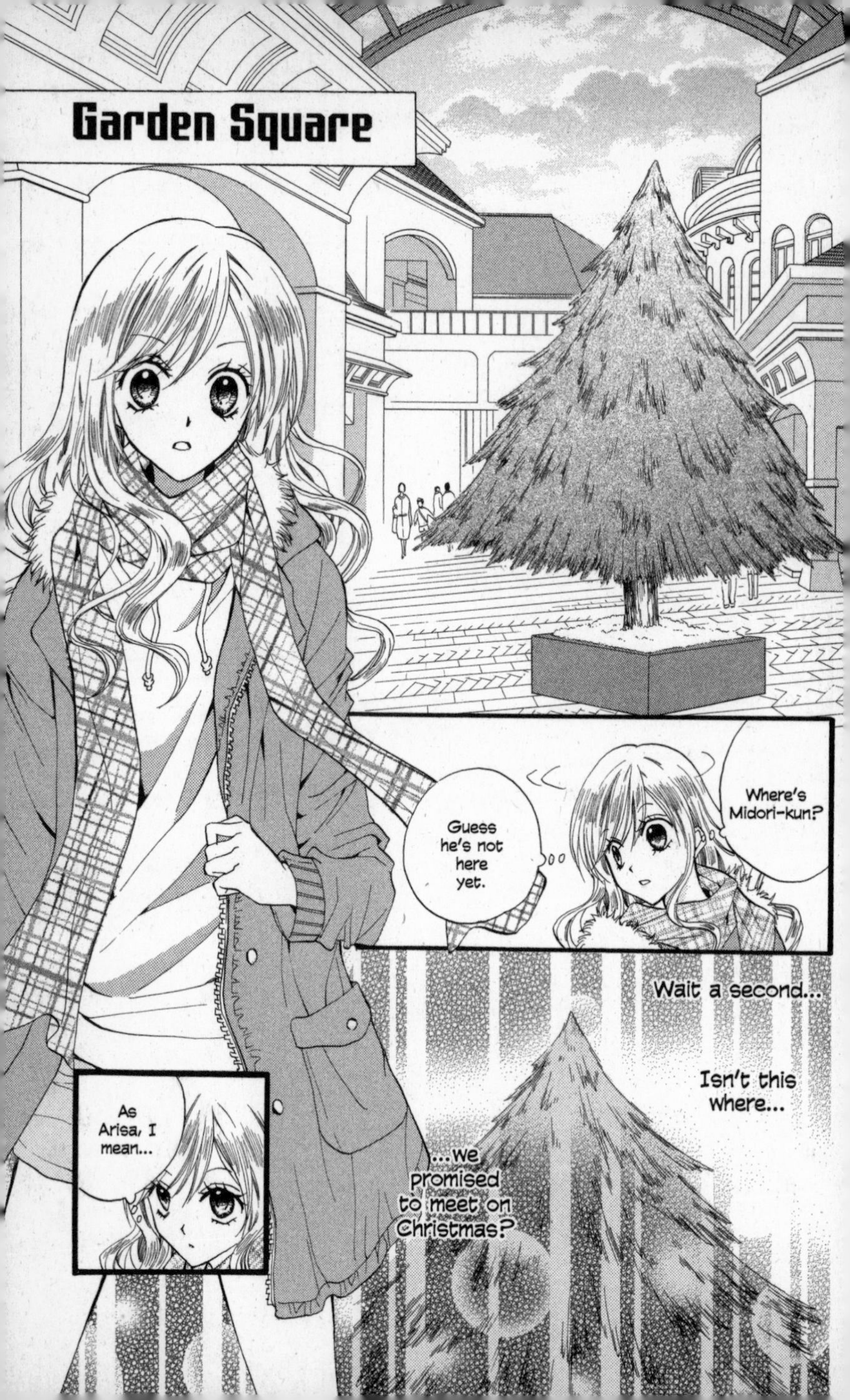

Garden Square
Where's Midori-kun?
Guess he's not here yet.
Wait a second...
Isn't this where...
...we promised to meet on Christmas?
As Arisa, I mean...

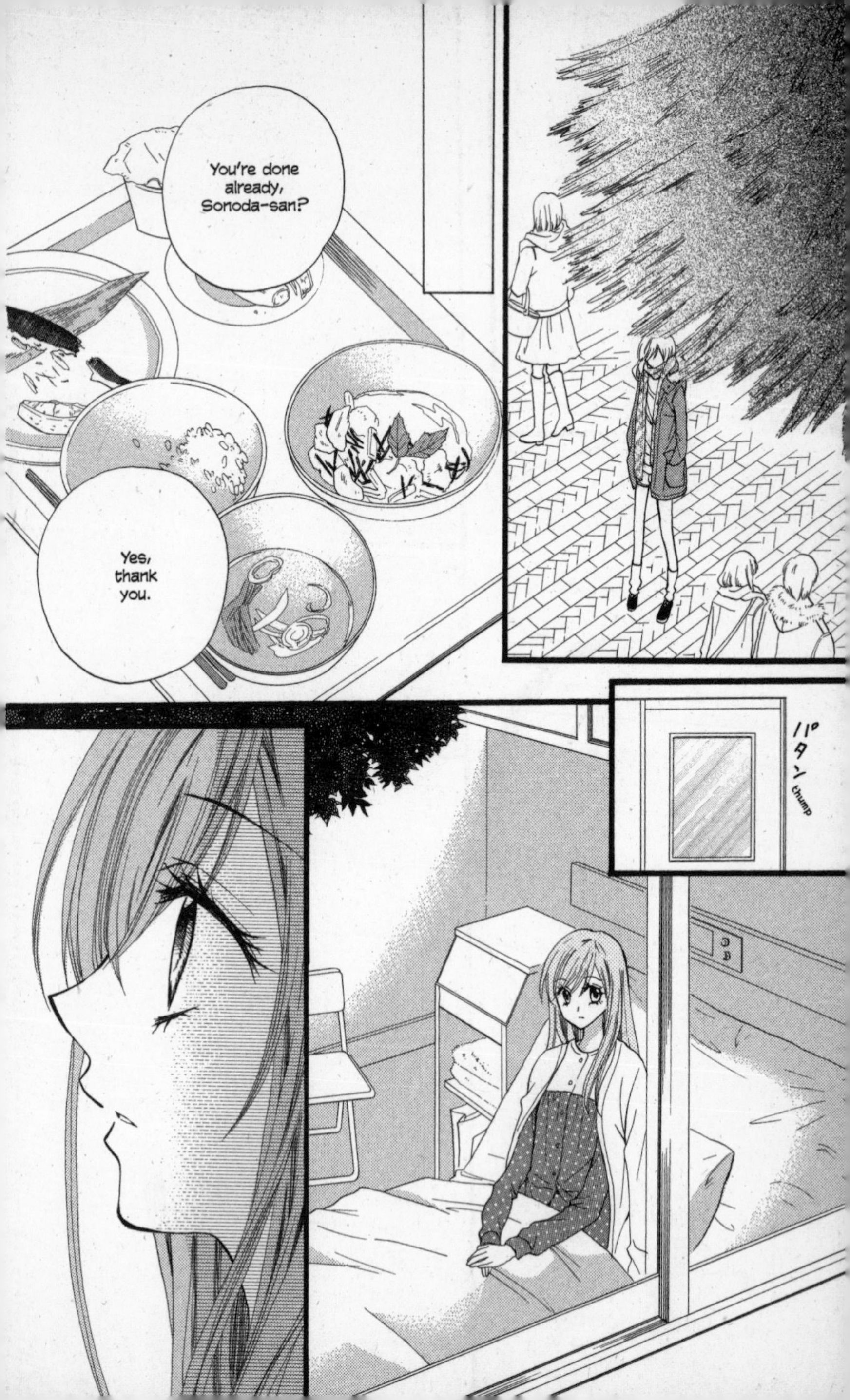
You're done already, Sonoda-san?
Yes, thank you.
パタン
thump

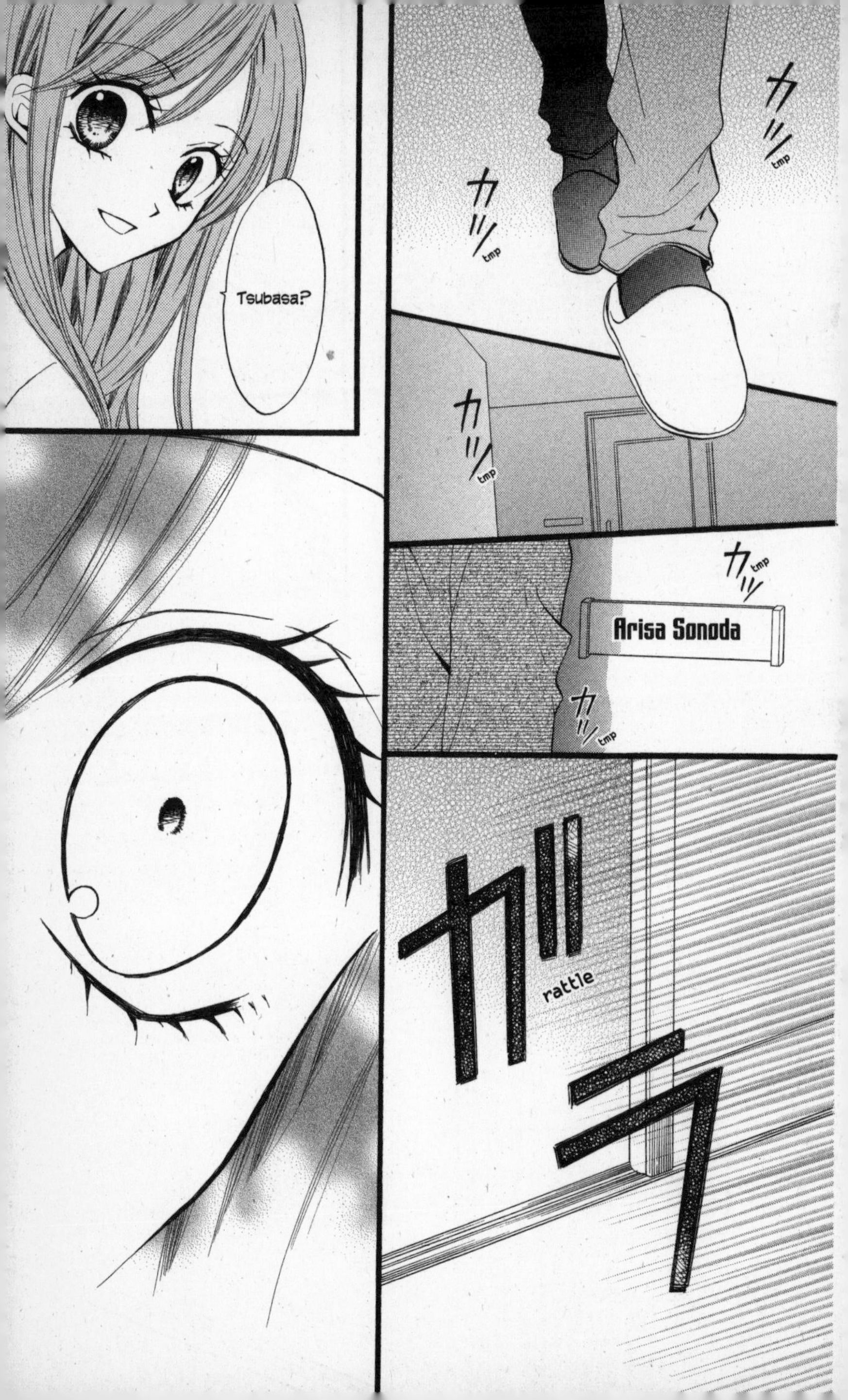
tmp
tmp
tmp
Tsubasa?
tmp
Arisa Sonoda
tmp
rattle

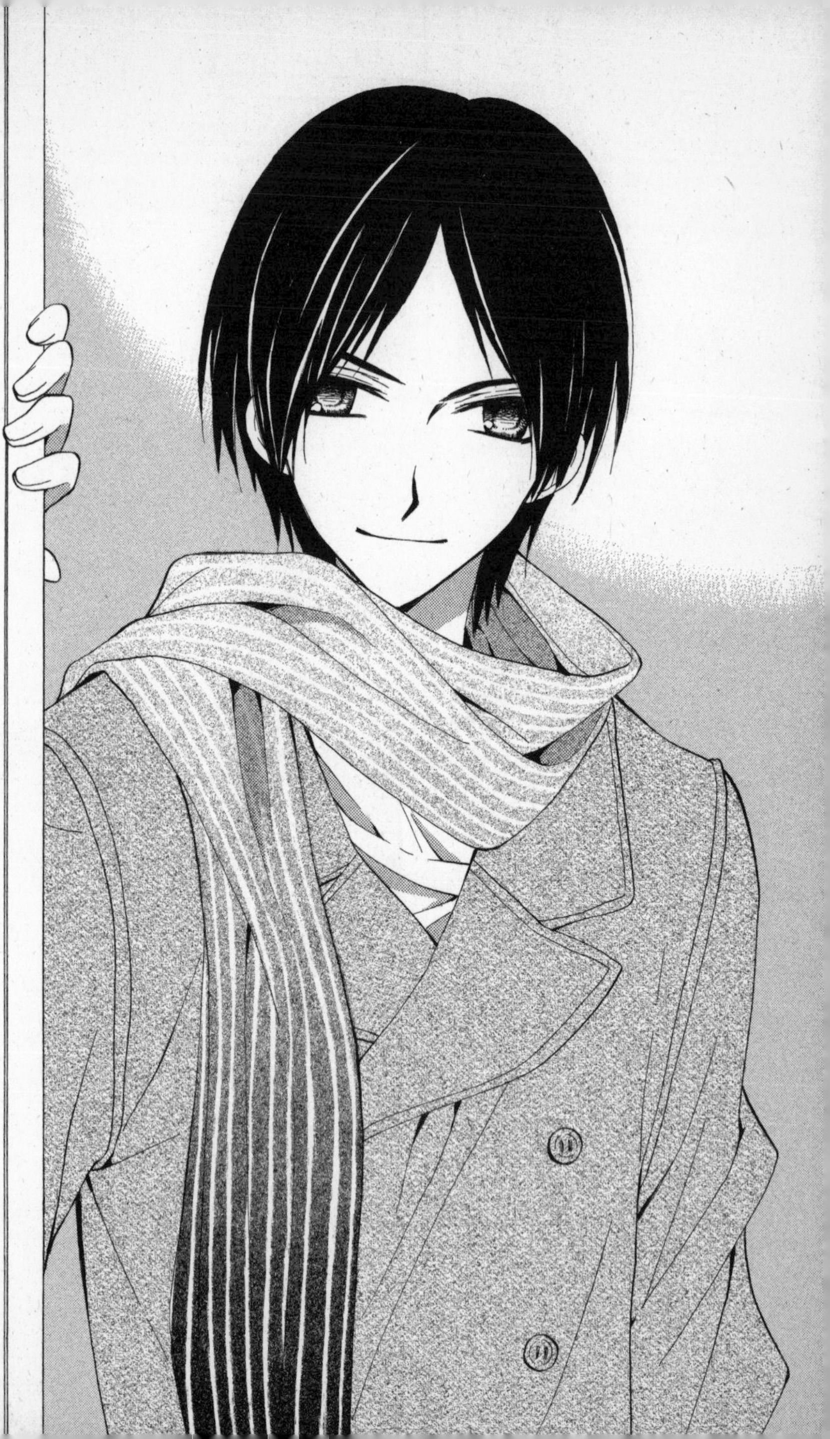

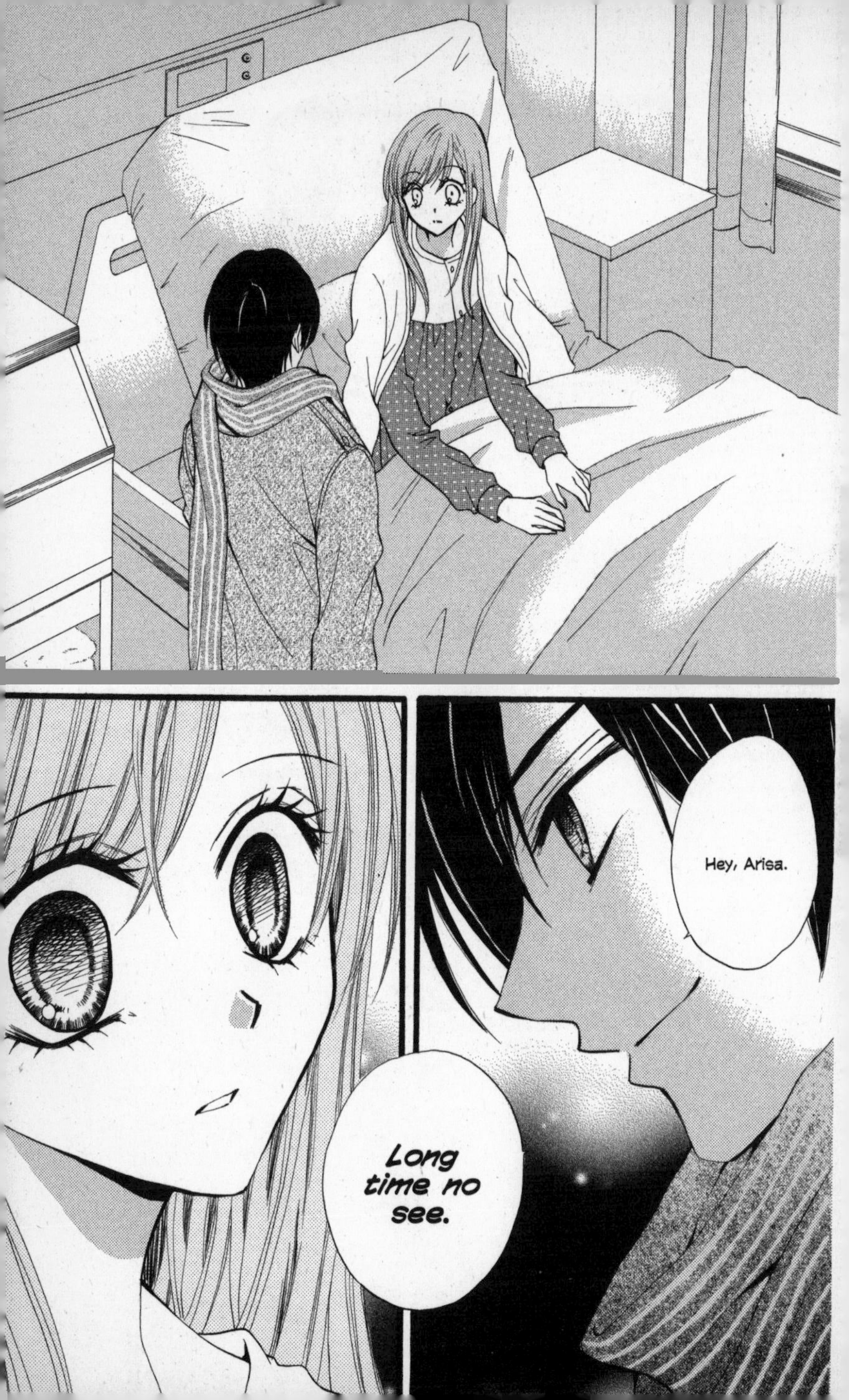
Hey, Arisa.
Long time no see.

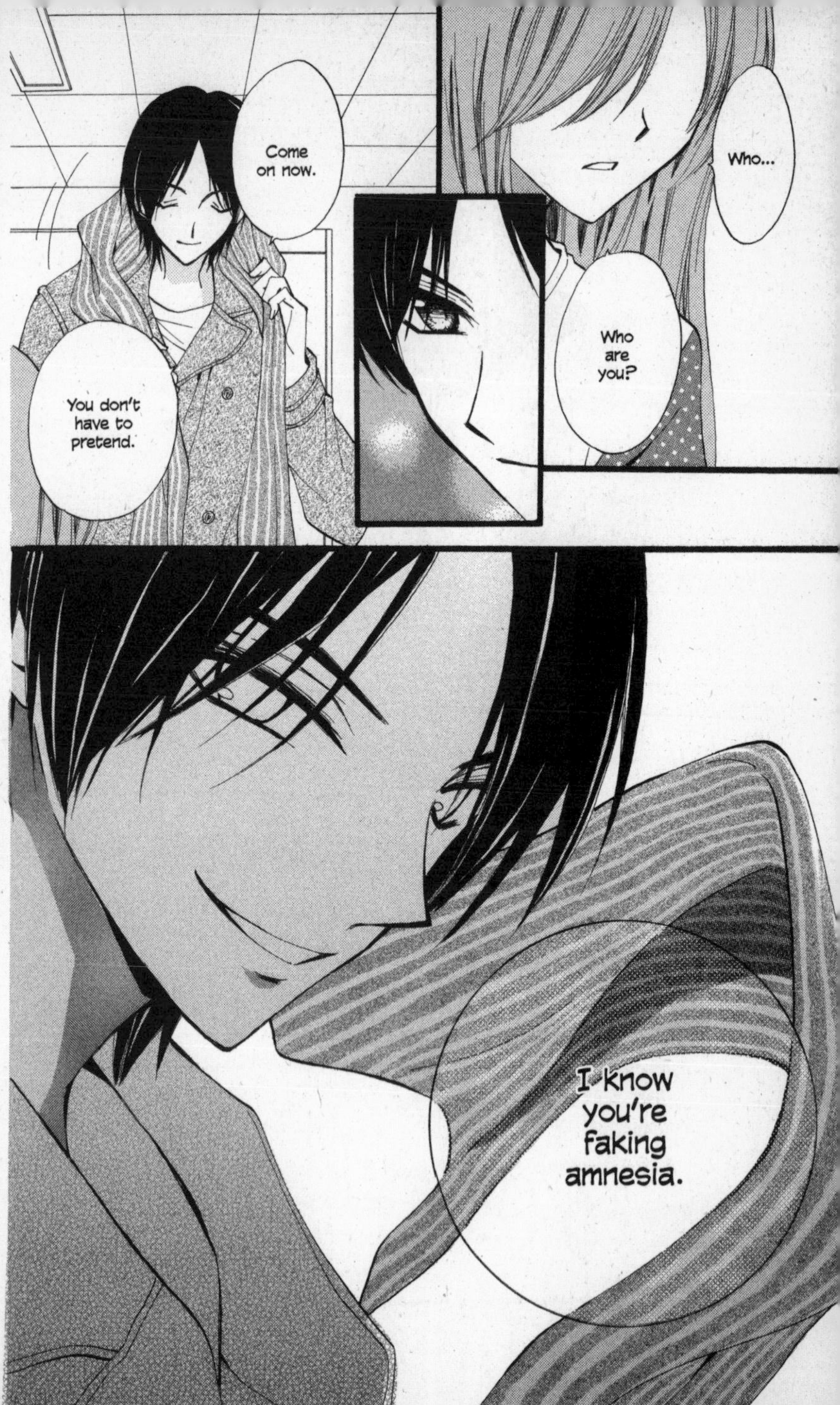
Who...
Who are you?
Come on now.
You don't have to pretend.
I know you're faking amnesia.

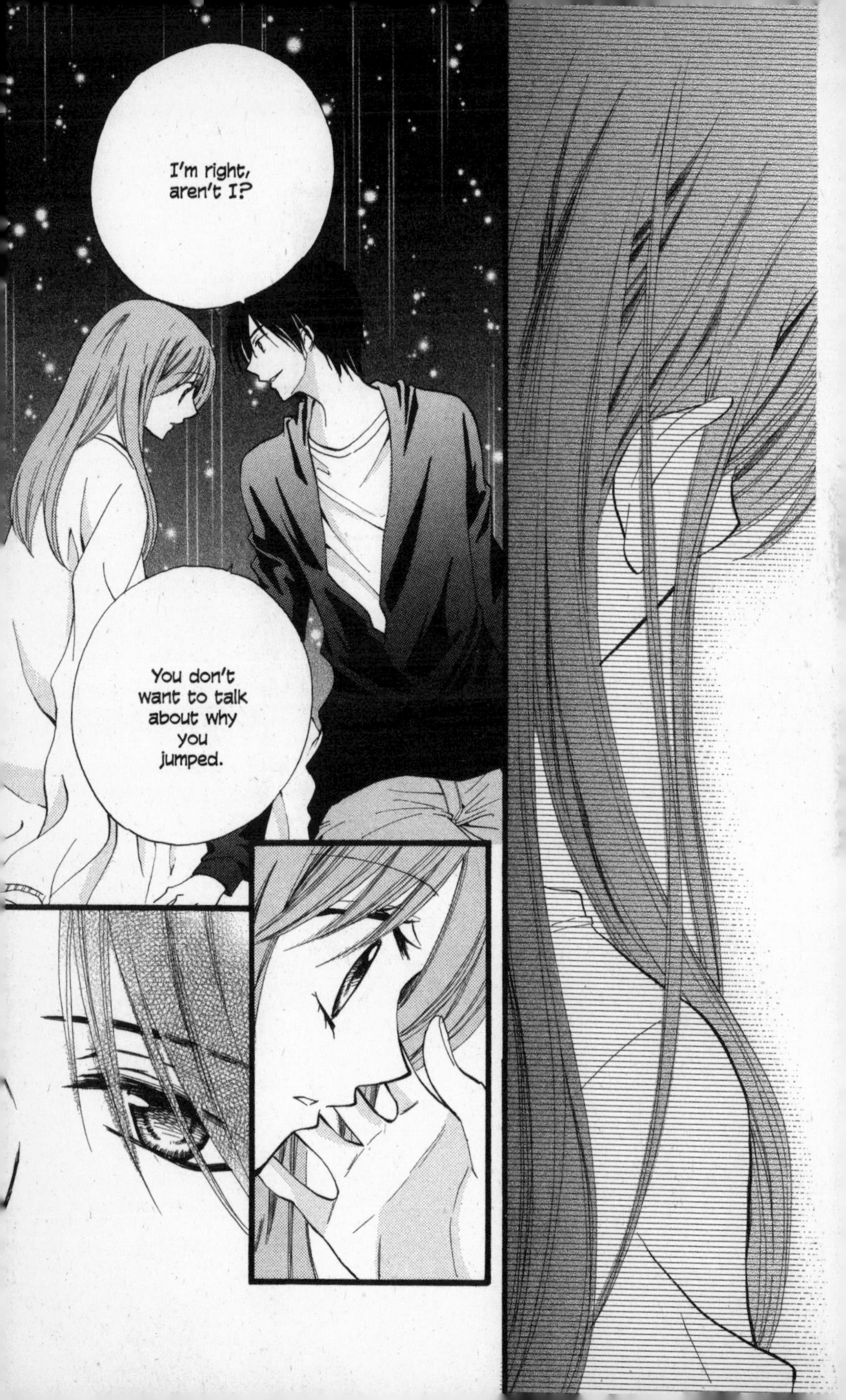
I'm right, aren't I?
You don't want to talk about why you jumped.

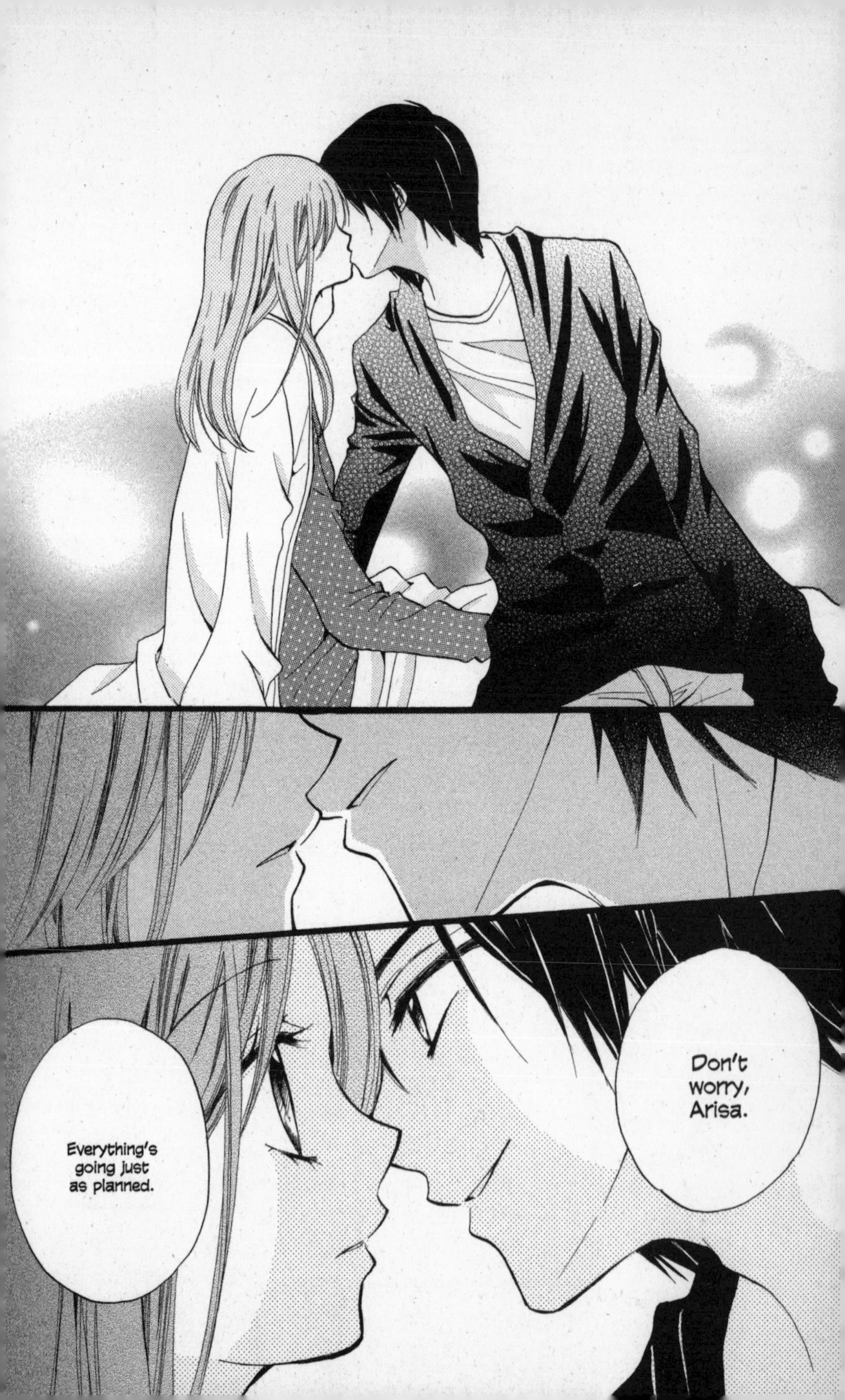
Don't worry, Arisa.
Everything's going just as planned.

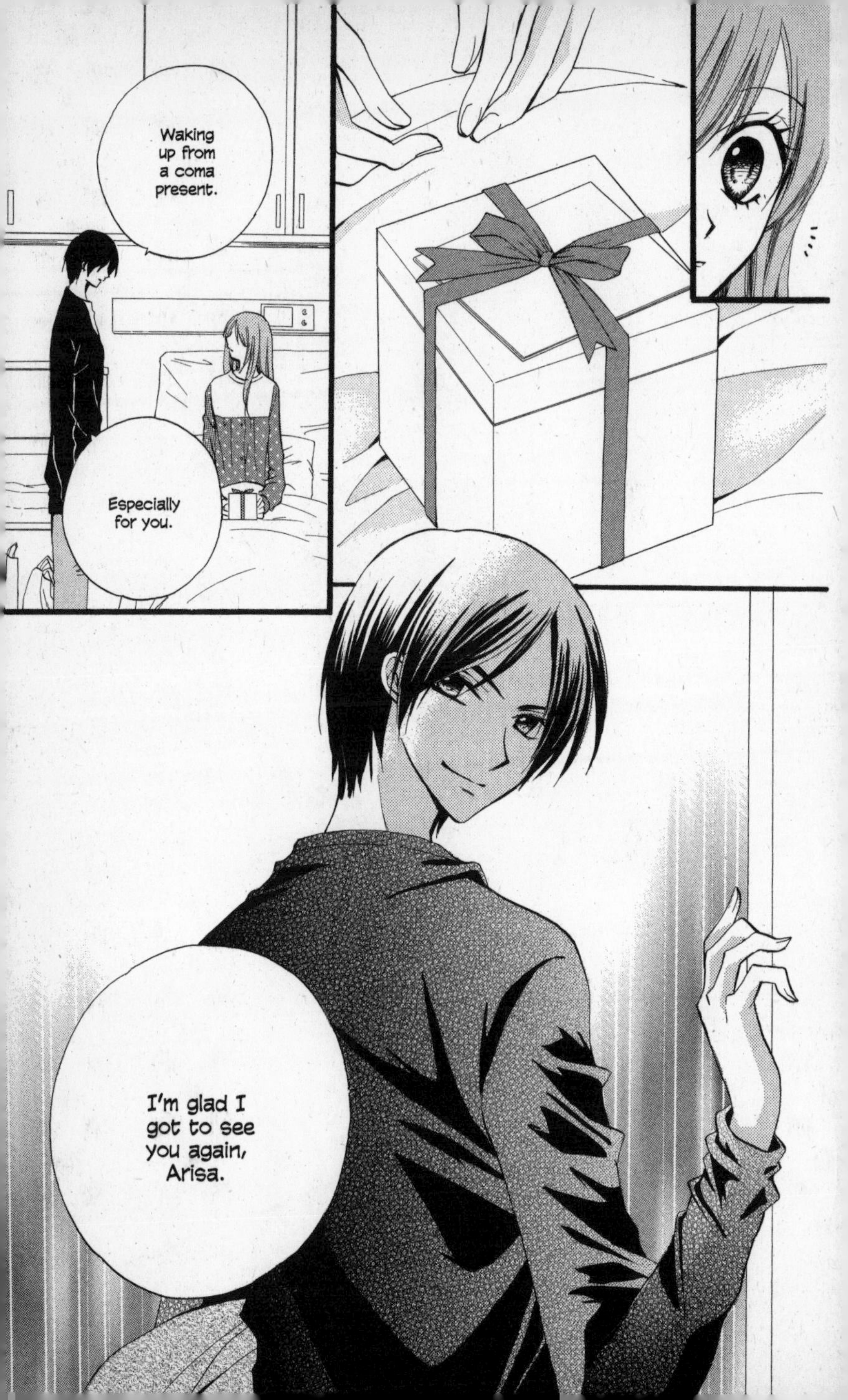
Waking up from a coma present.
Especially for you.
I'm glad I got to see you again, Arisa.

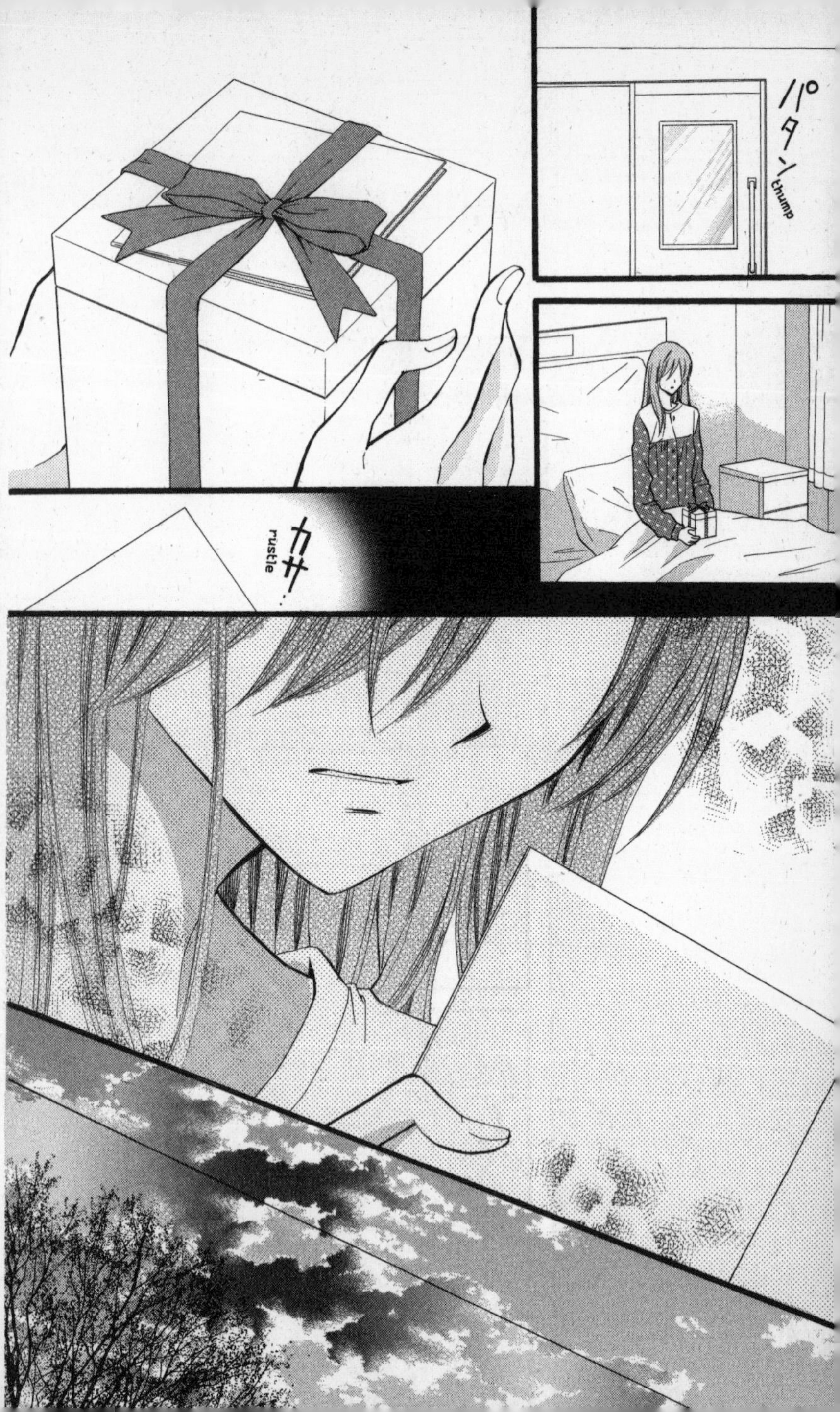
パタン
thump
カサッ
rustle

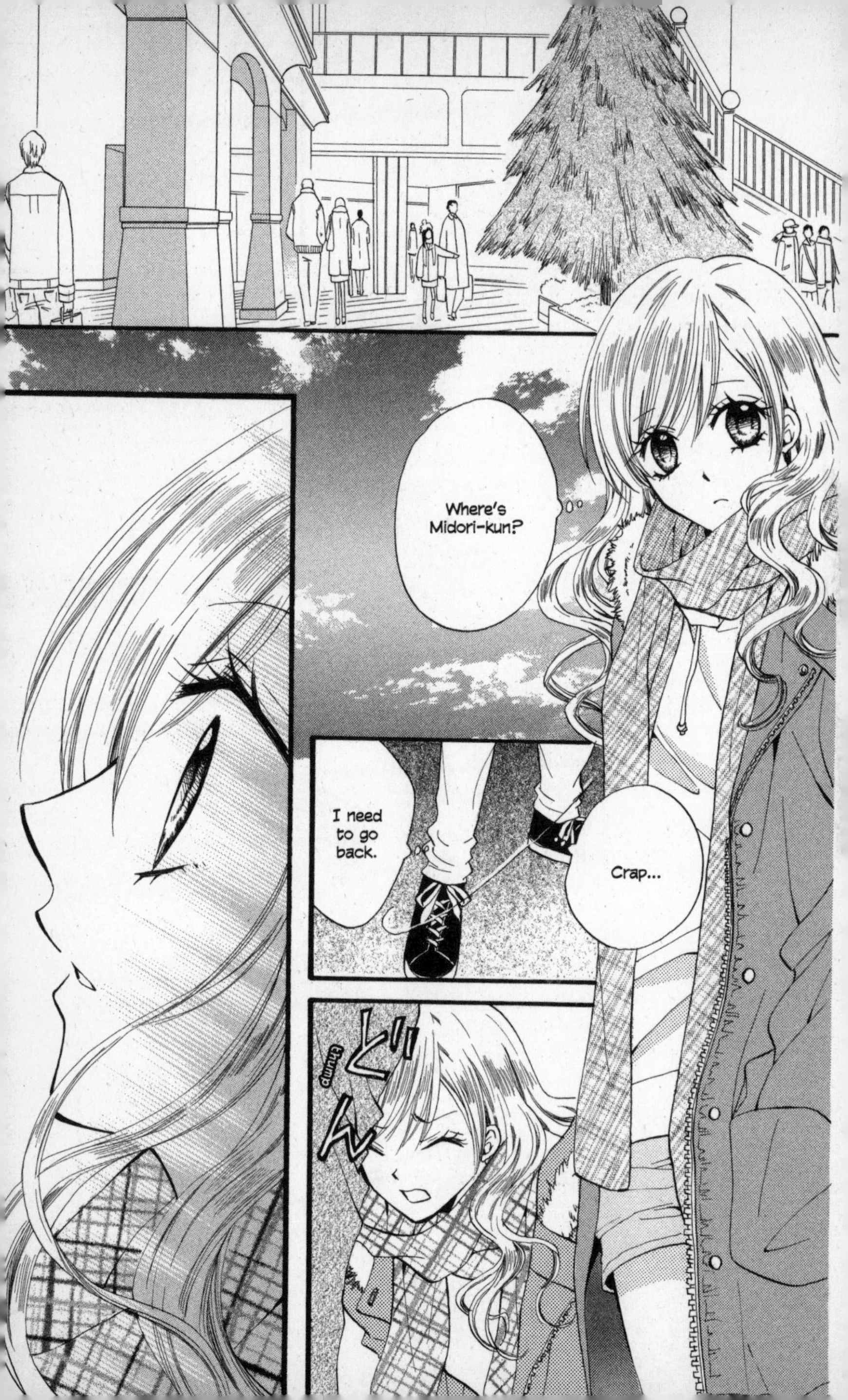

Where's Midori-kun?
Crap...
I need to go back.
thump

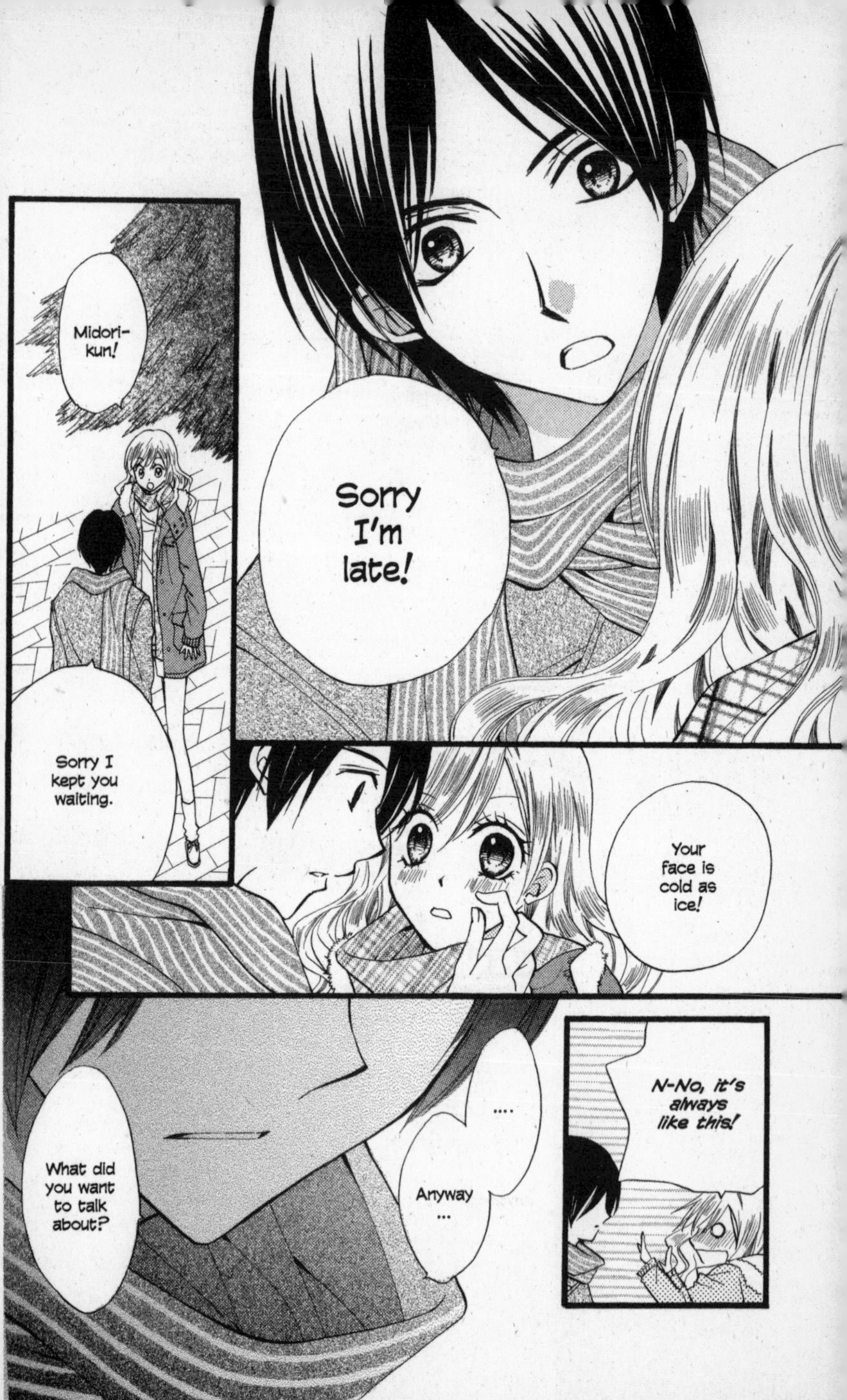

Sorry I'm late!
Midori-kun!
Sorry I kept you waiting.
Your face is cold as ice!
N-No, it's always like this!
....
Anyway ...
What did you want to talk about?

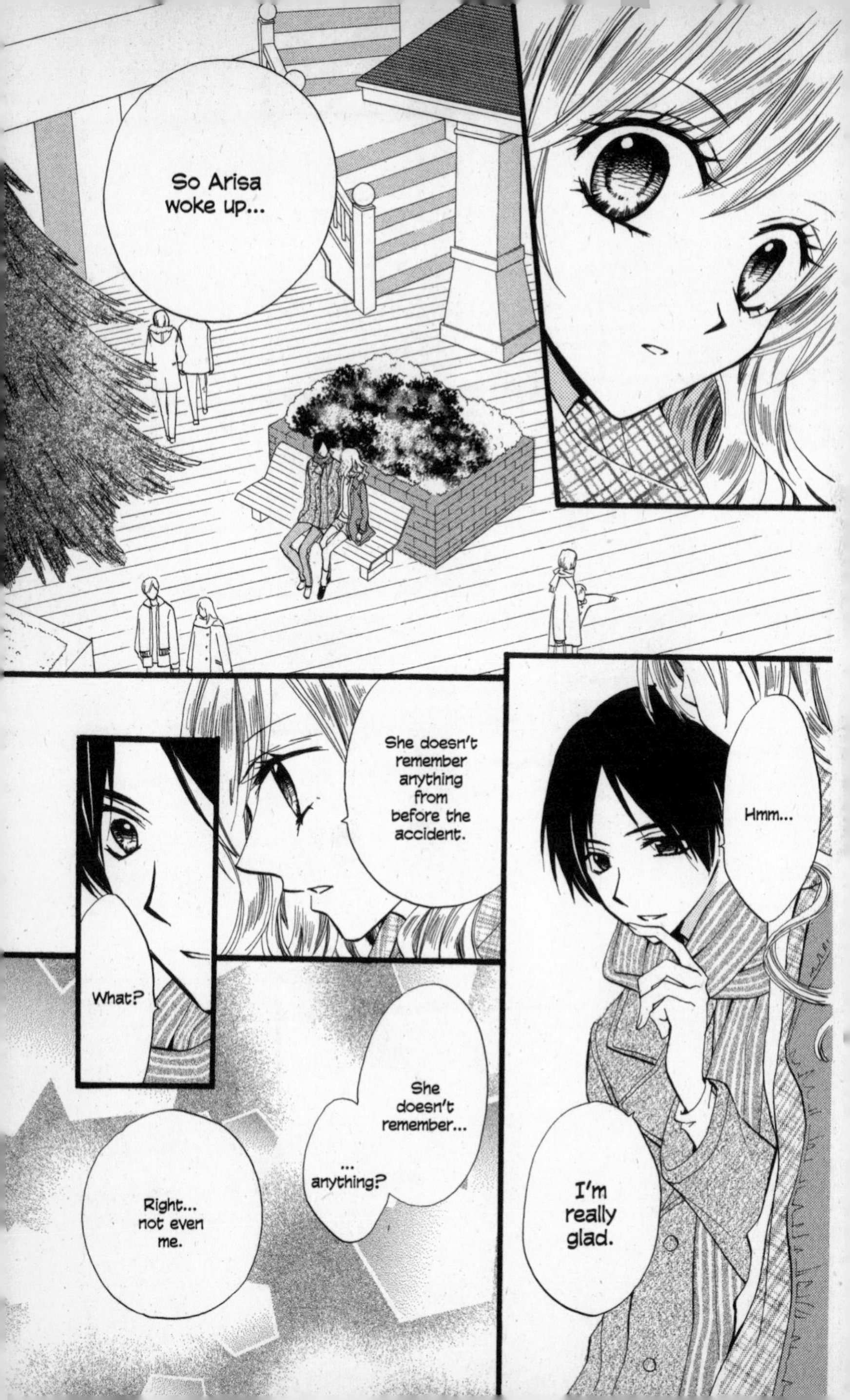
So Arisa woke up...
Hmm...
I'm really glad.
She doesn't remember anything from before the accident.
What?
She doesn't remember...
... anything?
Right... not even me.

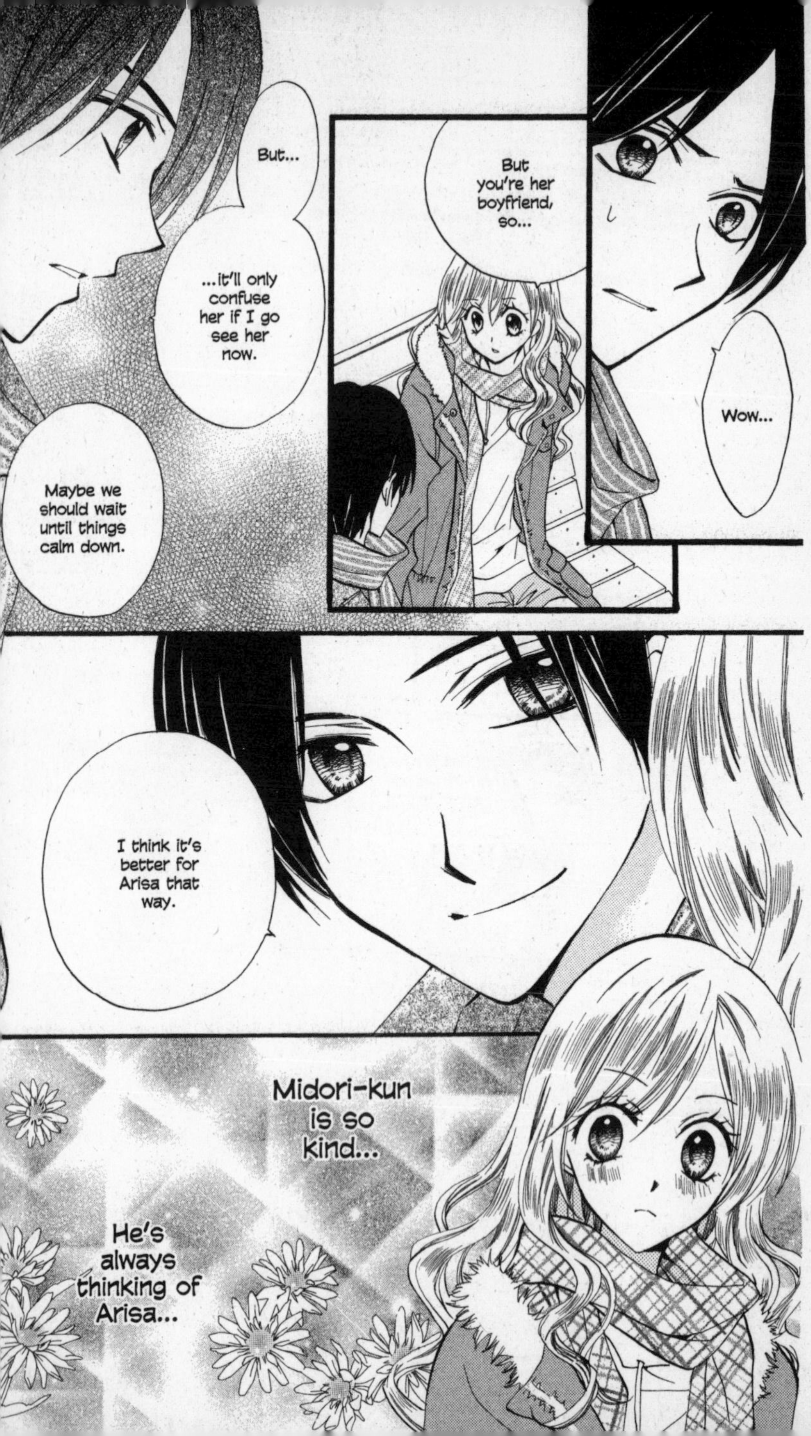
Wow...
But you're her boyfriend, so...
But...
...it'll only confuse her if I go see her now.
Maybe we should wait until things calm down.
I think it's better for Arisa that way.
Midori-kun is so kind...
He's always thinking of Arisa...

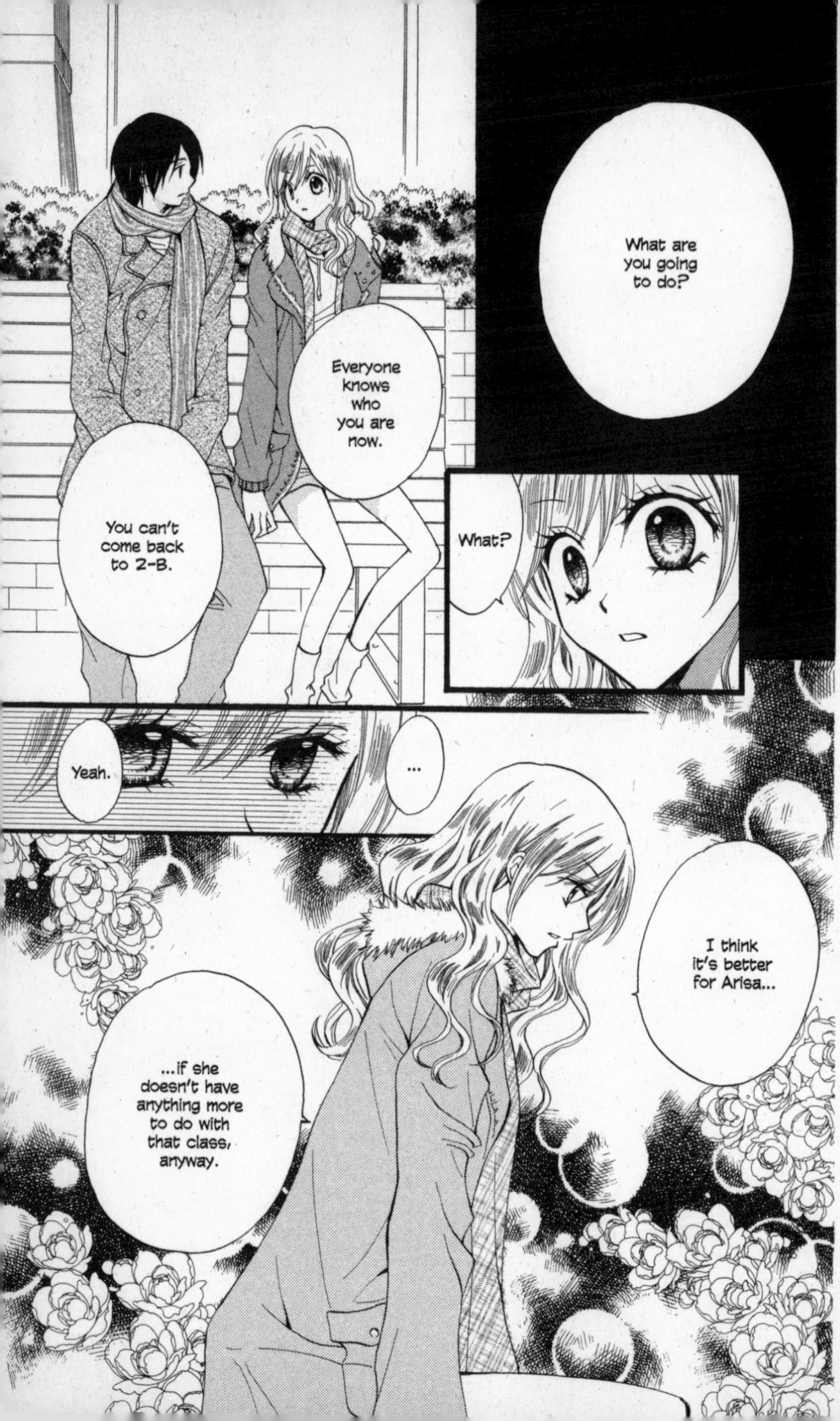

What are you going to do?
Everyone knows who you are now.
You can't come back to 2-B.
What?
...
Yeah.
I think it's better for Arisa...
...if she doesn't have anything more to do with that class, anyway.

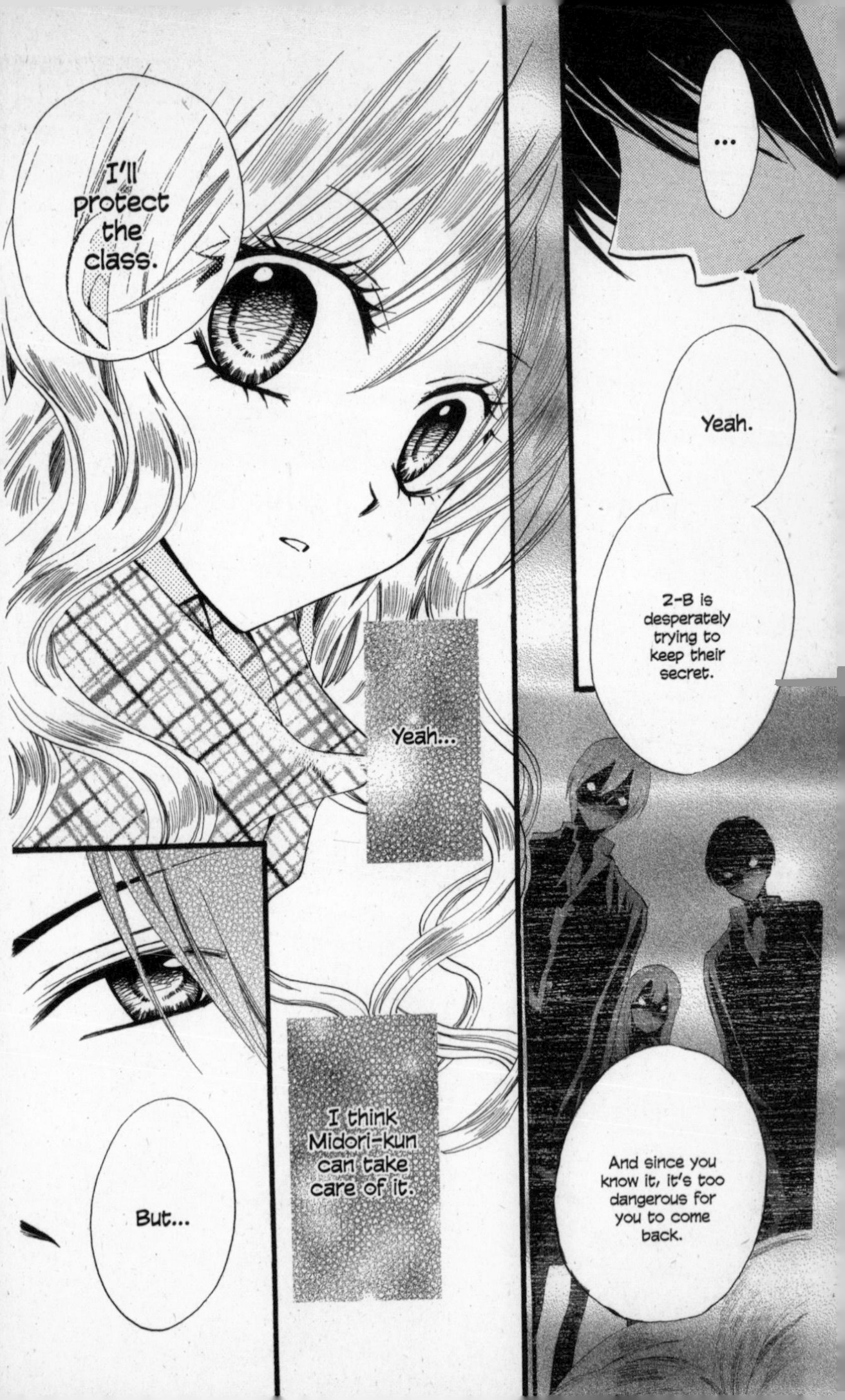
...
Yeah.
2-B is desperately trying to keep their secret.
And since you know it, it's too dangerous for you to come back.
I'll protect the class.
Yeah...
I think Midori-kun can take care of it.
But...

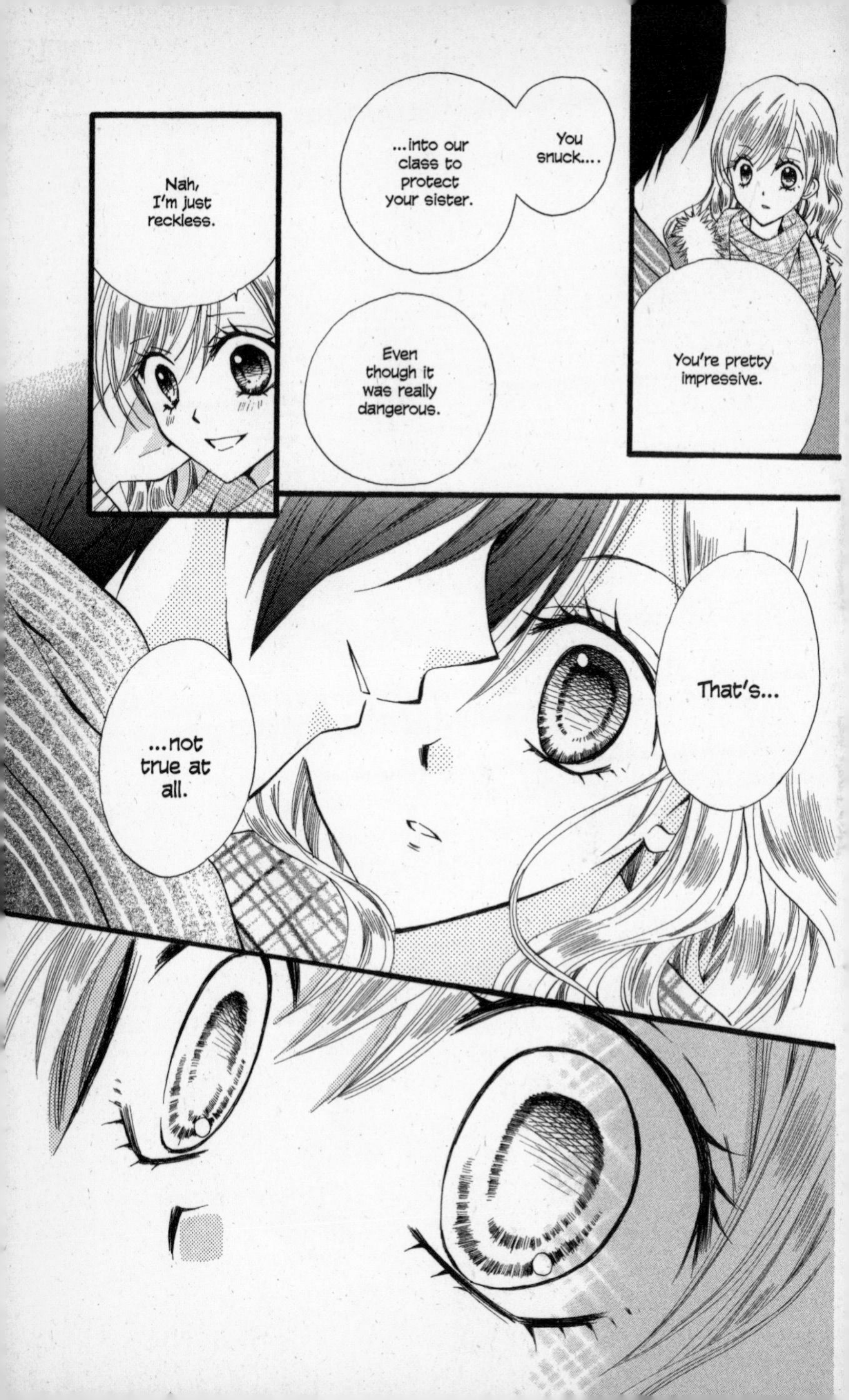
You snuck....
...into our class to protect your sister.
You're pretty impressive.
Even though it was really dangerous.
Nah, I'm just reckless.
That's...
...not true at all.

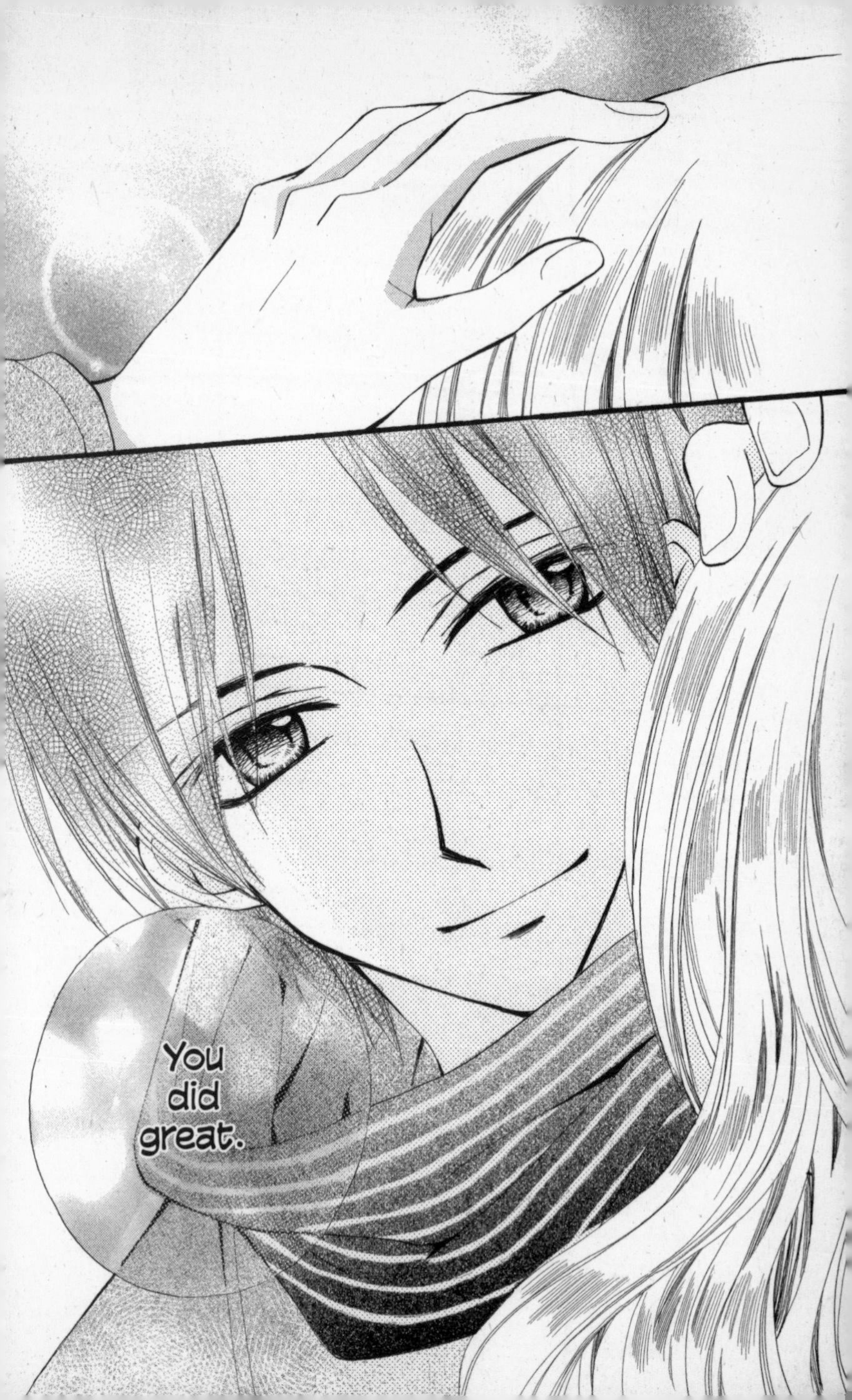
You did great.

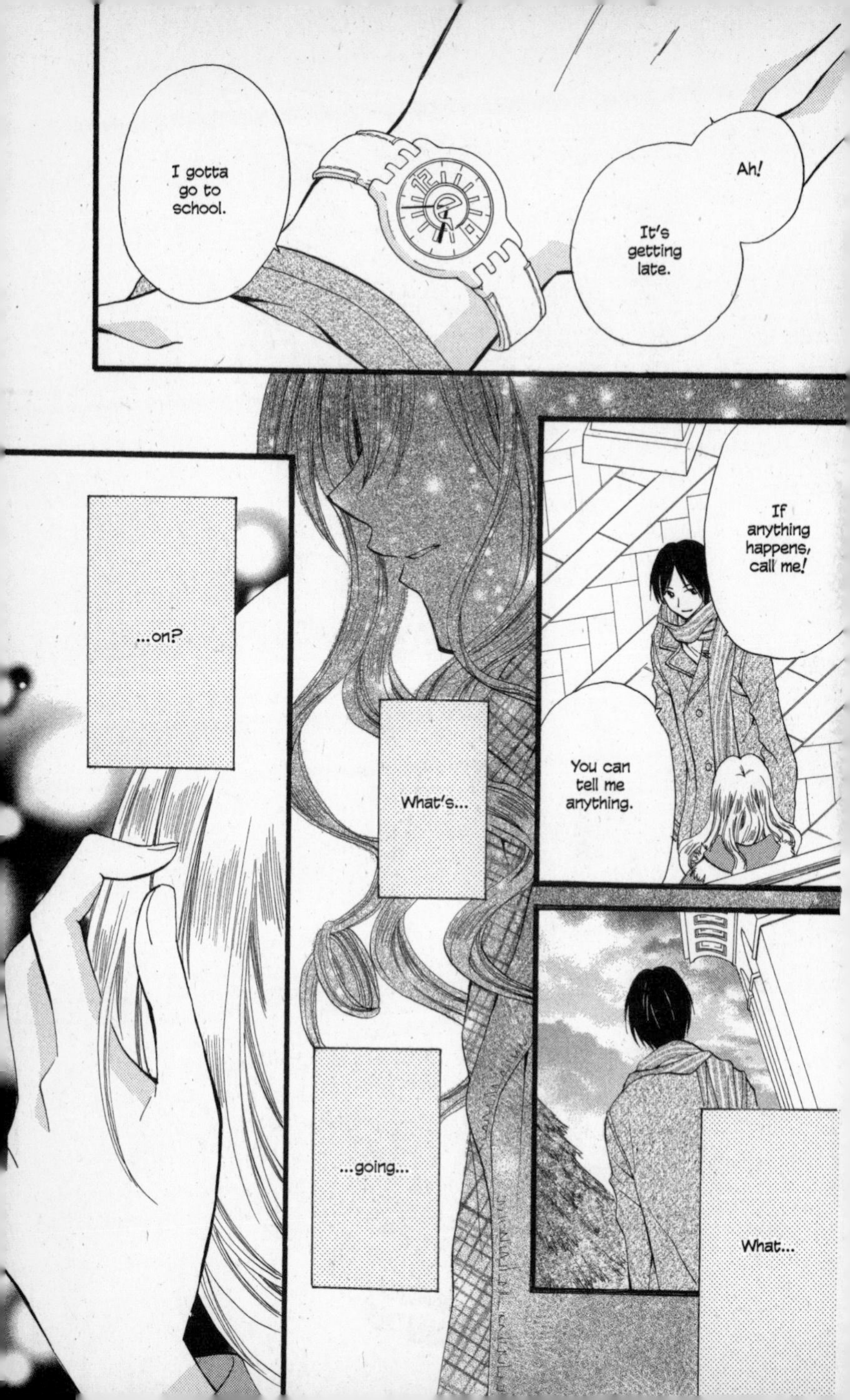
Ah! It's getting late.
I gotta go to school.
If anything happens, call me!
You can tell me anything.
What...
What's...
...going...
...on?

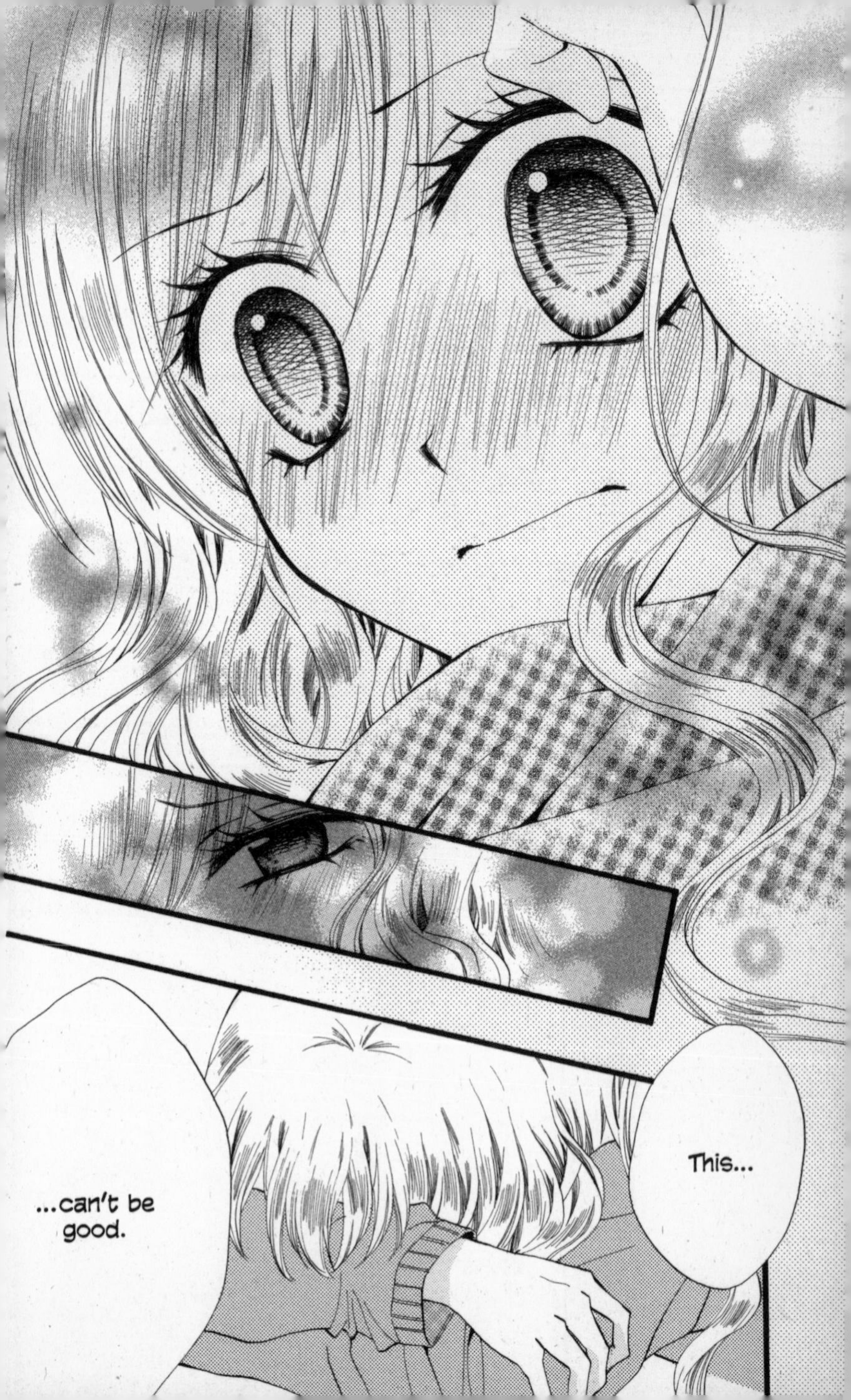
This...
...can't be good.

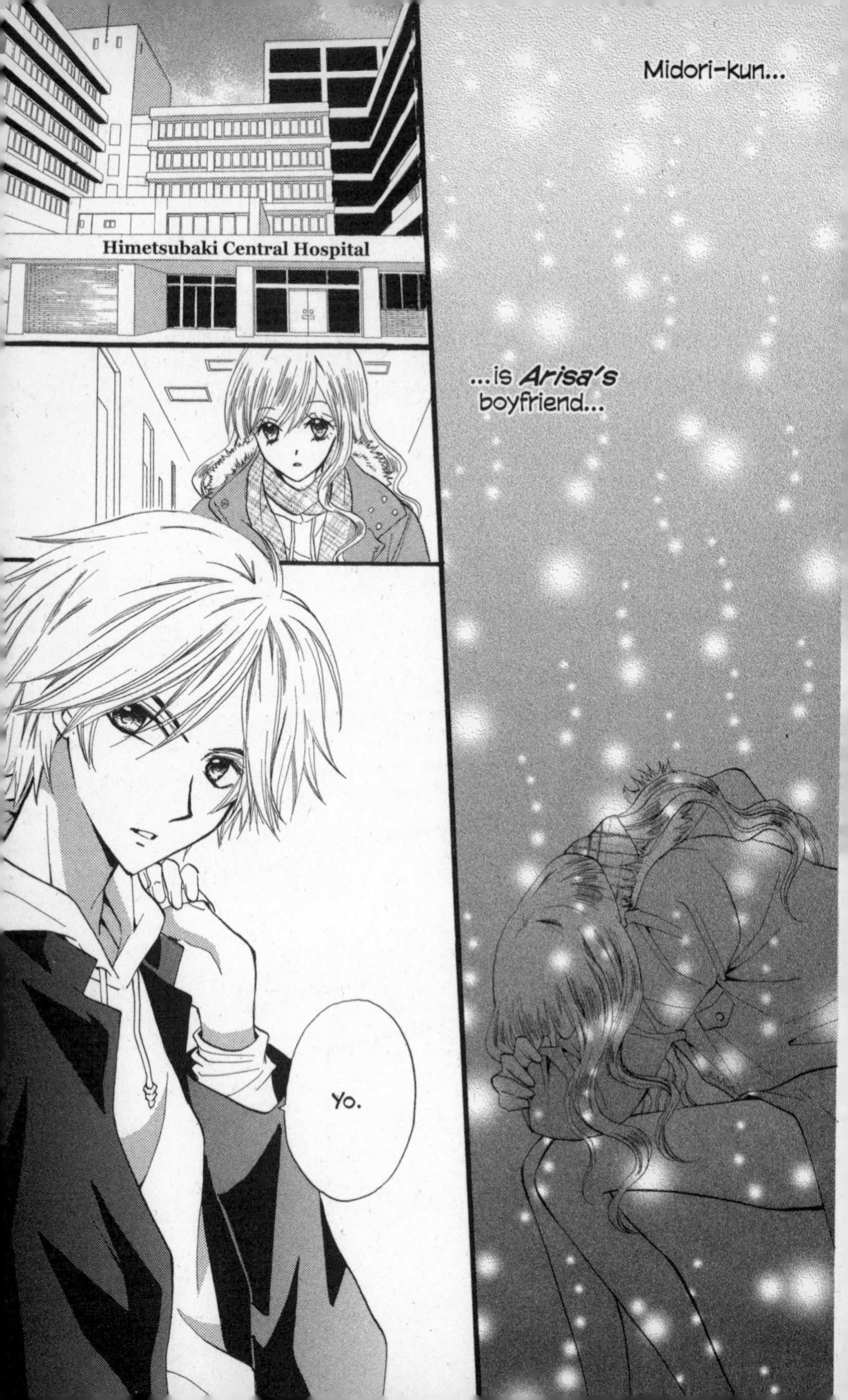
Midori-kun...
...is Arisa's boyfriend...
Himetsubaki Central Hospital
Yo.

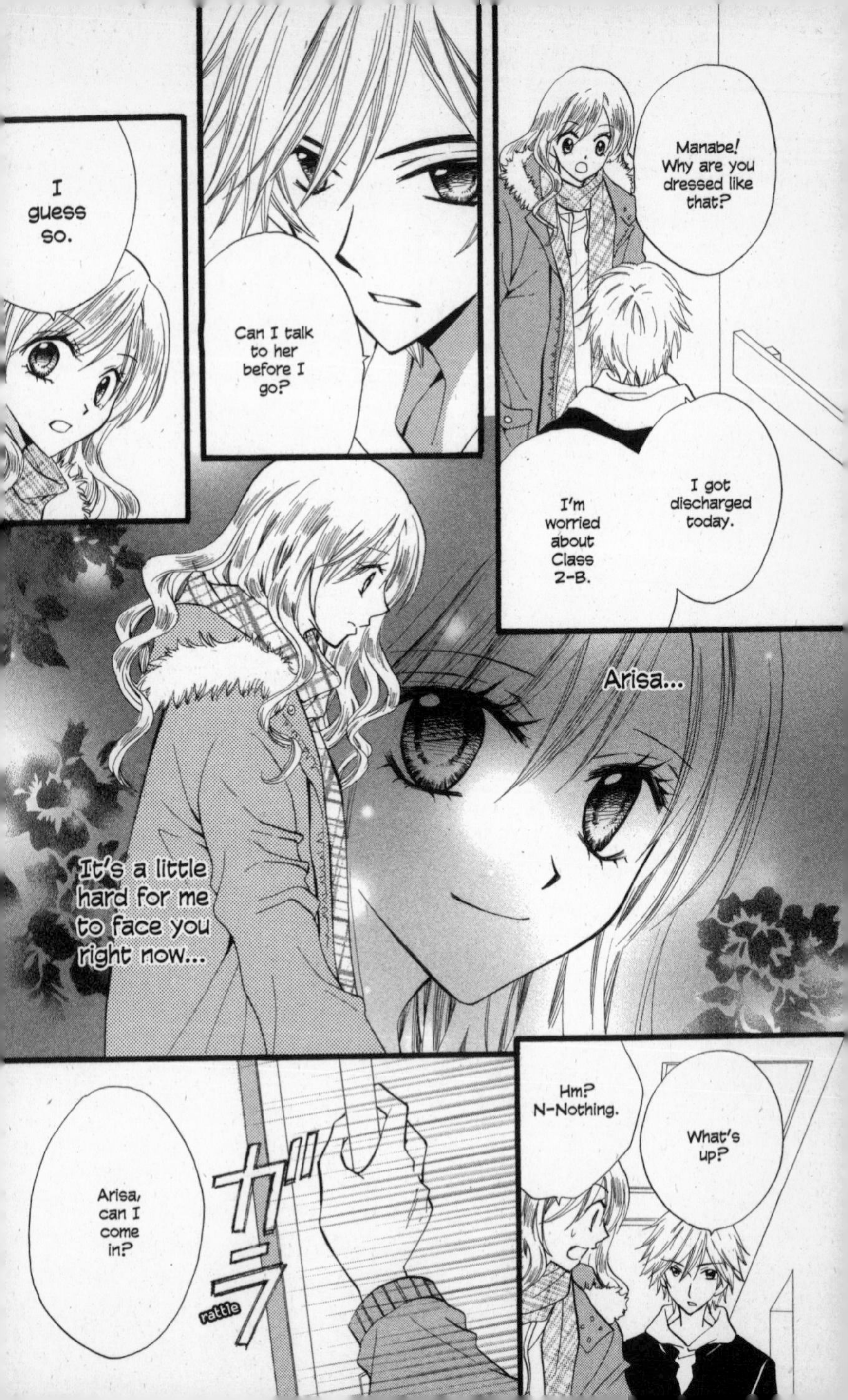
Manabe! Why are you dressed like that?
I got discharged today.
I'm worried about Class 2-B.
Can I talk to her before I go?
I guess so.
Arisa...
It's a little hard for me to face you right now...
What's up?
Hm? N-Nothing.
rattle
Arisa, can I come in?

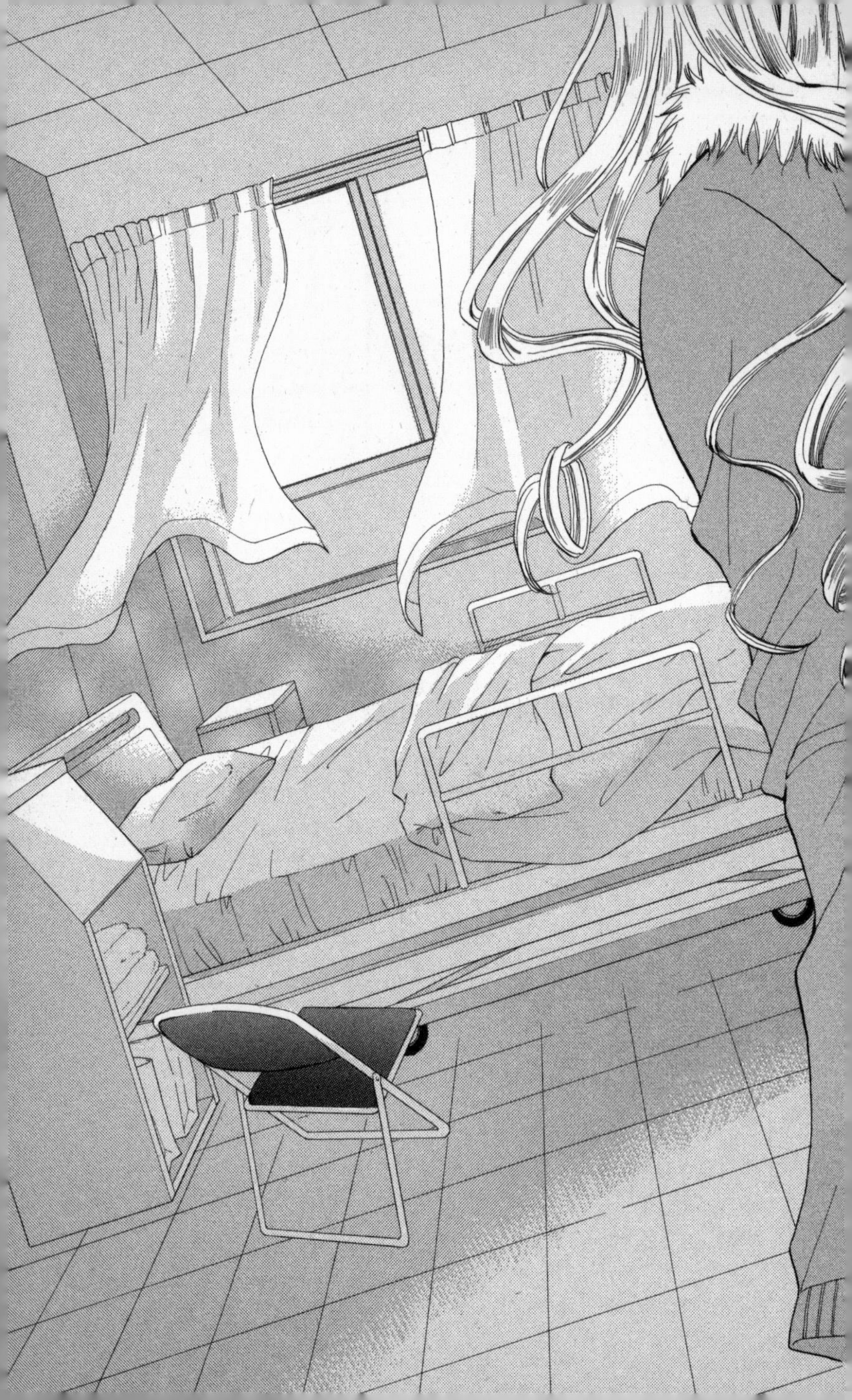

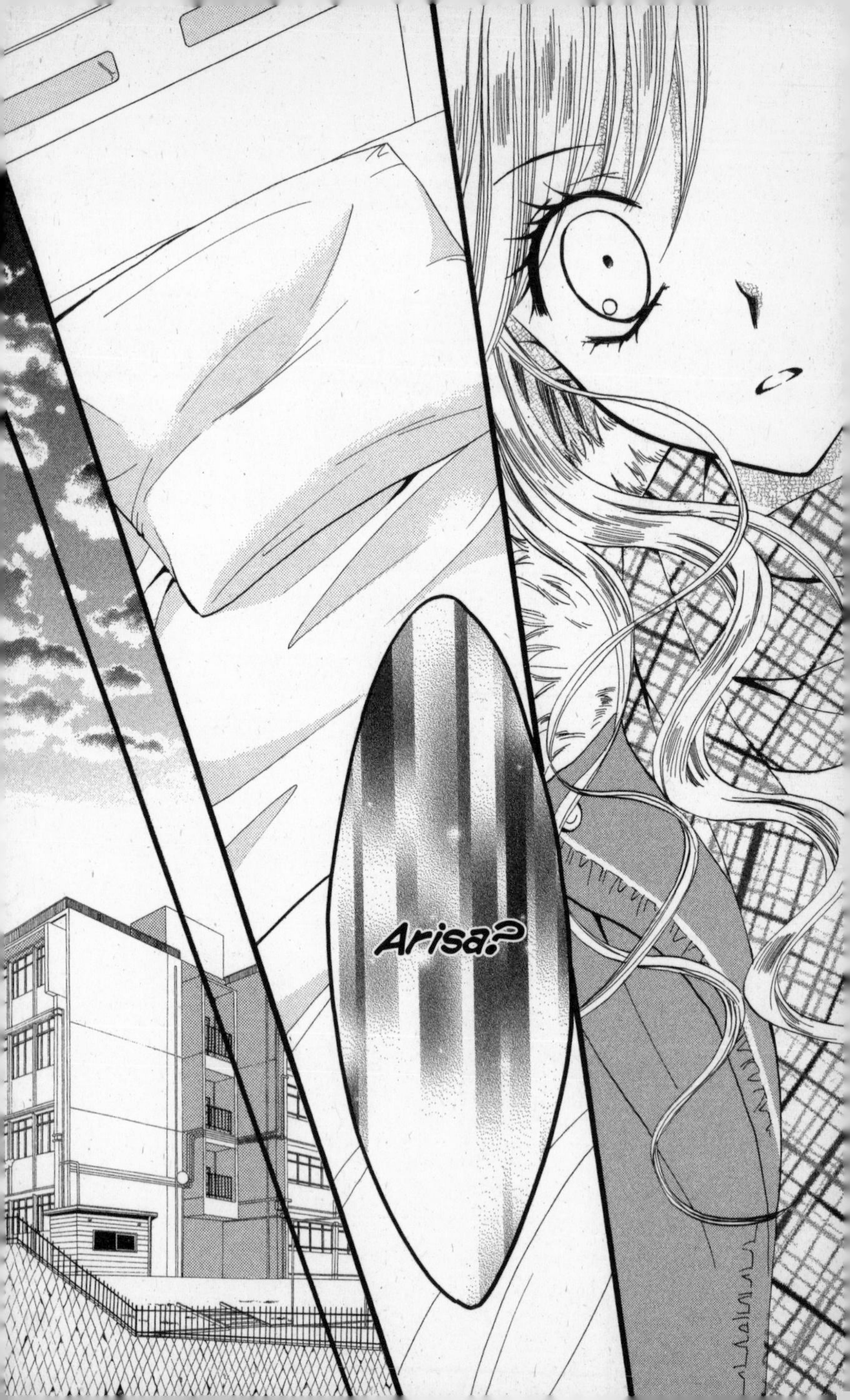
Arisa?

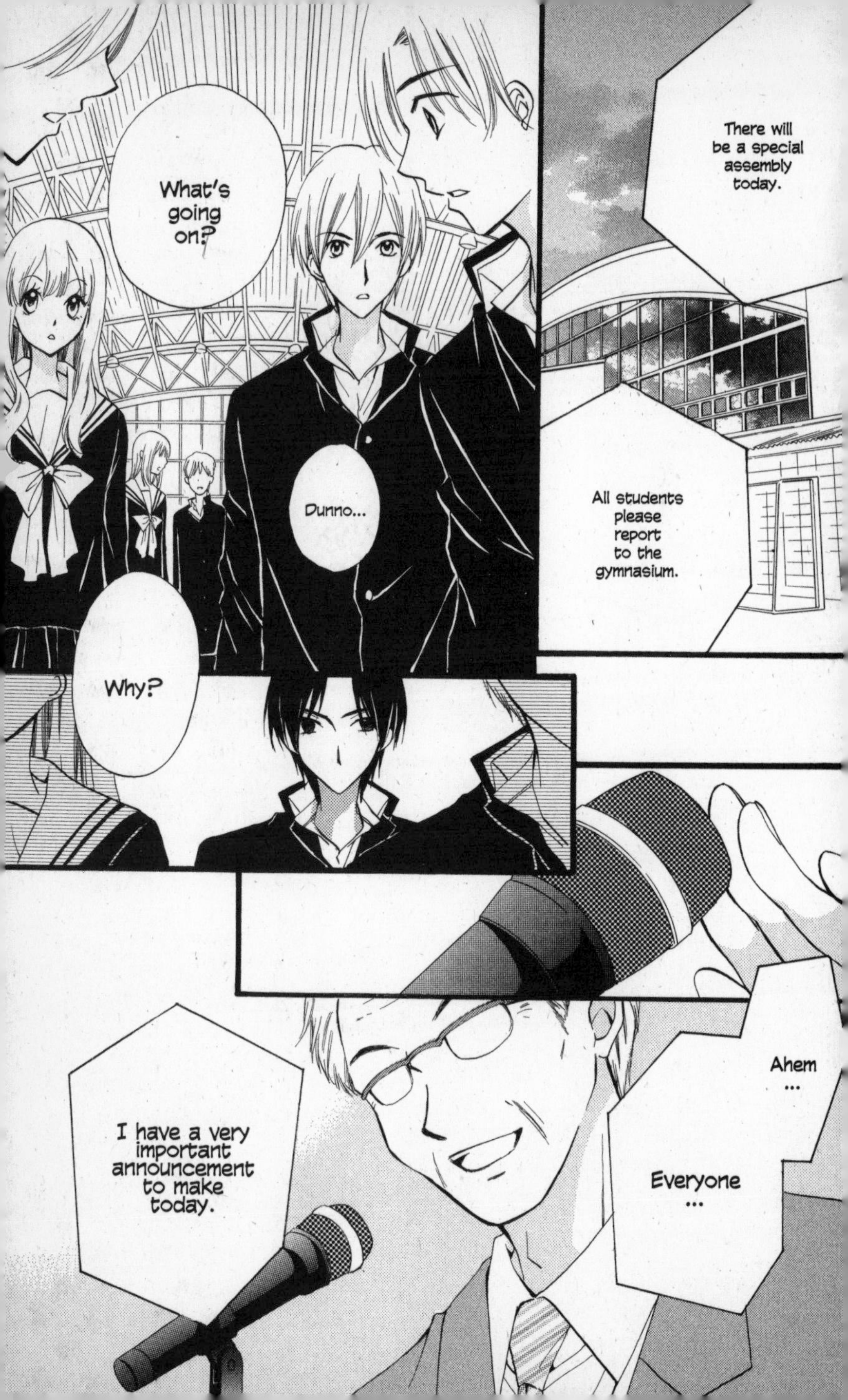
There will be a special assembly today.
All students please report to the gymnasium.
What's going on?
Dunno...
Why?
Ahem ...
Everyone ...
I have a very important announcement to make today.

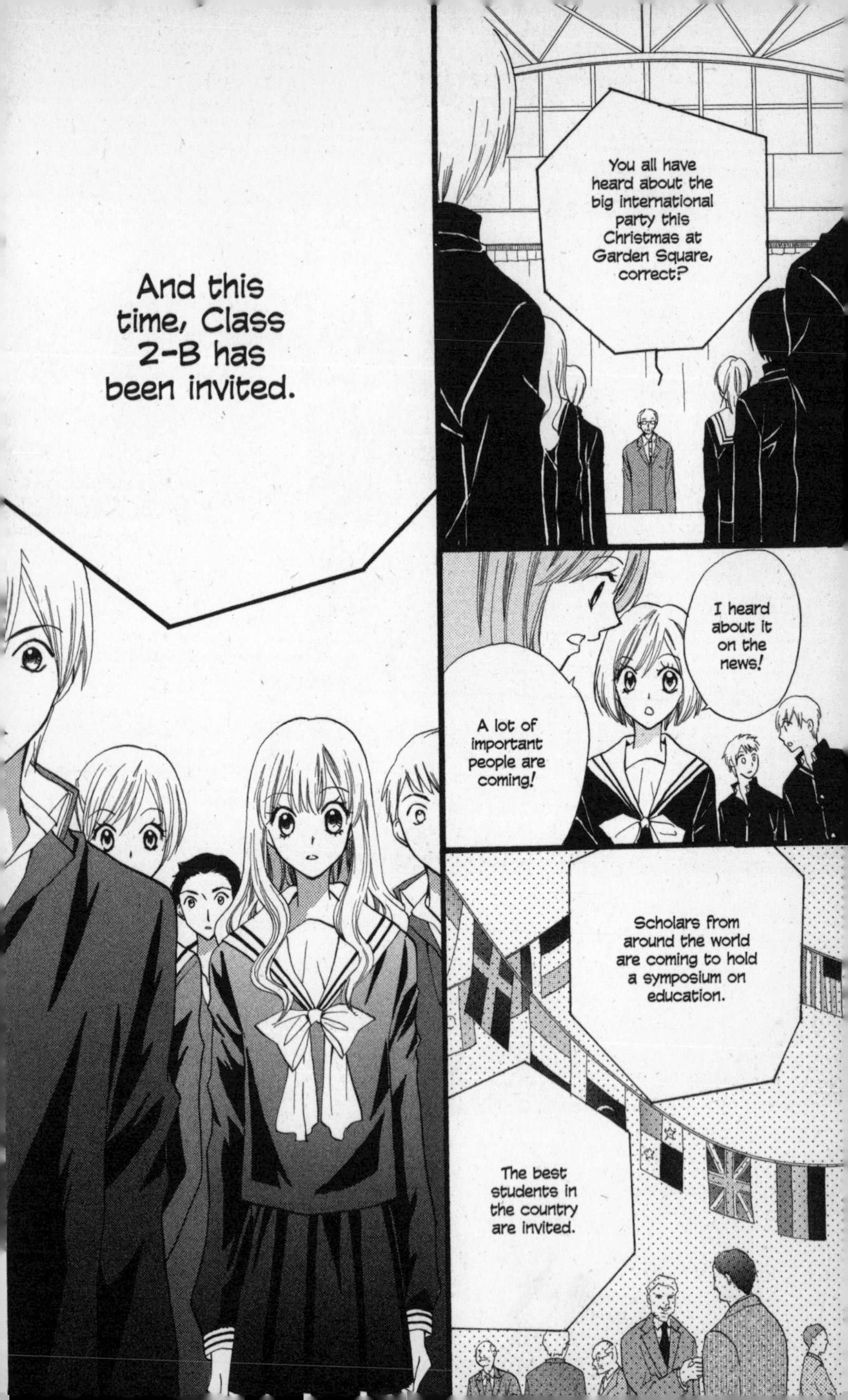
You all have heard about the big international party this Christmas at Garden Square, correct?
I heard about it on the news!
A lot of important people are coming!
Scholars from around the world are coming to hold a symposium on education.
The best students in the country are invited.
And this time, Class 2-B has been invited.

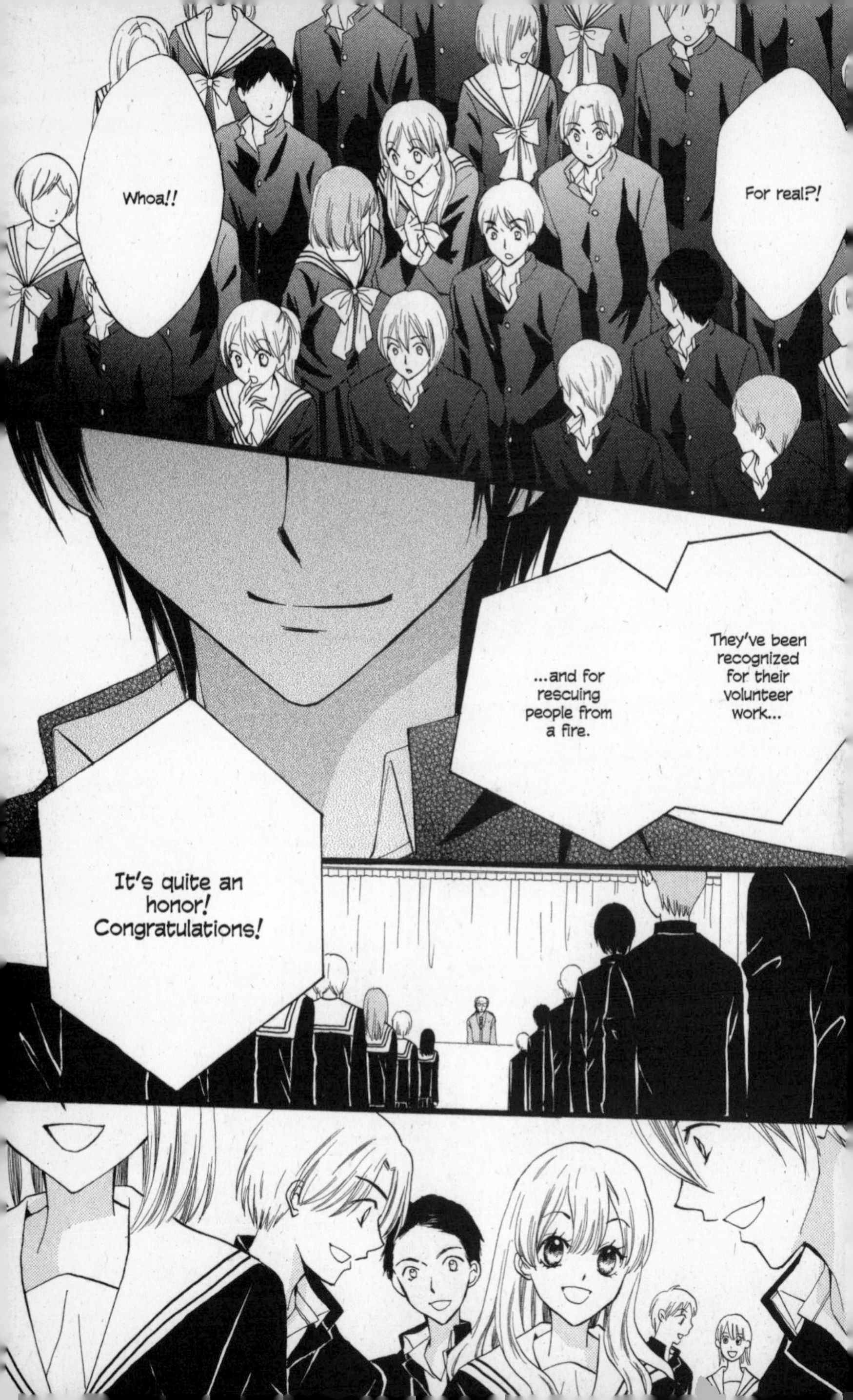
For real?!
Whoa!!
They've been recognized for their volunteer work...
...and for rescuing people from a fire.
It's quite an honor! Congratulations!

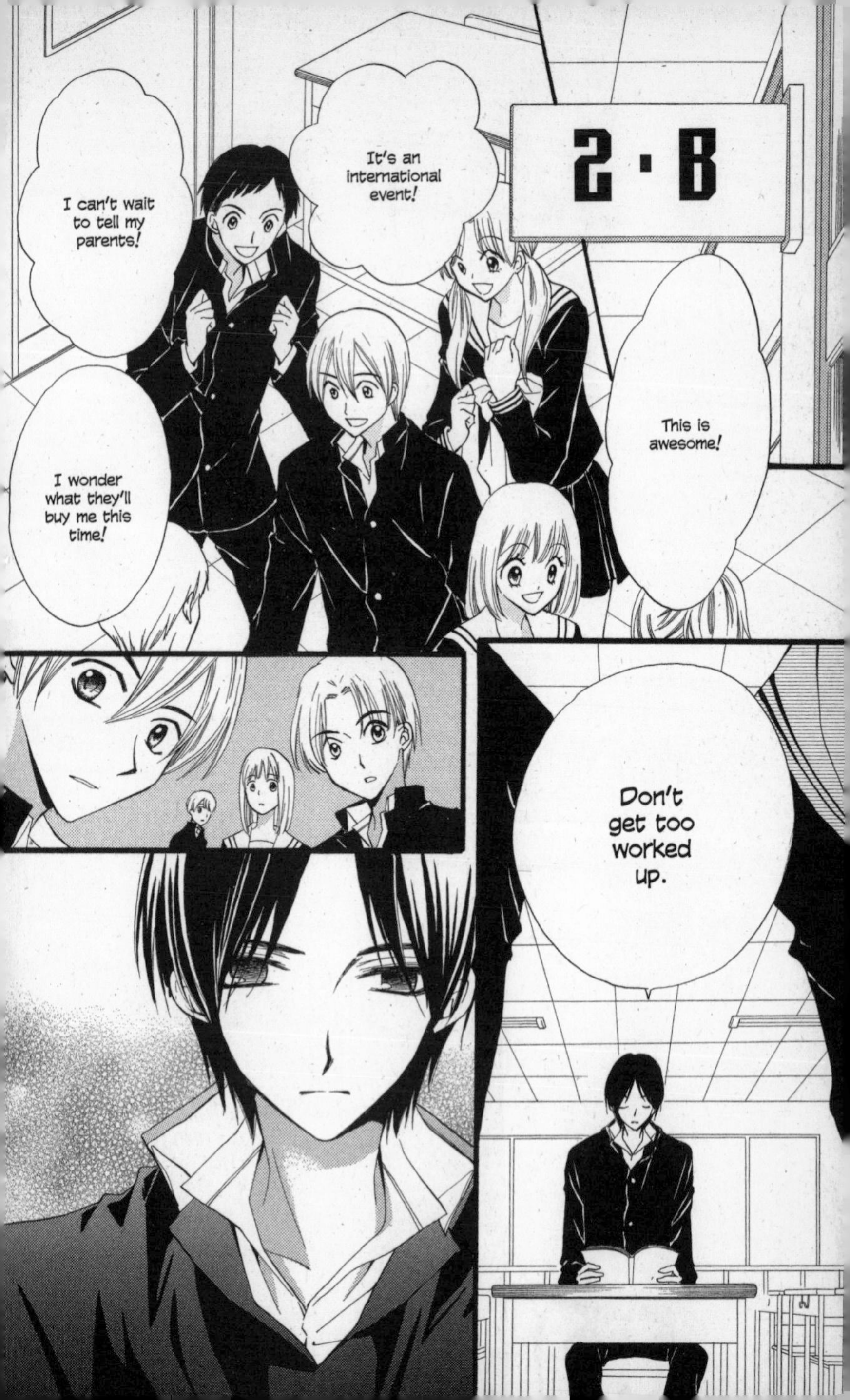
2·B
This is awesome!
It's an international event!
I can't wait to tell my parents!
I wonder what they'll buy me this time!
Don't get too worked up.

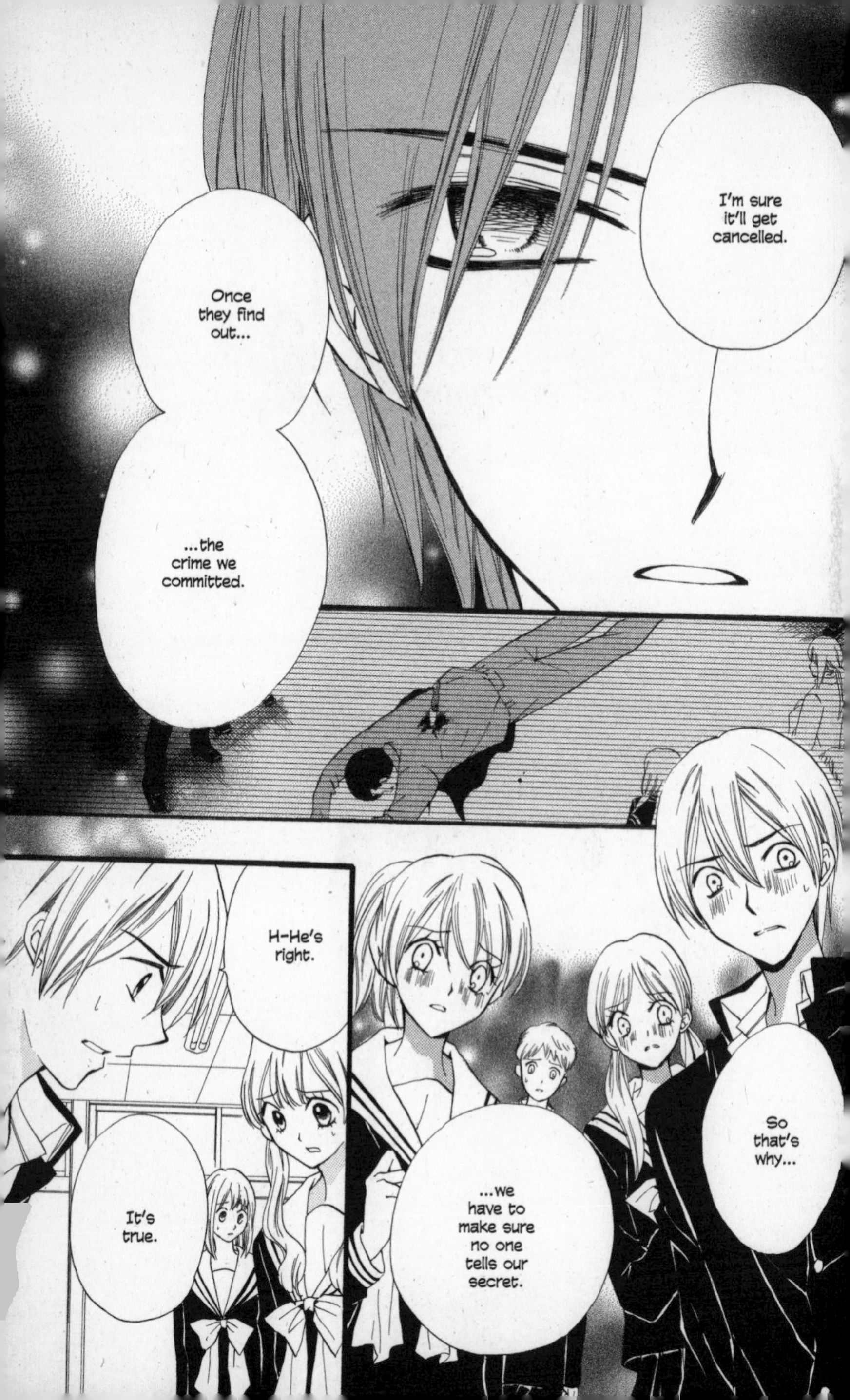
I'm sure it'll get cancelled.
Once they find out...
...the crime we committed.
So that's why...
...we have to make sure no one tells our secret.
H-He's right.
It's true.

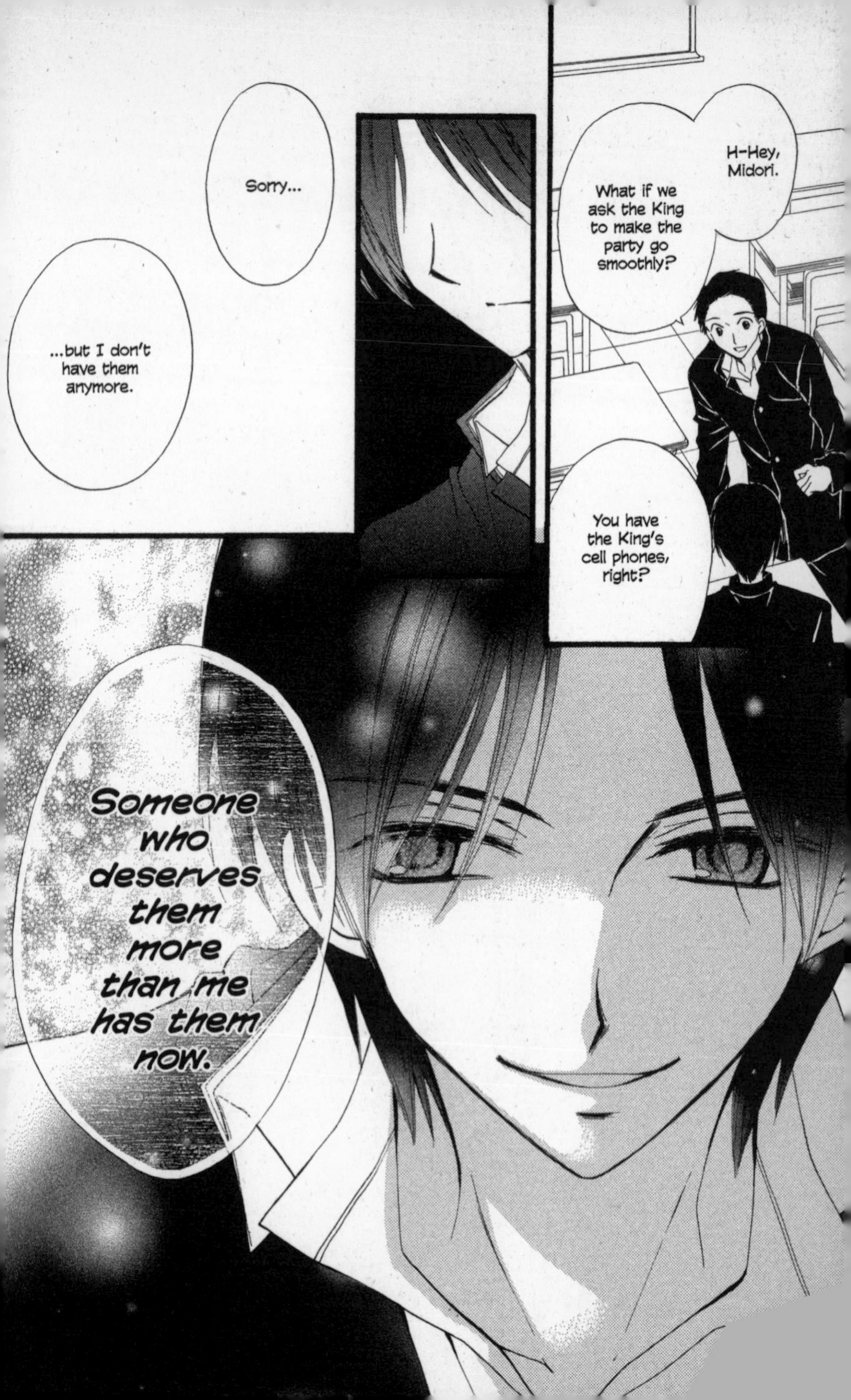
H-Hey, Midori.
What if we ask the King to make the party go smoothly?
You have the King's cell phones, right?
Sorry...
...but I don't have them anymore.
Someone who deserves them more than me has them now.

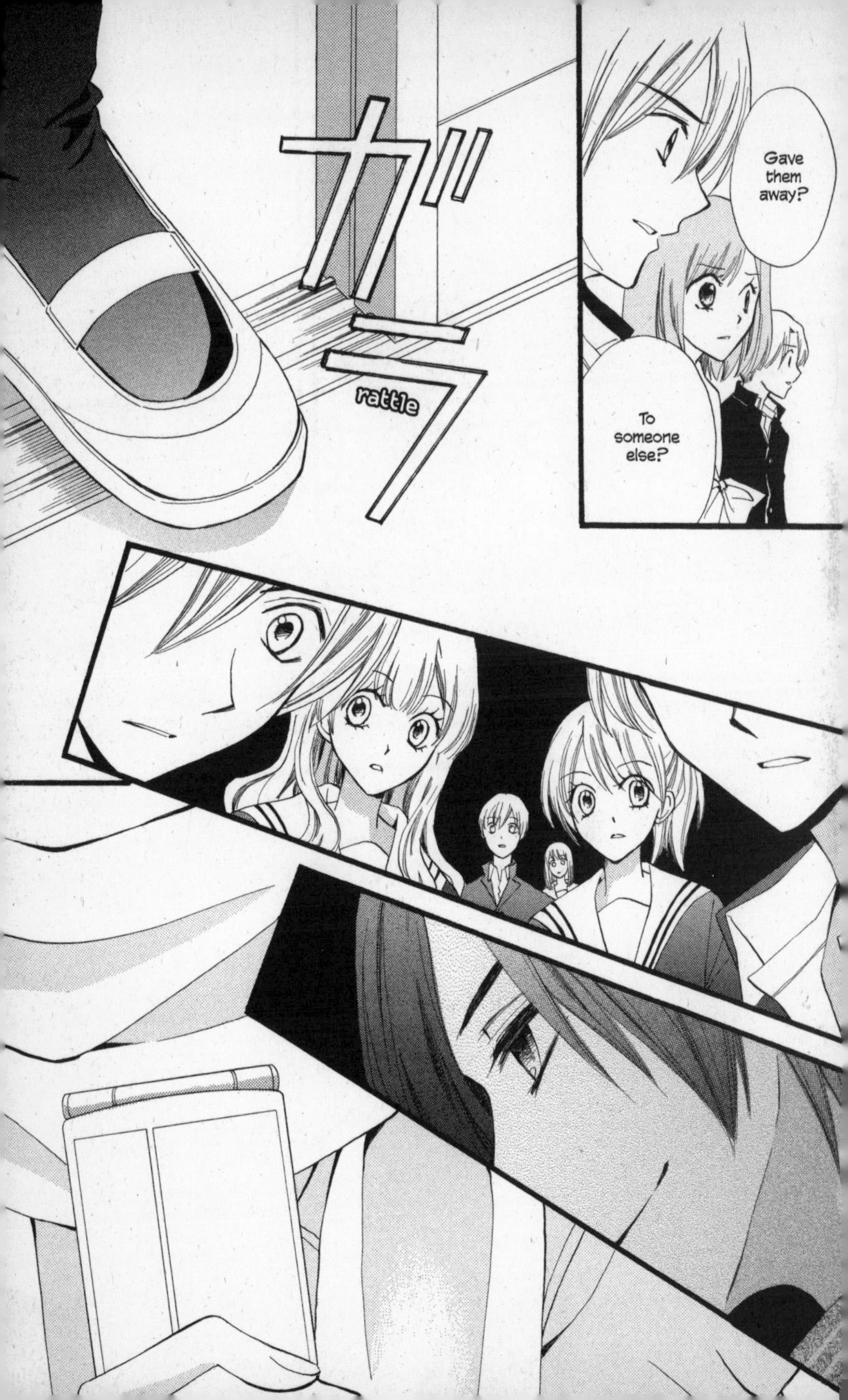
Gave them away?
To someone else?
ガラ
rattle

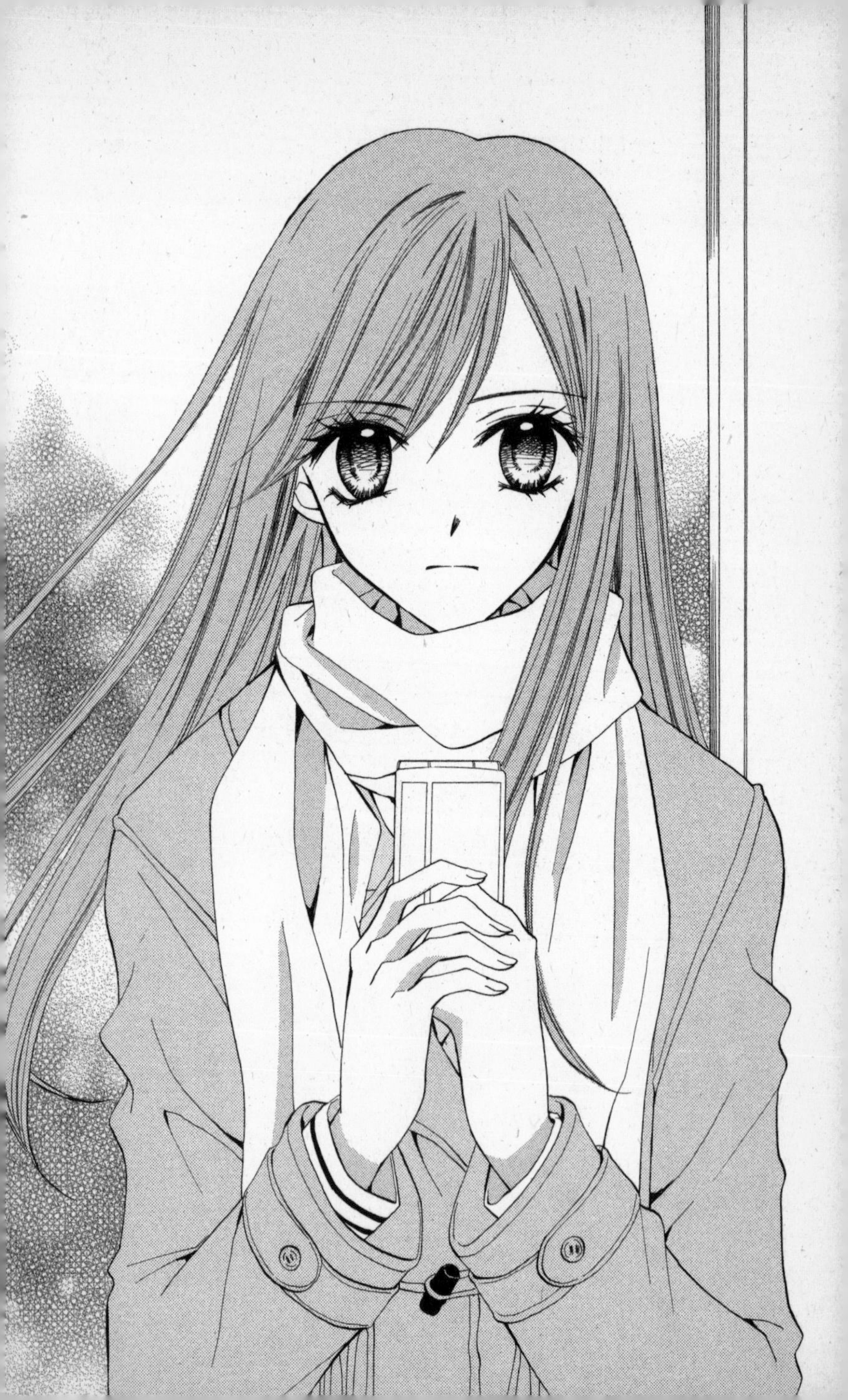

ARISA

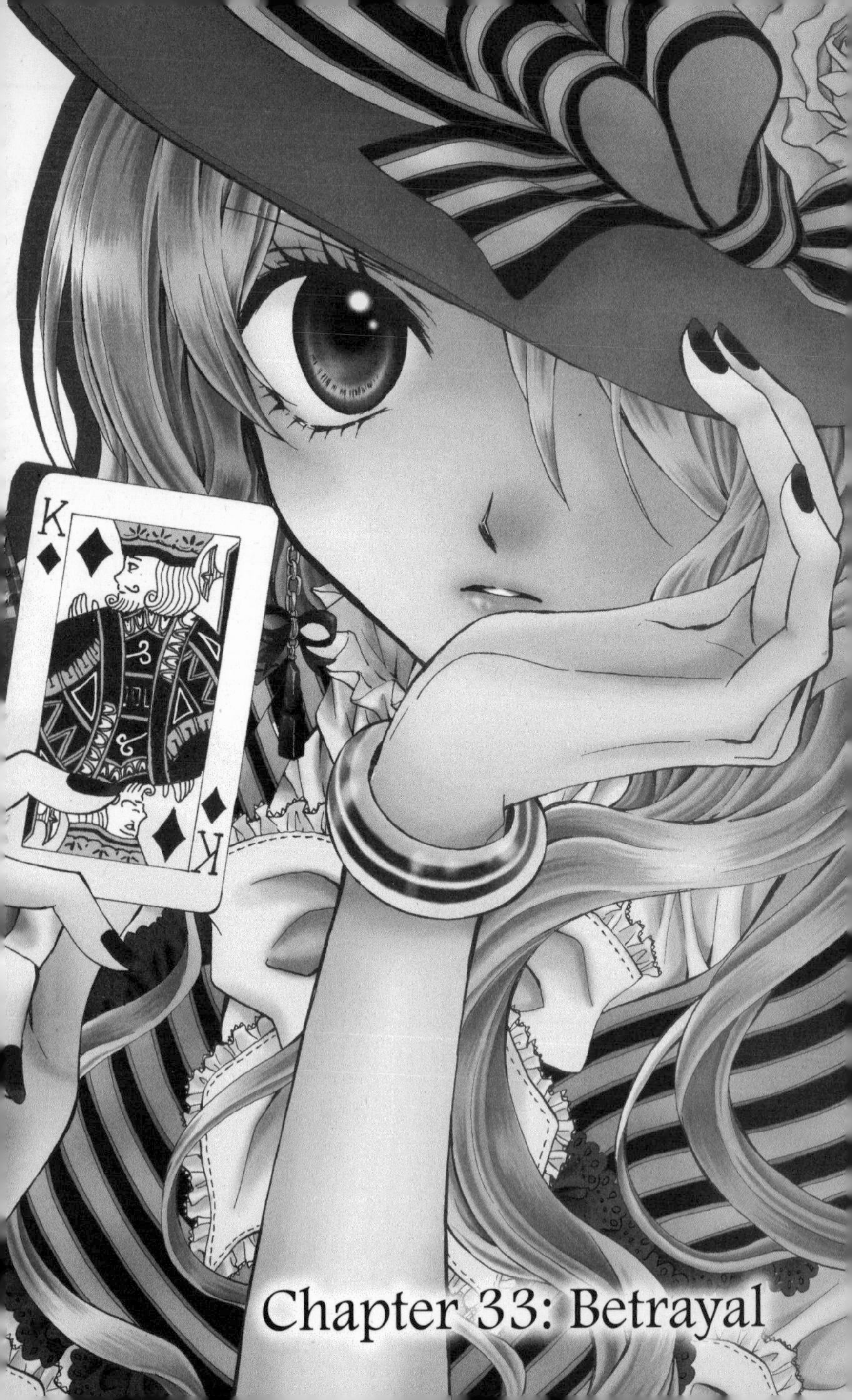

Chapter 33: Betrayal

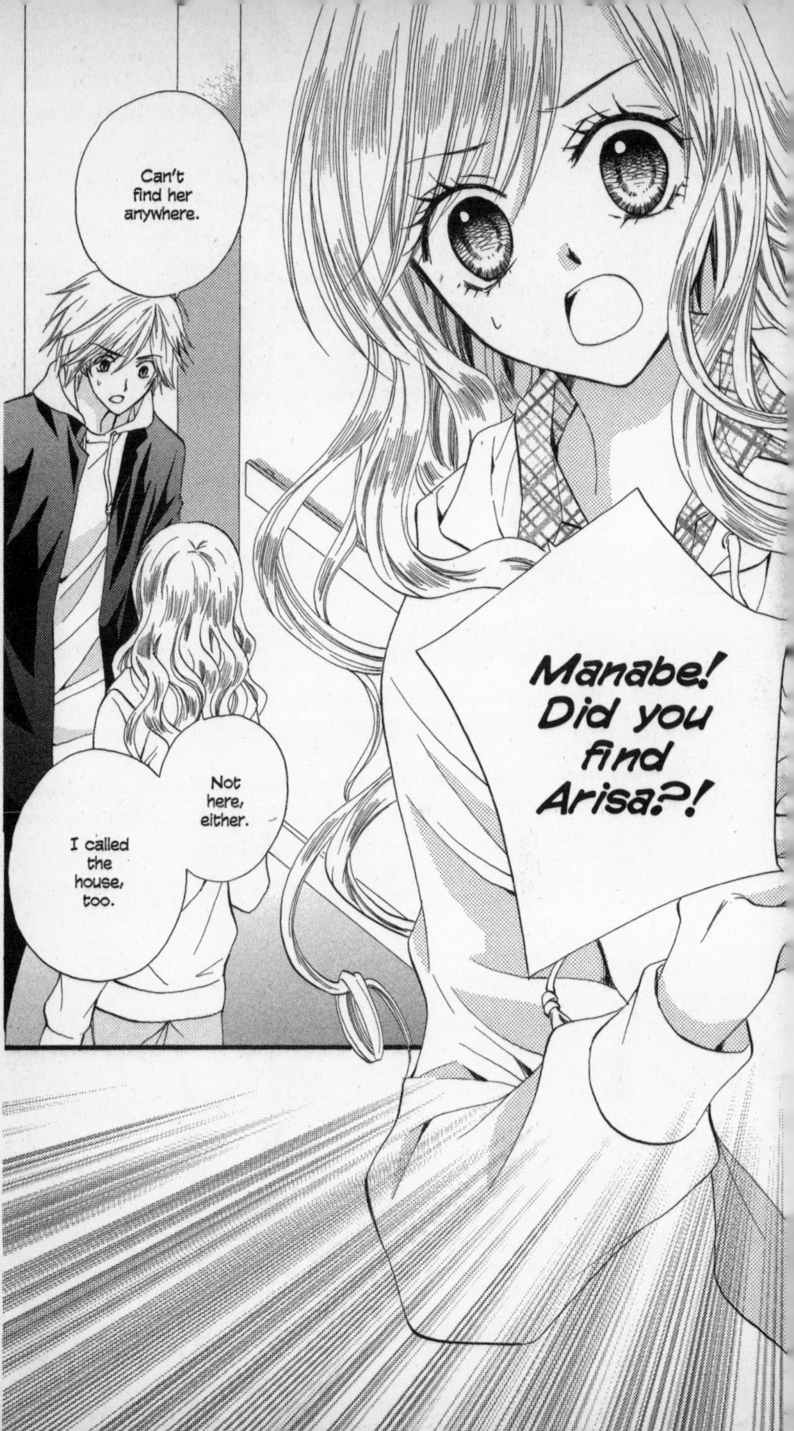
Manabe! Did you find Arisa?!
Can't find her anywhere.
Not here, either.
I called the house, too.

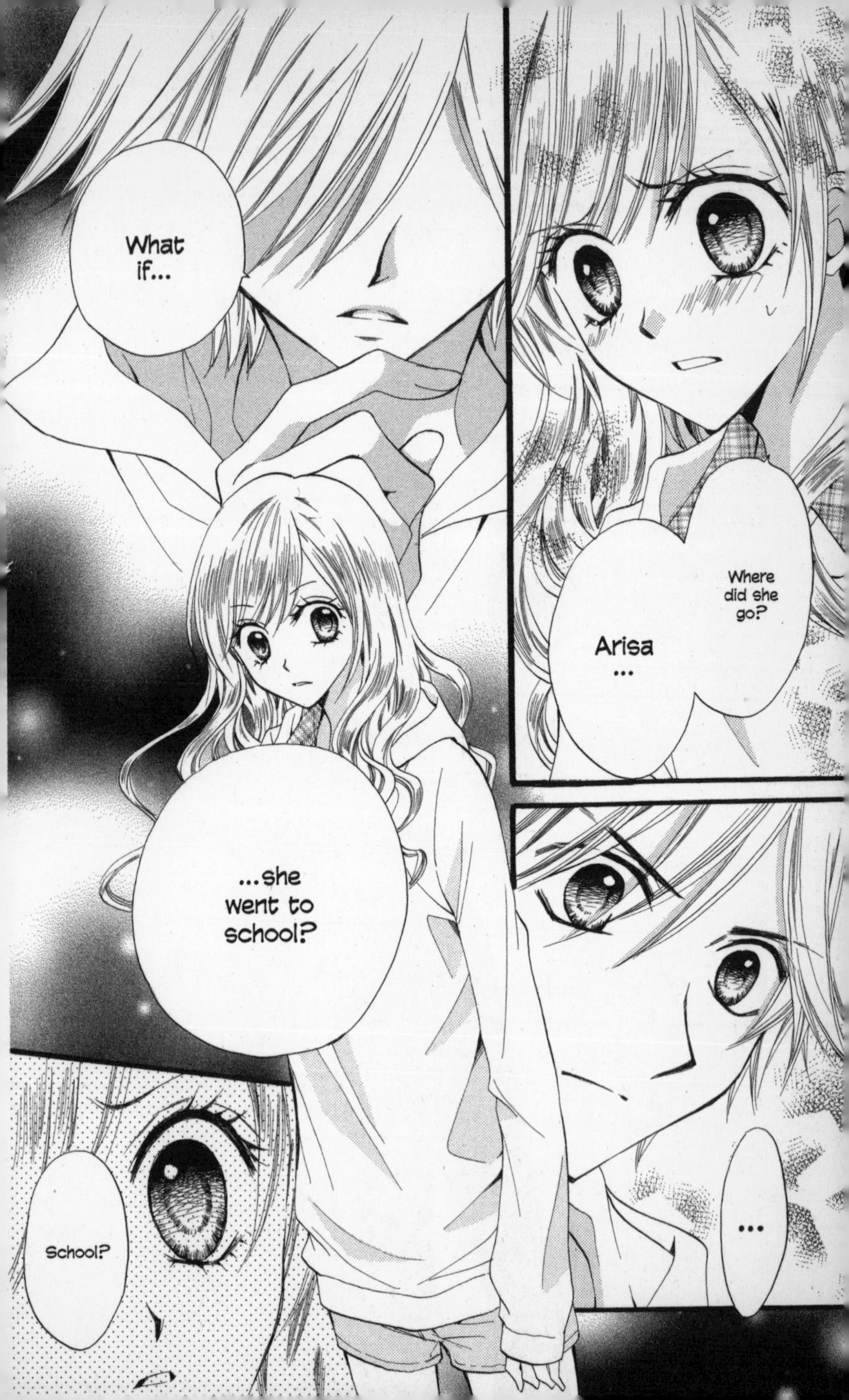
Where did she go?
Arisa...
...
What if...
...she went to school?
School?

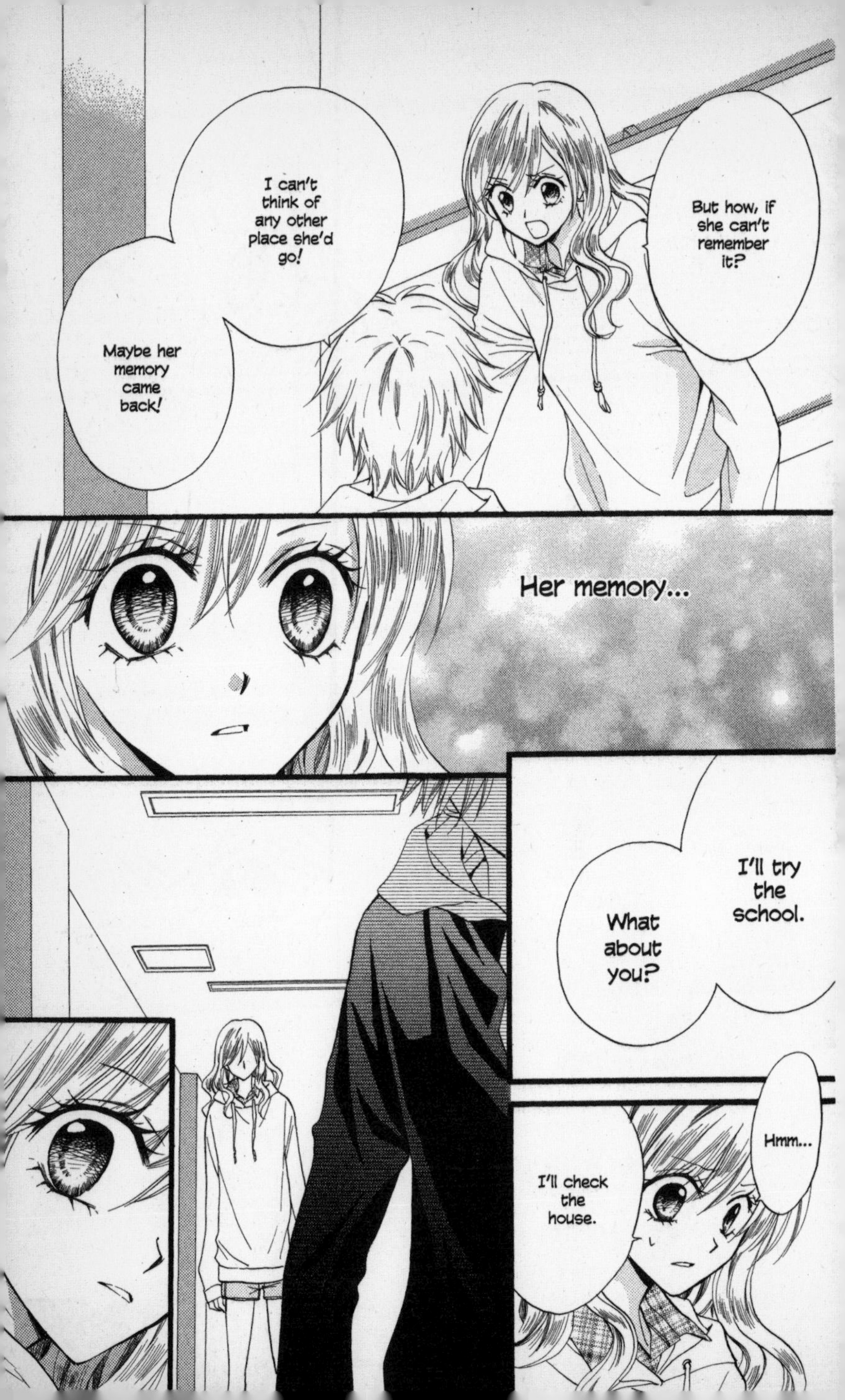
I can't think of any other place she'd go!
Maybe her memory came back!
But how, if she can't remember it?
Her memory...
I'll try the school.
What about you?
Hmm...
I'll check the house.

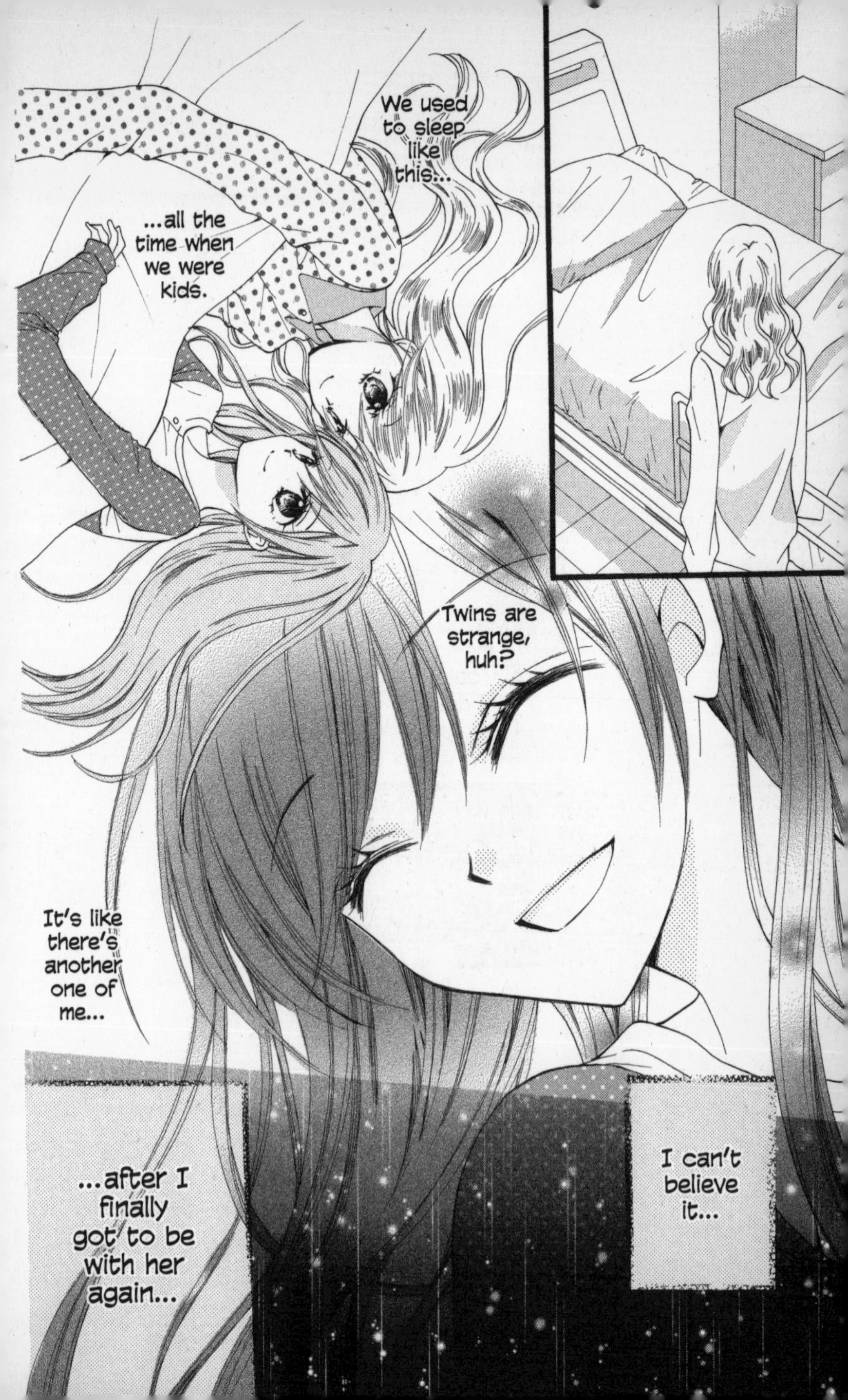
We used to sleep like this...
...all the time when we were kids.
Twins are strange, huh?
It's like there's another one of me...
I can't believe it...
...after I finally got to be with her again...

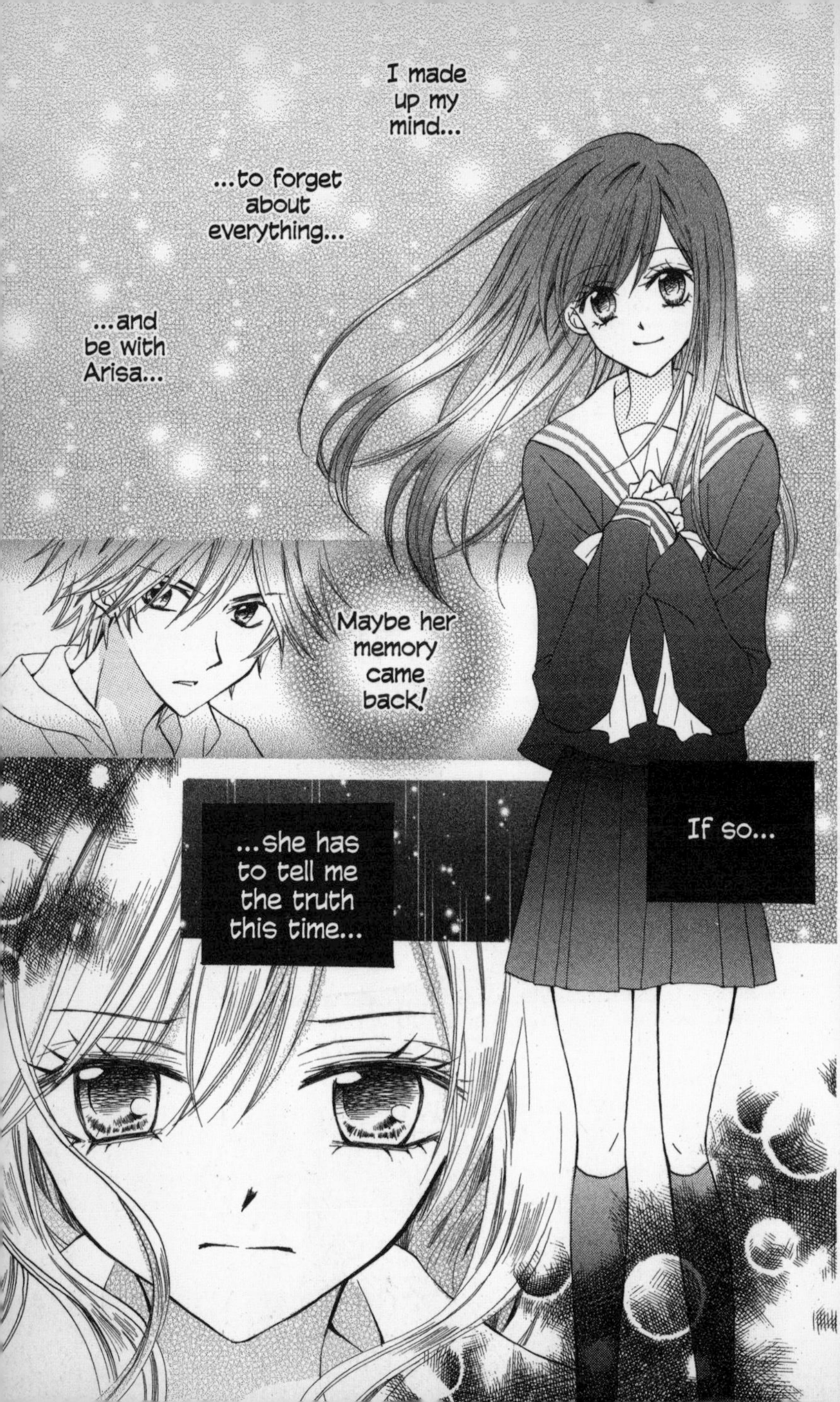
I made up my mind...
...to forget about everything...
...and be with Arisa...
Maybe her memory came back!
If so...
...she has to tell me the truth this time...

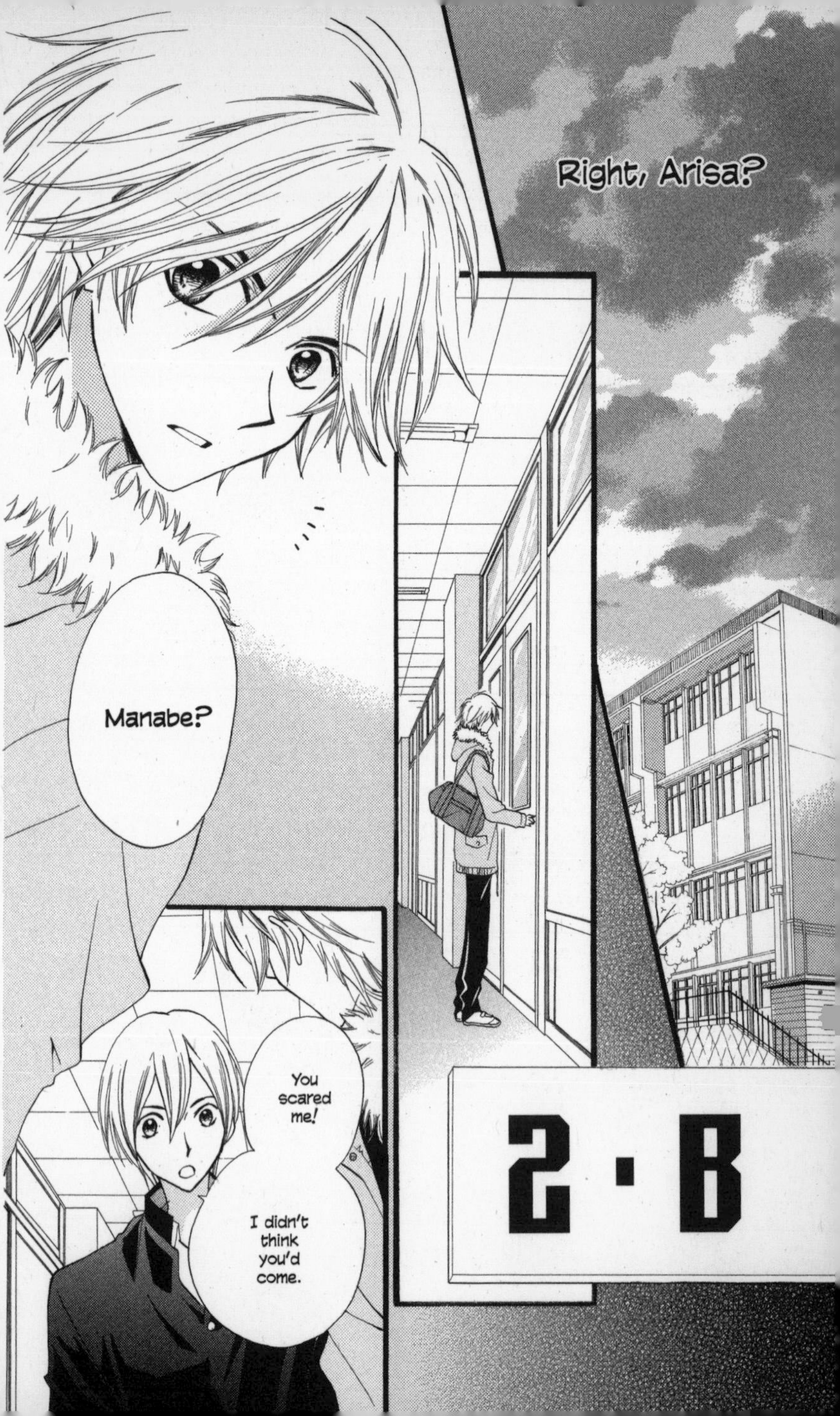
Right, Arisa?
2 · B
Manabe?
You scared me!
I didn't think you'd come.

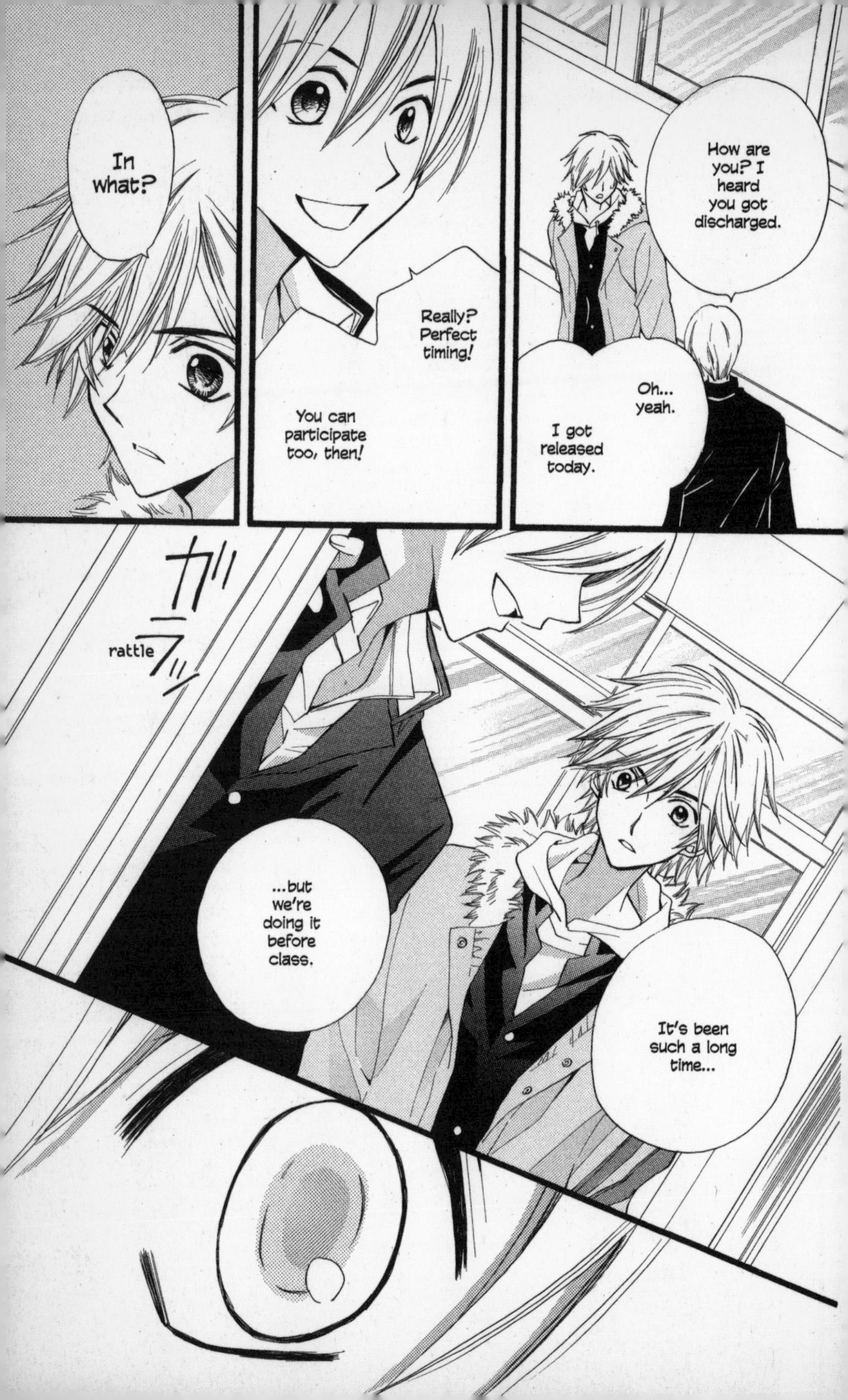
How are you? I heard you got discharged.
Oh... yeah.
I got released today.
Really? Perfect timing!
You can participate too, then!
In what?
ガラッ
rattle
...but we're doing it before class.
It's been such a long time...

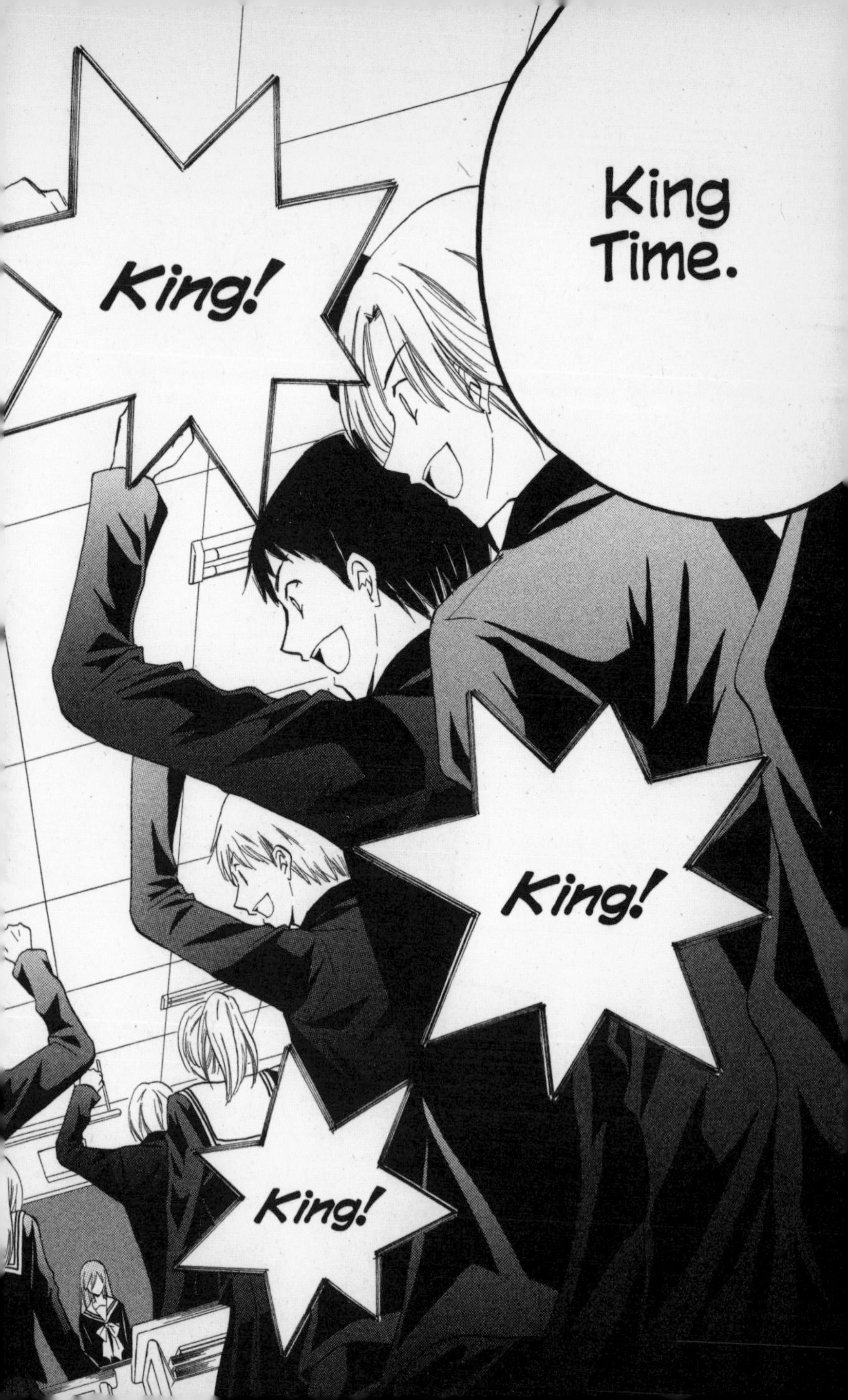
King Time.
King!
King!
King!

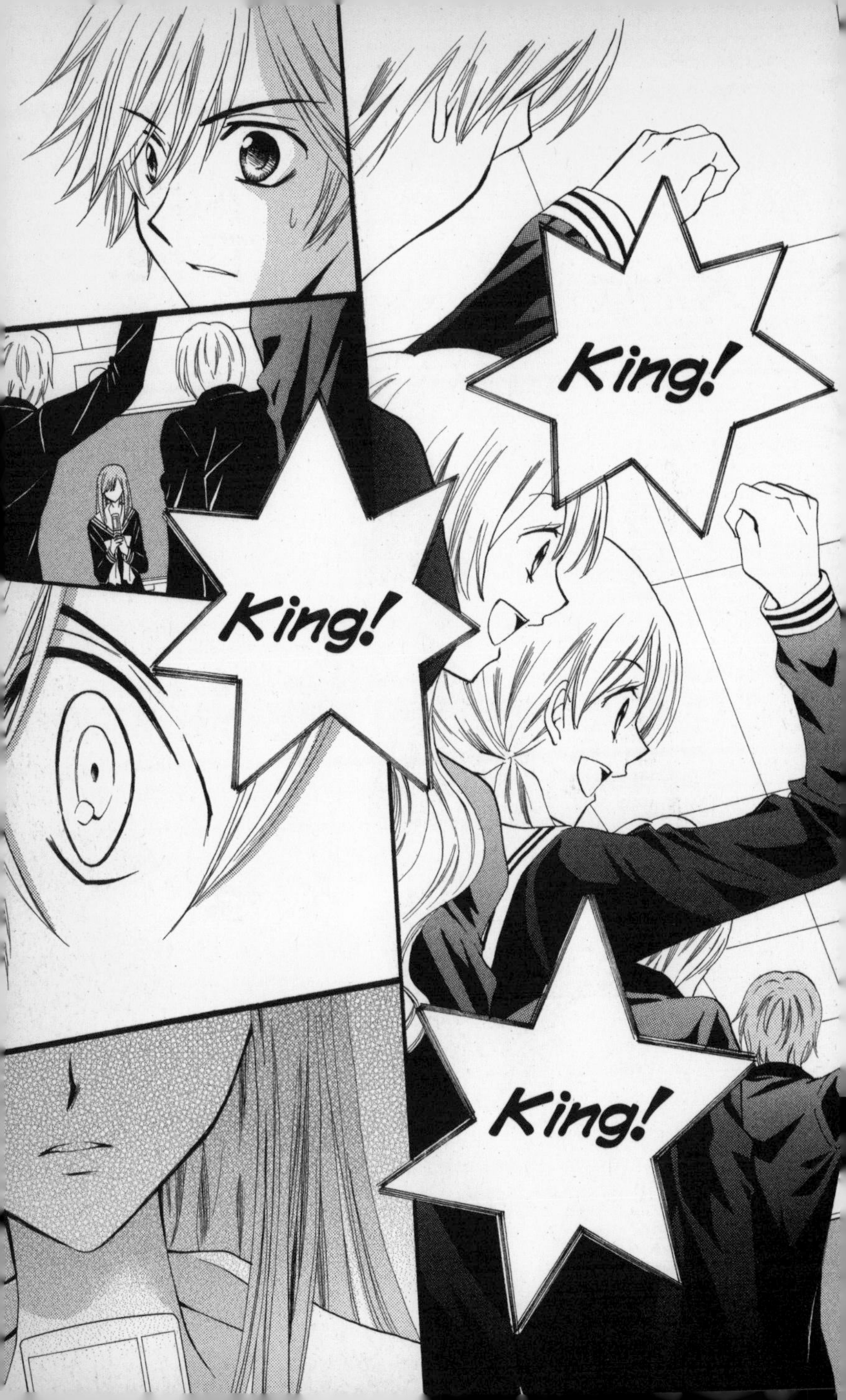
King!
King!
King!

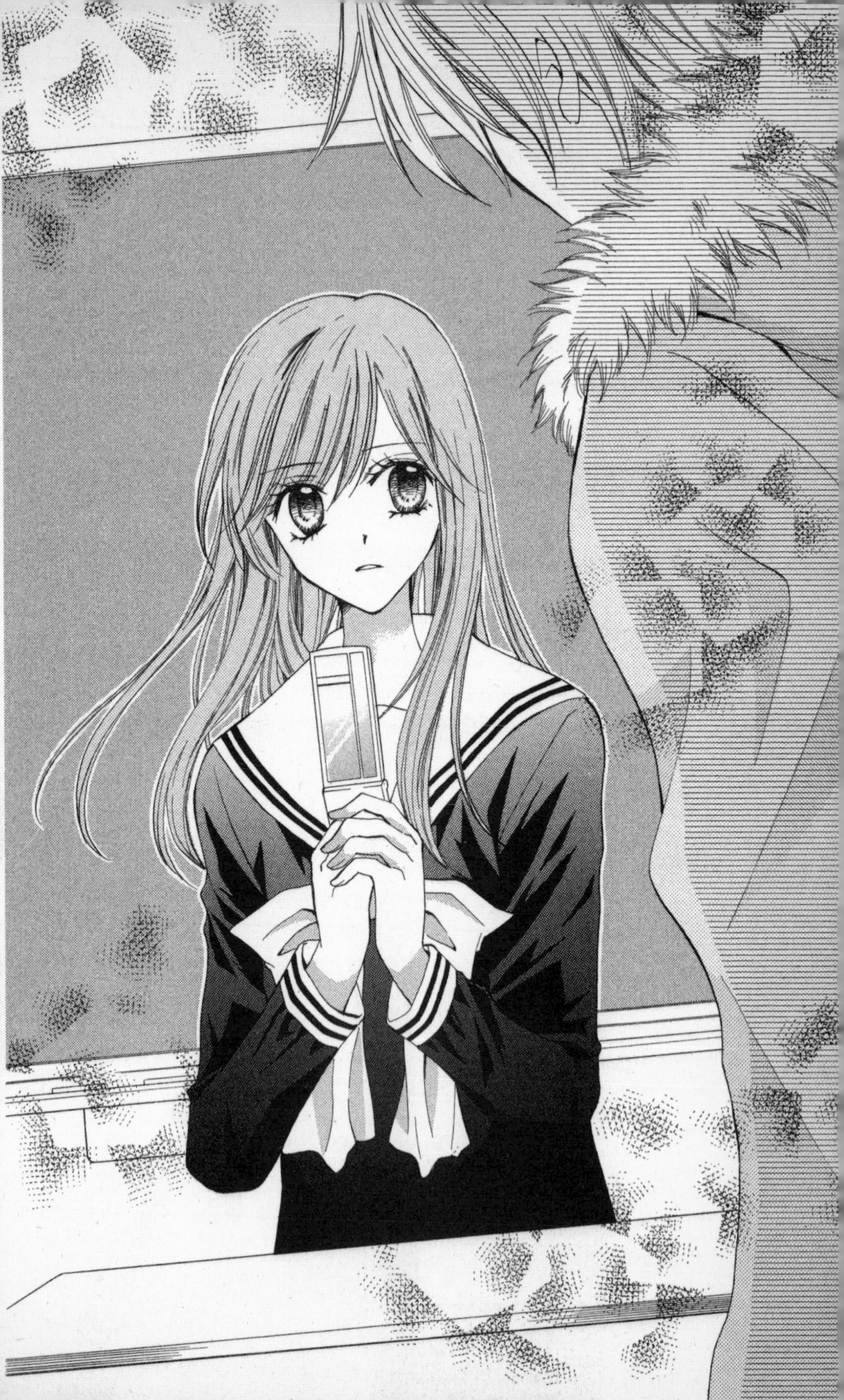

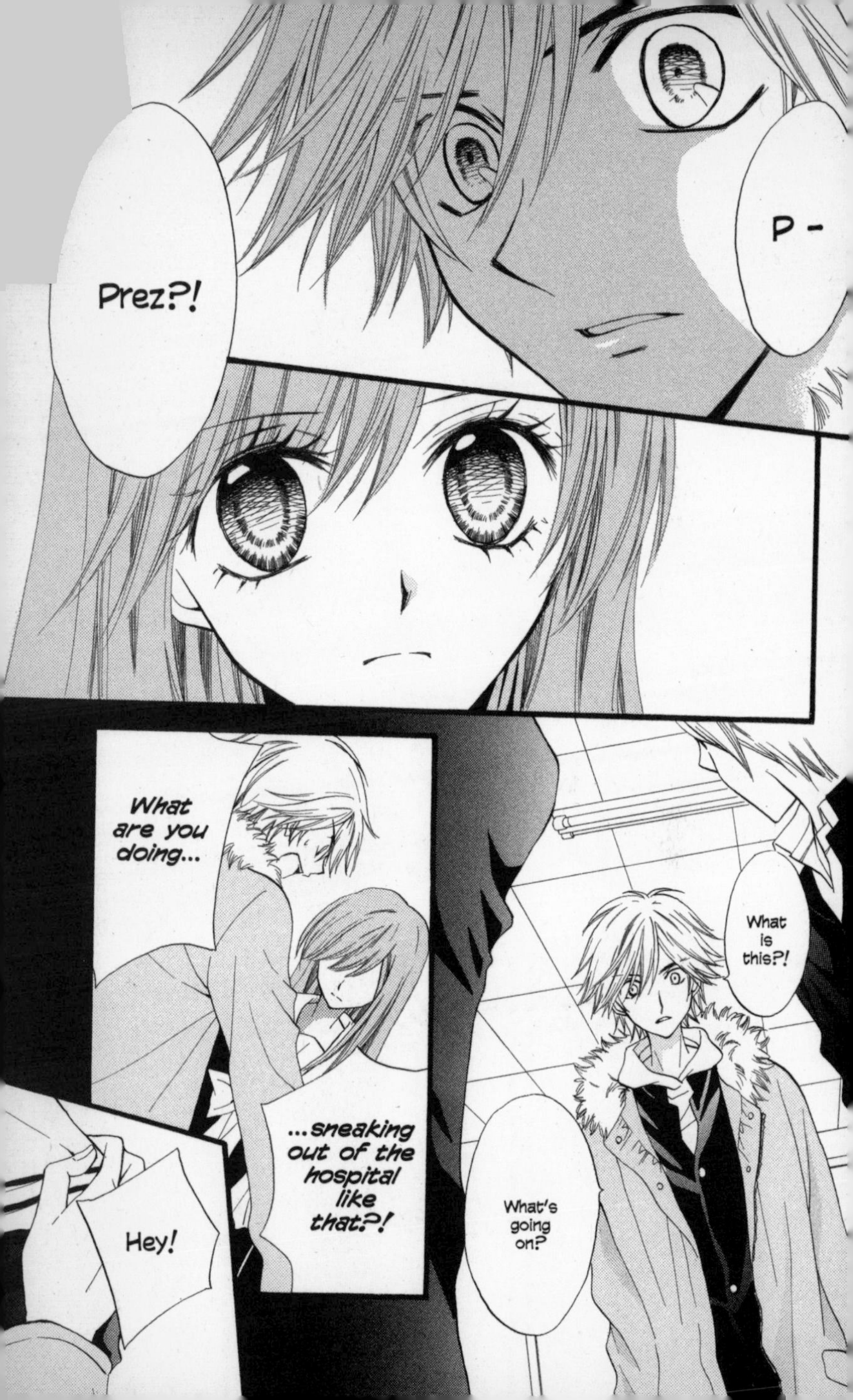
P -
Prez?!
What is this?!
What's going on?
What are you doing...
...sneaking out of the hospital like that?!
Hey!

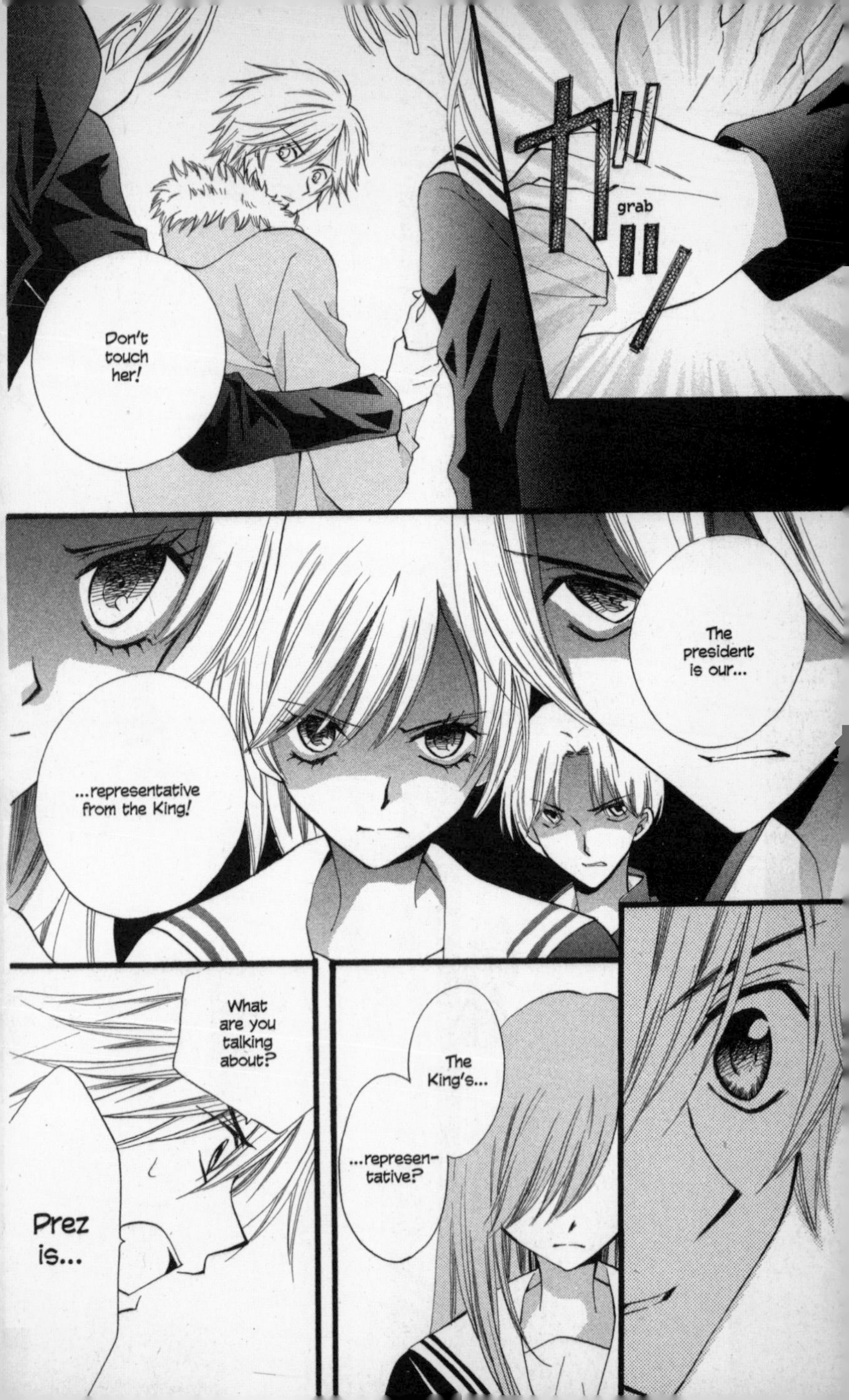
grab
Don't touch her!
The president is our...
...representative from the King!
The King's...
...represen-tative?
What are you talking about?
Prez is...

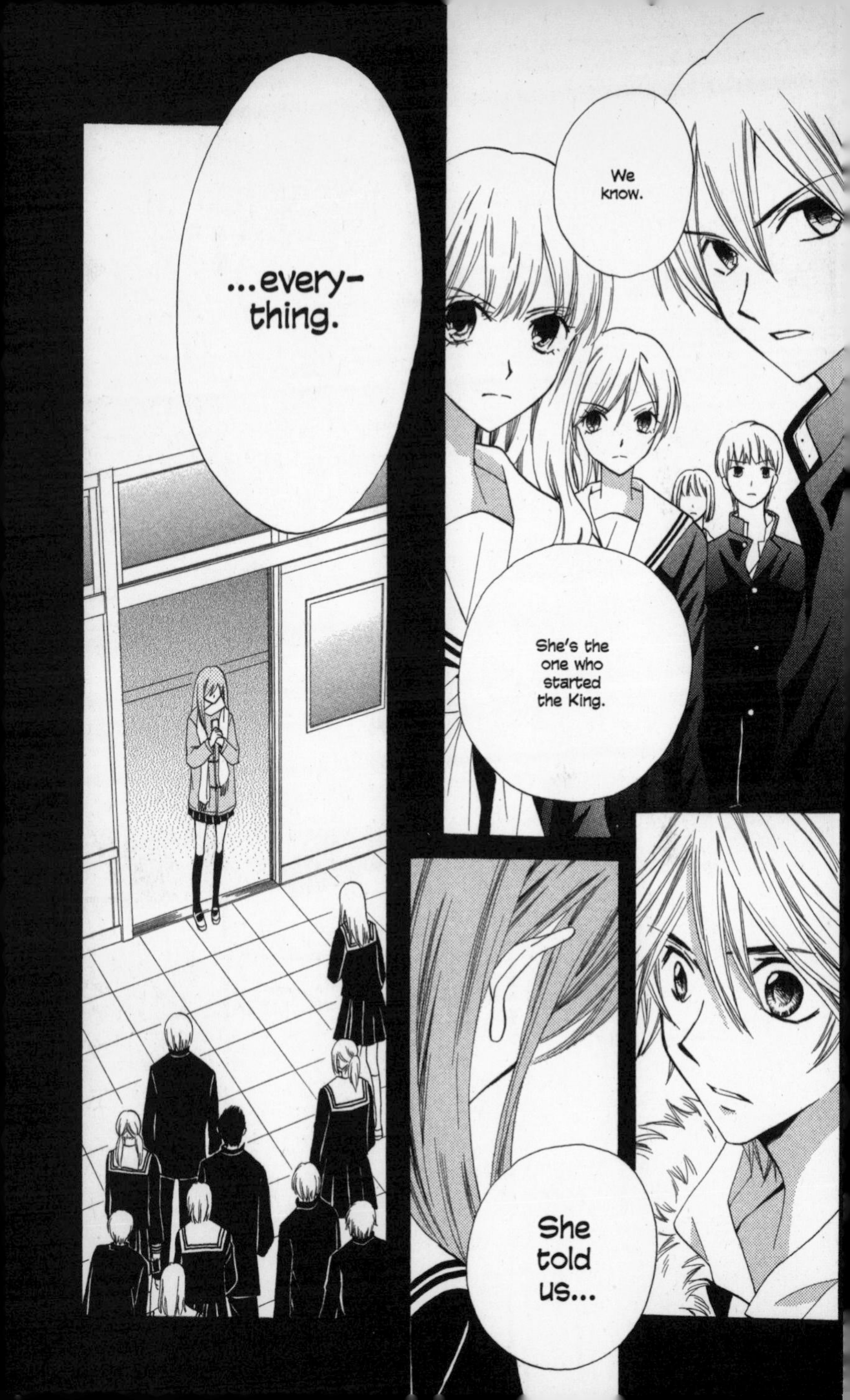
We know.
She's the one who started the King.
She told us...
...every-thing.

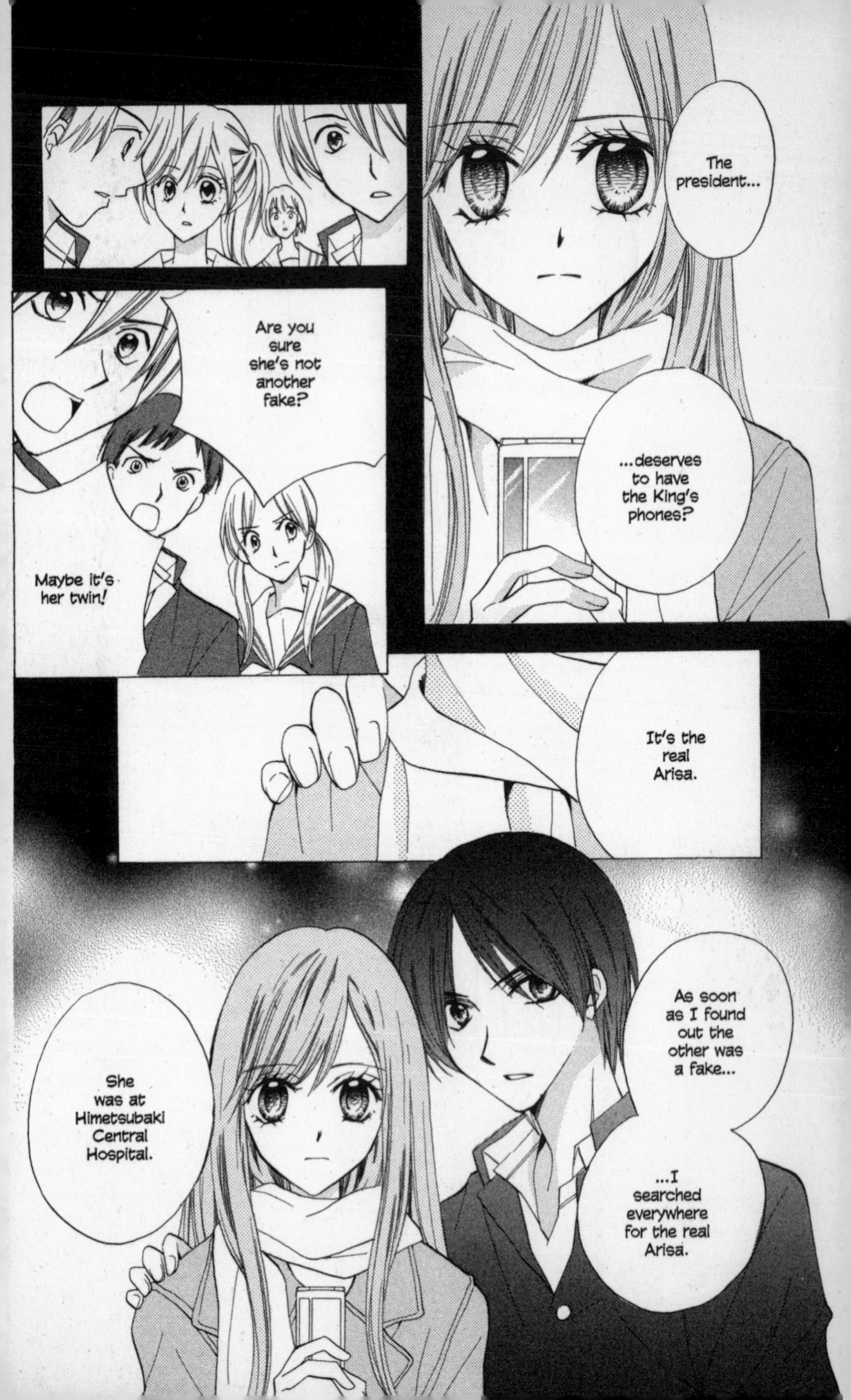
The president...
...deserves to have the King's phones?
Are you sure she's not another fake?
Maybe it's her twin!
It's the real Arisa.
As soon as I found out the other was a fake...
...I searched everywhere for the real Arisa.
She was at Himetsubaki Central Hospital.

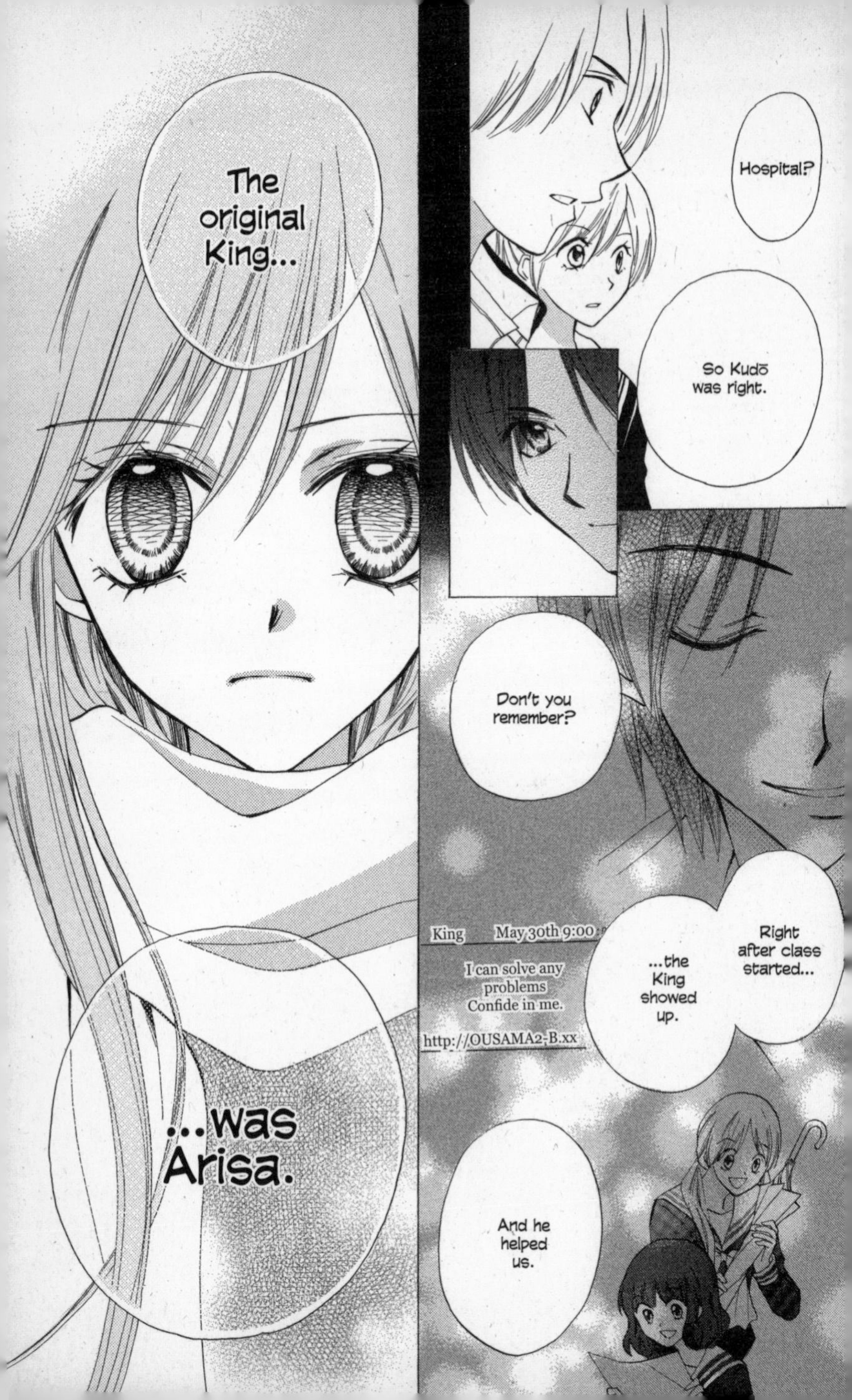
Hospital?
So Kudō was right.
Don't you remember?
Right after class started...
...the King showed up.
King May 30th 9:00
I can solve any problems Confide in me.
http://OUSAMA2-B.xx
And he helped us.
The original King...
...was Arisa.

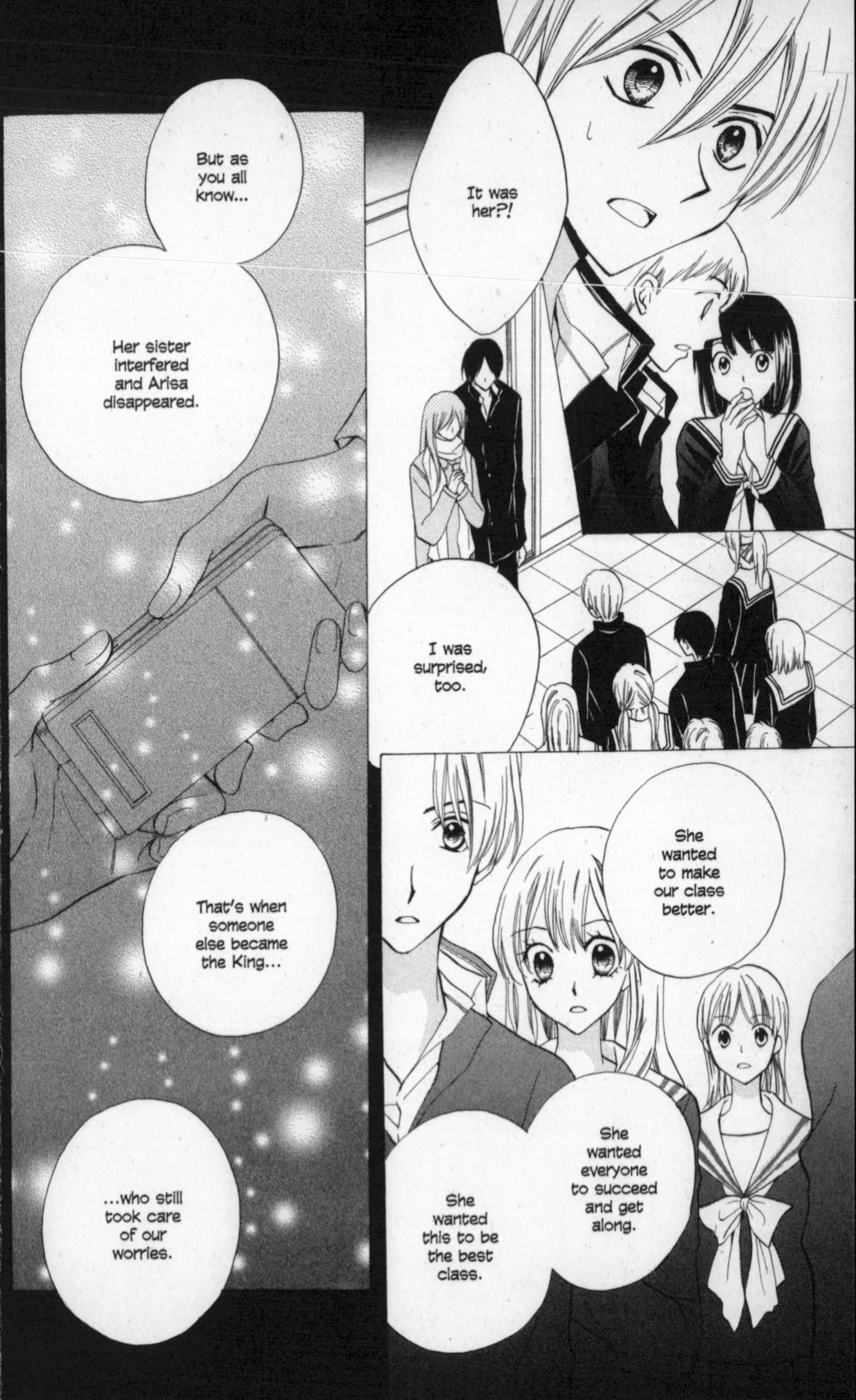
It was her?!
I was surprised, too.
She wanted to make our class better.
She wanted everyone to succeed and get along.
She wanted this to be the best class.
But as you all know...
Her sister interfered and Arisa disappeared.
That's when someone else became the King...
...who still took care of our worries.

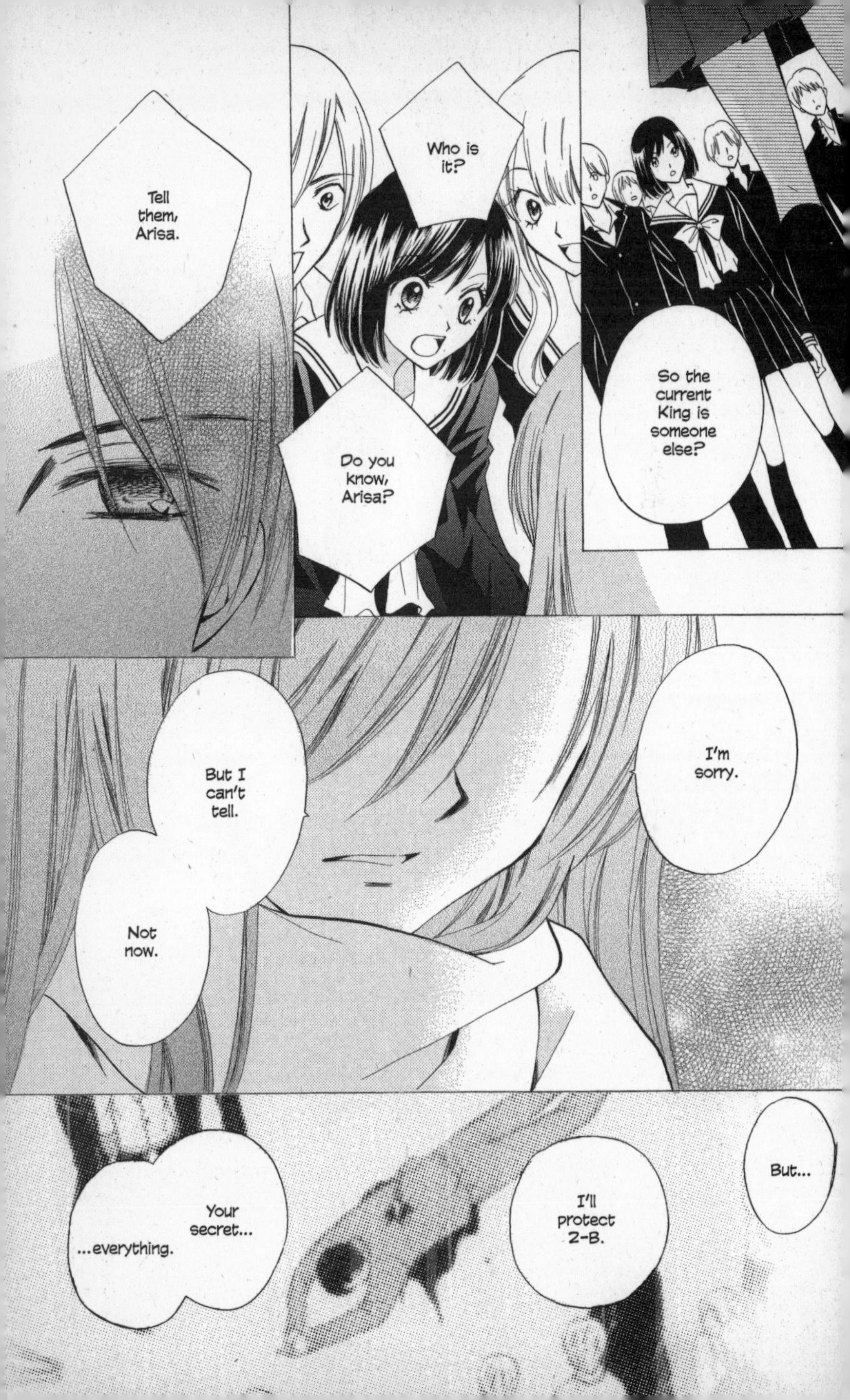
So the current King is someone else?
Who is it?
Do you know, Arisa?
Tell them, Arisa.
I'm sorry.
But I can't tell.
Not now.
But...
I'll protect 2-B.
Your secret...
...everything.

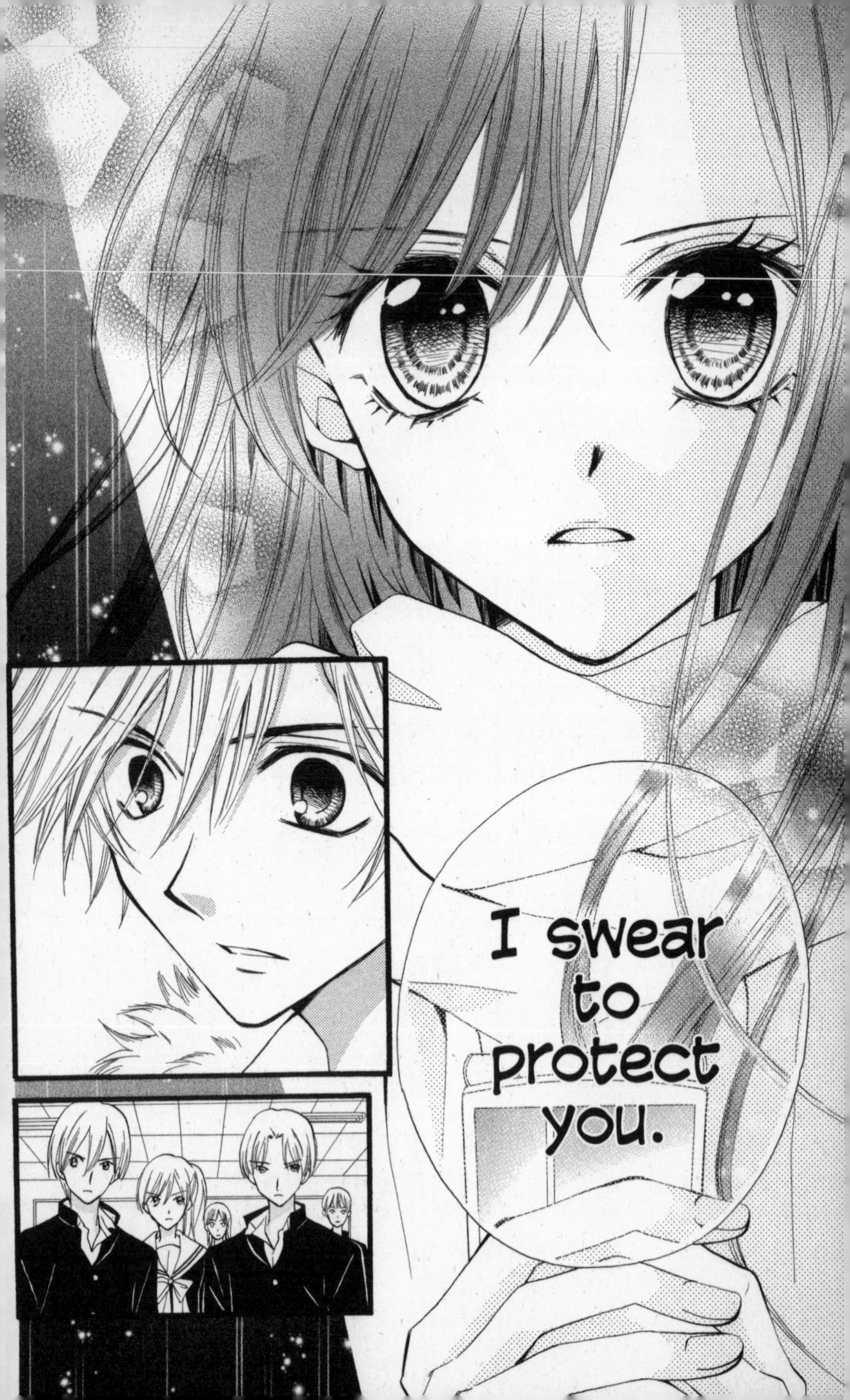
I swear to protect you.

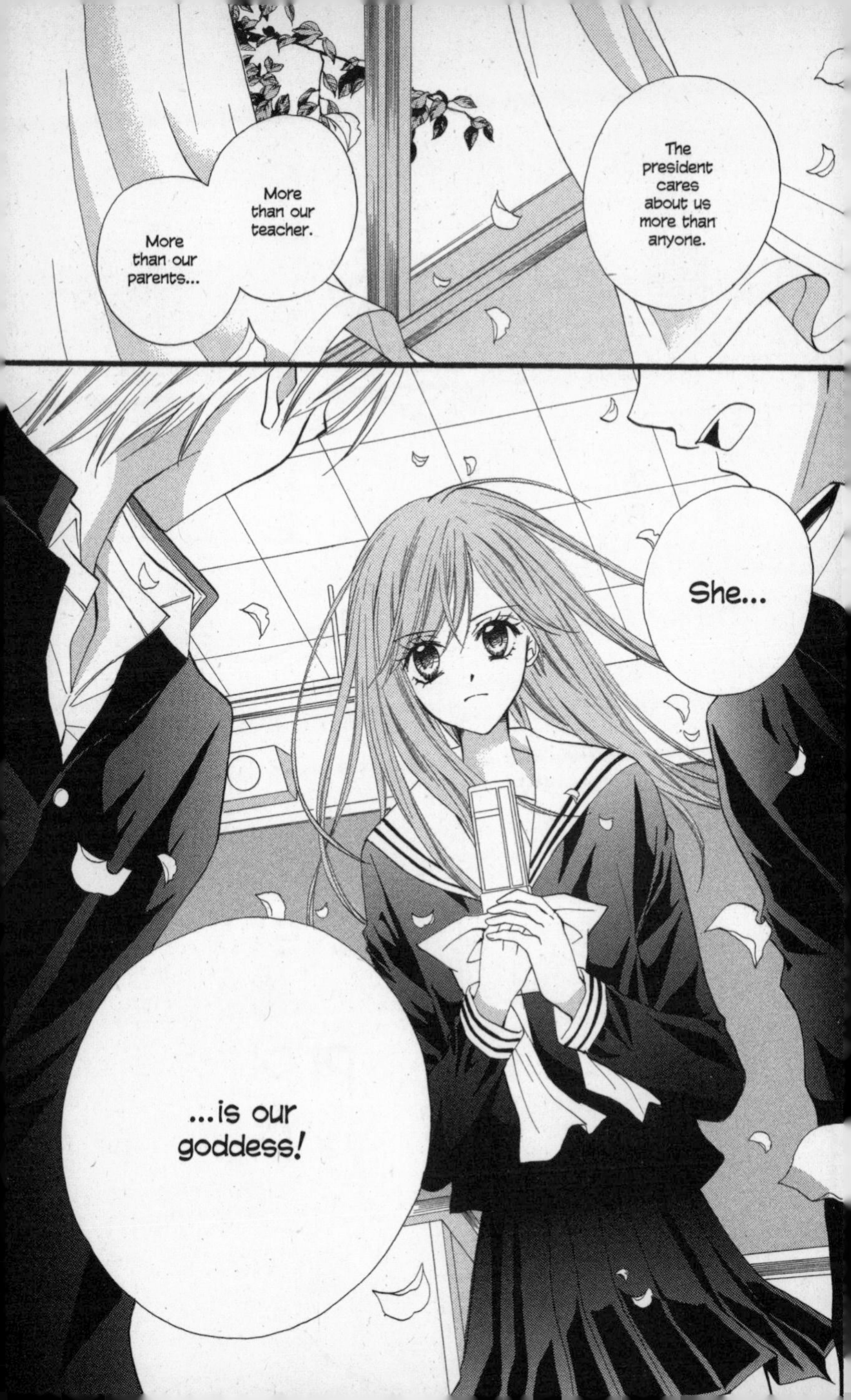
The president cares about us more than anyone.
More than our teacher.
More than our parents...
She...
...is our goddess!

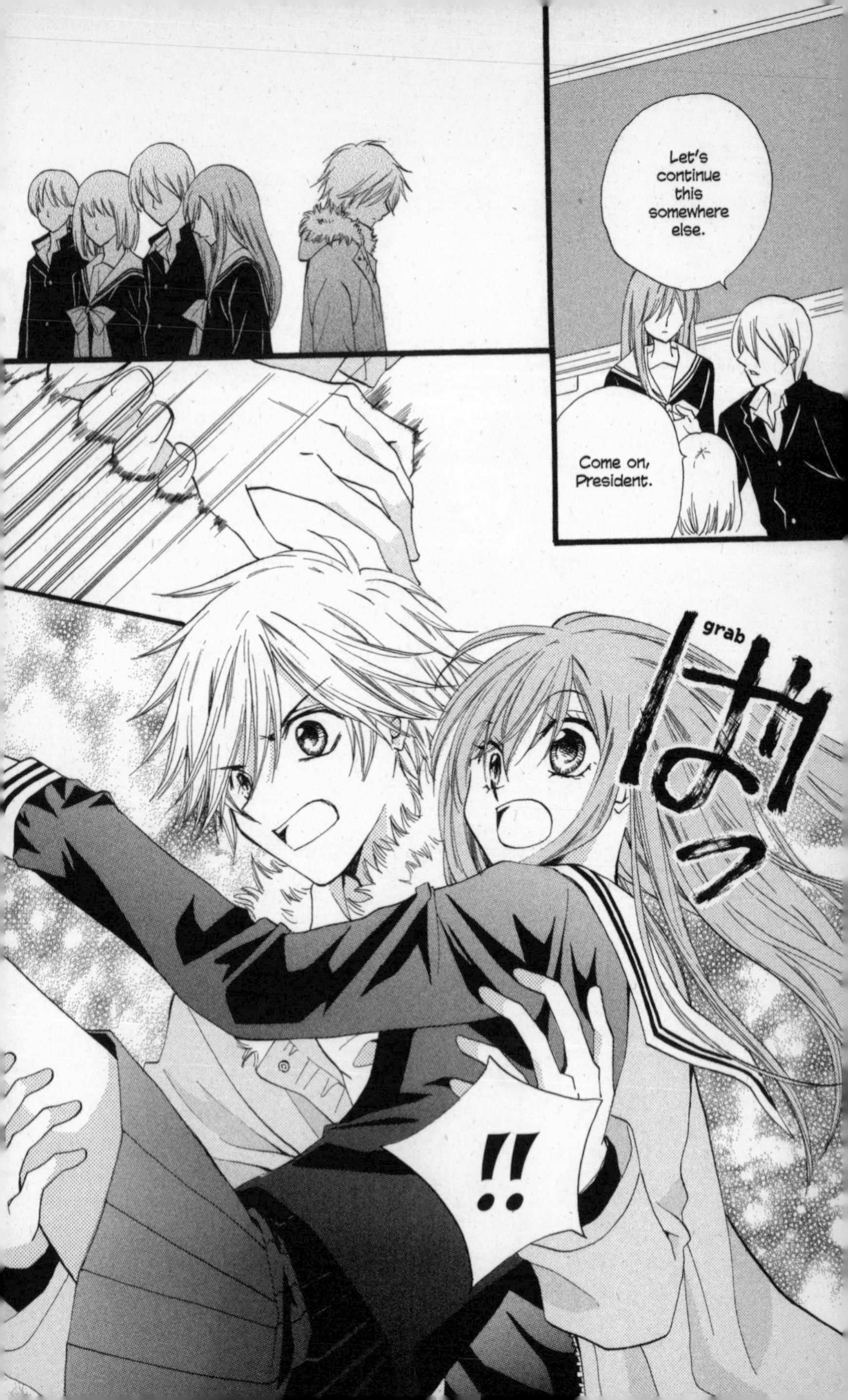
Let's continue this somewhere else.
Come on, President.
grab
はっ
!!

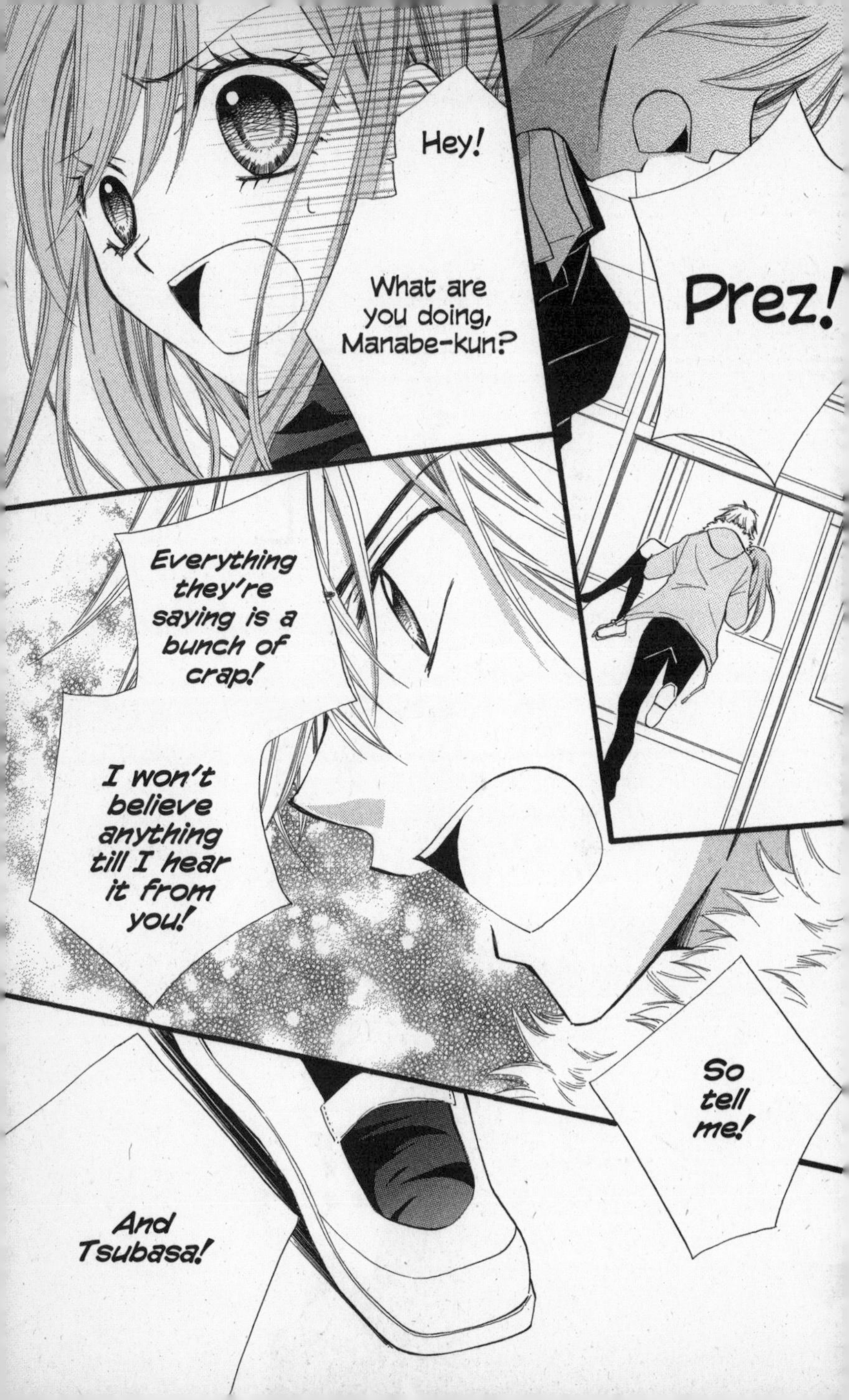
Prez!
Hey!
What are you doing, Manabe-kun?
Everything they're saying is a bunch of crap!
I won't believe anything till I hear it from you!
So tell me!
And Tsubasa!

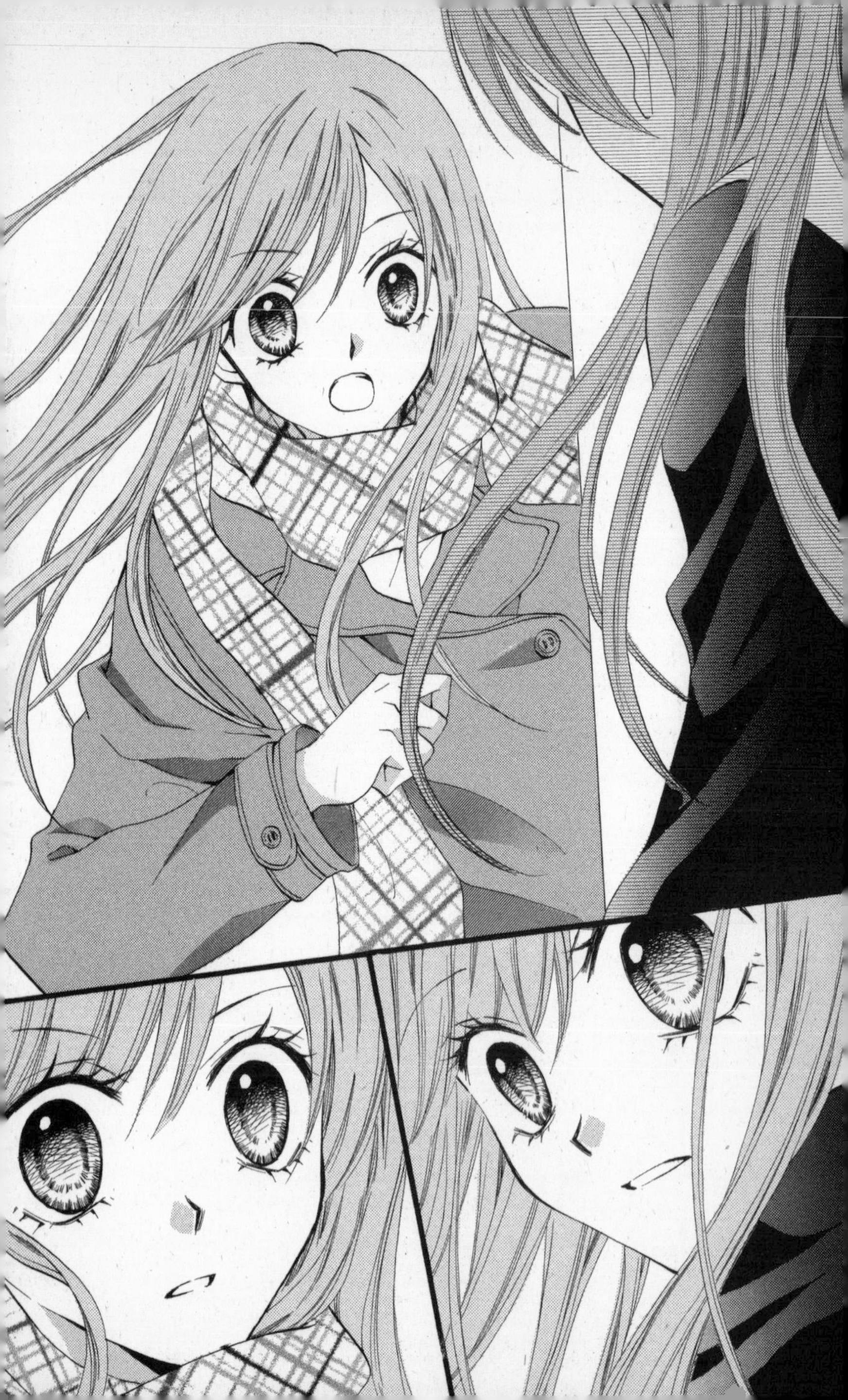

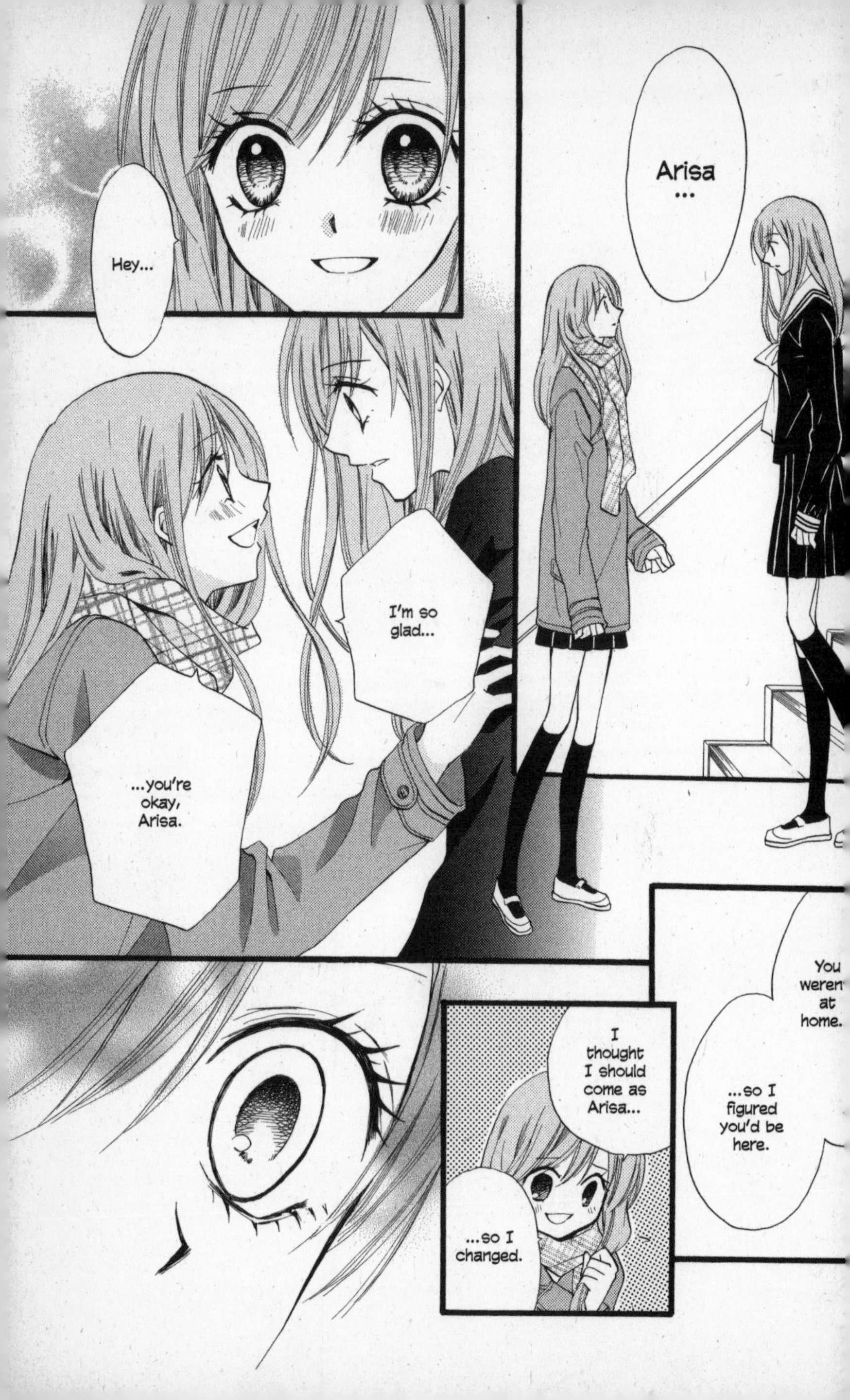
Arisa ...
Hey...
I'm so glad...
...you're okay, Arisa.
You weren at home.
...so I figured you'd be here.
I thought I should come as Arisa...
...so I changed.

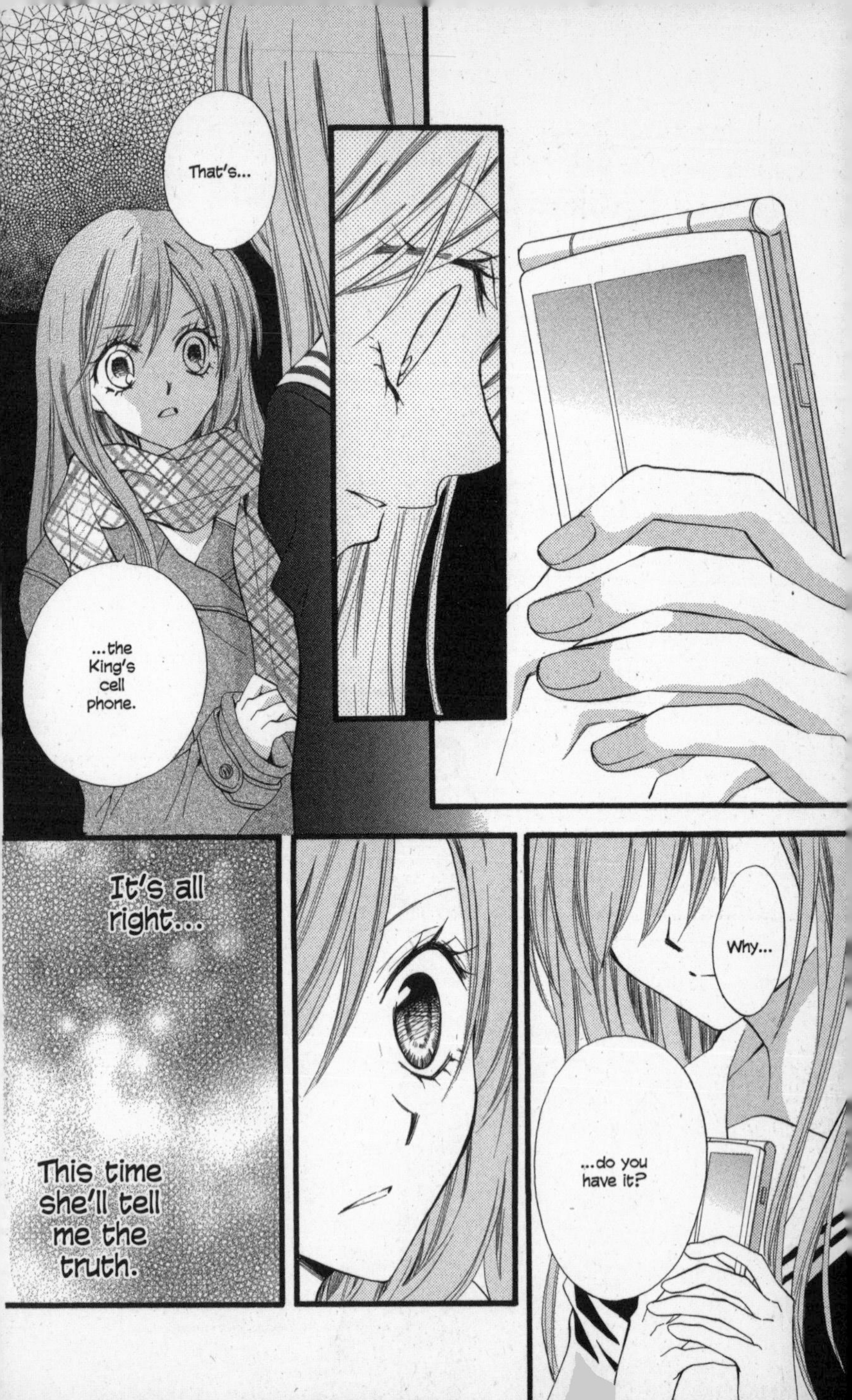
That's...
...the King's cell phone.
Why...
...do you have it?
It's all right...
This time she'll tell me the truth.

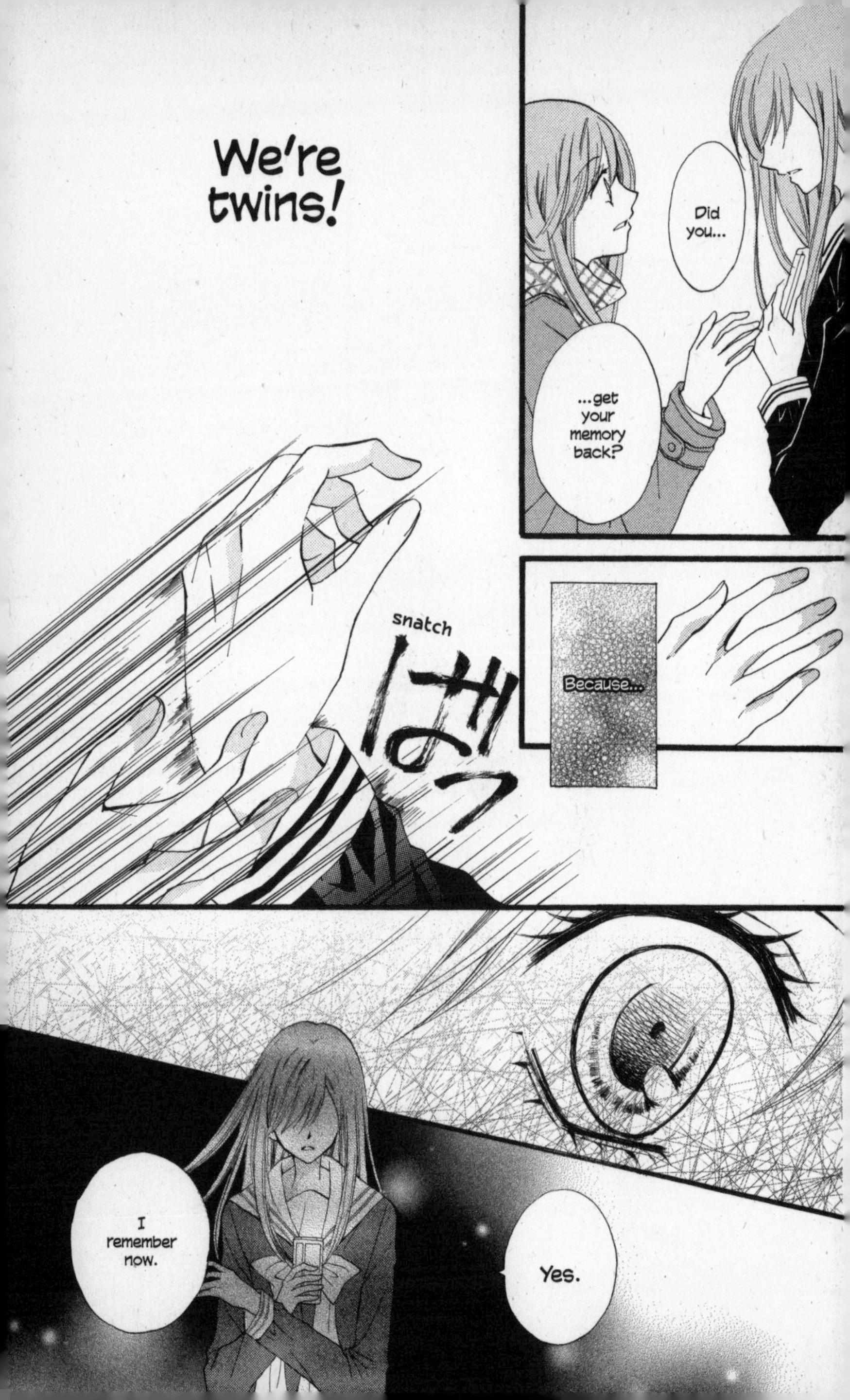

Did you...
...get your memory back?
Because...
We're twins!
snatch
Yes.
I remember now.

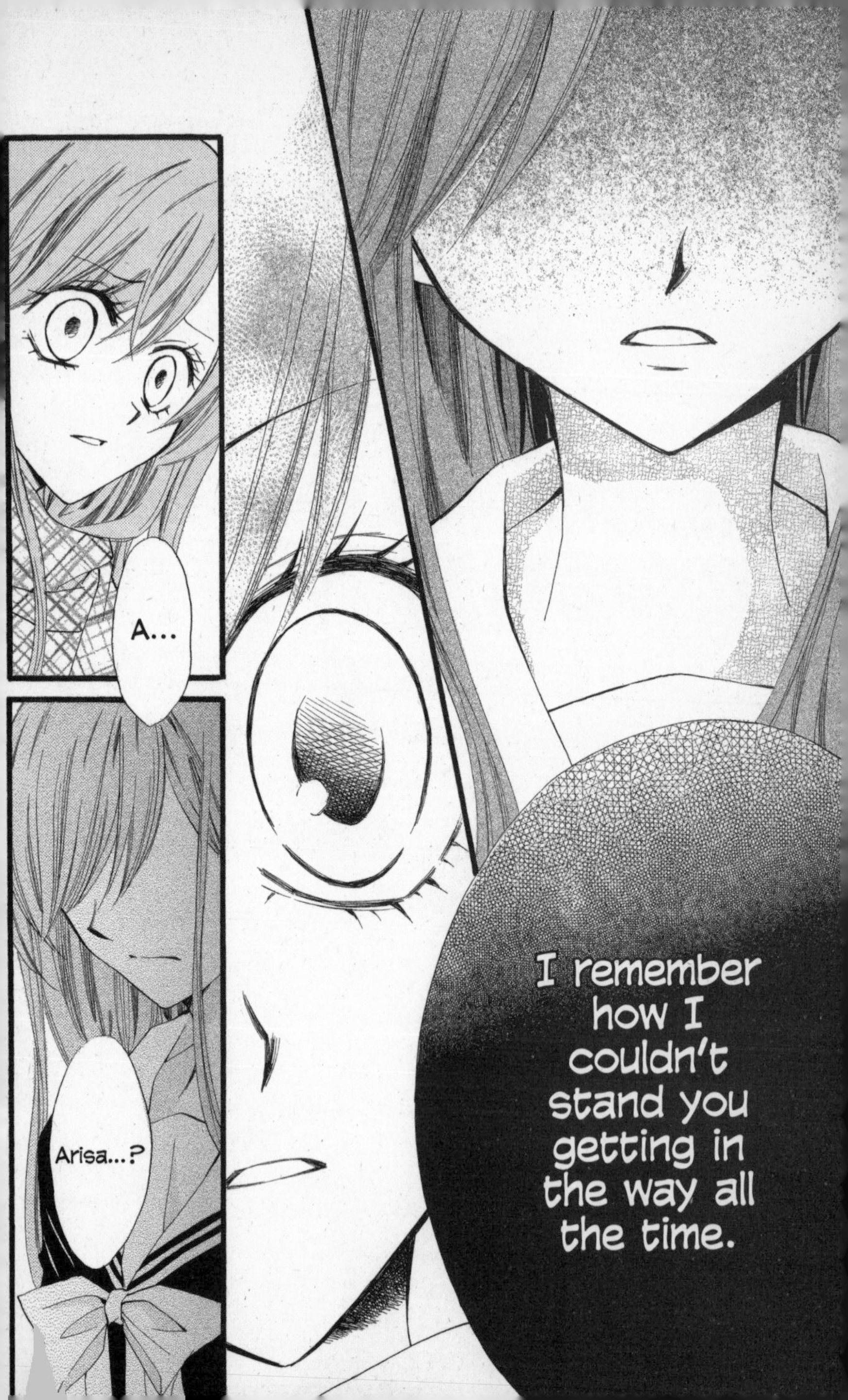
I remember how I couldn't stand you getting in the way all the time.
A...
Arisa...?

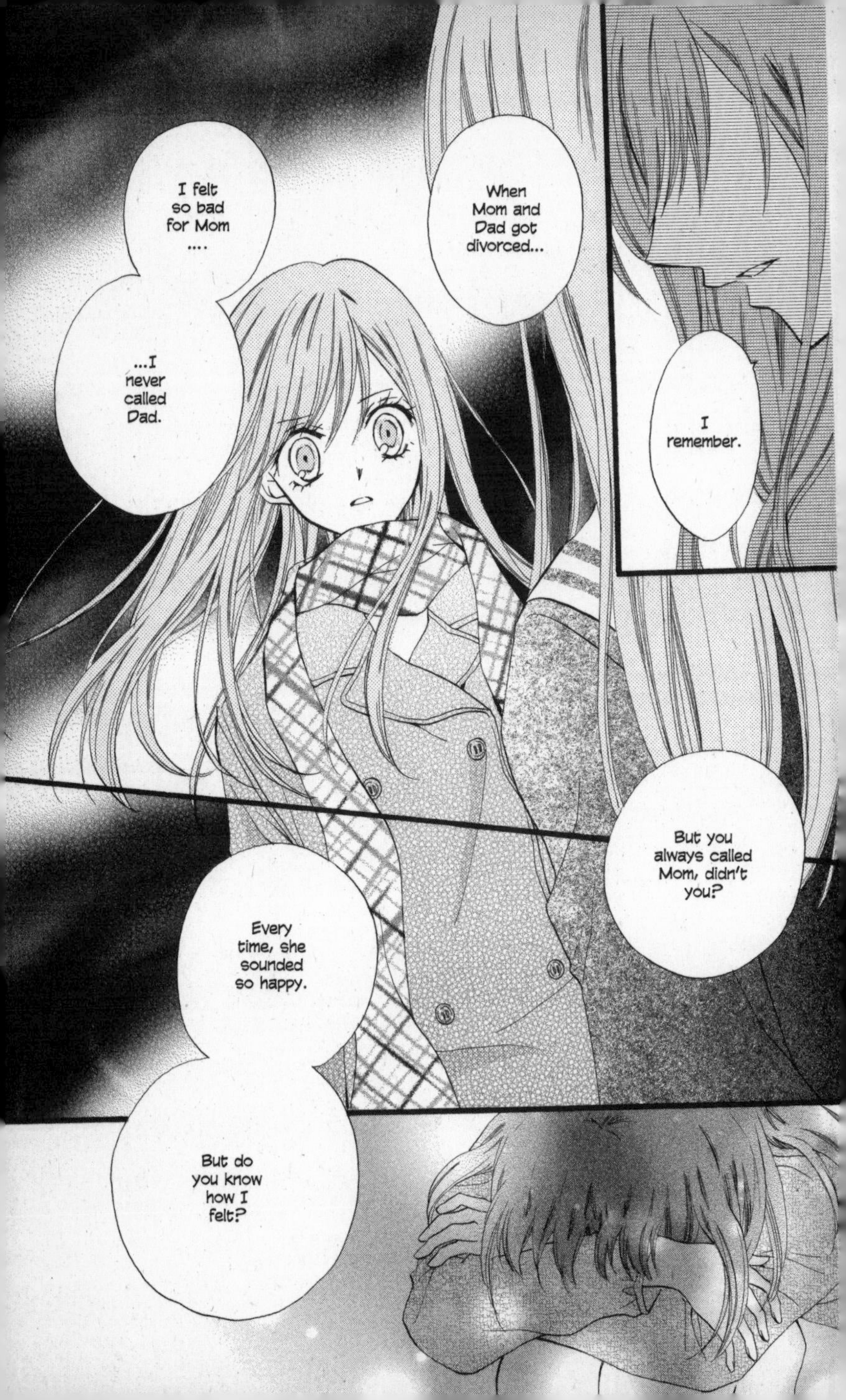
I remember.
When Mom and Dad got divorced...
I felt so bad for Mom ....
...I never called Dad.
But you always called Mom, didn't you?
Every time, she sounded so happy.
But do you know how I felt?

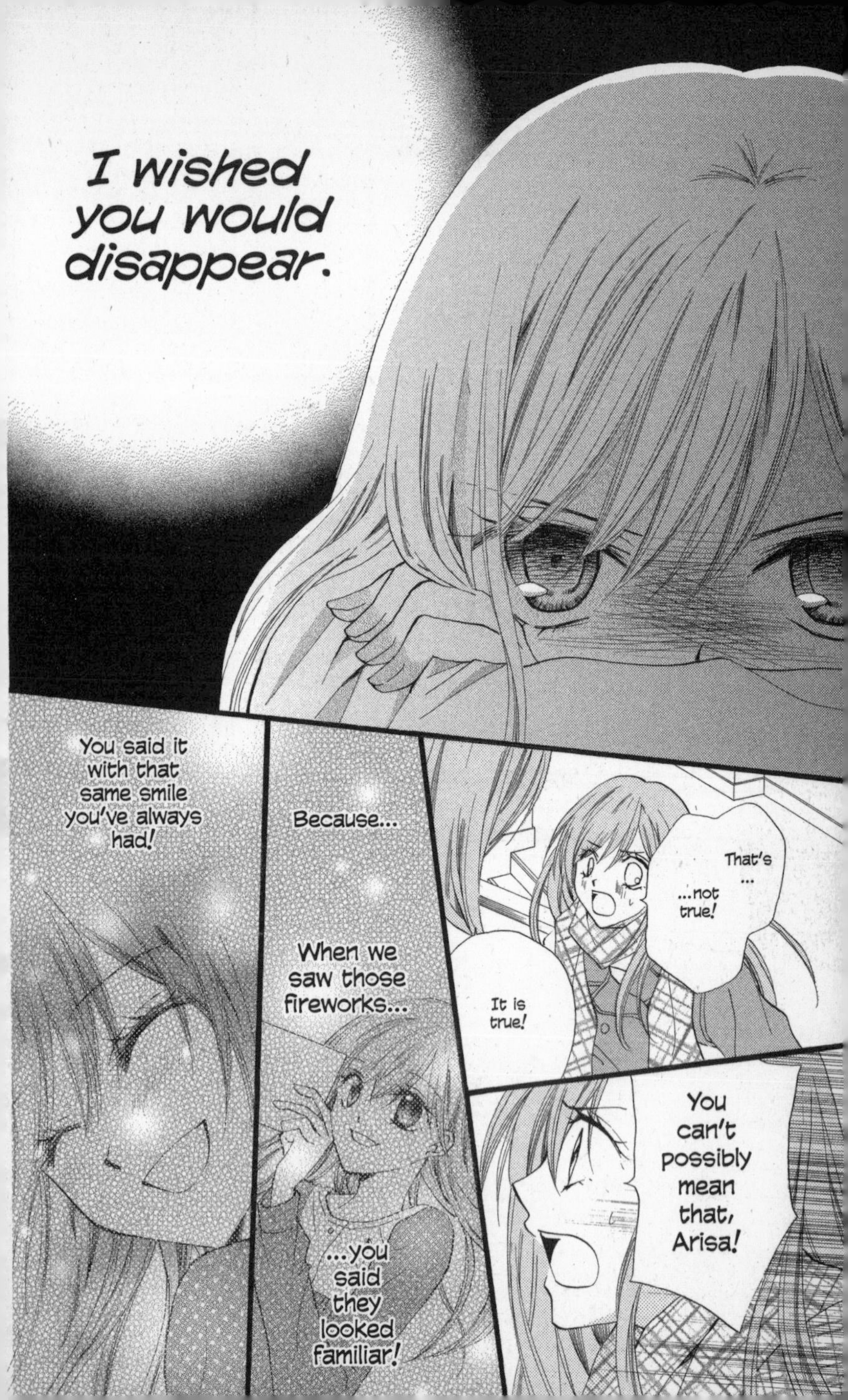
I wished you would disappear.
That's...
...not true!
It is true!
You can't possibly mean that, Arisa!
Because...
When we saw those fireworks...
...you said they looked familiar!
You said it with that same smile you've always had!

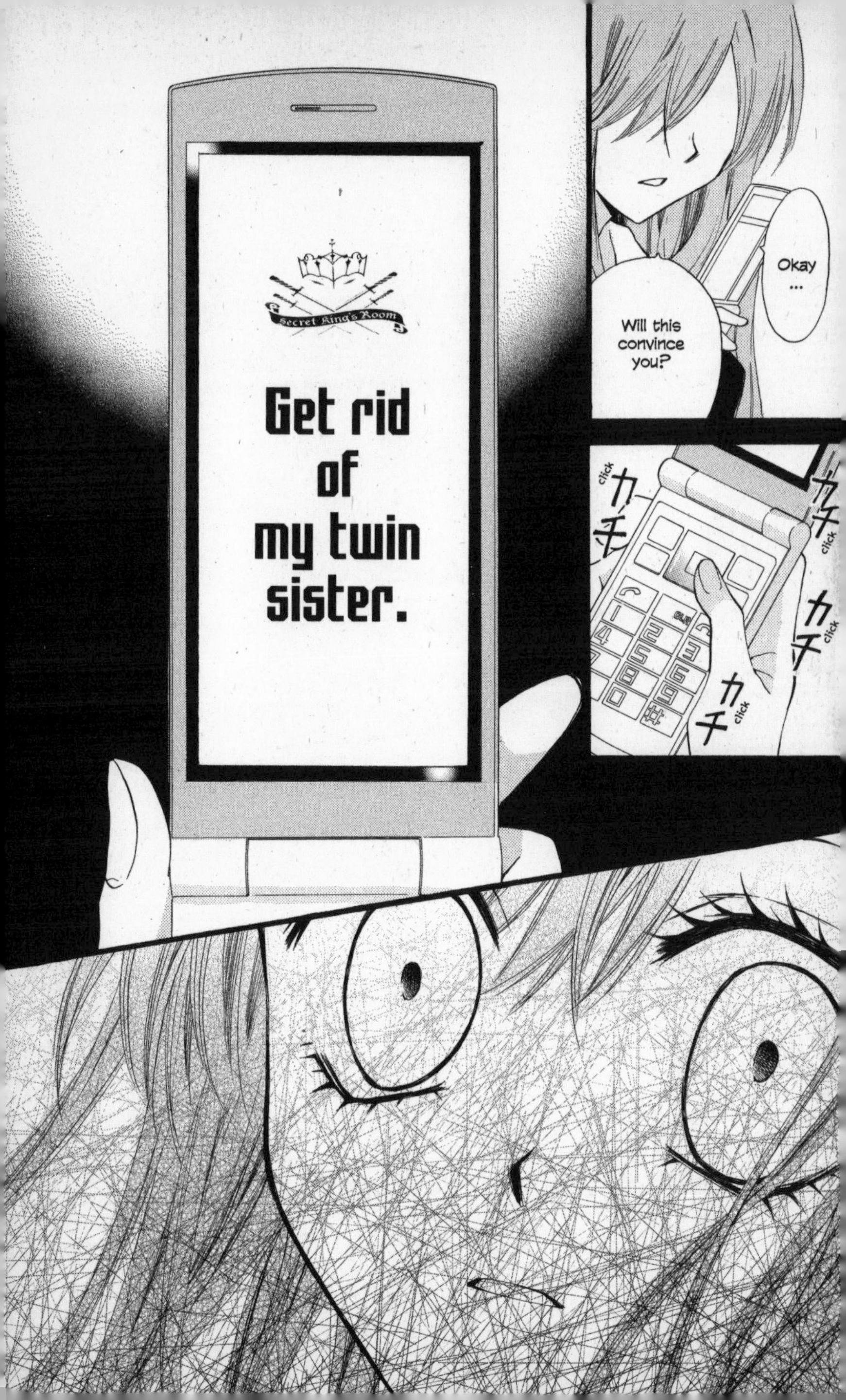
Okay ...
Will this convince you?
カチ click
カチ click
カチ click
カチ click
Secret King's Room
Get rid of my twin sister.

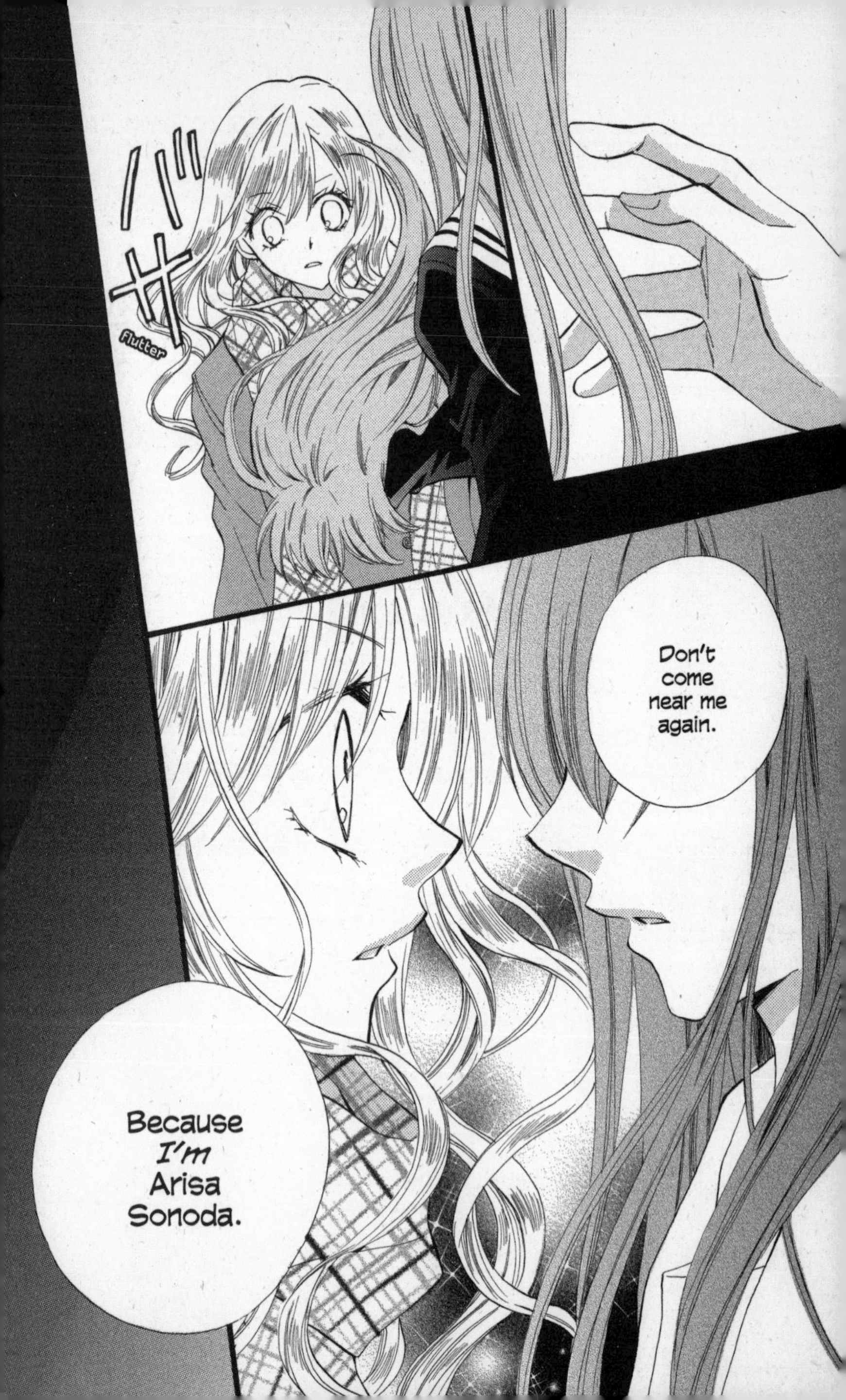
バサ
Flutter
Don't come near me again.
Because *I'm* Arisa Sonoda.

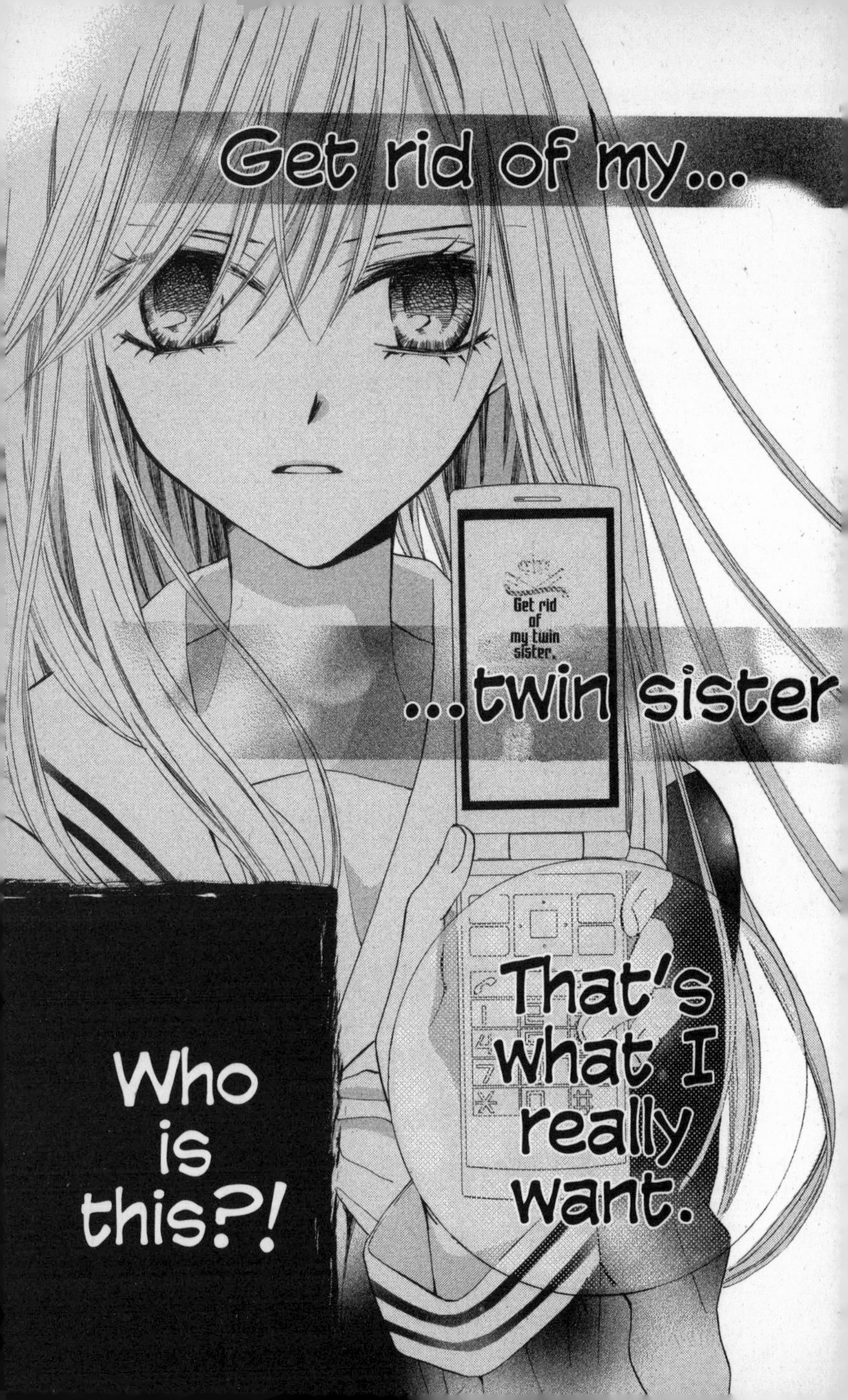
Get rid of my...
Get rid of my twin sister.
...twin sister
That's what I really want.
Who is this?!

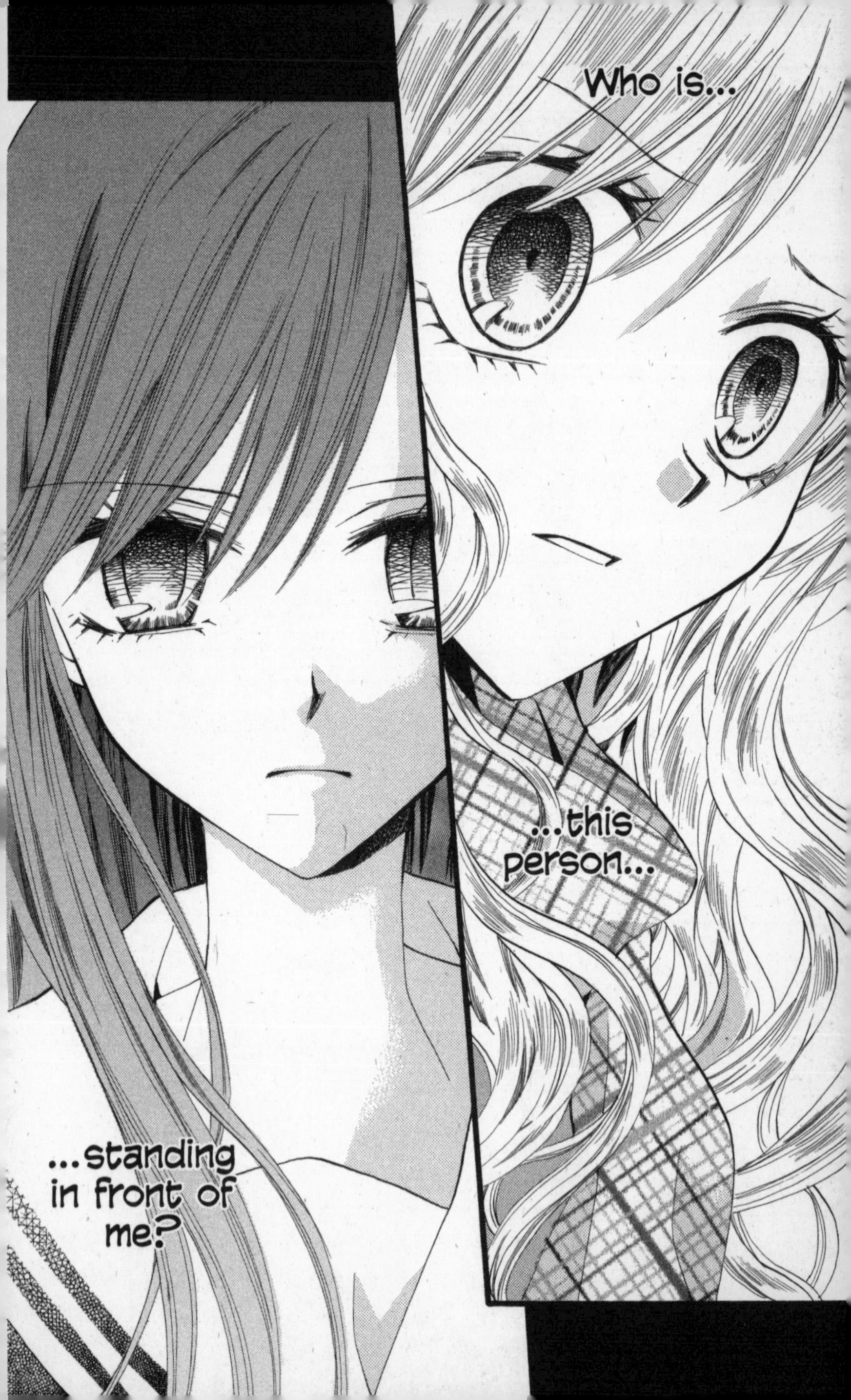
Who is...
...this person...
...standing in front of me?

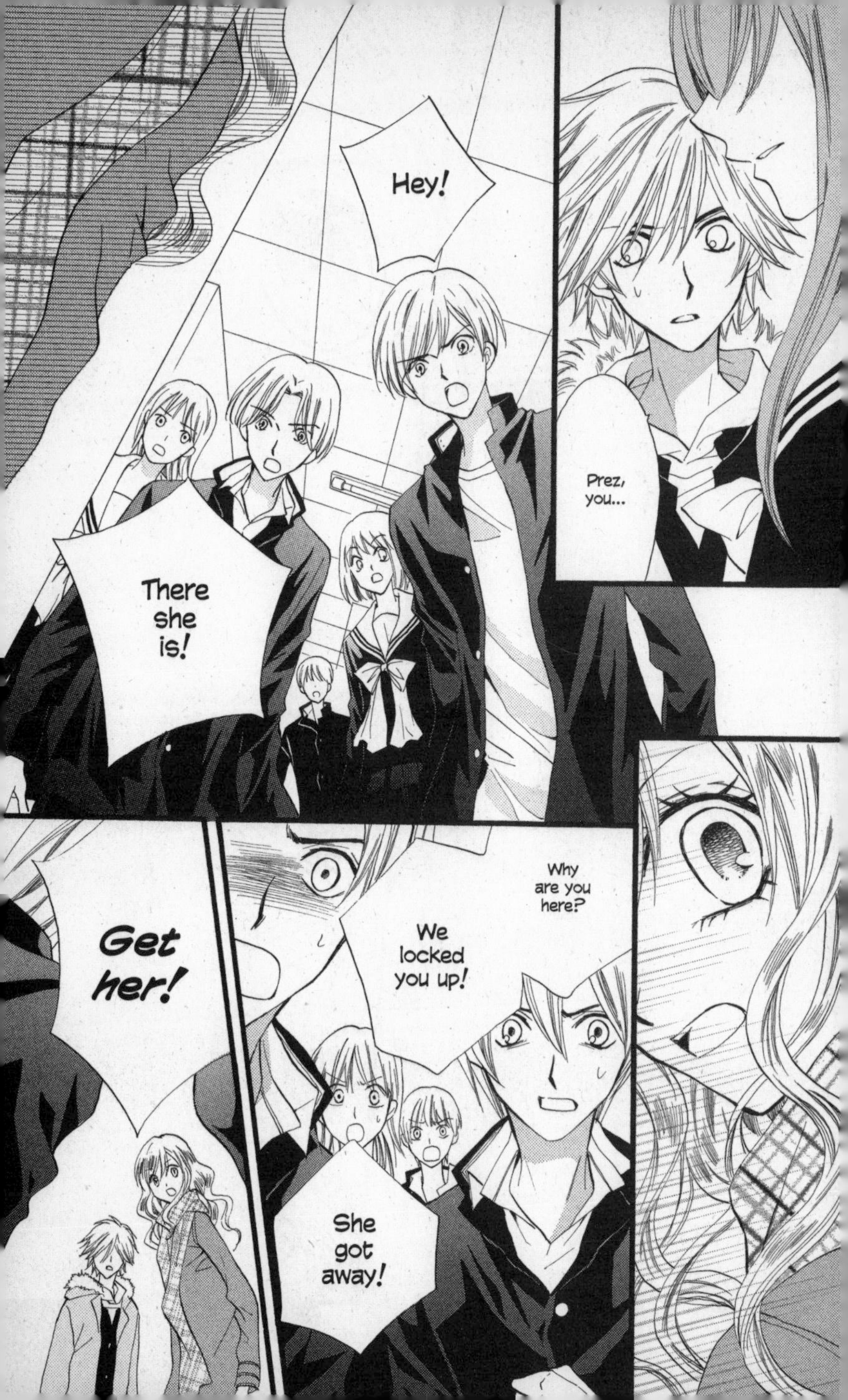
Prez, you...
Hey!
There she is!
Why are you here?
We locked you up!
She got away!
Get her!

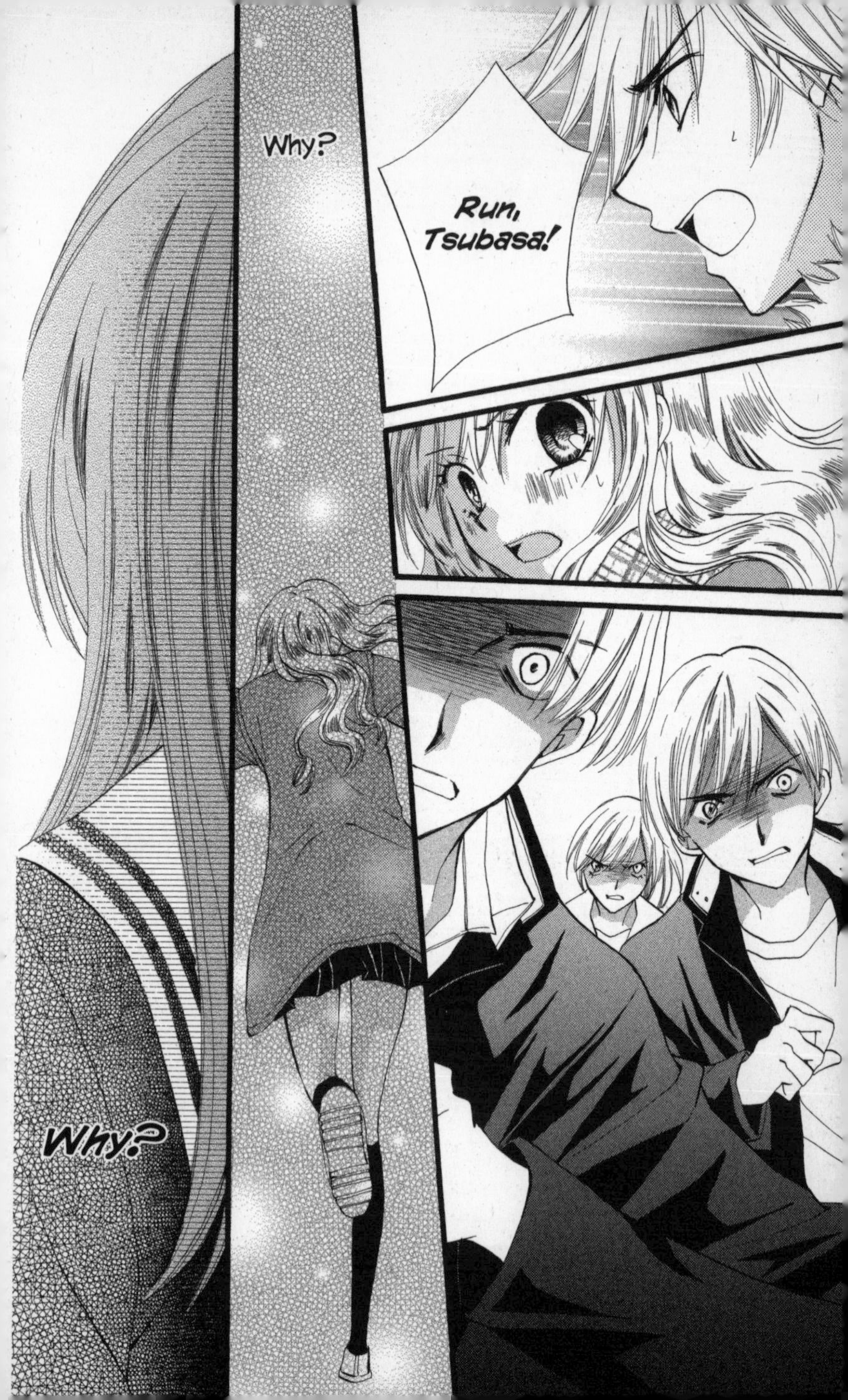
Run, Tsubasa!
Why?
Why?

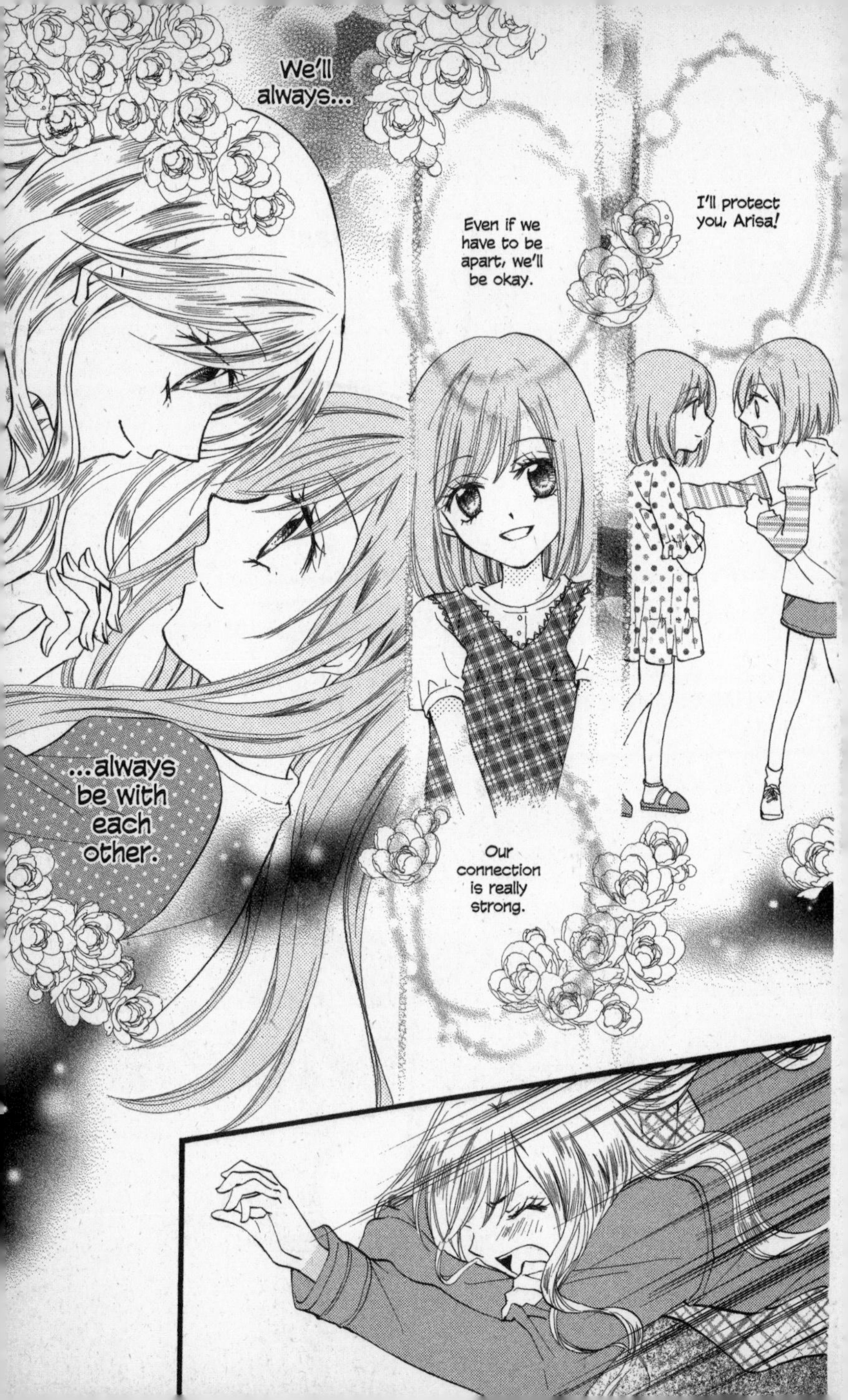
I'll protect you, Arisa!
Even if we have to be apart, we'll be okay.
Our connection is really strong.
We'll always...
...always be with each other.

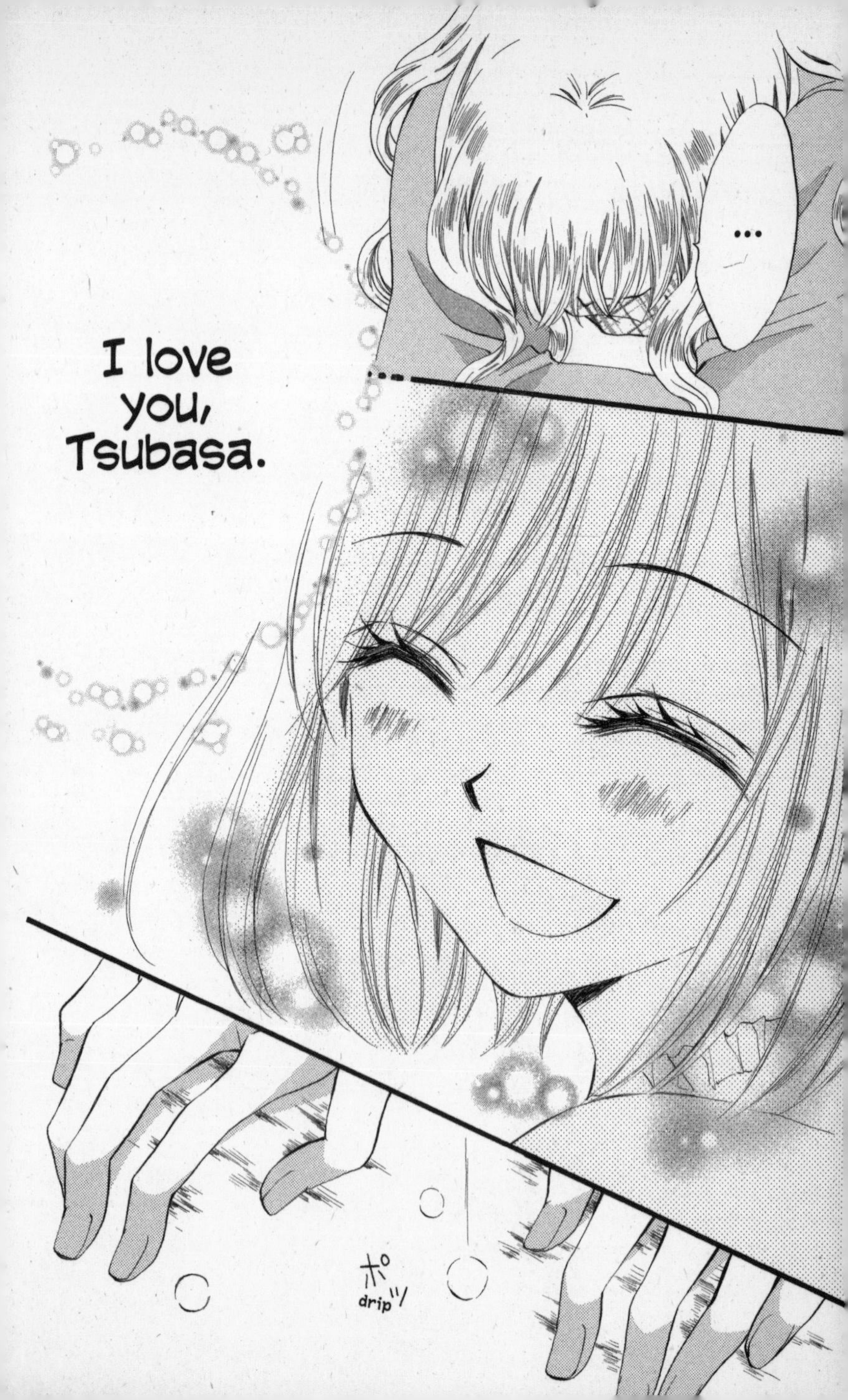
...
I love you, Tsubasa.
ポツ
drip

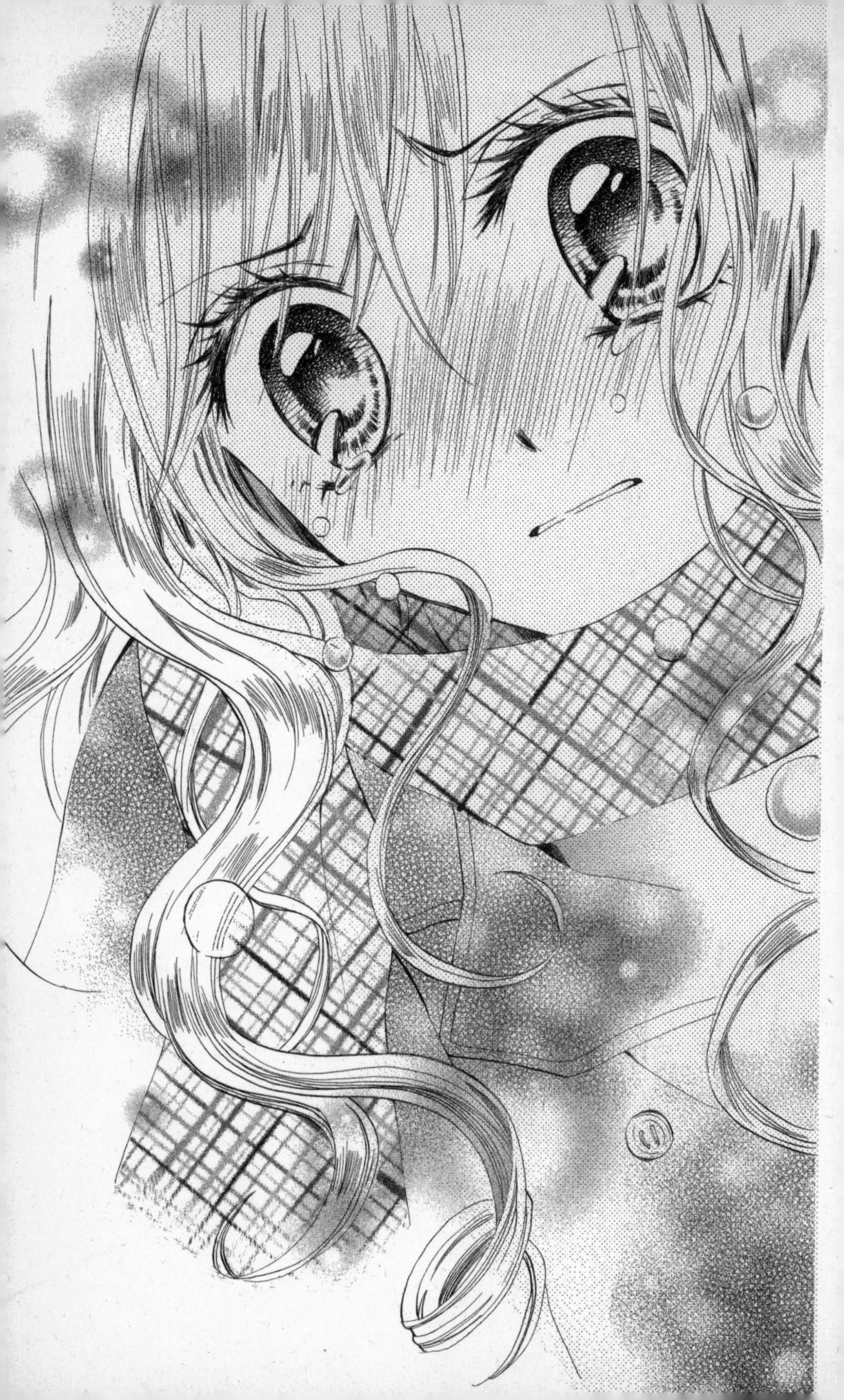

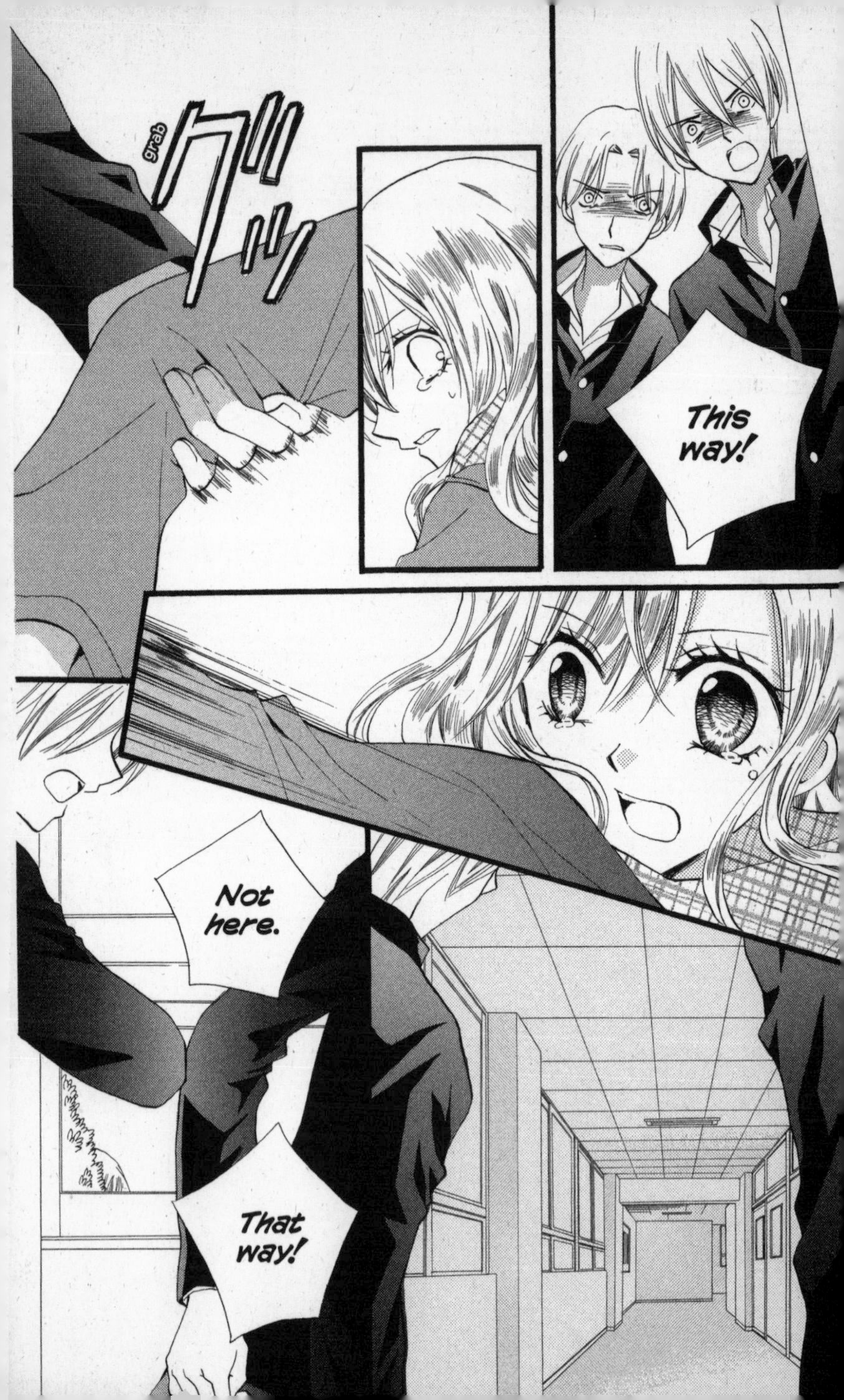
This way!
grab
Not here.
That way!

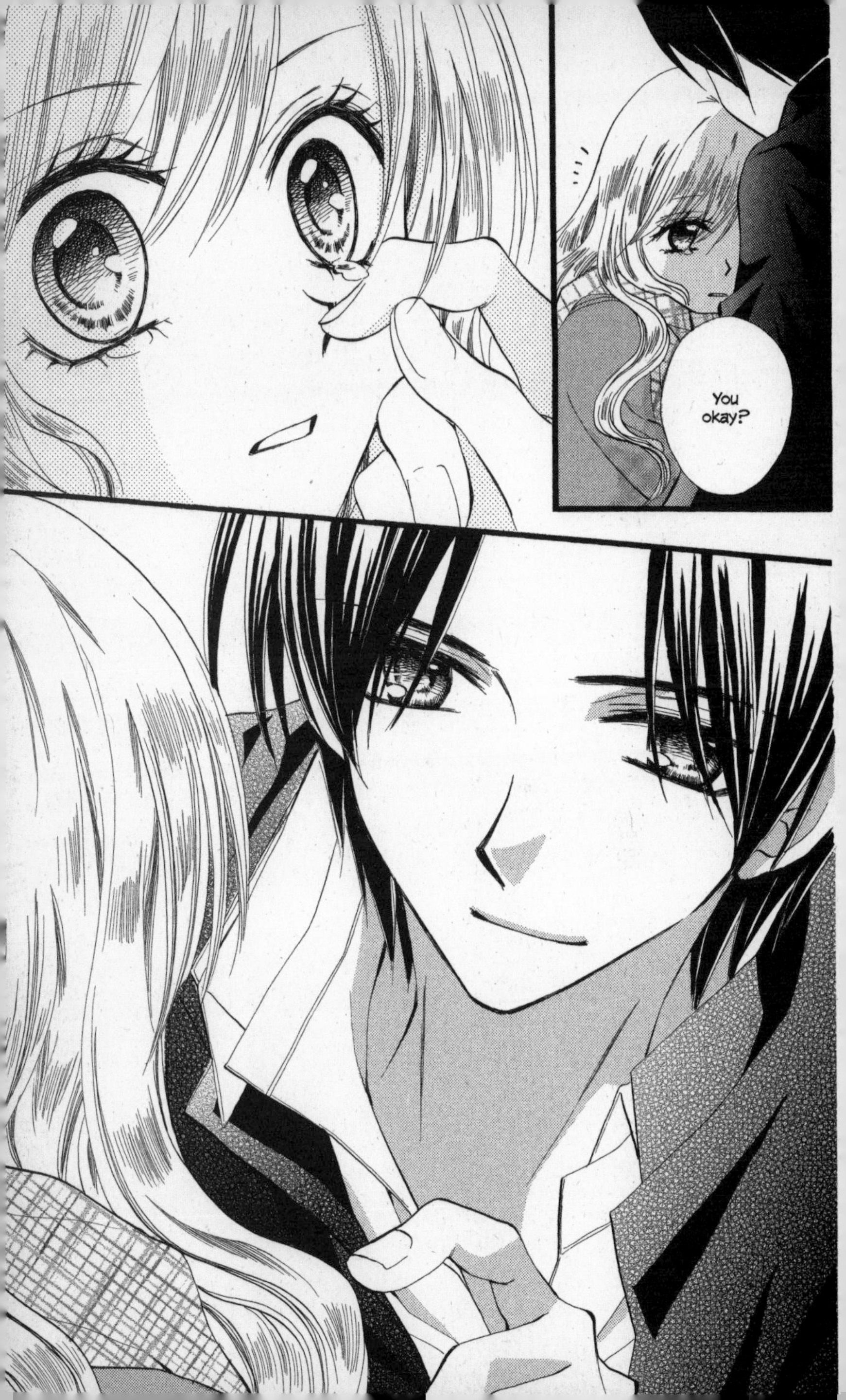
You okay?

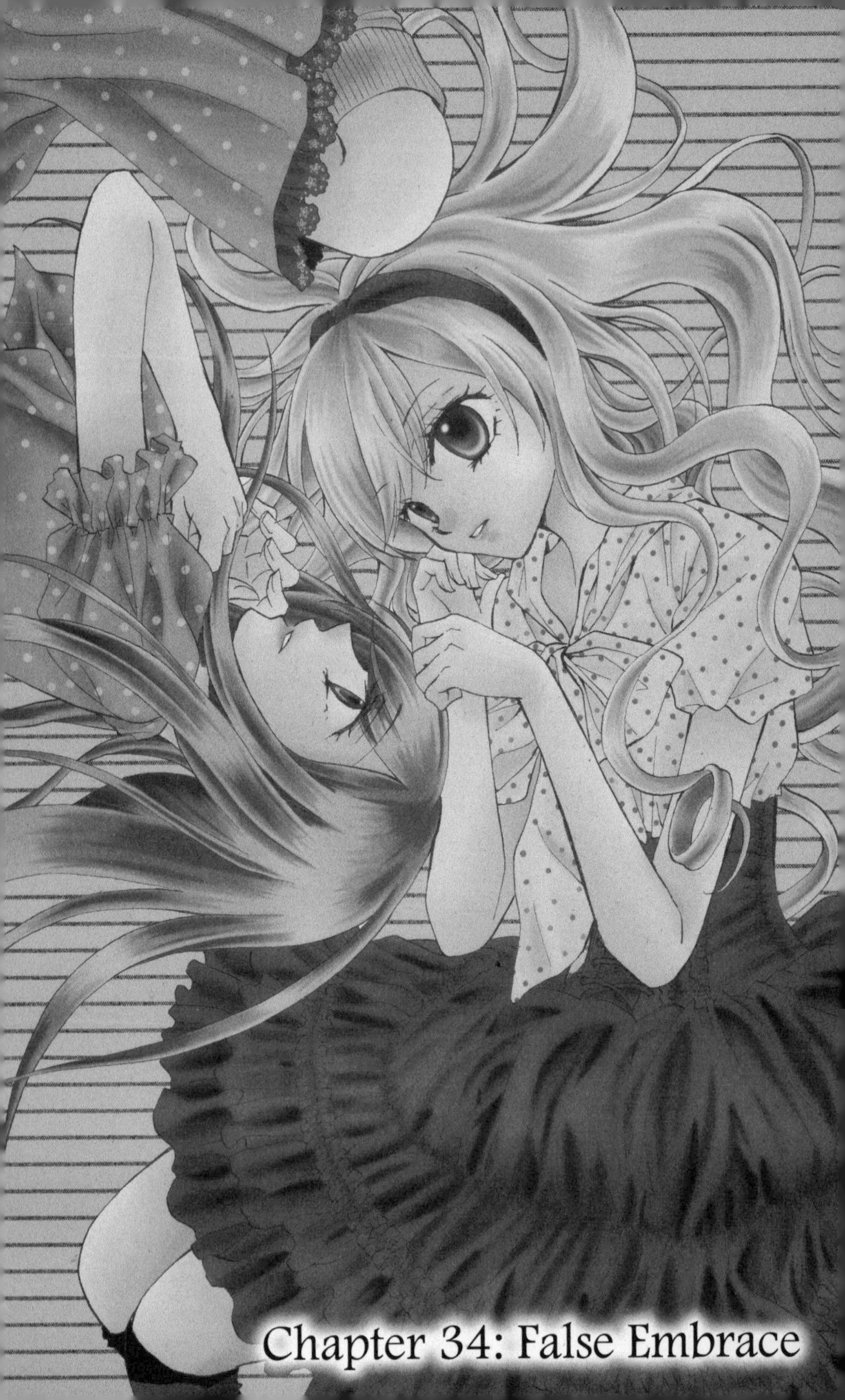

Chapter 34: False Embrace

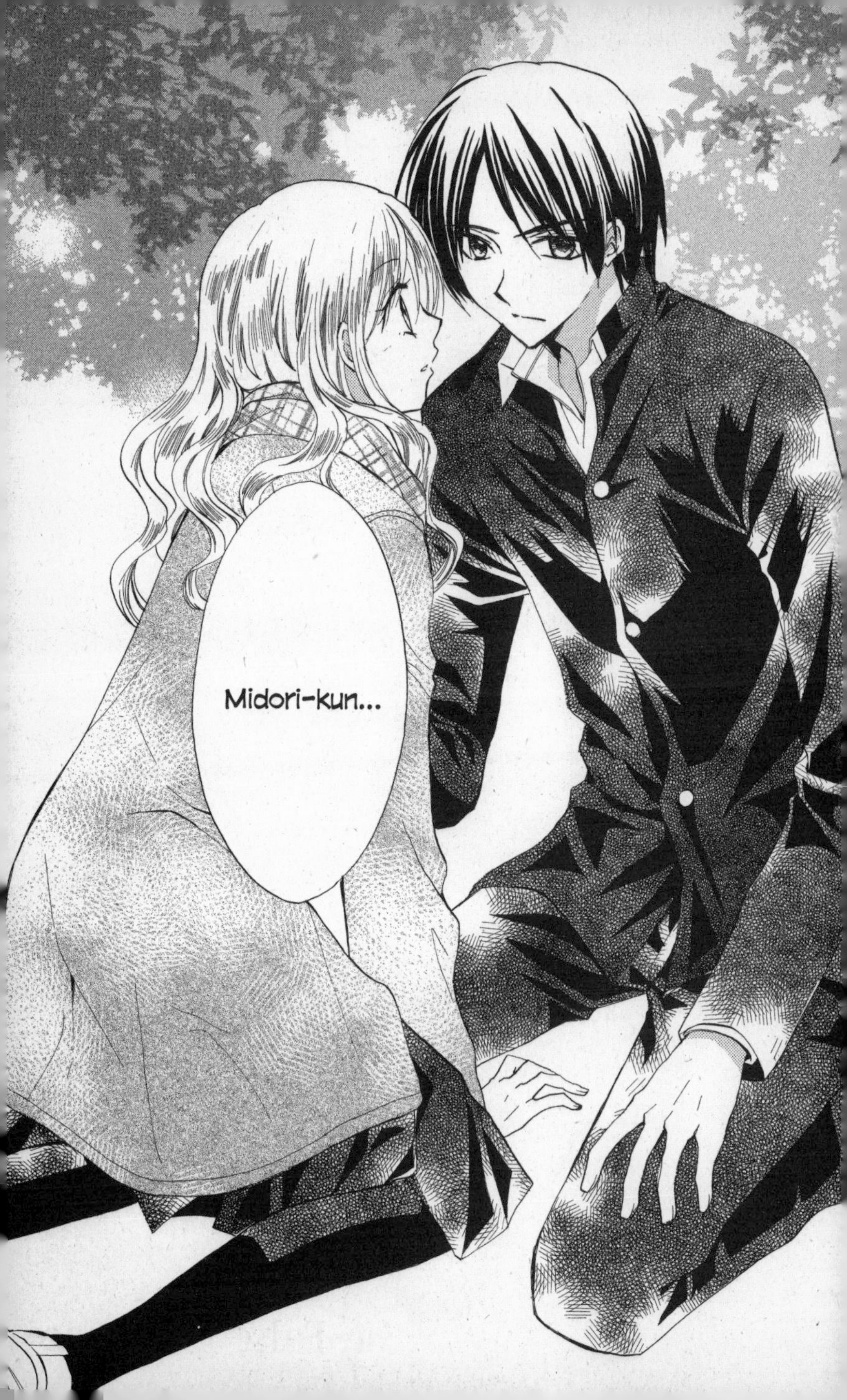
Midori-kun...

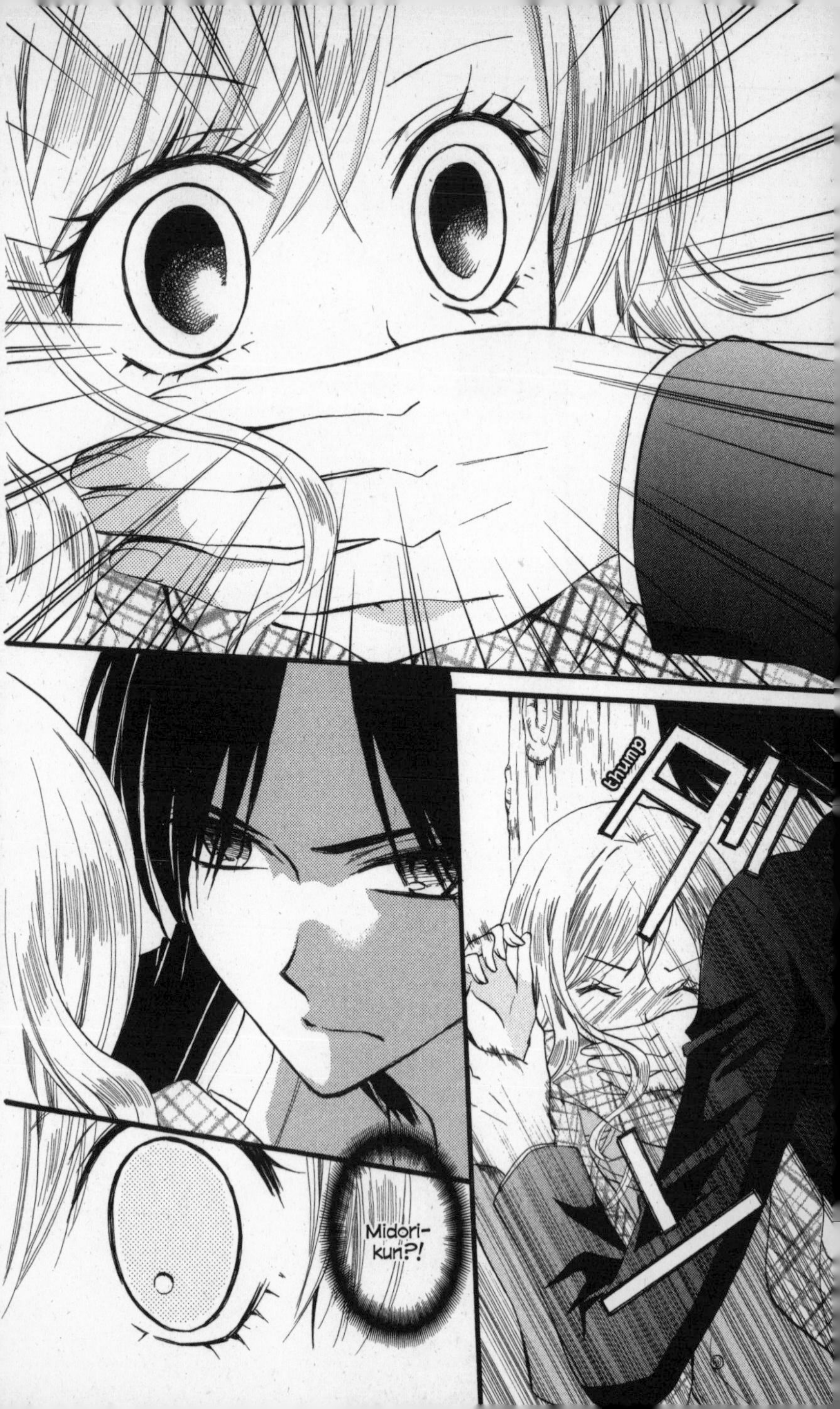
thump
Midori-kun?!

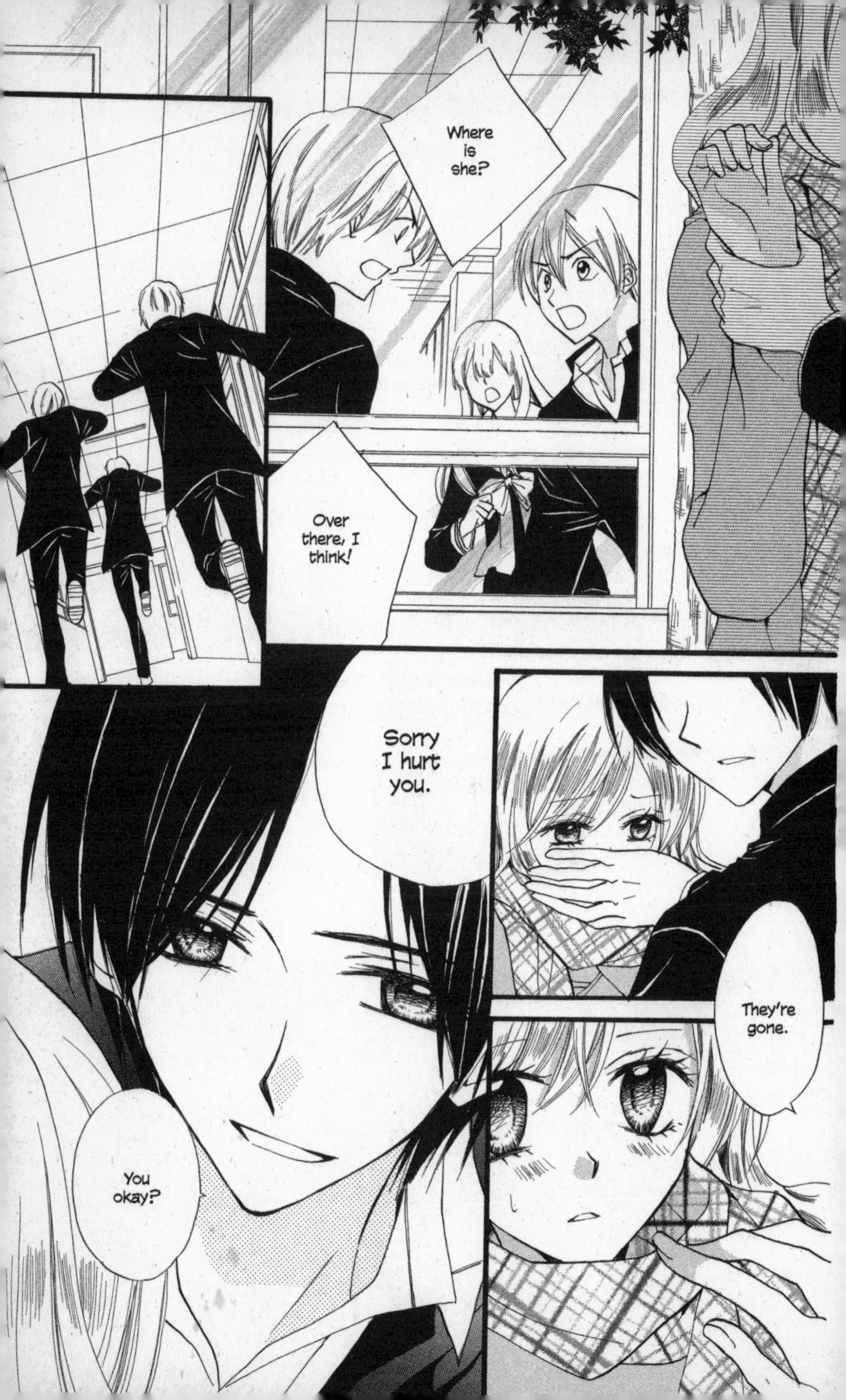
Where is she?
Over there, I think!
They're gone.
Sorry I hurt you.
You okay?

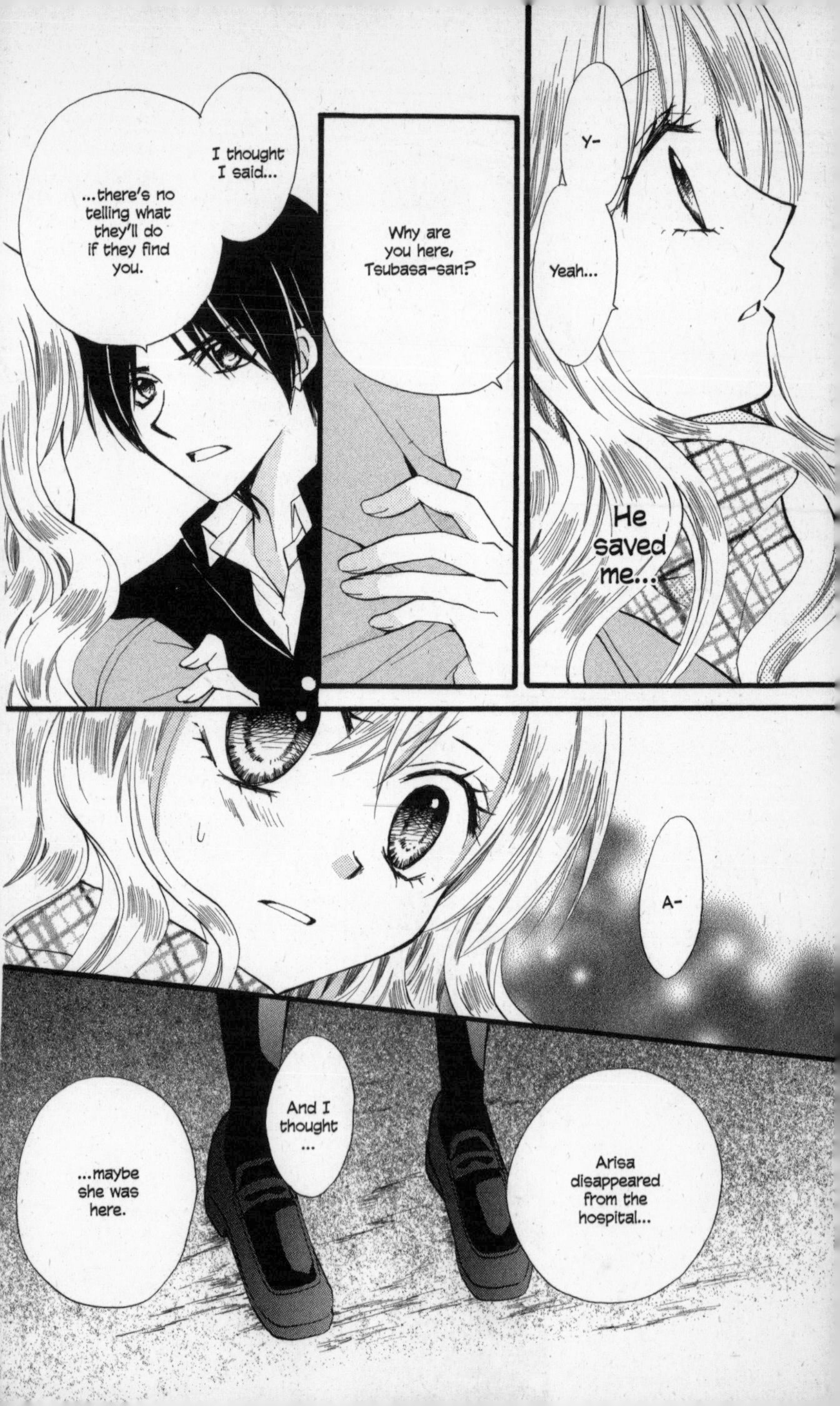
Y-
Yeah...
He saved me...
Why are you here, Tsubasa-san?
I thought I said...
...there's no telling what they'll do if they find you.
A-
Arisa disappeared from the hospital...
And I thought...
...maybe she was here.

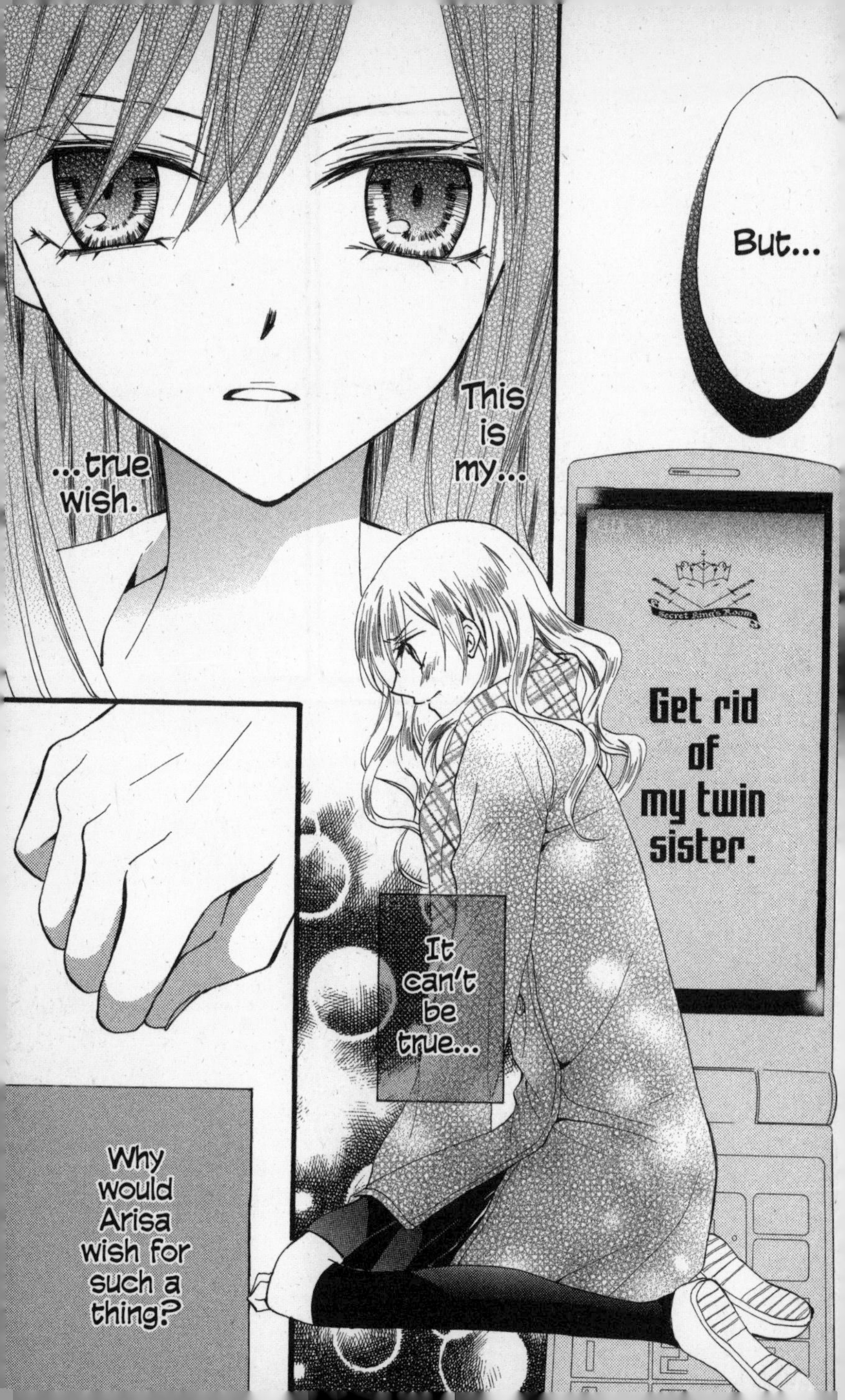
But...
Get rid of my twin sister.
This is my...
...true wish.
It can't be true...
Why would Arisa wish for such a thing?

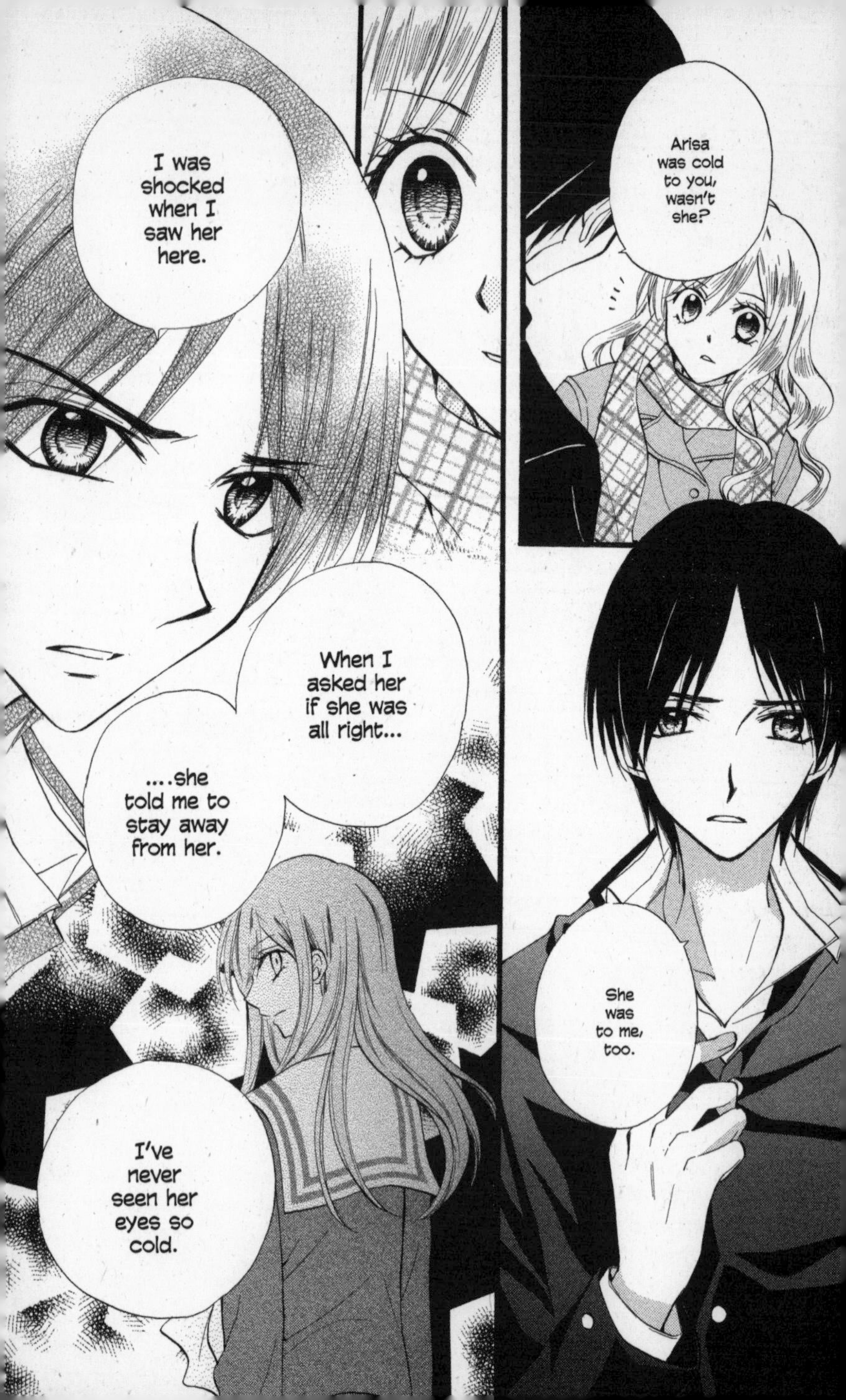
Arisa was cold to you, wasn't she?
She was to me, too.
I was shocked when I saw her here.
When I asked her if she was all right...
....she told me to stay away from her.
I've never seen her eyes so cold.

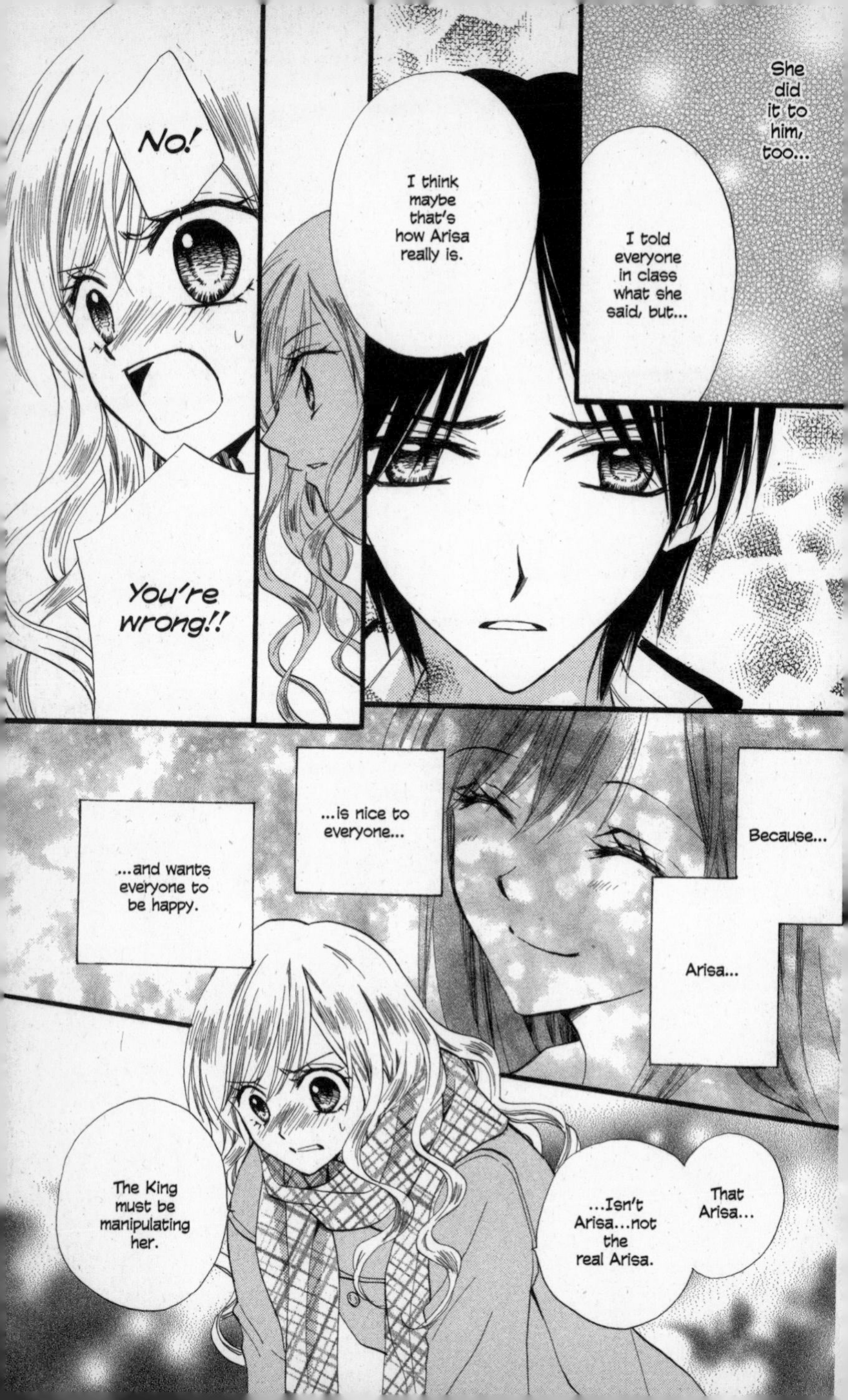
She did it to him, too...
I told everyone in class what she said, but...
I think maybe that's how Arisa really is.
No!
You're wrong!!
Because...
Arisa...
...is nice to everyone...
...and wants everyone to be happy.
That Arisa...
...Isn't Arisa...not the real Arisa.
The King must be manipulating her.

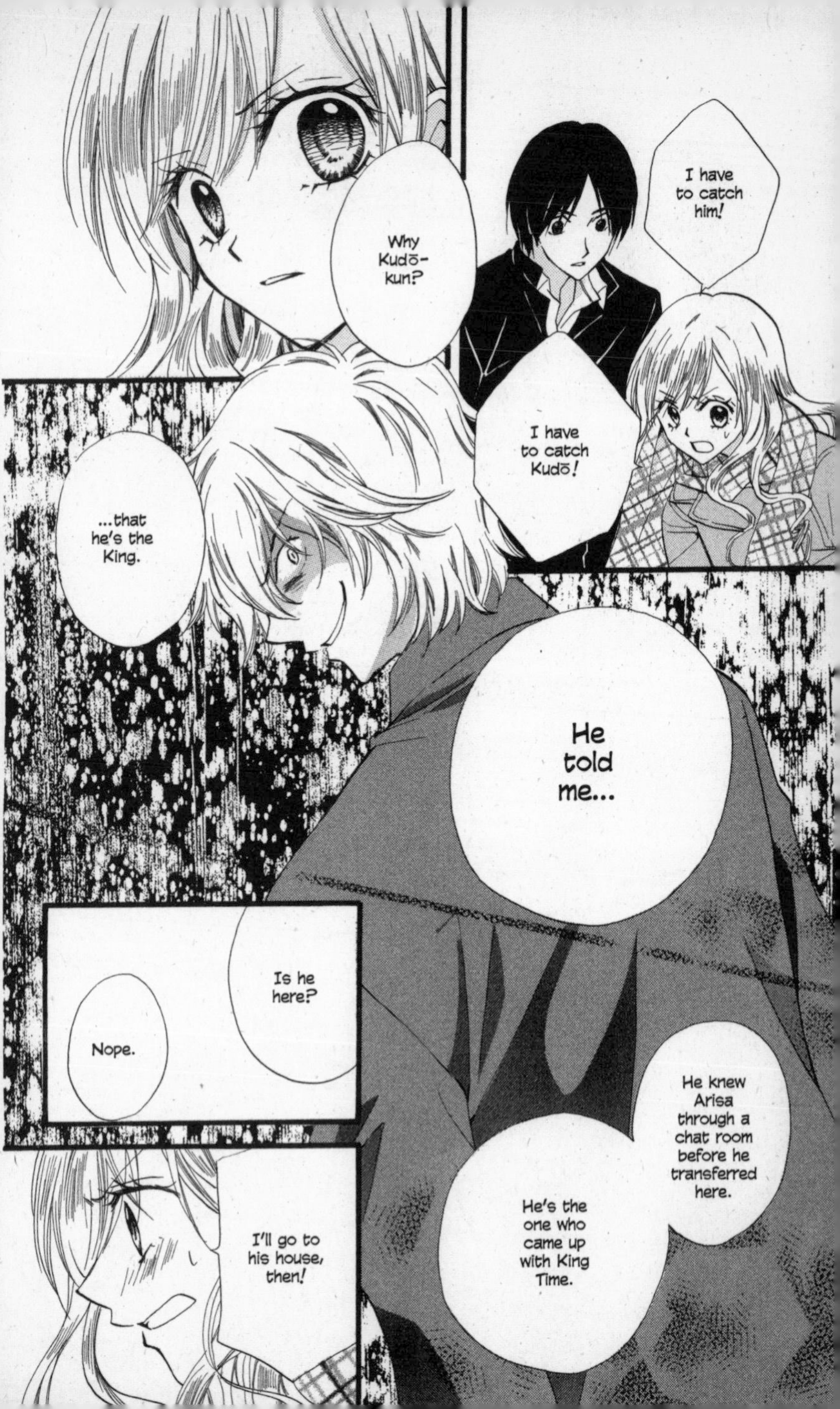
I have to catch him!
I have to catch Kudō!
Why Kudō-kun?
He told me...
...that he's the King.
He knew Arisa through a chat room before he transferred here.
He's the one who came up with King Time.
Is he here?
Nope.
I'll go to his house, then!

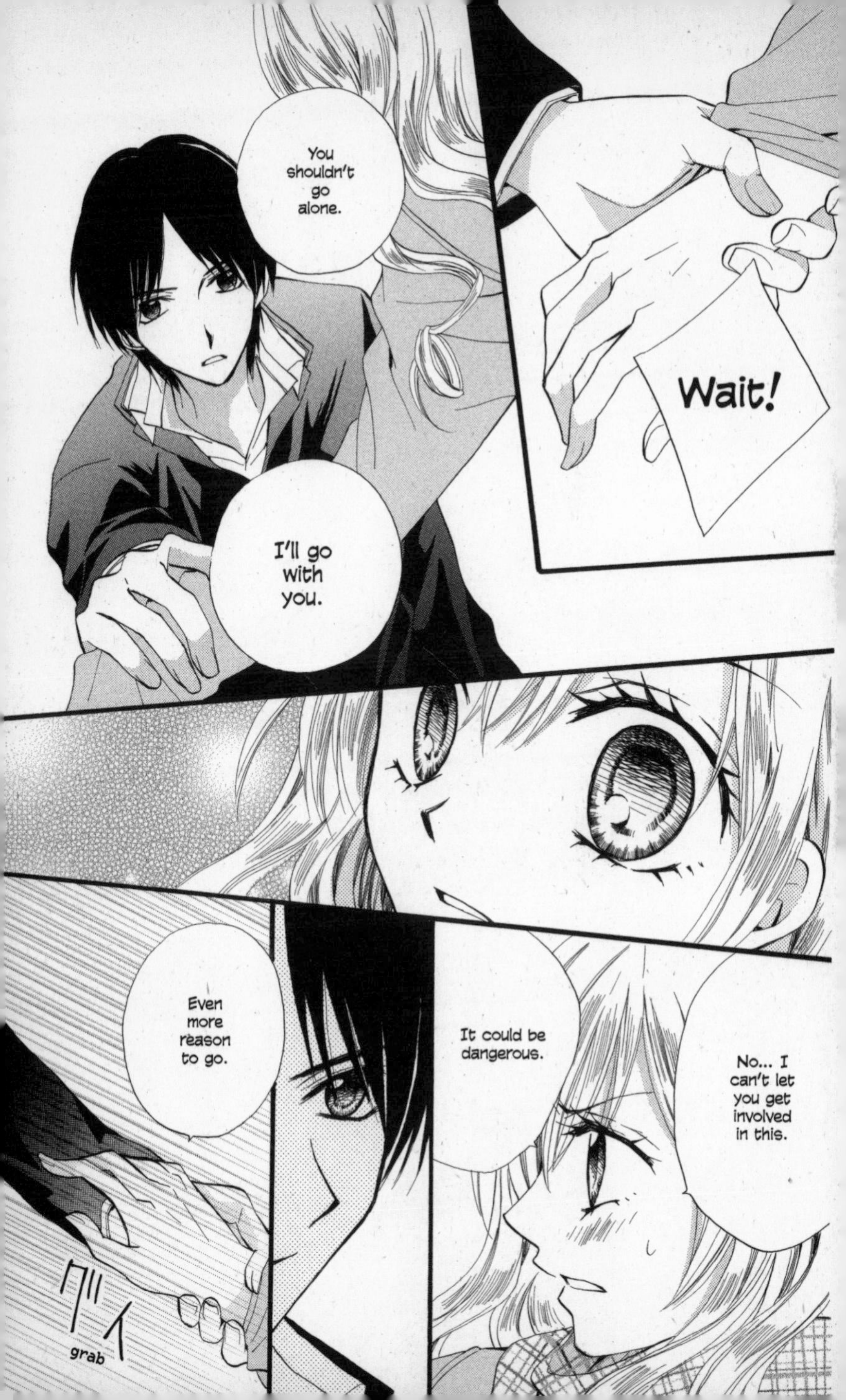
Wait!
You shouldn't go alone.
I'll go with you.
No... I can't let you get involved in this.
It could be dangerous.
Even more reason to go.
グイ
grab

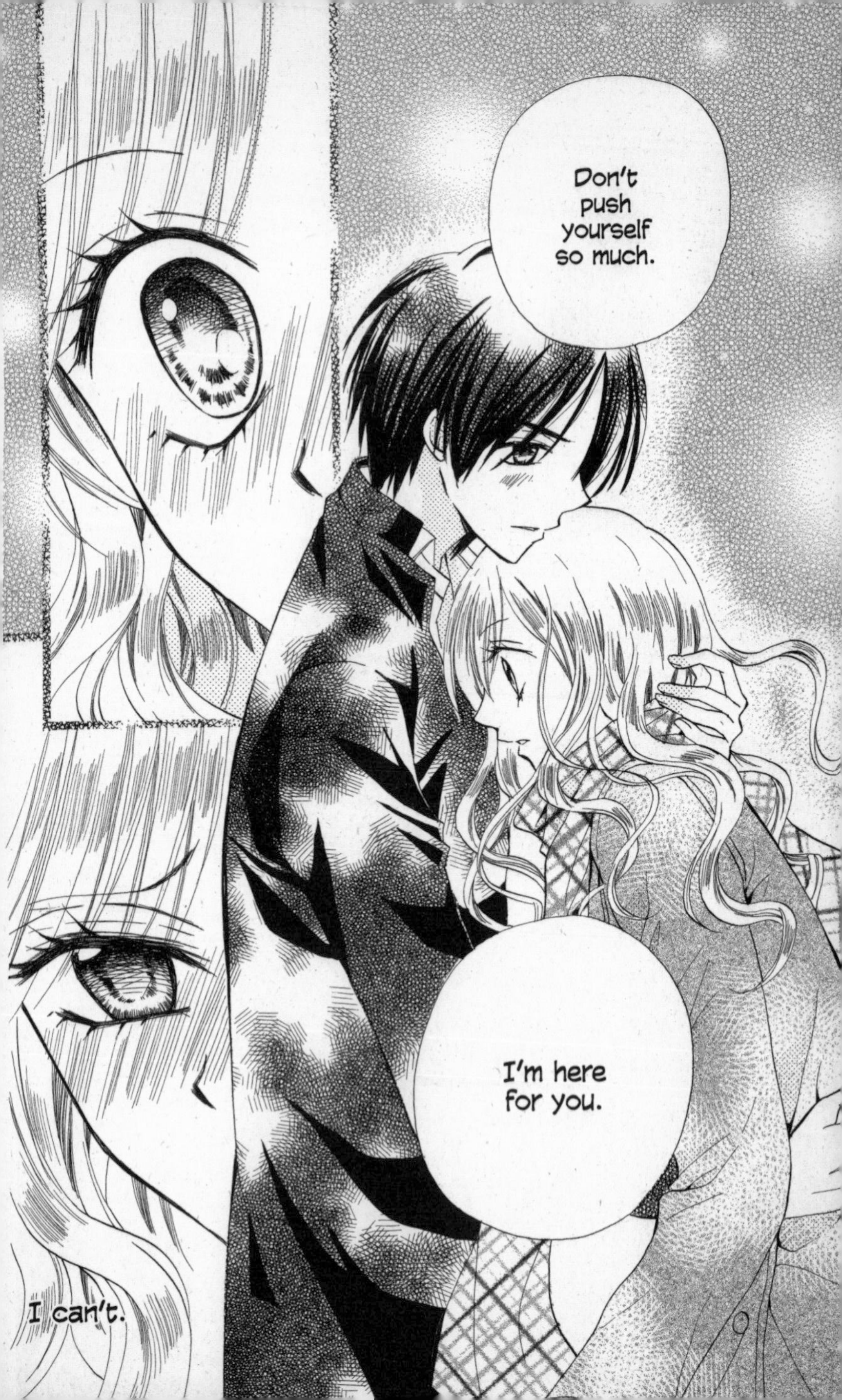
Don't push yourself so much.
I'm here for you.
I can't.

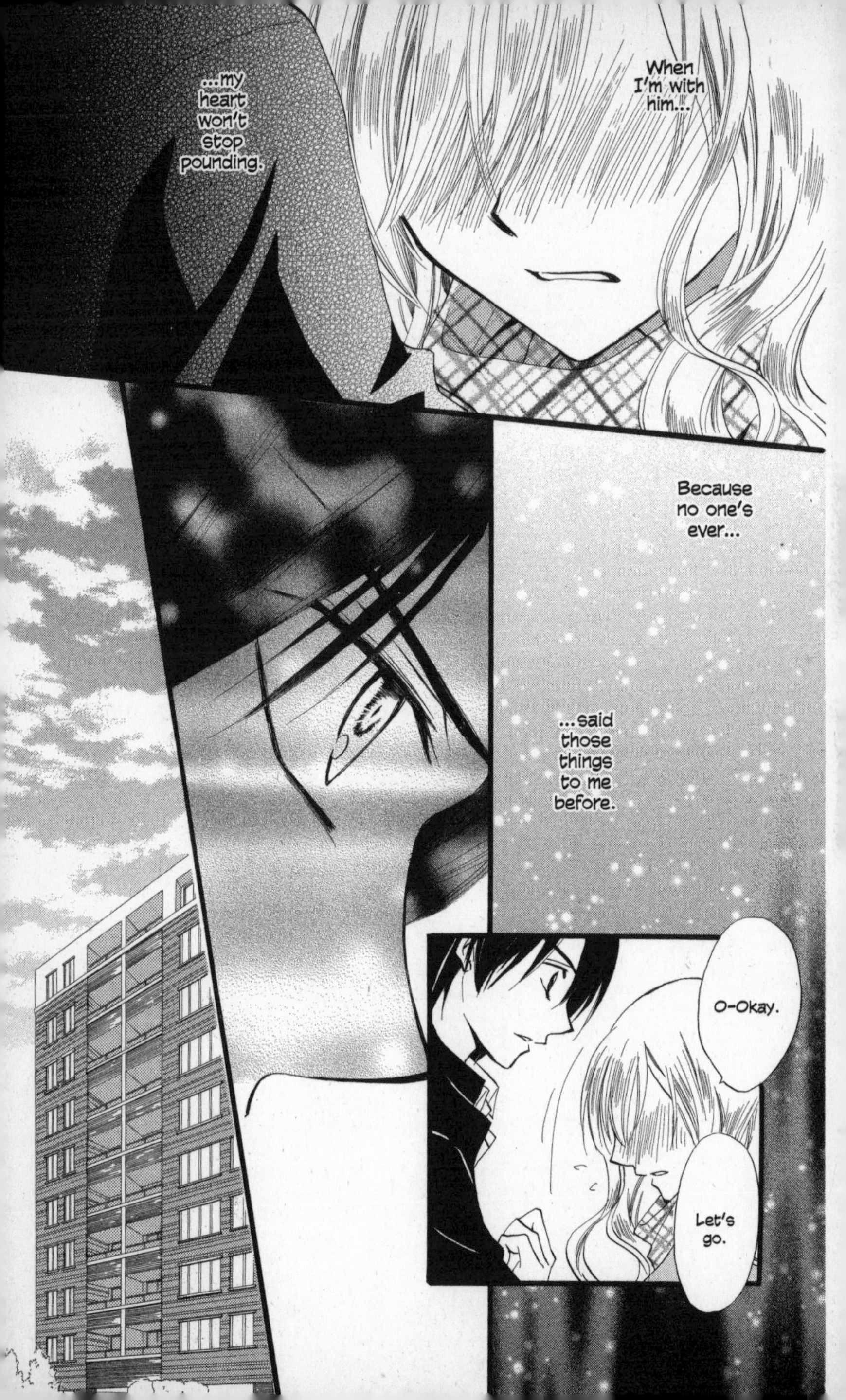
When I'm with him...
...my heart won't stop pounding.
Because no one's ever...
...said those things to me before.
O-Okay.
Let's go.

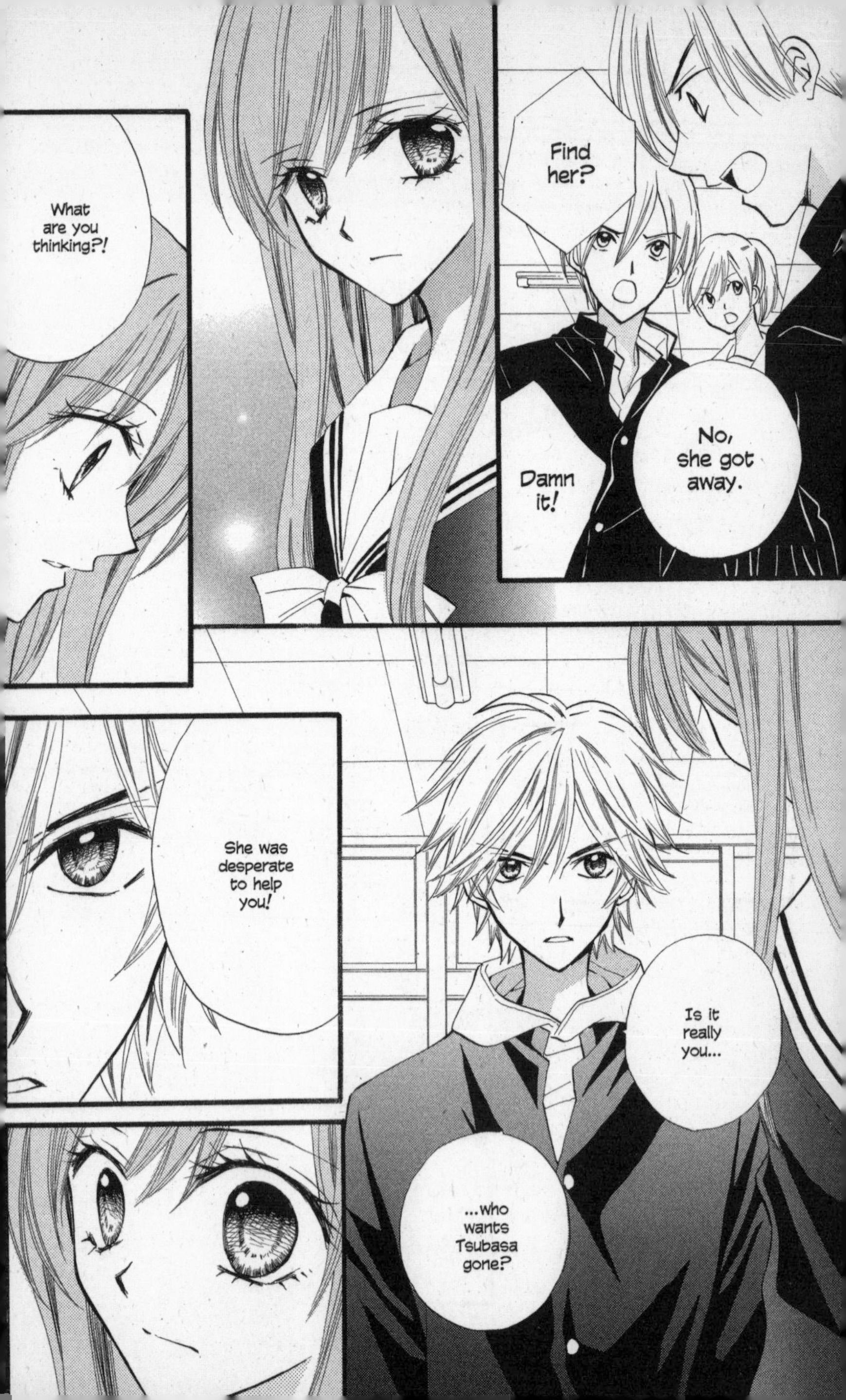
Find her?
No, she got away.
Damn it!
What are you thinking?!
Is it really you...
...who wants Tsubasa gone?
She was desperate to help you!

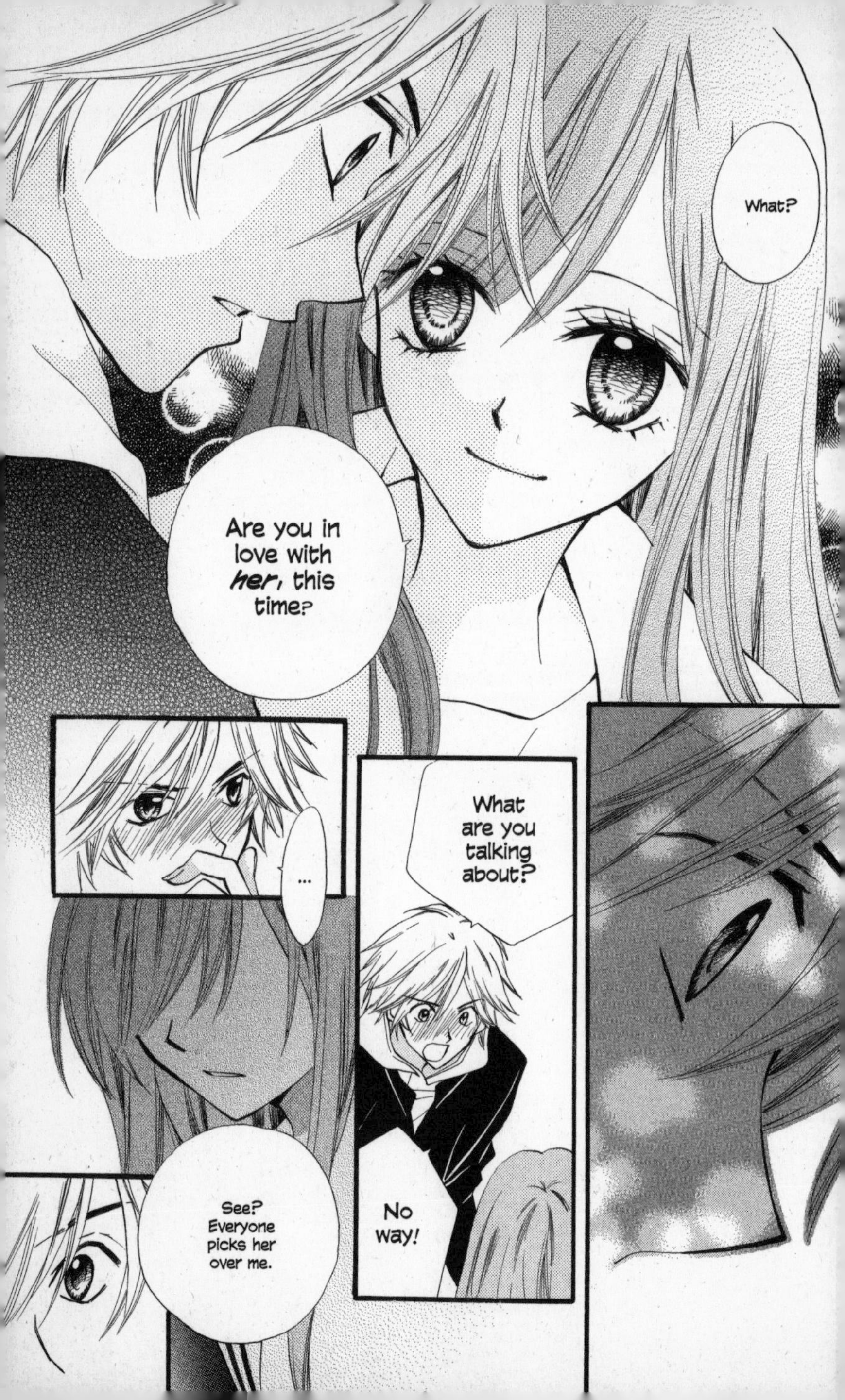
What?
Are you in love with *her*, this time?
What are you talking about?
No way!
...
See? Everyone picks her over me.

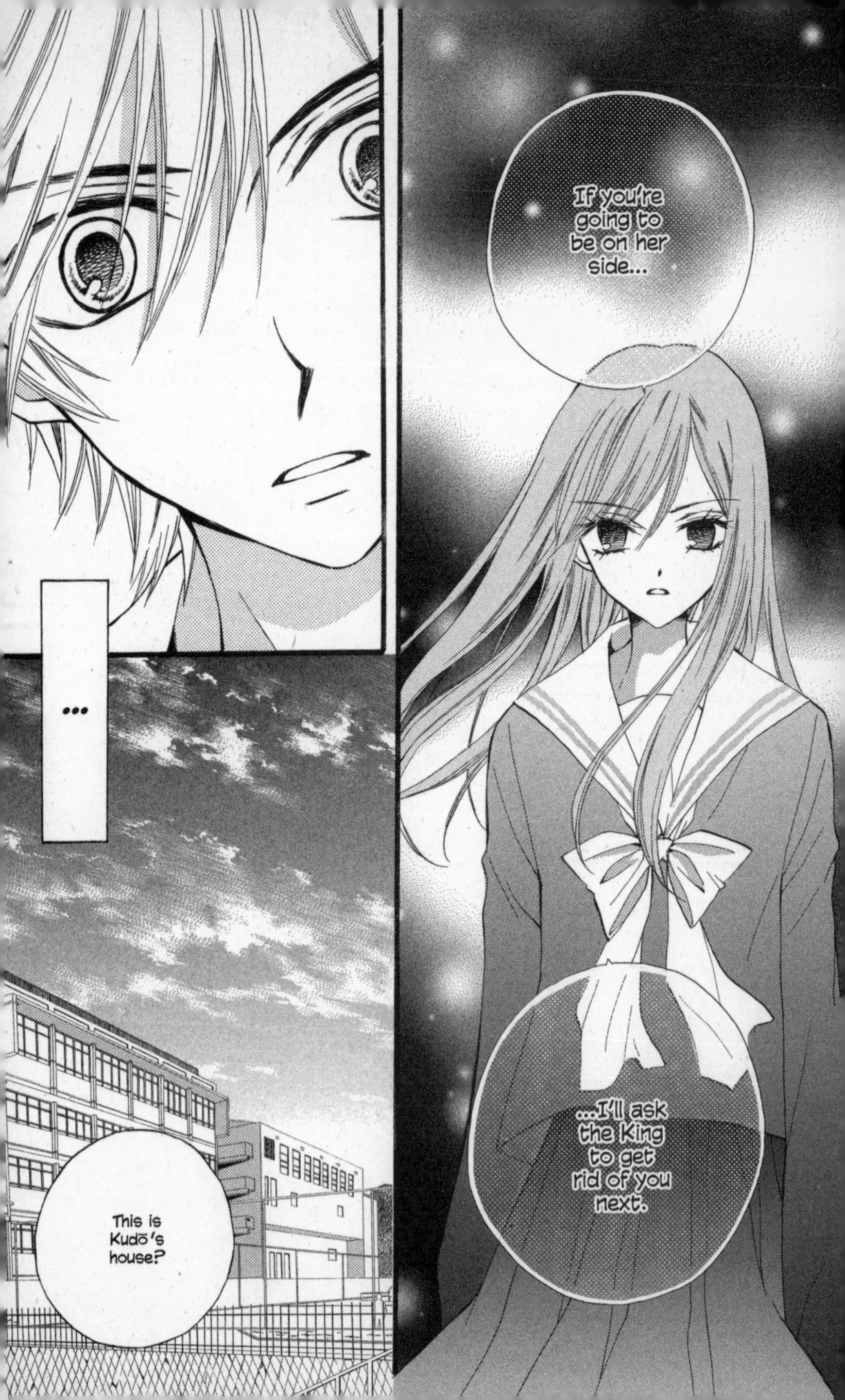
If you're going to be on her side...
...I'll ask the King to get rid of you next.
...
This is Kudō's house?

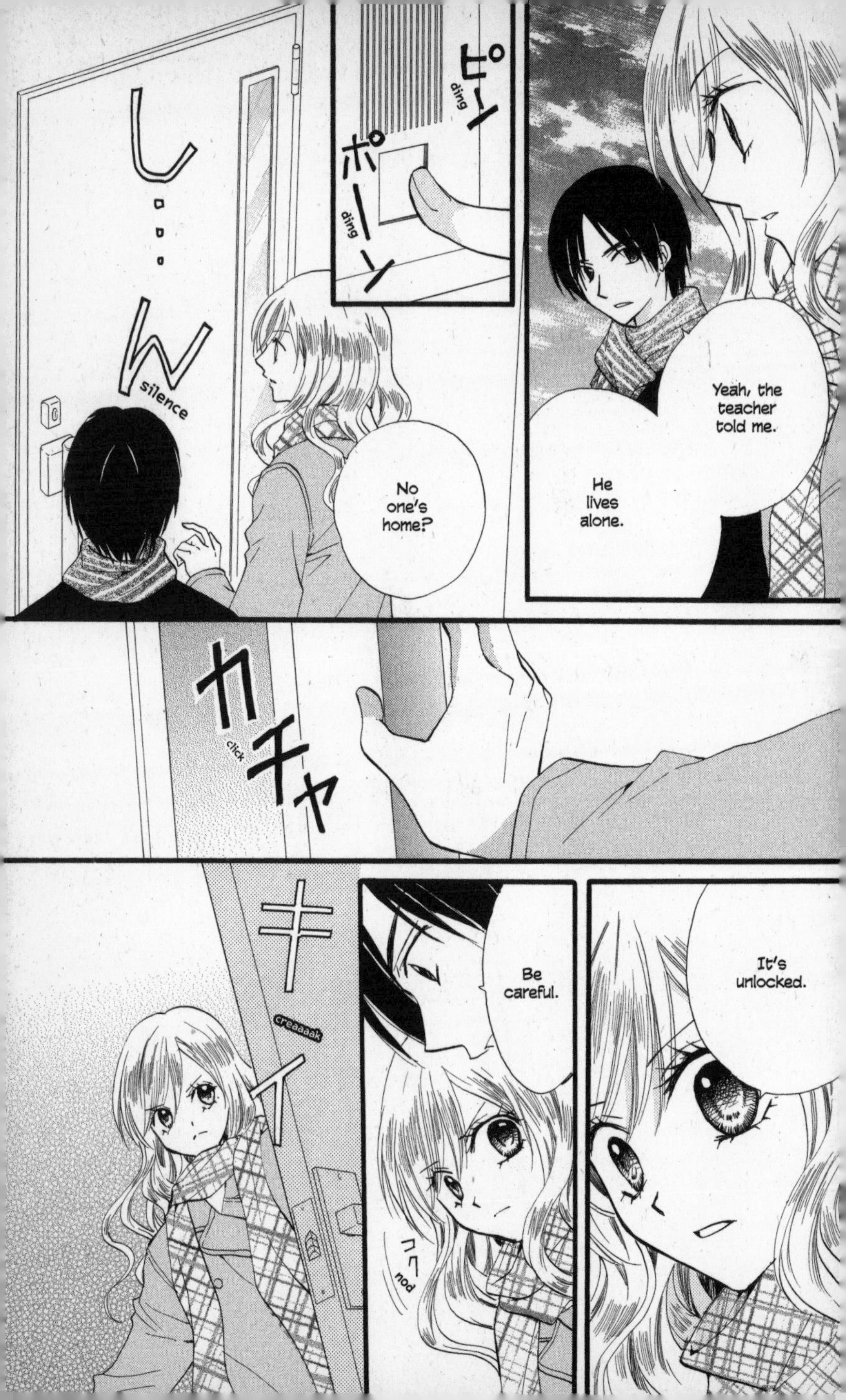
Yeah, the teacher told me.
He lives alone.
ピーン
ding
ポーン
ding
し…ん
silence
No one's home?
カチャ
click
It's unlocked.
Be careful.
コク
nod
キイ
creaaaak

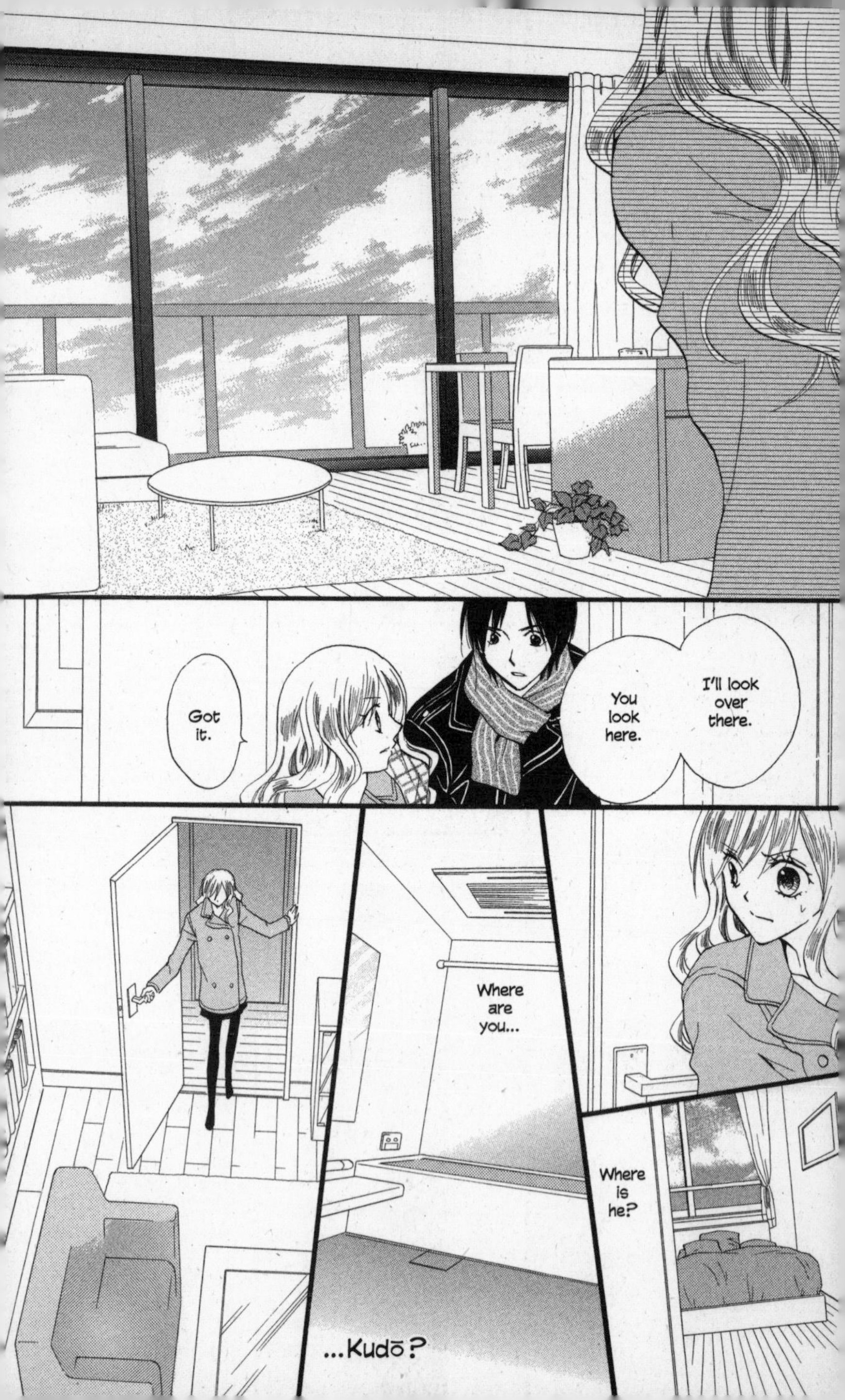
You look here. I'll look over there.
Got it.
Where is he?
Where are you...
...Kudō?

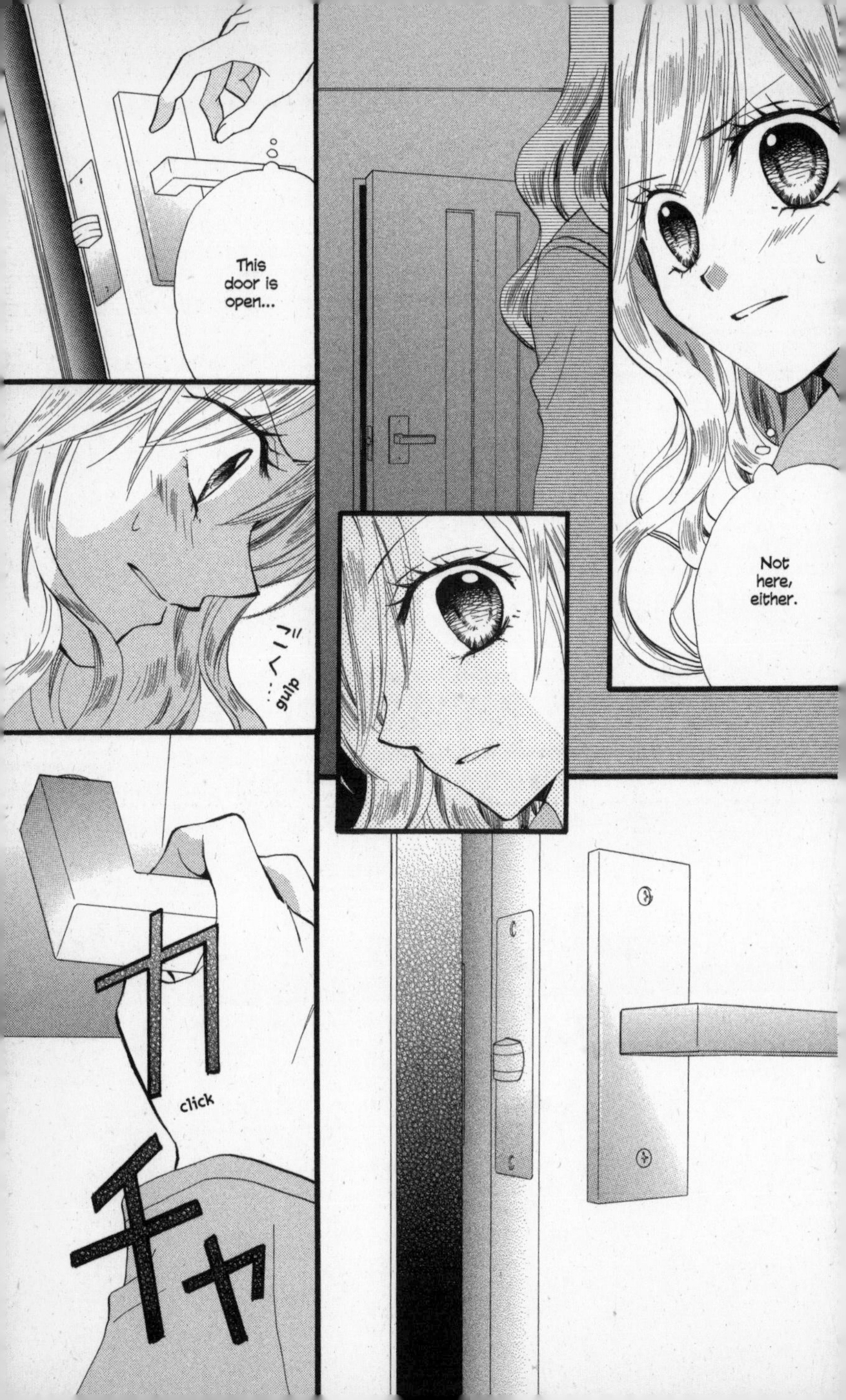
Not here, either.
This door is open...
gulp
カチャ
click

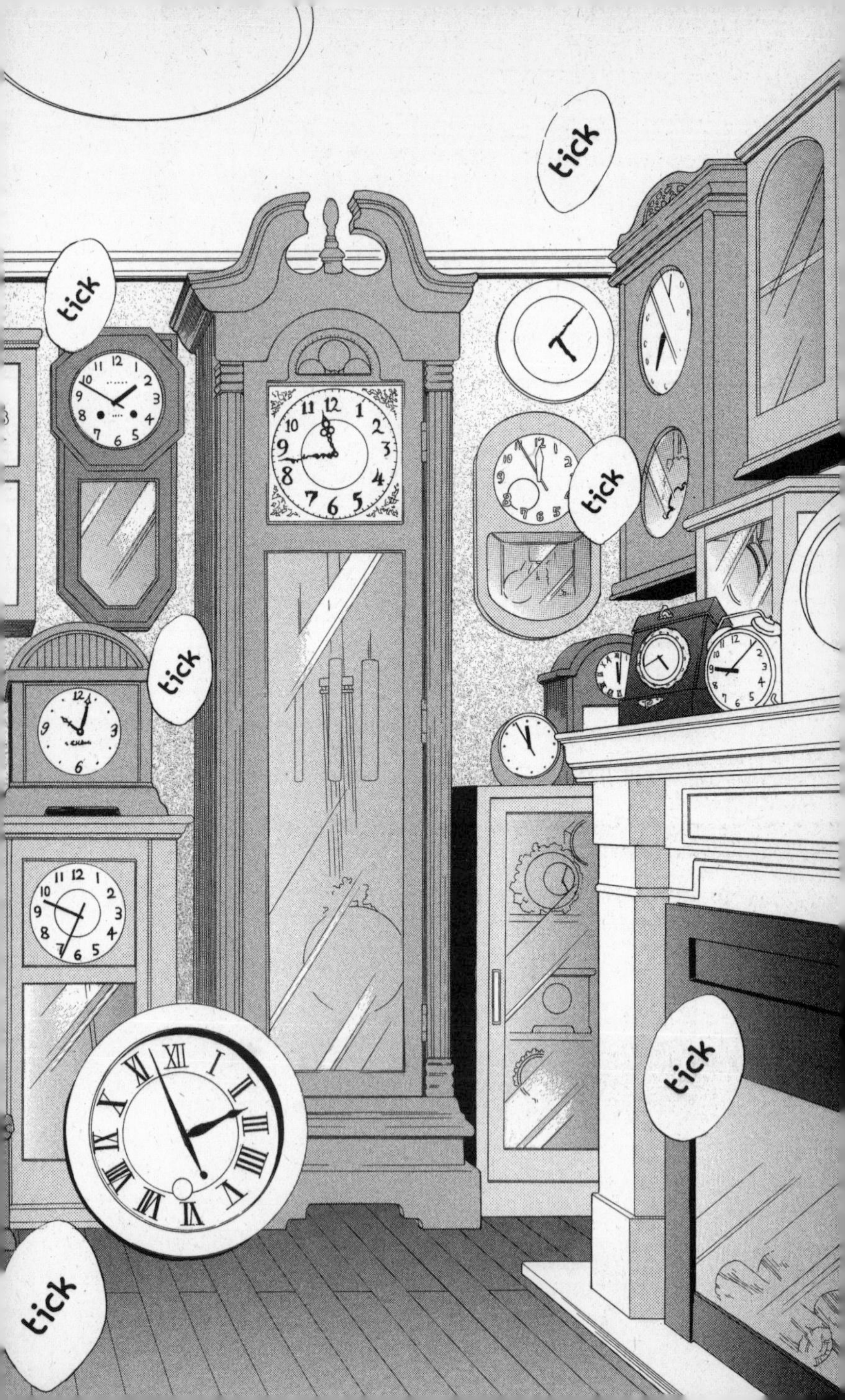
tick
tick
tick
tick
tick
tick

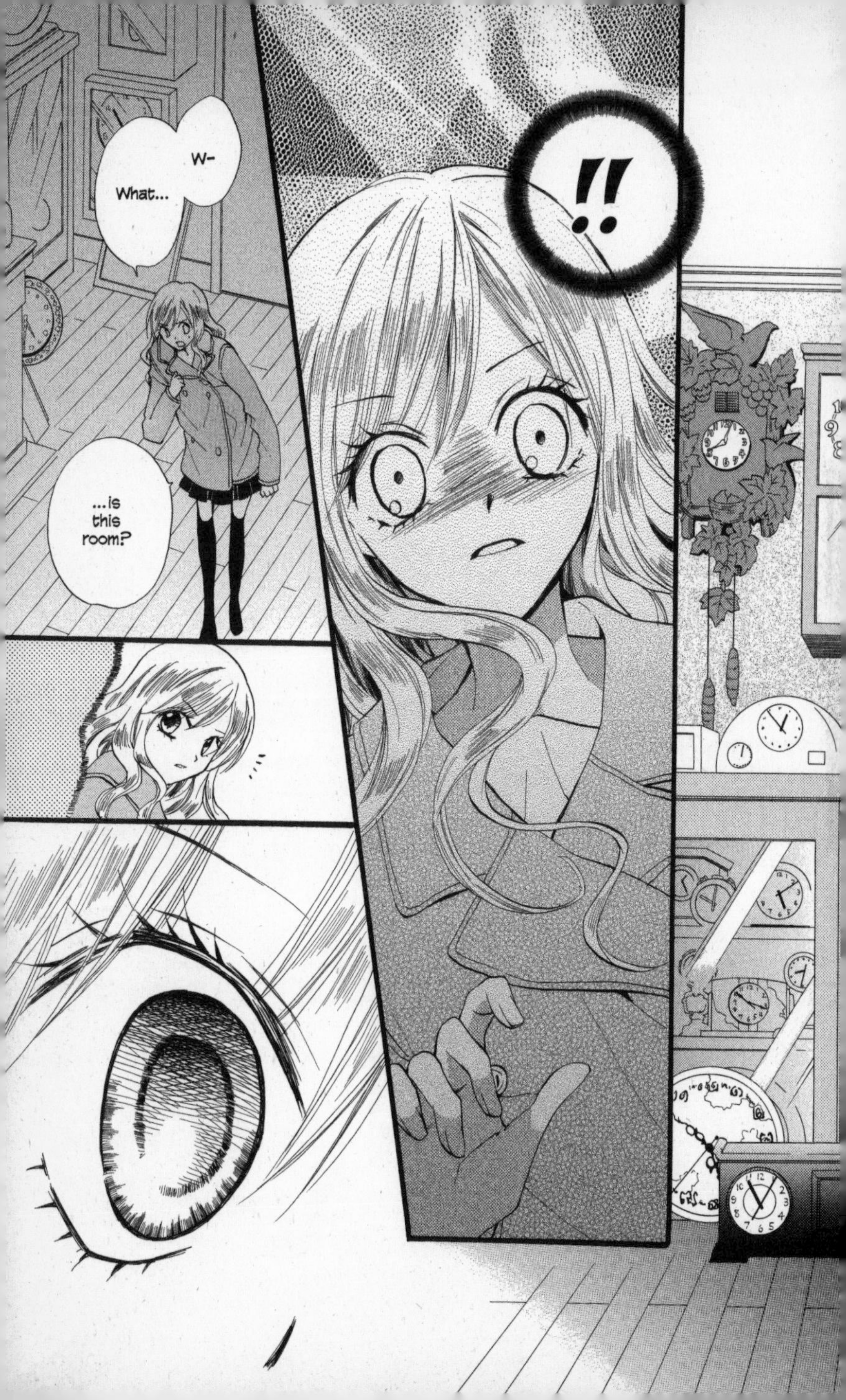
!!
W-
What...
...is this room?
...

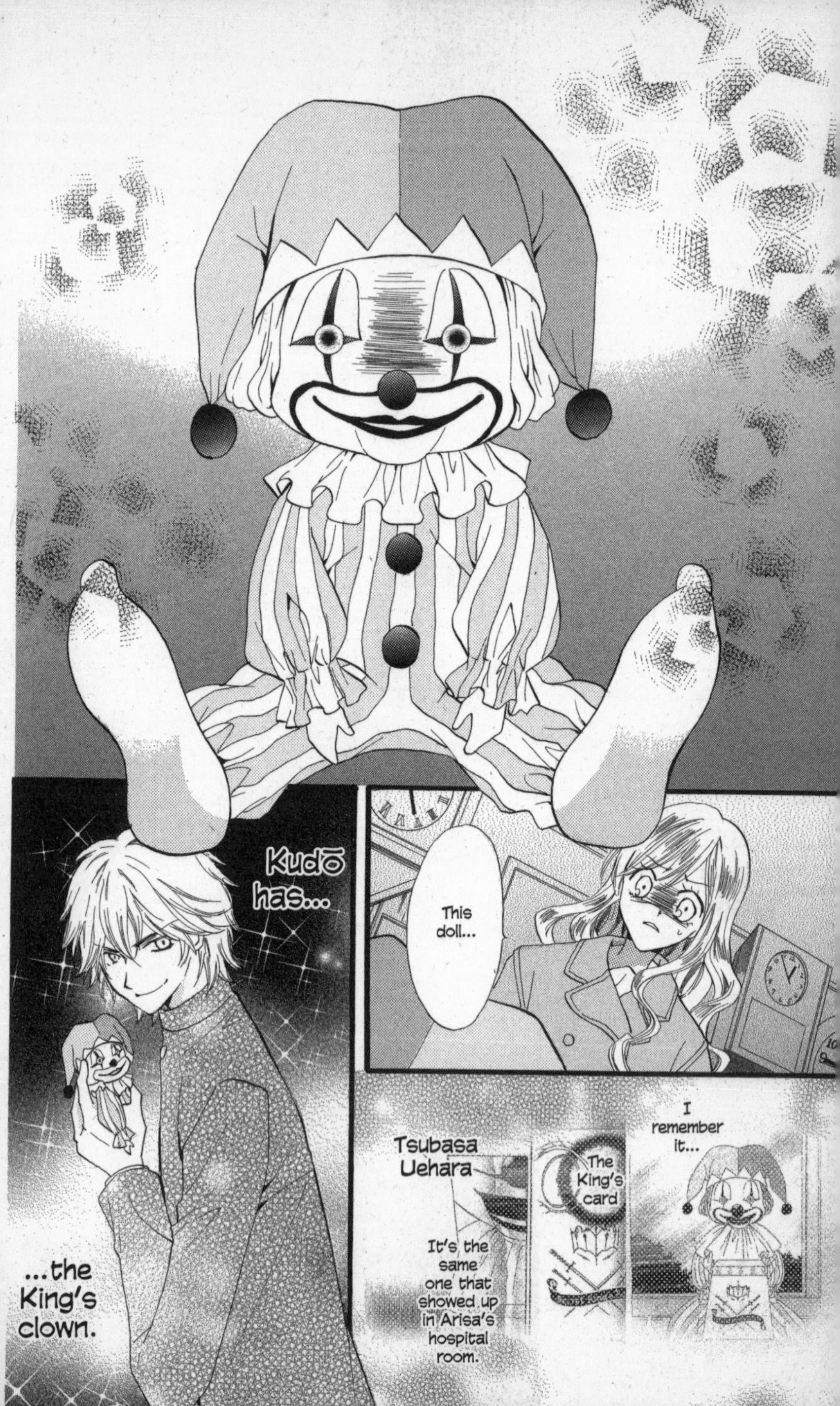
This doll...
I remember it...
The King's card
Tsubasa Uehara
It's the same one that showed up in Arisa's hospital room.
Kudō has...
...the King's clown.

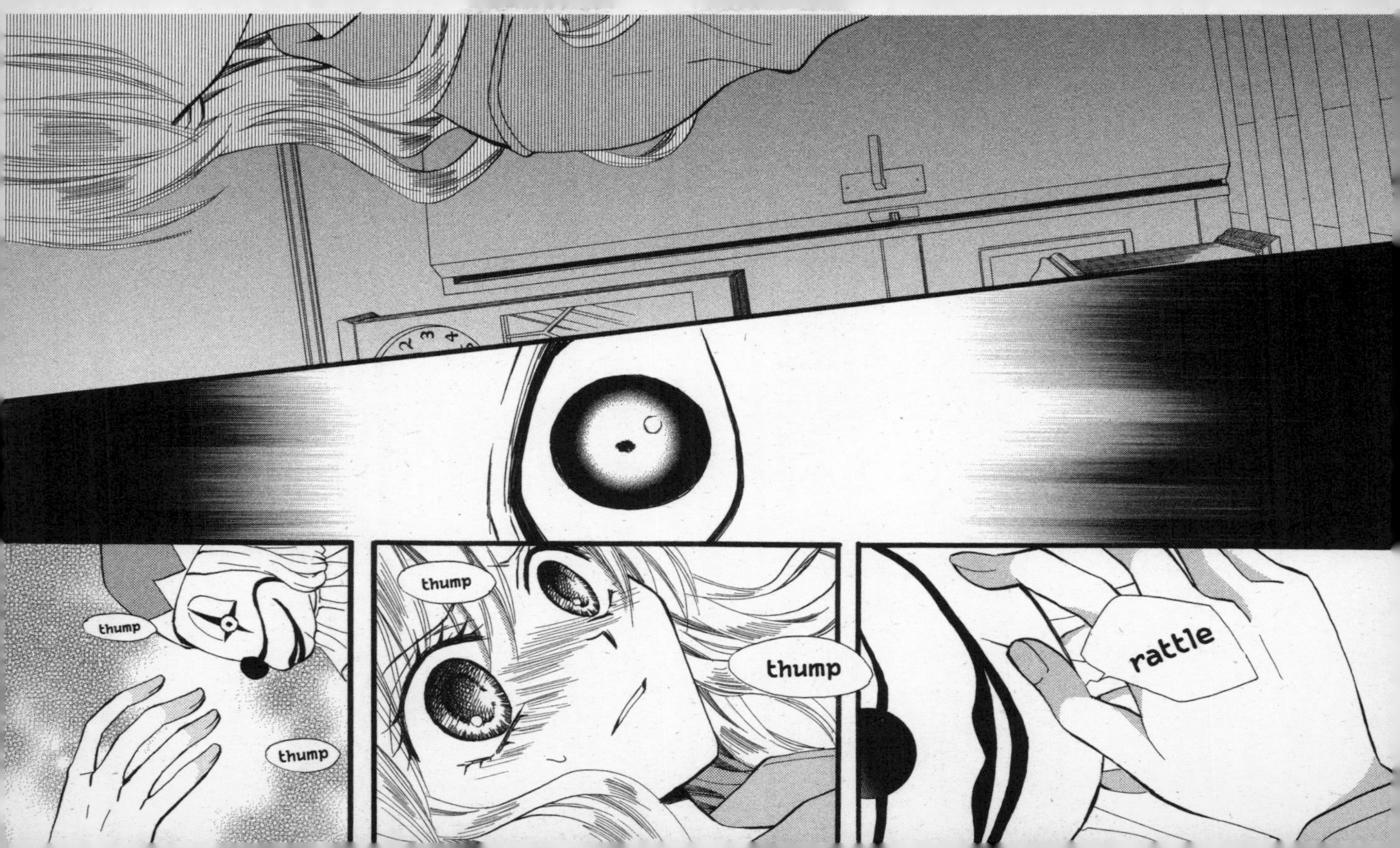
rattle
thump
thump
thump
thump

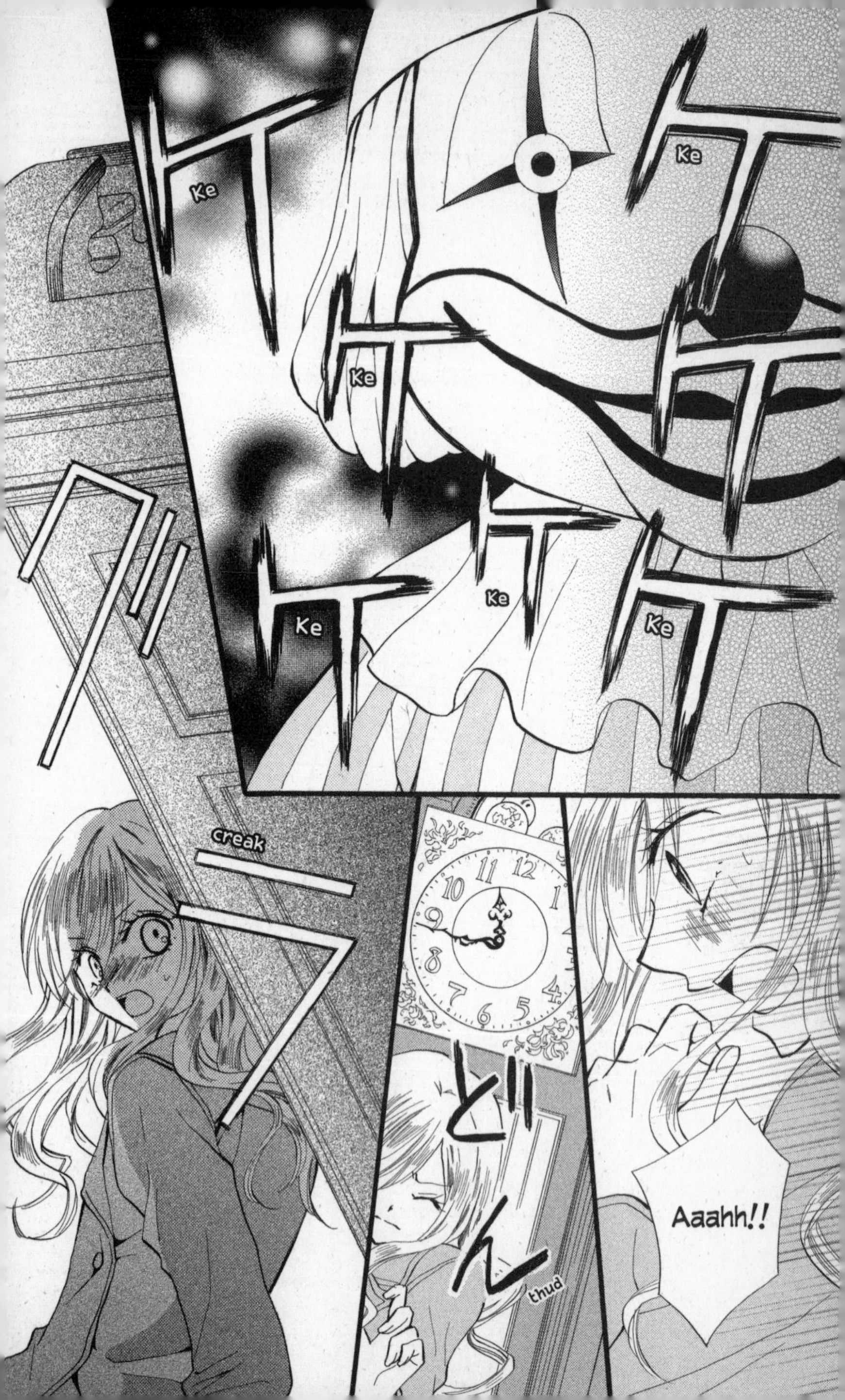
Ke
Ke
Ke
Ke
Ke
Ke
Aaahh!!
thud
creak

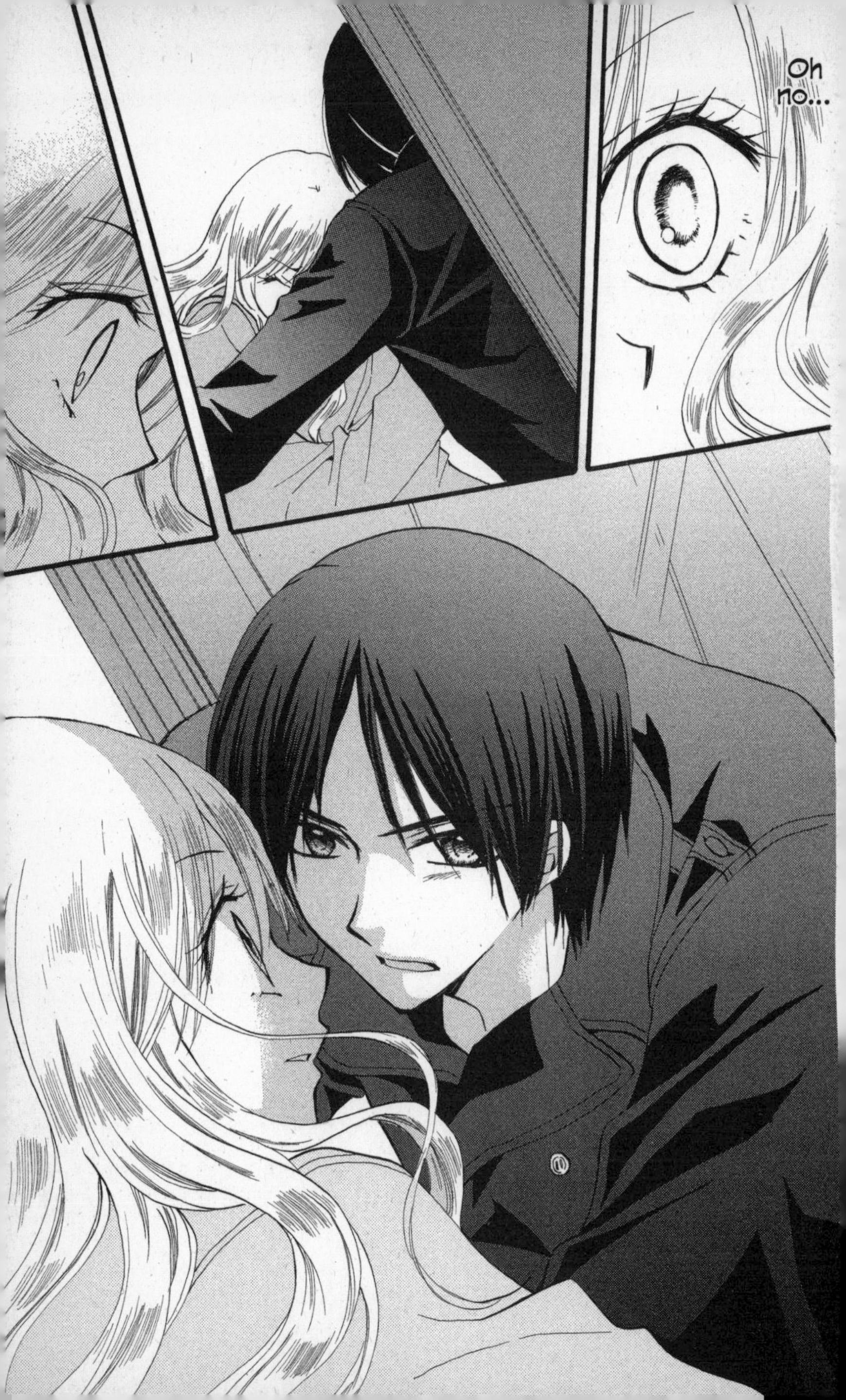
Oh no...

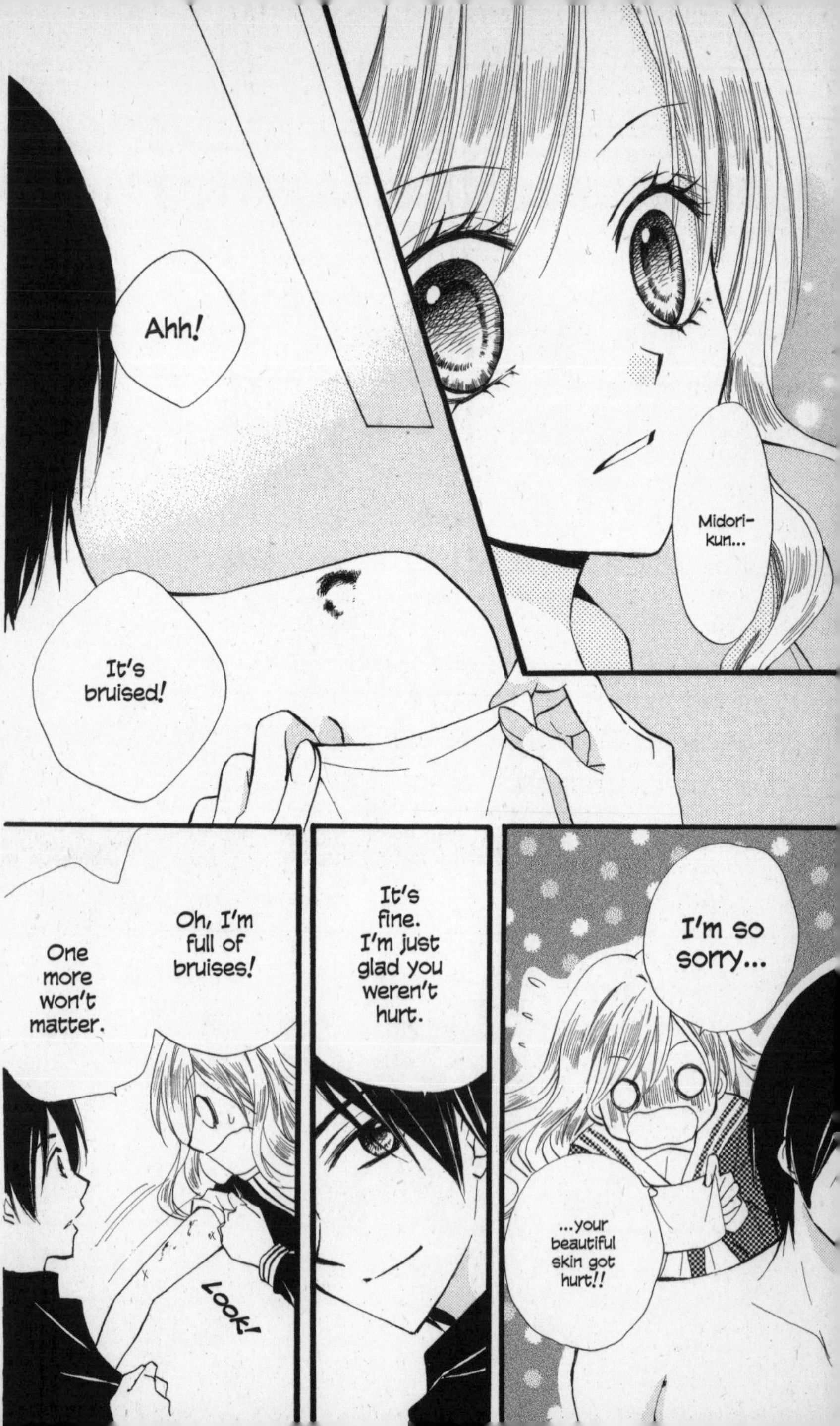
Midori-kun...
Ahh!
It's bruised!
I'm so sorry...
...your beautiful skin got hurt!!
It's fine. I'm just glad you weren't hurt.
Oh, I'm full of bruises!
One more won't matter.
Look!

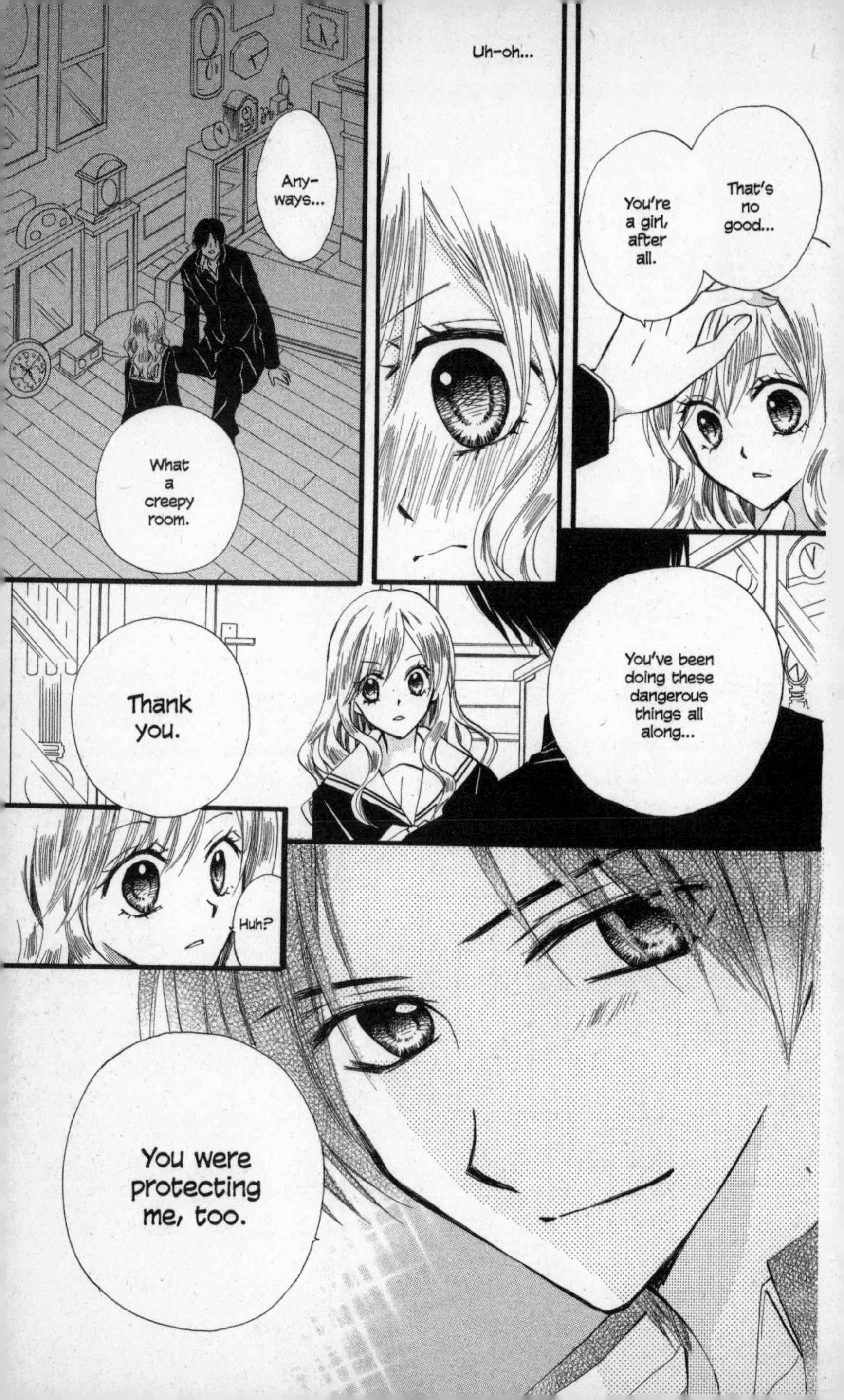
That's no good...
You're a girl, after all.
Uh-oh...
Any-ways...
What a creepy room.
You've been doing these dangerous things all along...
Thank you.
Huh?
You were protecting me, too.

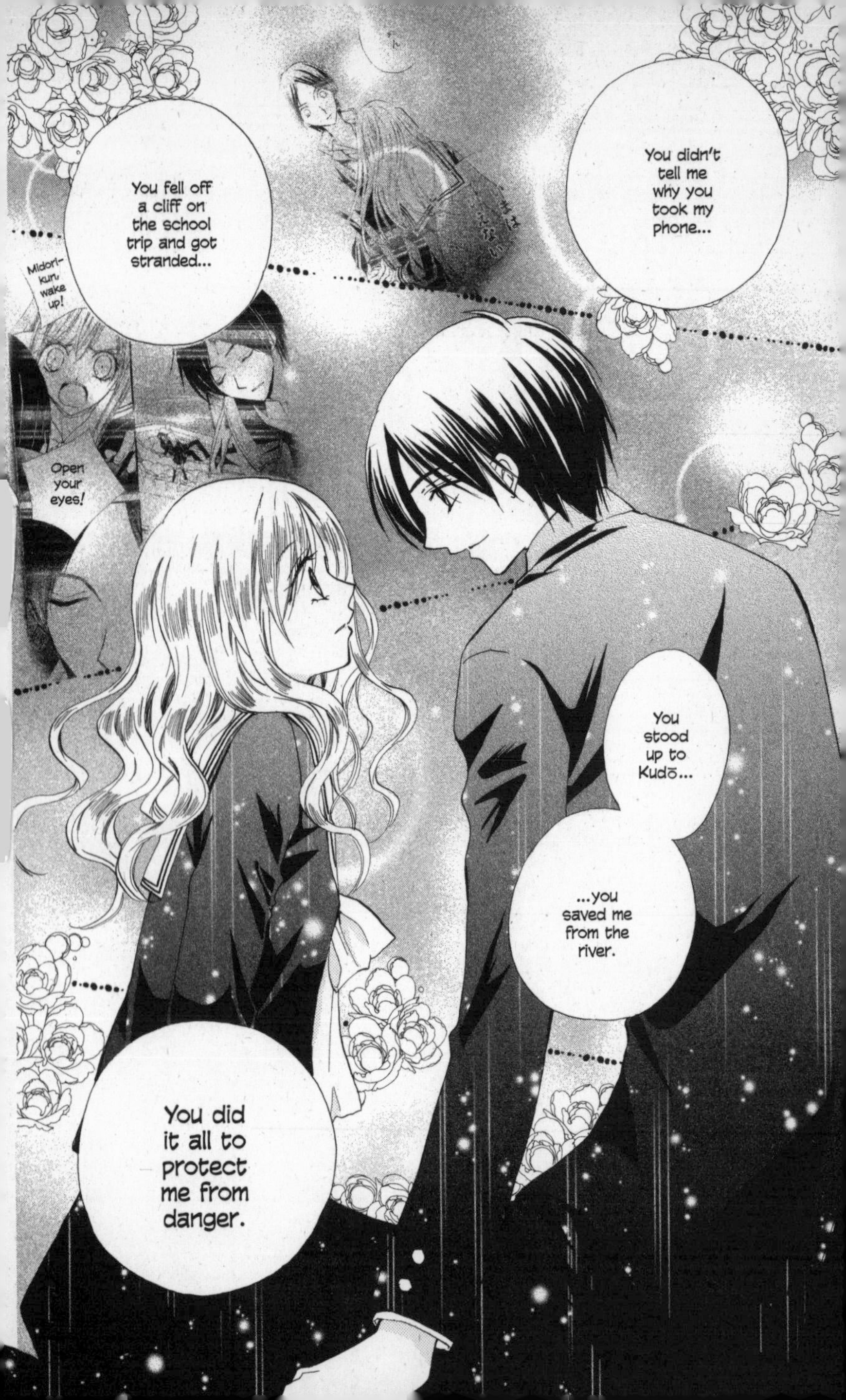
You didn't tell me why you took my phone...
You fell off a cliff on the school trip and got stranded...
Midori-kun, wake up!
Open your eyes!
You stood up to Kudō...
...you saved me from the river.
You did it all to protect me from danger.

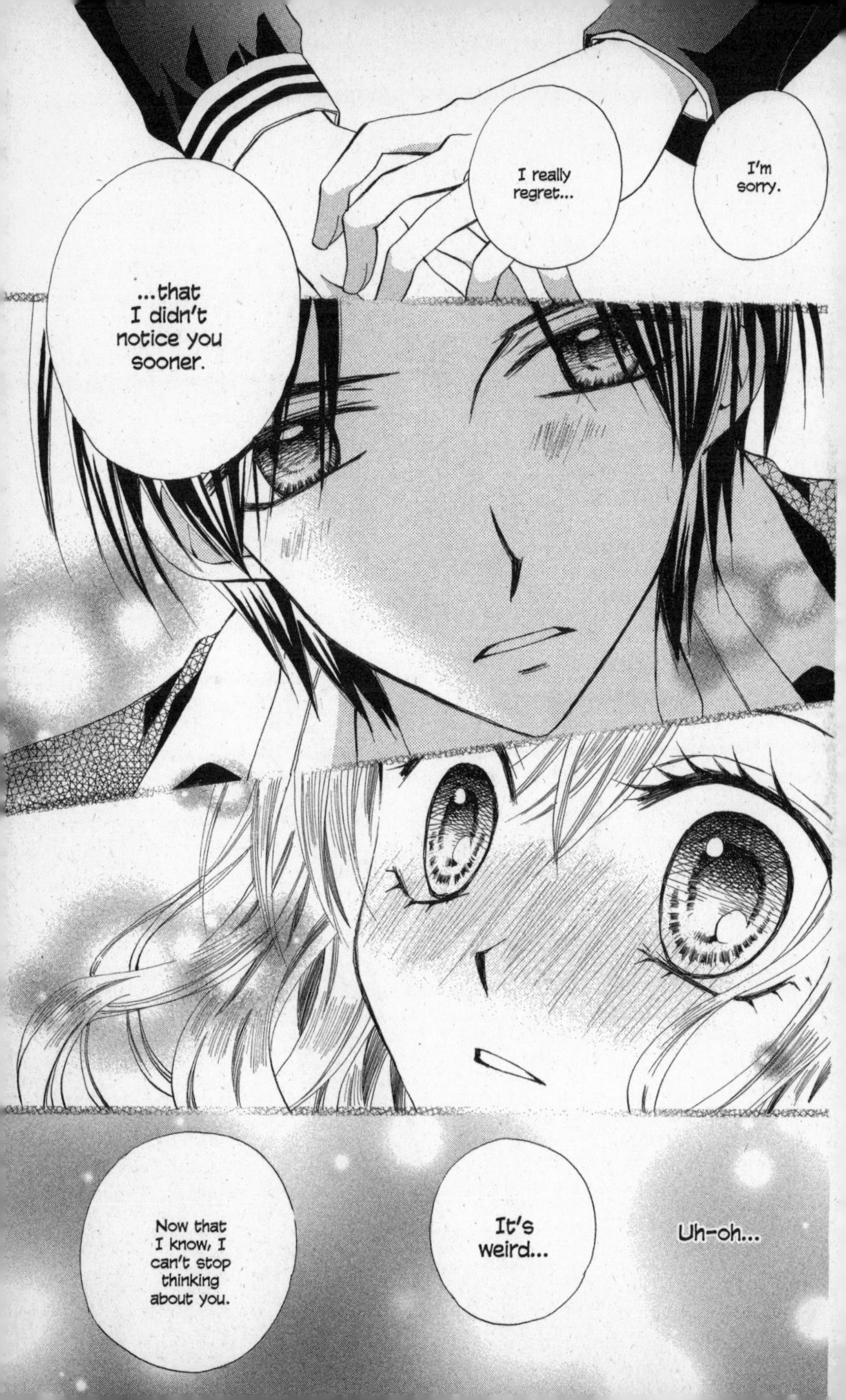
I'm sorry.
I really regret...
...that I didn't notice you sooner.
Uh-oh...
It's weird...
Now that I know, I can't stop thinking about you.

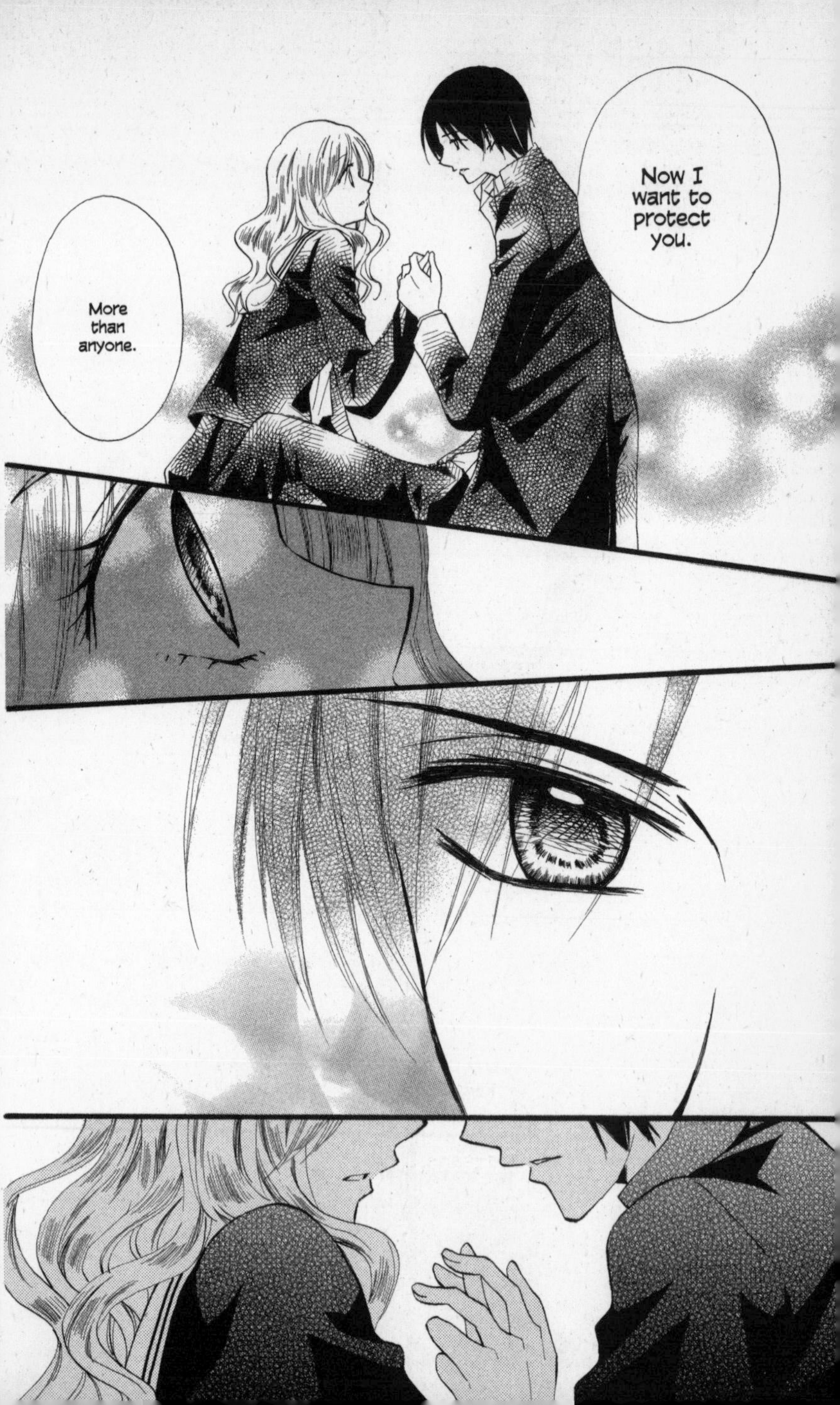
Now I want to protect you.
More than anyone.

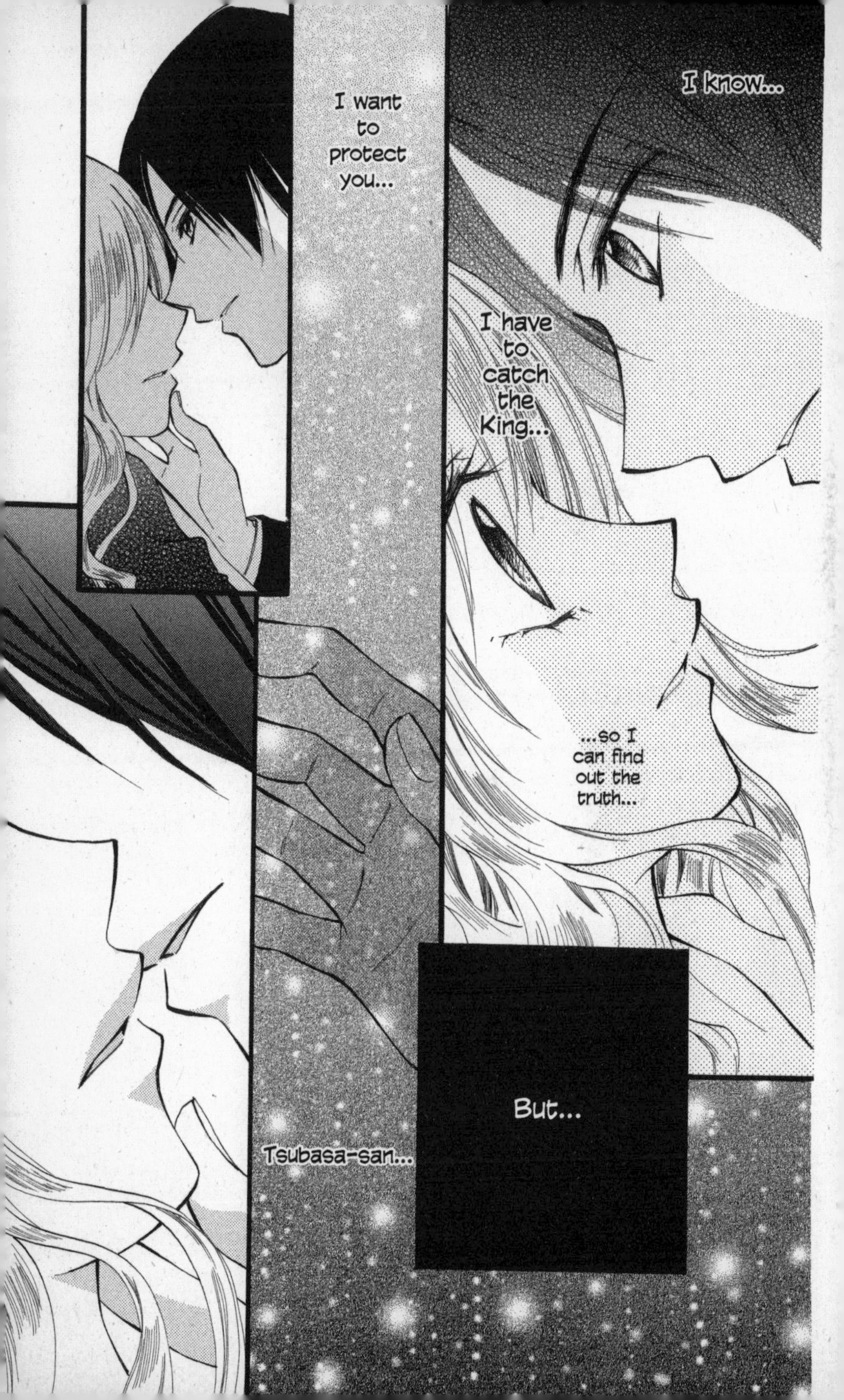
I know...
I have to catch the King...
...so I can find out the truth...
I want to protect you...
But...
Tsubasa-san...

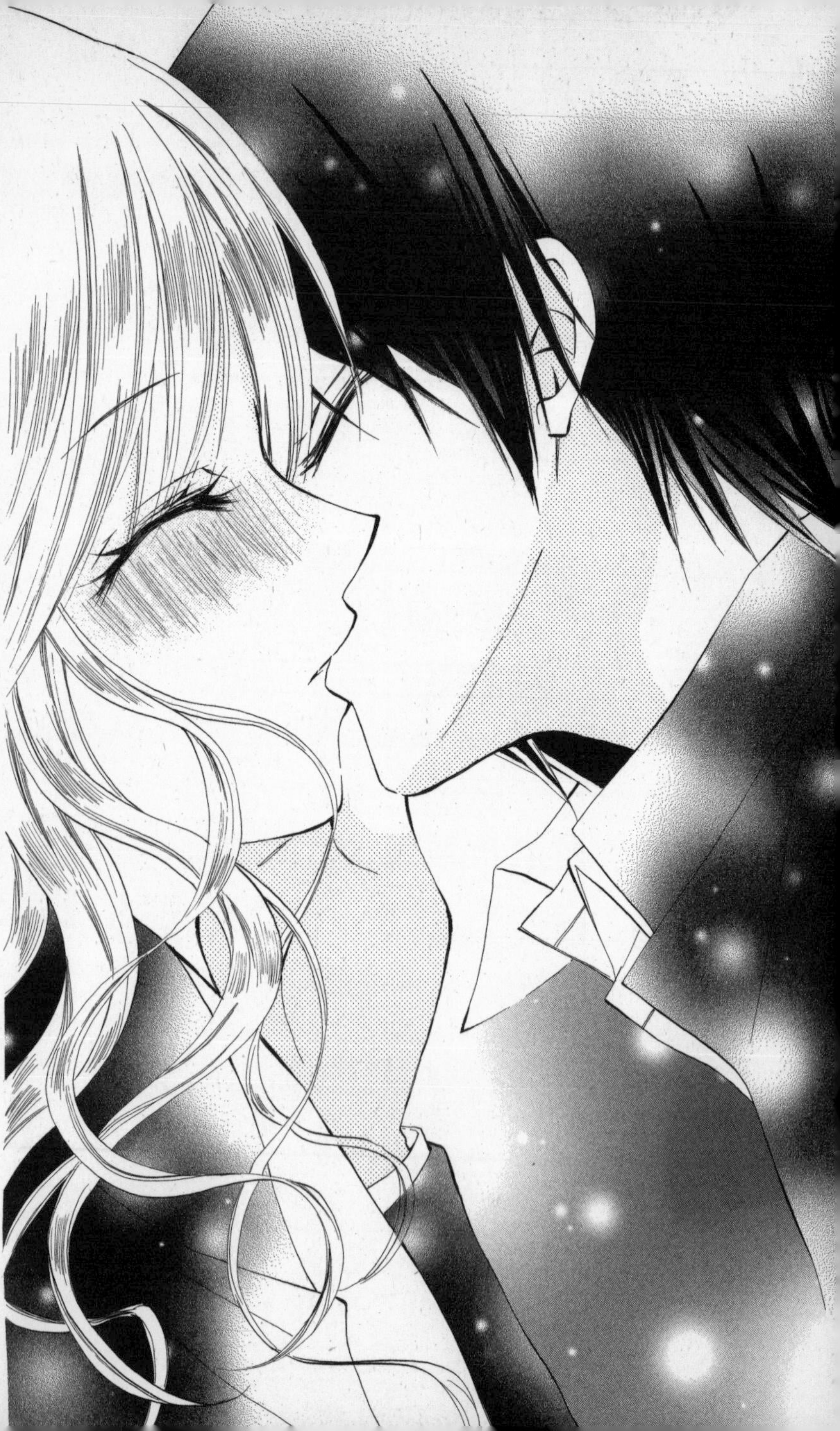

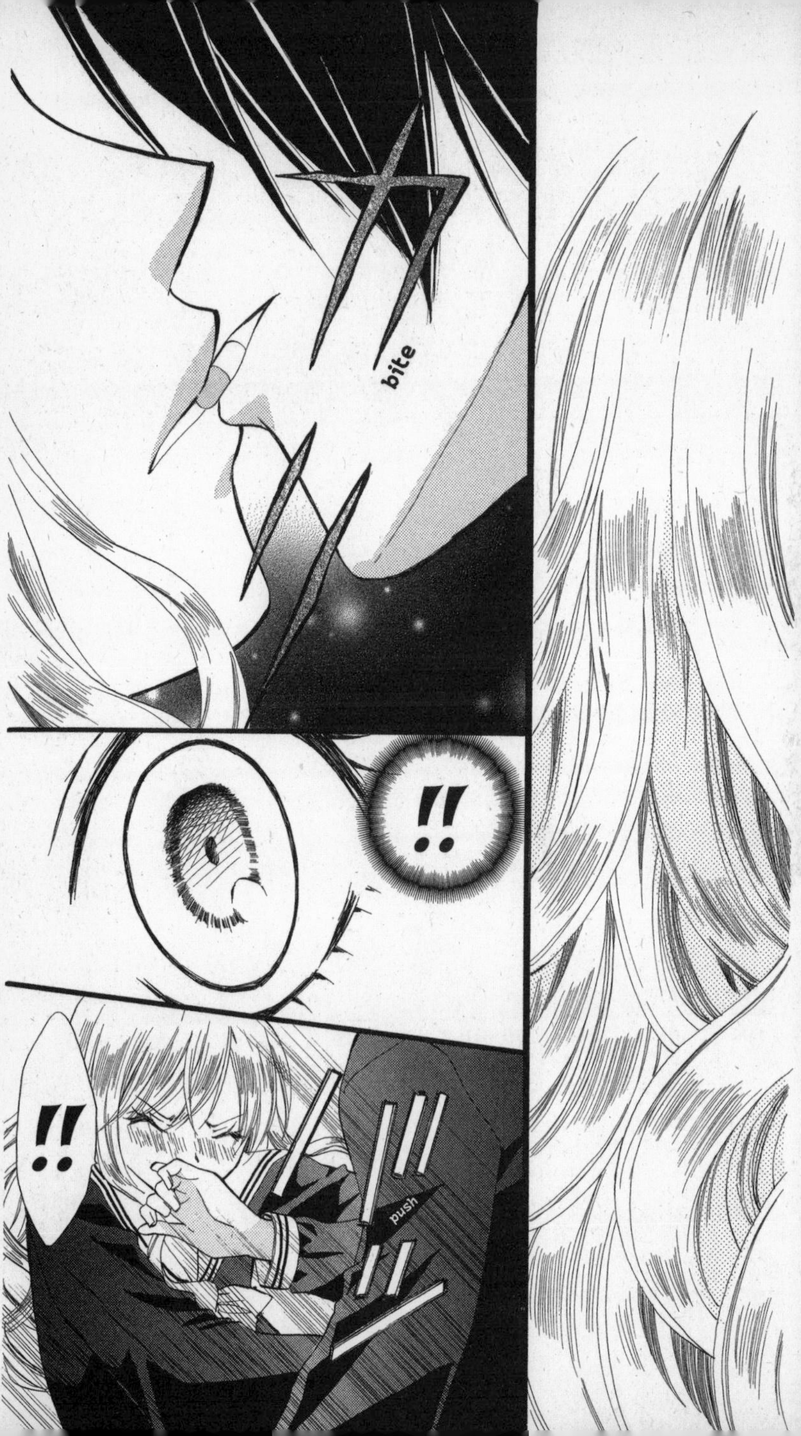
bite
!!
push
!!

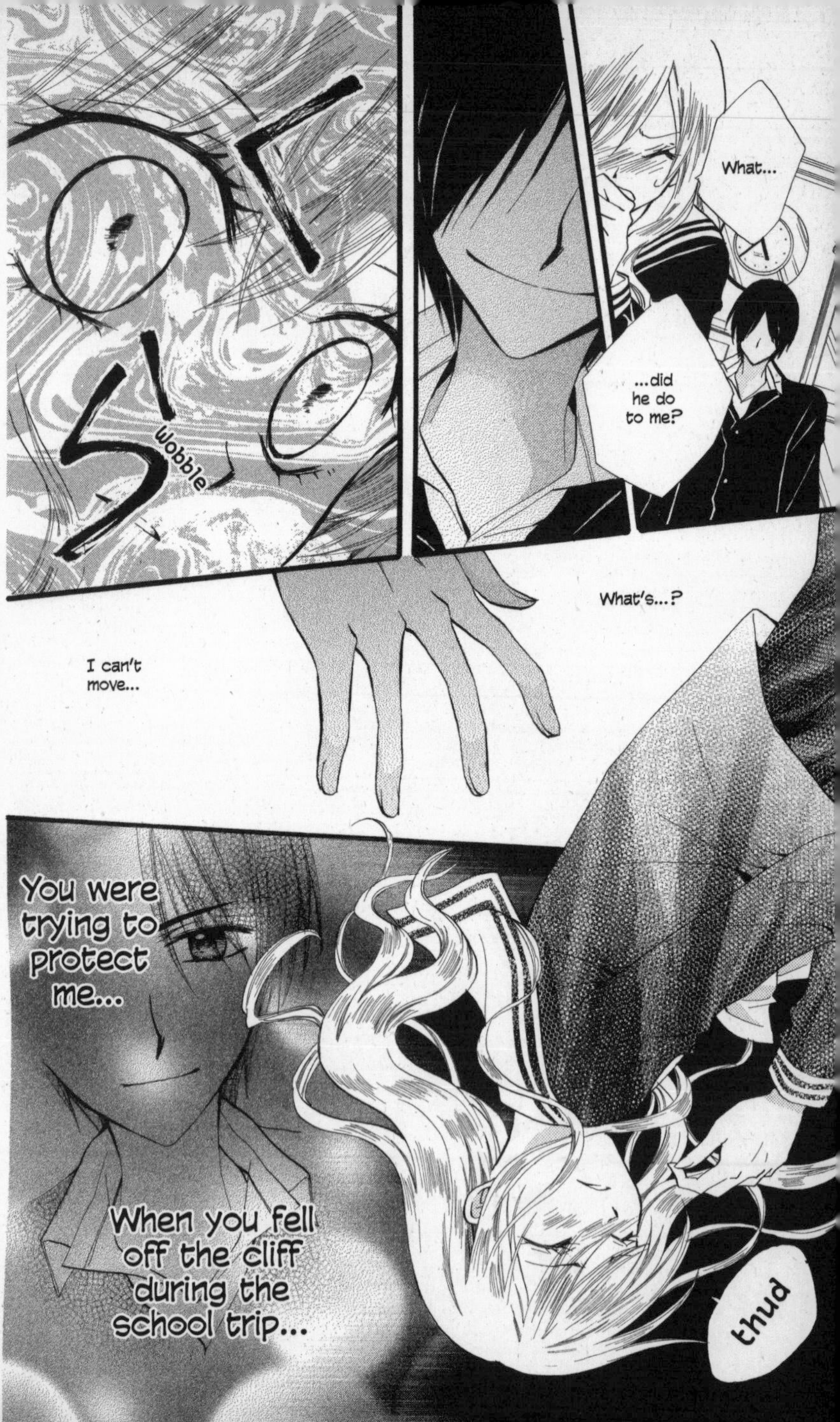
What...
...did he do to me?
Wobble
What's...?
I can't move...
You were trying to protect me...
When you fell off the cliff during the school trip...
thud

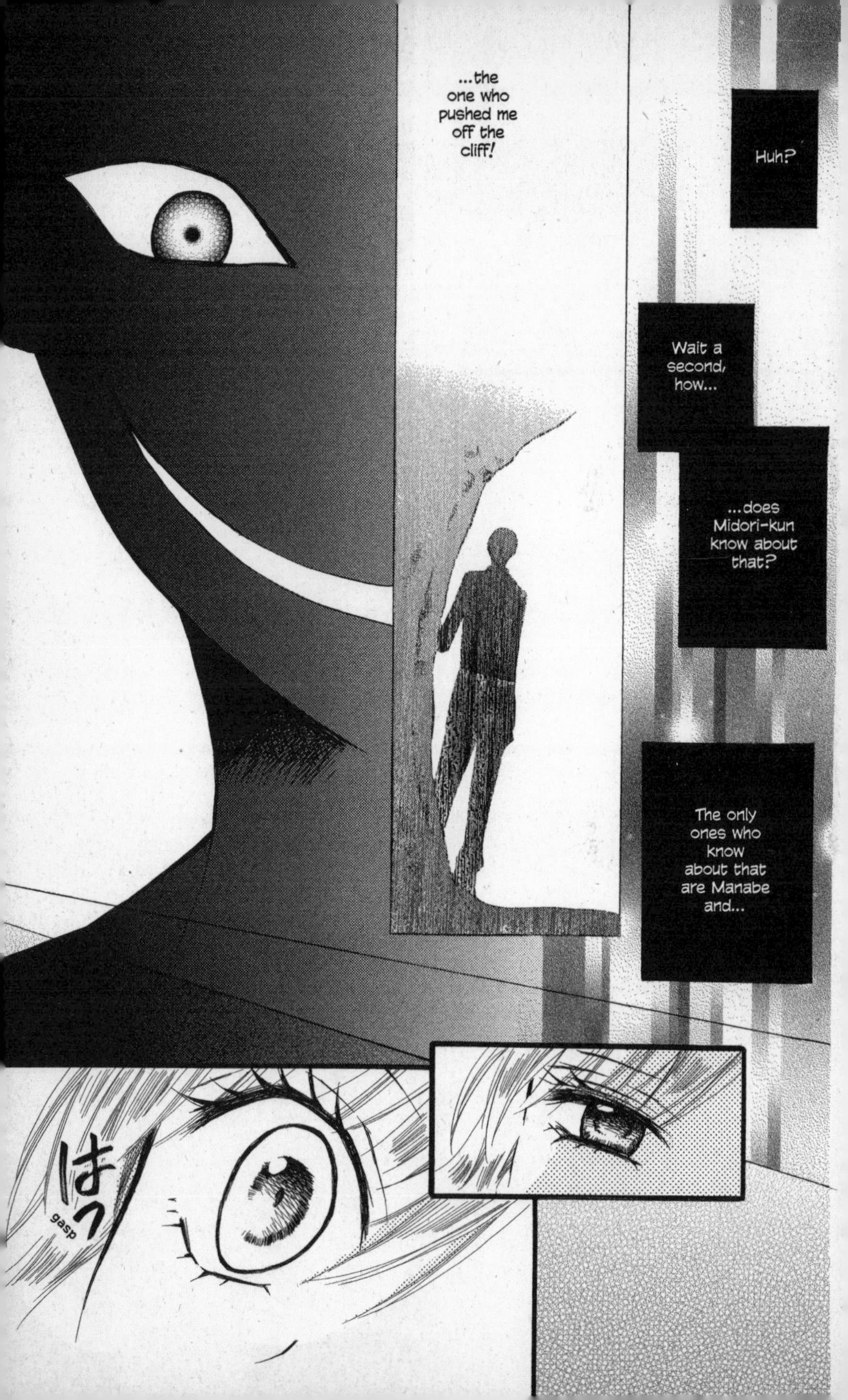
Huh?
Wait a second, how...
...does Midori-kun know about that?
The only ones who know about that are Manabe and...
...the one who pushed me off the cliff!
はっ
gasp

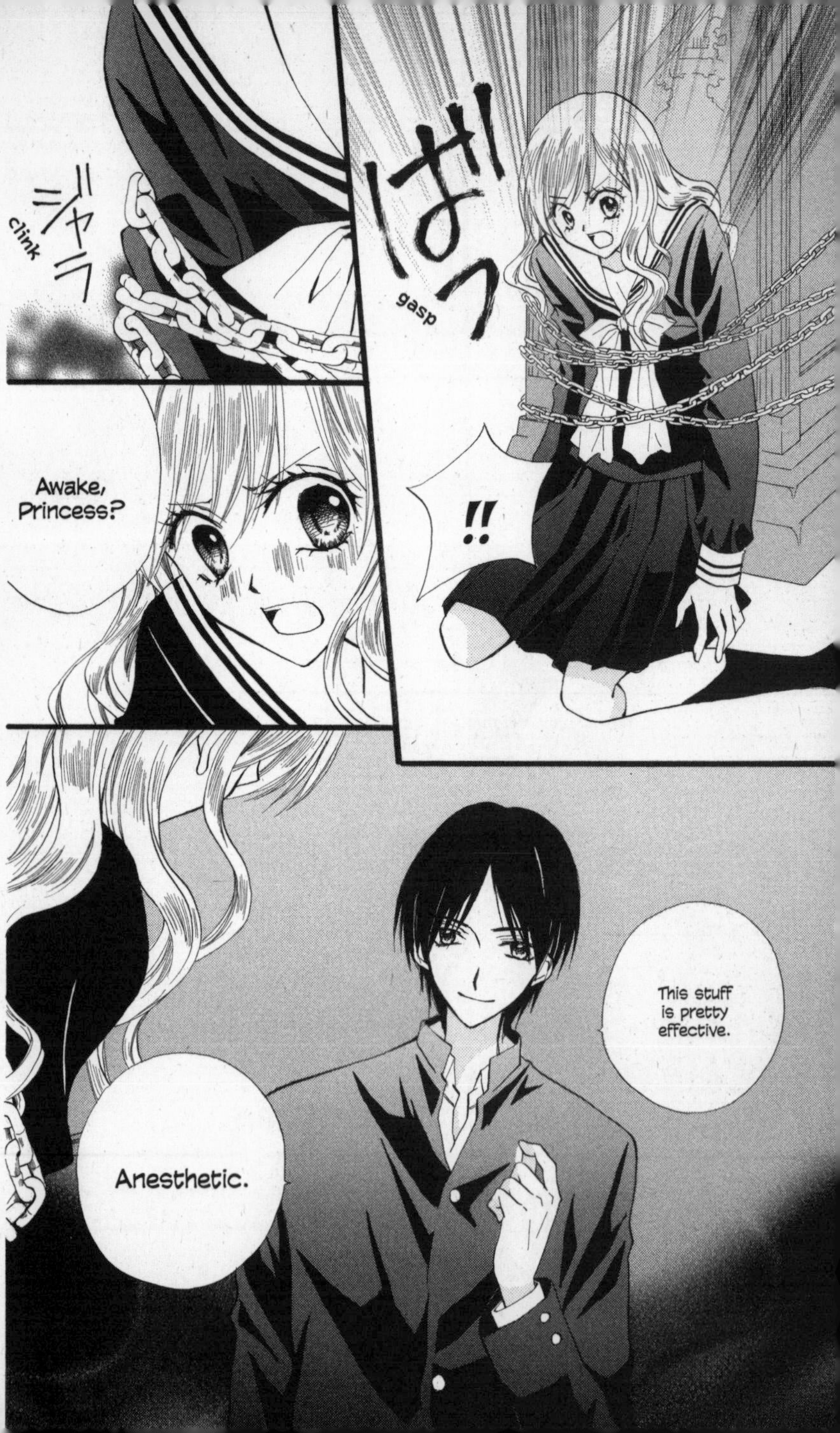
ばっ
gasp
!!
ジャラ
clink
Awake, Princess?
This stuff is pretty effective.
Anesthetic.

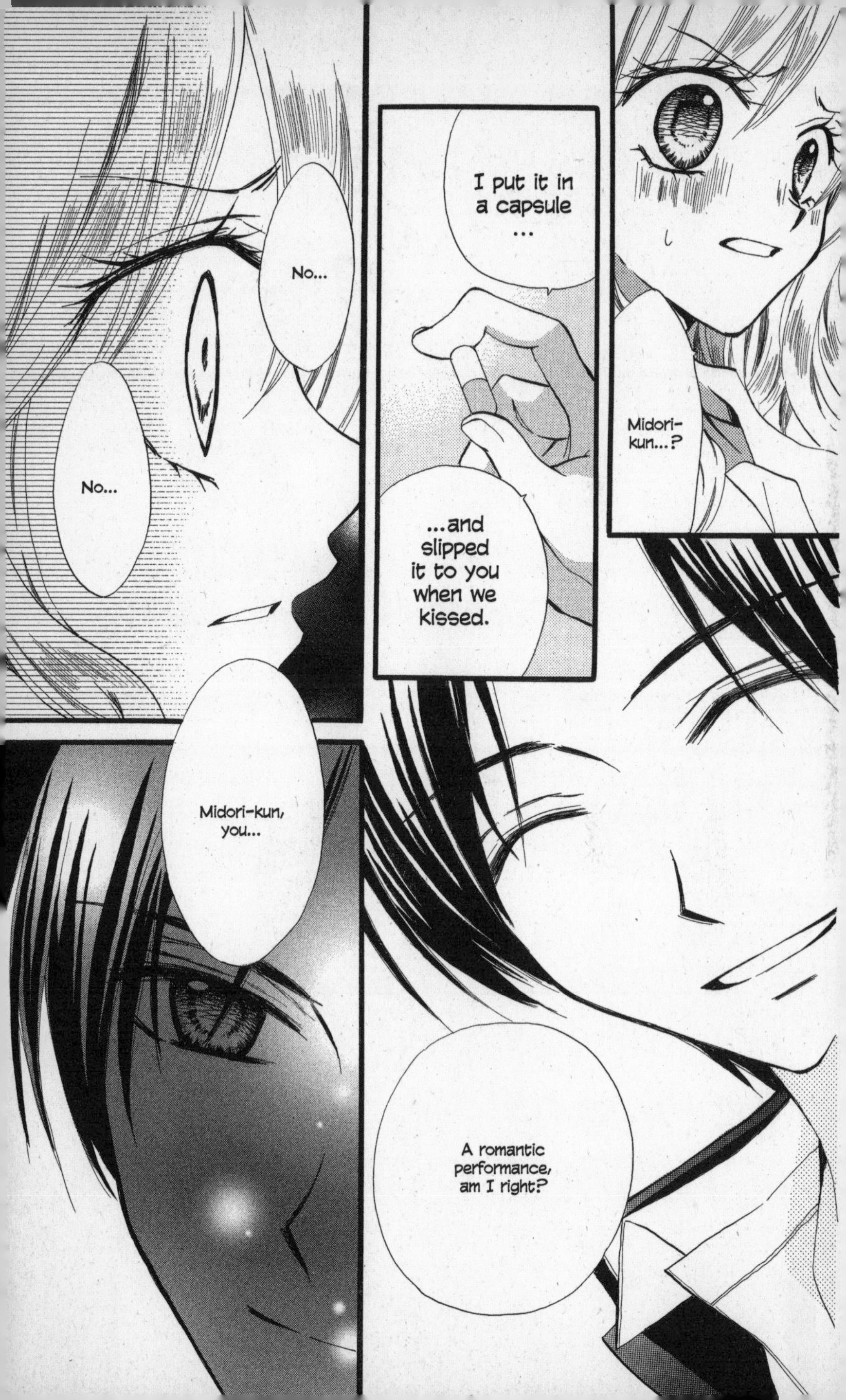
Midori-kun...?
I put it in a capsule ...
...and slipped it to you when we kissed.
No...
No...
Midori-kun, you...
A romantic performance, am I right?

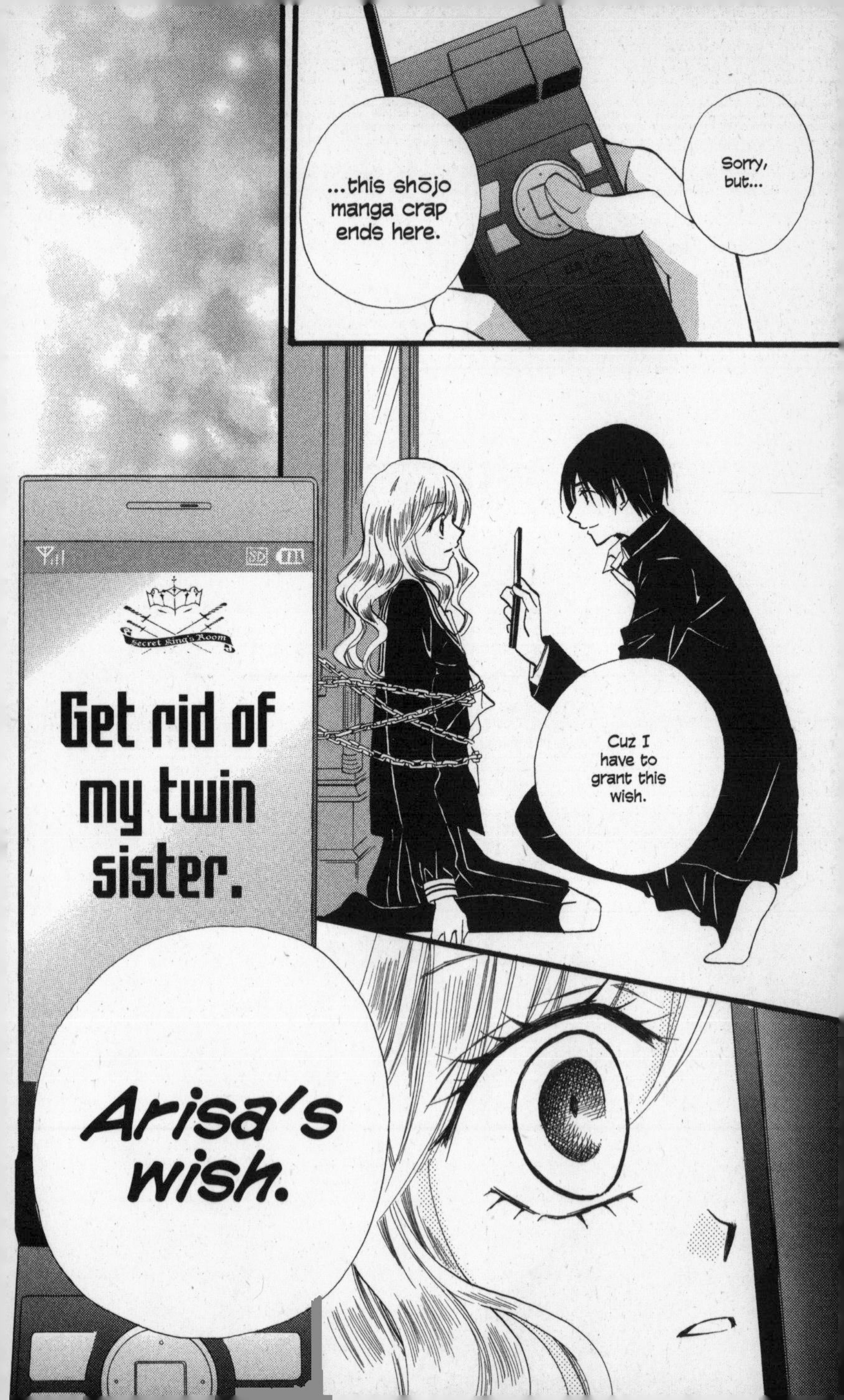
Sorry, but...
...this shōjo manga crap ends here.
Cuz I have to grant this wish.
Secret King's Room
Get rid of my twin sister.
Arisa's wish.

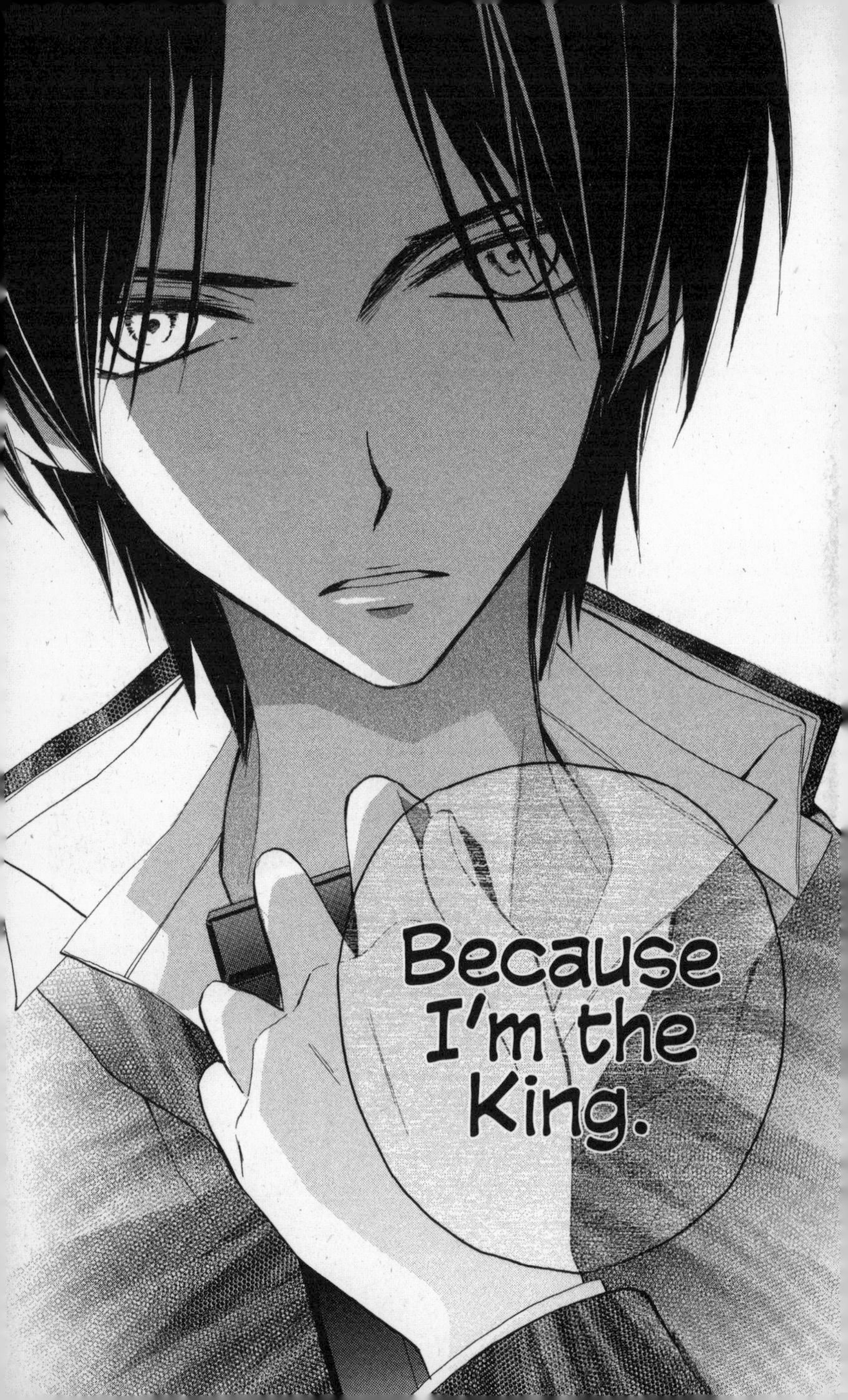
Because I'm the King.

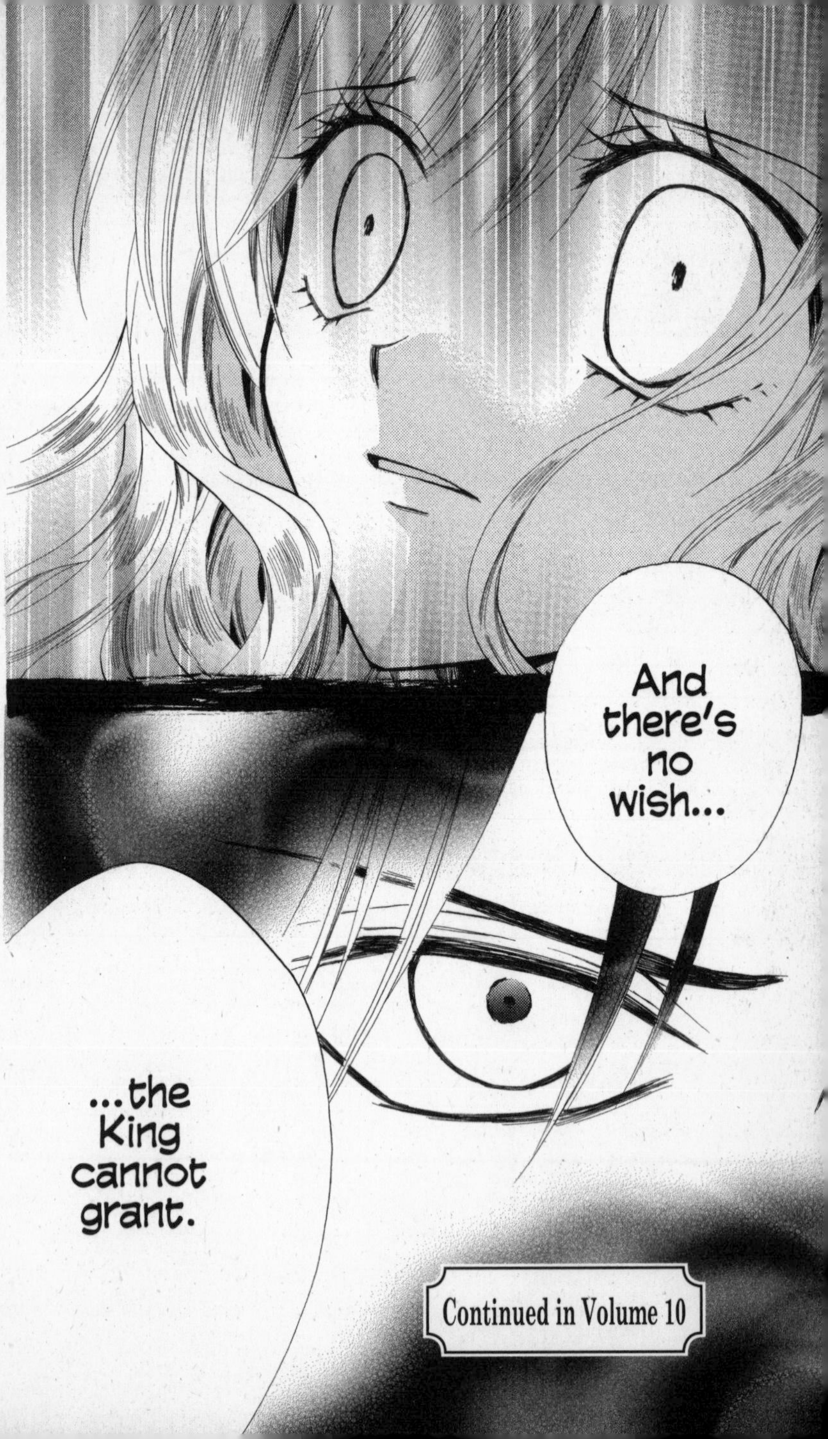
And there's no wish...
...the King cannot grant.
Continued in Volume 10

Special Thanks:
T. Nakamura   H. Kishimoto
M. Nakata   M. Shirasawa

My assistants and editors at Nakayoshi
Takeda-sama
Red rooster
Takashi Shimoyama
GINNANSHA

And all my readers
who support me.

Please send mail to:
Natsumi Andō
c/o Kodansha Comics
1745 Broadway
New York, NY 10019

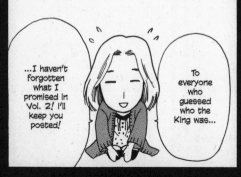

To everyone who guessed who the King was...
...I haven't forgotten what I promised in Vol. 2! I'll keep you posted!

What's Up with Andō

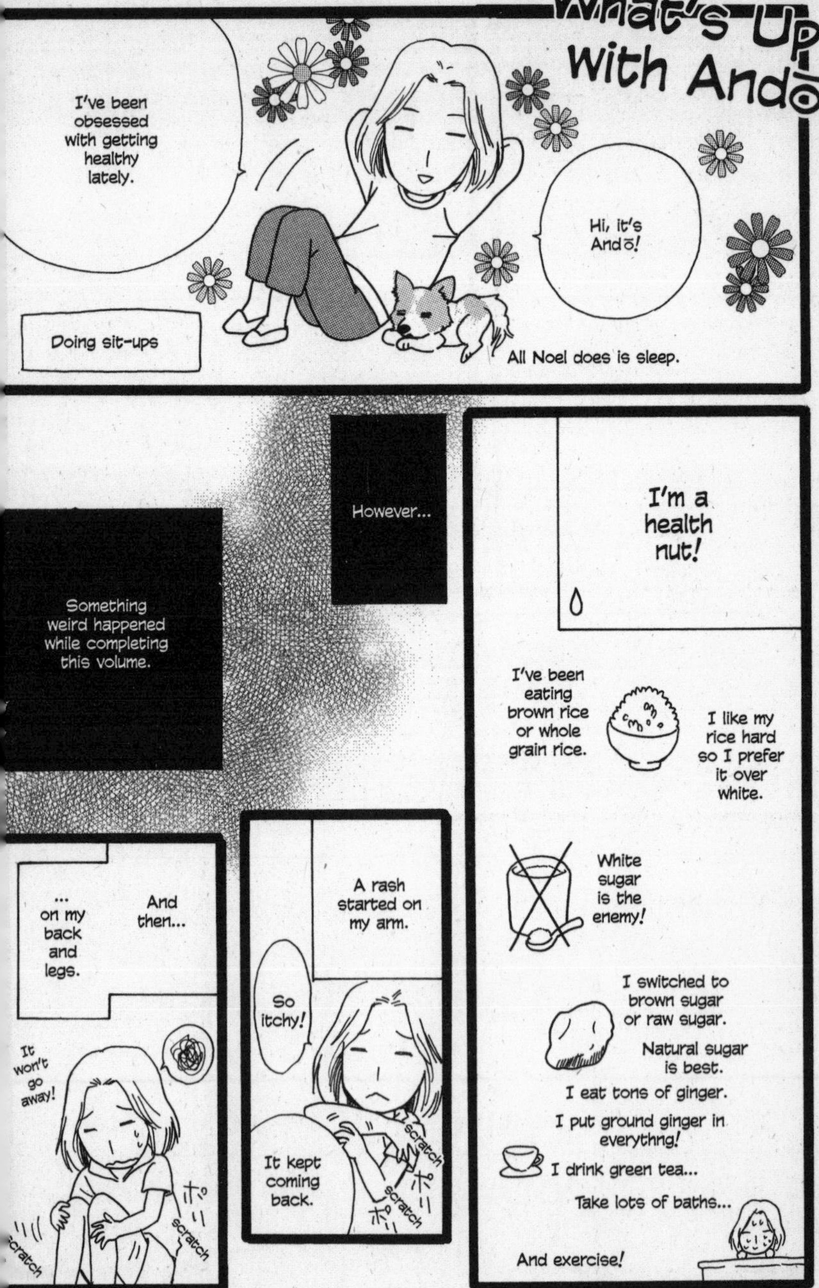
Hi, it's Andō!
I've been obsessed with getting healthy lately.
All Noel does is sleep.
Doing sit-ups
I'm a health nut!
I've been eating brown rice or whole grain rice.
I like my rice hard so I prefer it over white.
White sugar is the enemy!
I switched to brown sugar or raw sugar.
Natural sugar is best.
I eat tons of ginger.
I put ground ginger in everythng!
I drink green tea...
Take lots of baths...
And exercise!
However...
Something weird happened while completing this volume.
A rash started on my arm.
So itchy!
It kept coming back.
scratch
scratch
And then...
... on my back and legs.
It won't go away!
scratch
scratch

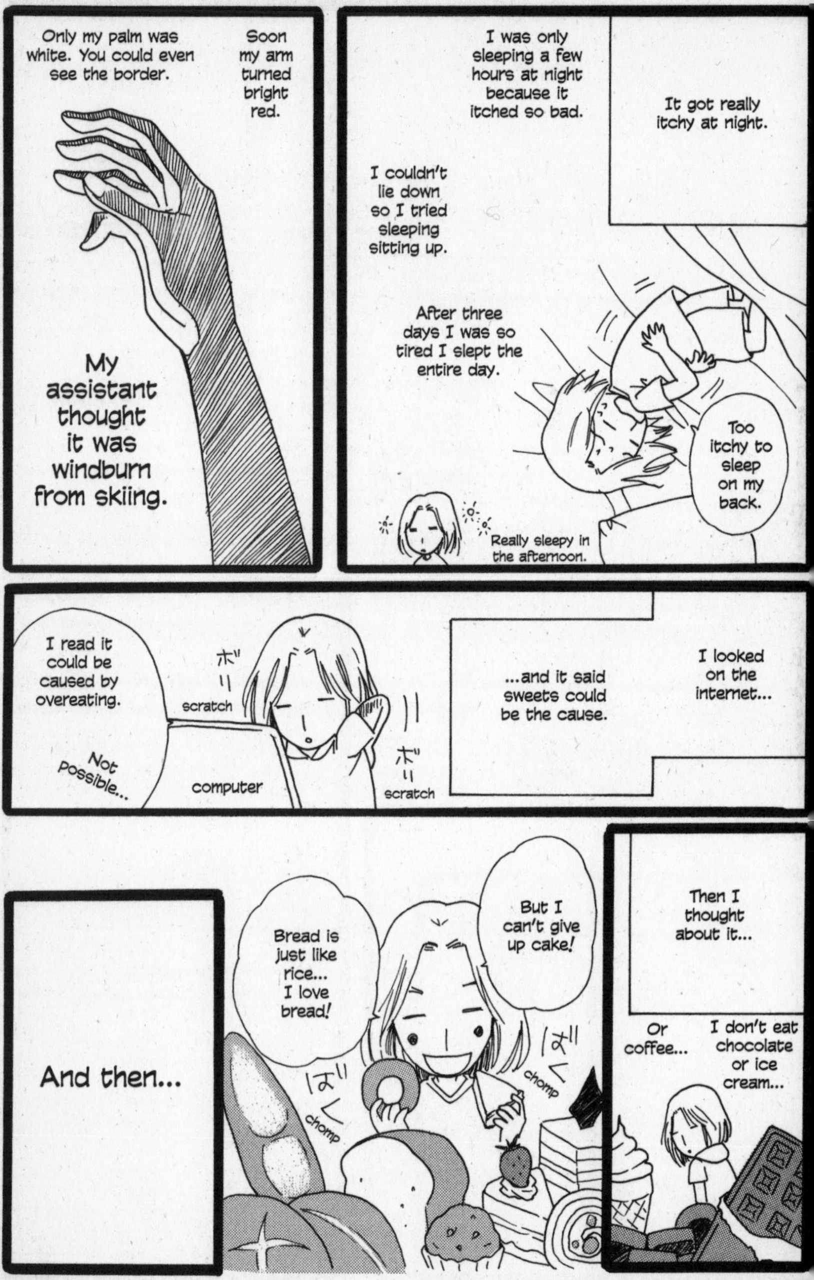
It got really itchy at night.
I was only sleeping a few hours at night because it itched so bad.
I couldn't lie down so I tried sleeping sitting up.
Too itchy to sleep on my back.
After three days I was so tired I slept the entire day.
Really sleepy in the afternoon.
Soon my arm turned bright red.
Only my palm was white. You could even see the border.
My assistant thought it was windburn from skiing.
I looked on the internet...
...and it said sweets could be the cause.
ボリ
scratch
ボリ
scratch
I read it could be caused by overeating.
computer
Not Possible...
Then I thought about it...
I don't eat chocolate or ice cream...
Or coffee...
But I can't give up cake!
ばく
chomp
Bread is just like rice... I love bread!
ばく
chomp
And then...

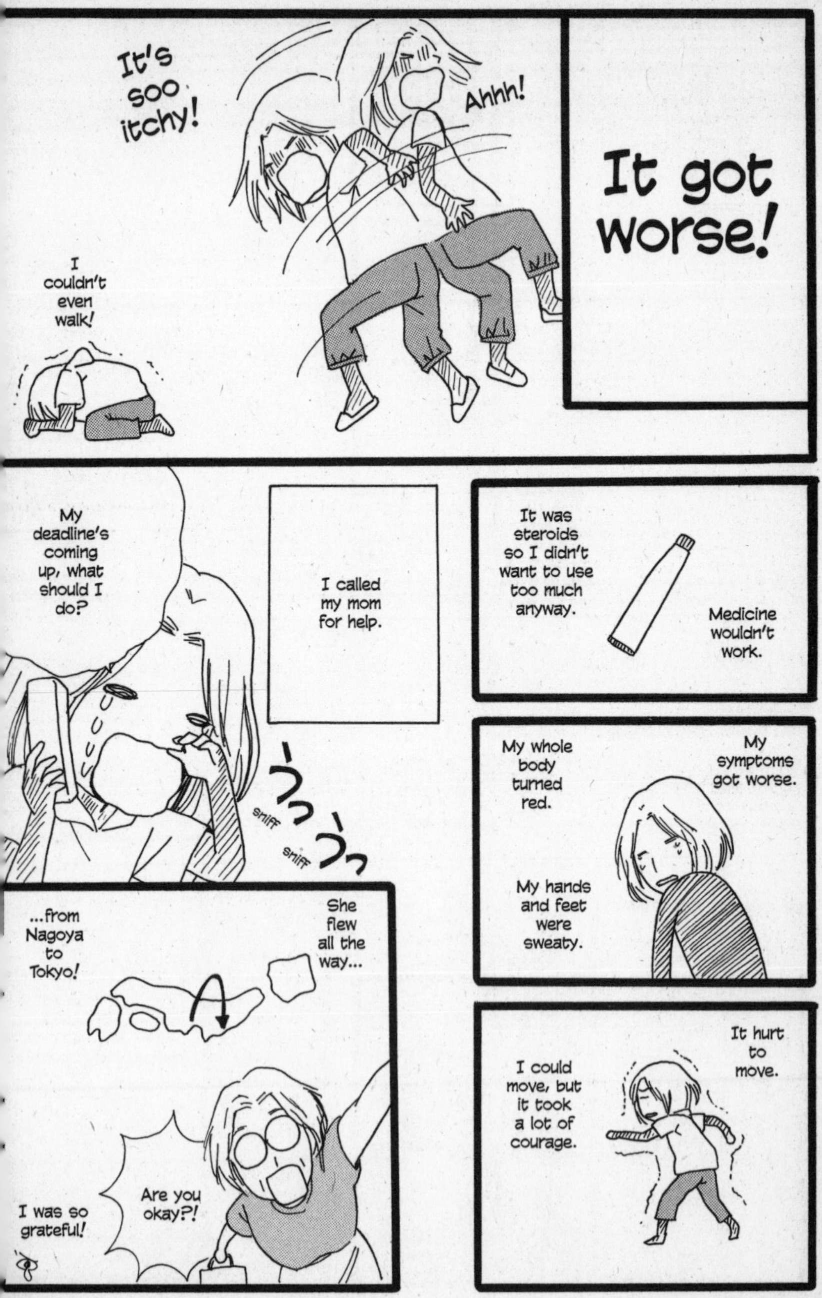
It got worse!
Ahhh!
It's soo itchy!
I couldn't even walk!
Medicine wouldn't work.
It was steroids so I didn't want to use too much anyway.
My symptoms got worse.
My whole body turned red.
My hands and feet were sweaty.
It hurt to move.
I could move, but it took a lot of courage.
I called my mom for help.
うっ
sniff
うっ
sniff
My deadline's coming up, what should I do?
She flew all the way...
...from Nagoya to Tokyo!
Are you okay?!
I was so grateful!

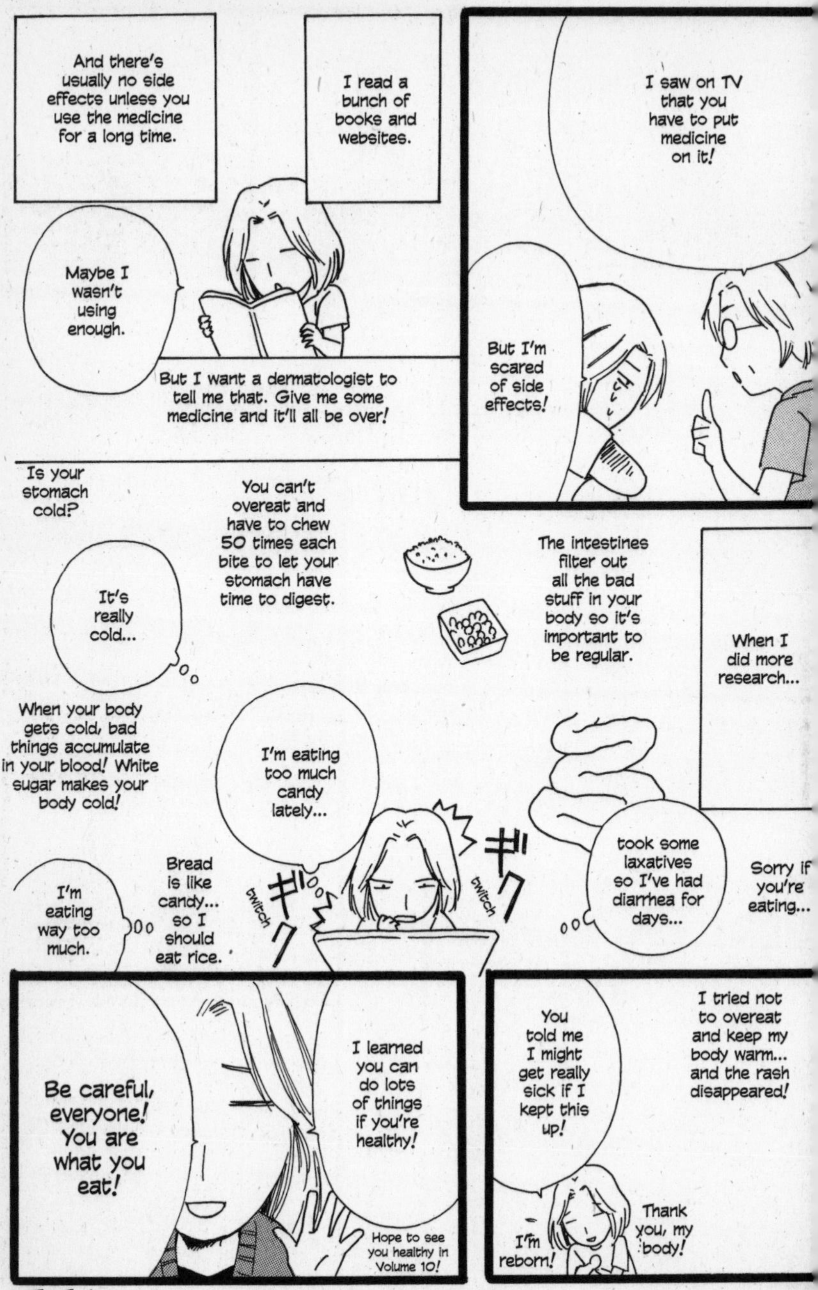
I saw on TV that you have to put medicine on it!
But I'm scared of side effects!
I read a bunch of books and websites.
And there's usually no side effects unless you use the medicine for a long time.
Maybe I wasn't using enough.
But I want a dermatologist to tell me that. Give me some medicine and it'll all be over!
When I did more research...
The intestines filter out all the bad stuff in your body so it's important to be regular.
Sorry if you're eating...
took some laxatives so I've had diarrhea for days...
You can't overeat and have to chew 50 times each bite to let your stomach have time to digest.
ギク
twitch
I'm eating too much candy lately...
ギク
twitch
Is your stomach cold?
It's really cold...
When your body gets cold, bad things accumulate in your blood! White sugar makes your body cold!
Bread is like candy... so I should eat rice.
I'm eating way too much.
I tried not to overeat and keep my body warm... and the rash disappeared!
You told me I might get really sick if I kept this up!
Thank you, my body!
I'm reborn!
I learned you can do lots of things if you're healthy!
Be careful, everyone! You are what you eat!
Hope to see you healthy in Volume 10!

The End

Preview of *Arisa* Volume 10

We're pleased to present you a preview from volume 10. Please check our website, www.kodanshacomics.com, to see when this volume will be available in English! For now you'll have to make do with Japanese!

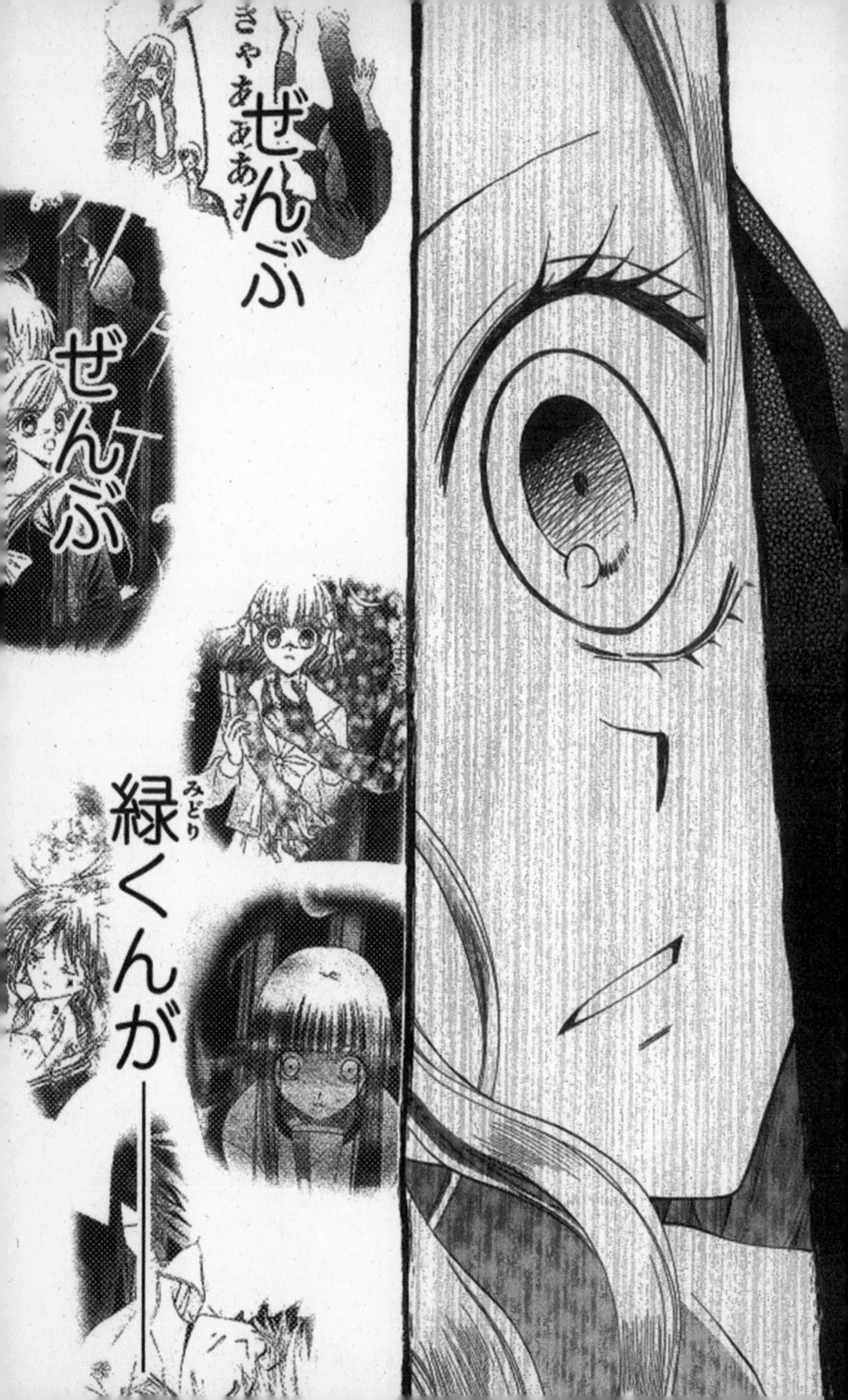
ぜんぶ
きゃあああ
ぜんぶ
緑くんが——

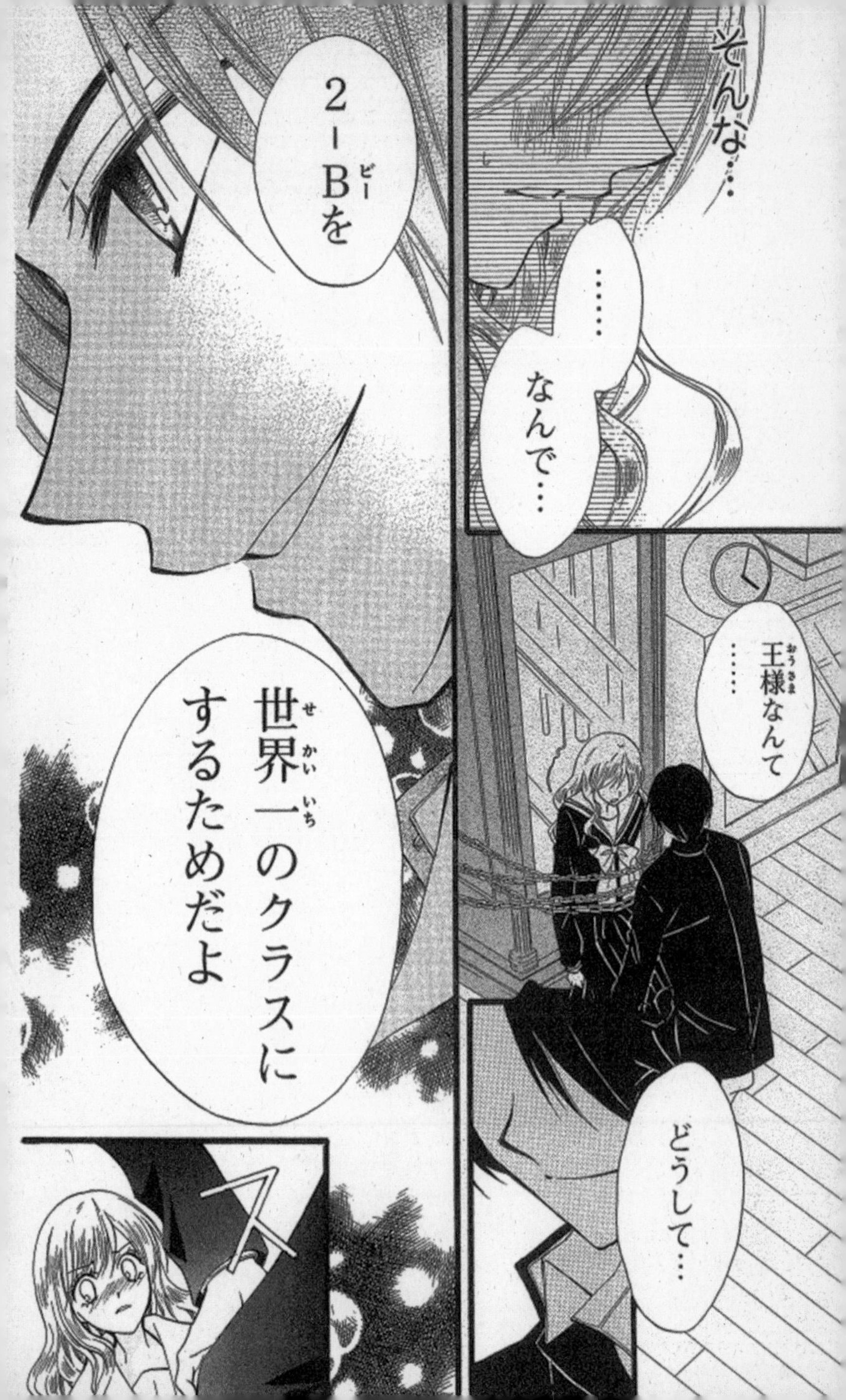
そんな…
……
なんで…
王様なんて……
どうして…
2-Bを
世界一のクラスにするためだよ

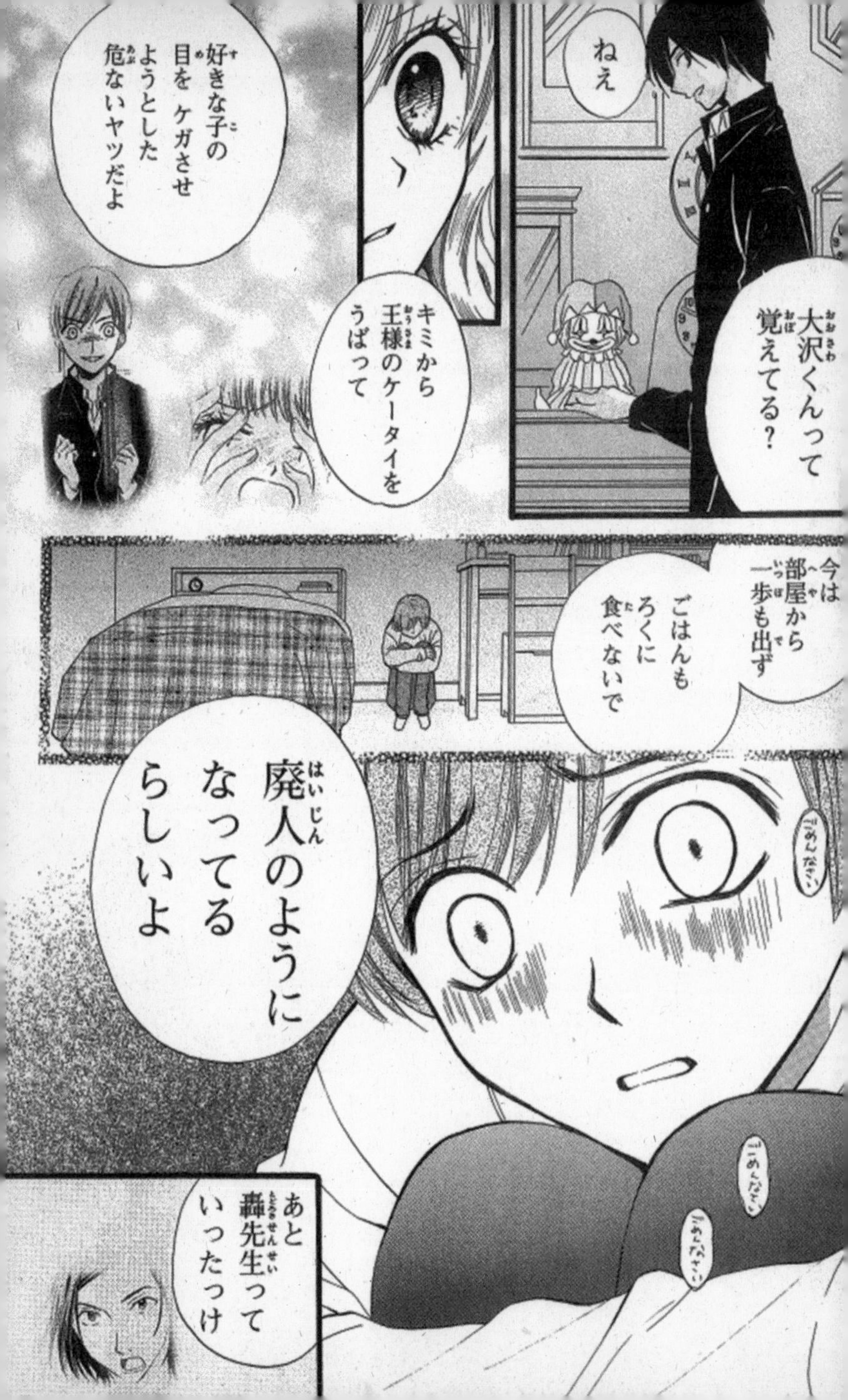

ねえ
大沢くんって覚えてる？
キミから王様のケータイをうばって
好きな子の目を ケガさせようとした危ないヤツだよ
今は部屋から一歩も出ず
ごはんもろくに食べないで
廃人のようになってるらしいよ
ごめんなさい
ごめんなさい
ごめんなさい
あと轟先生っていったっけ

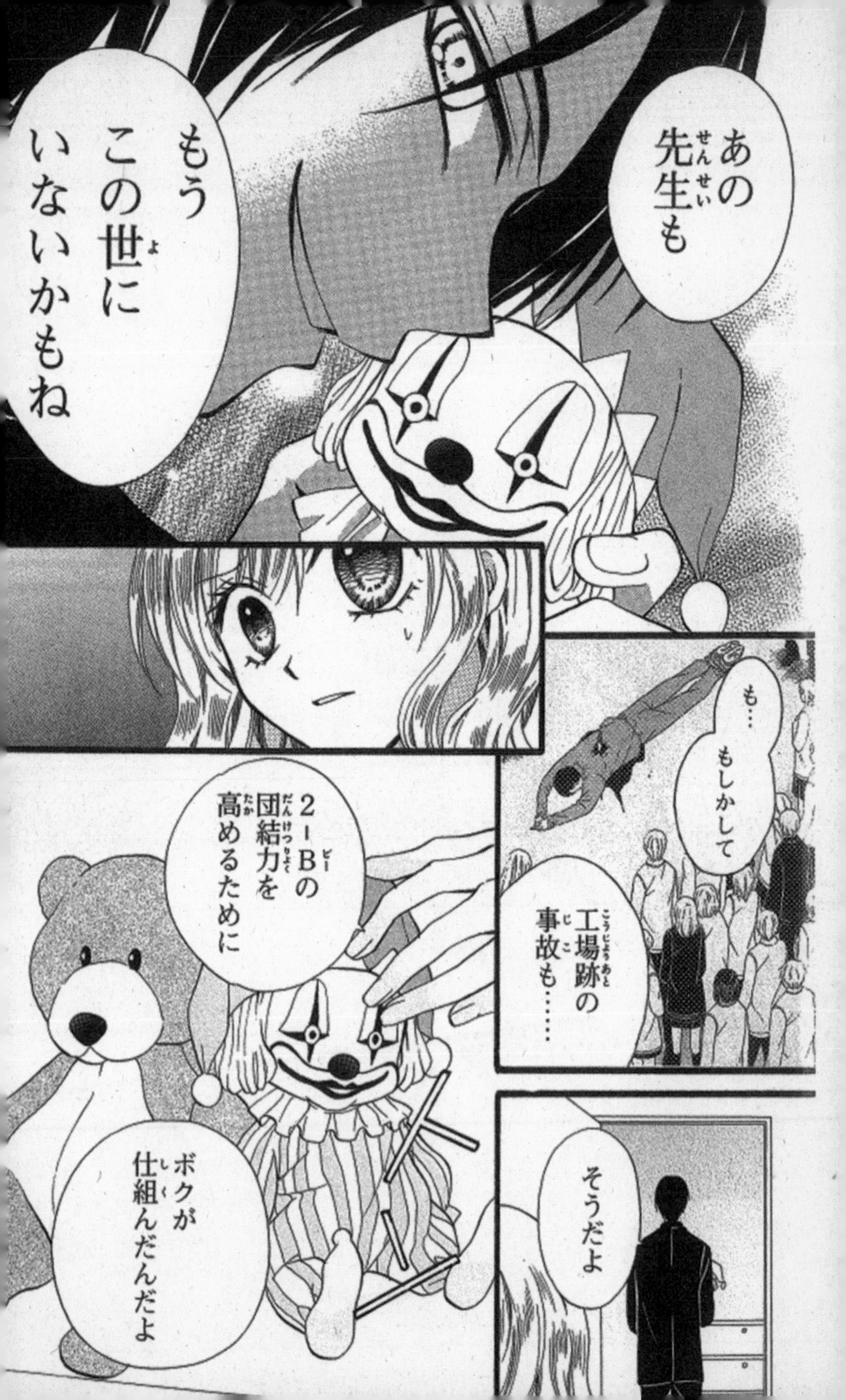
あの先生も
もうこの世にいないかもね
も…もしかして
工場跡の事故も……
そうだよ
2-Bの団結力を高めるために
ボクが仕組んだんだよ

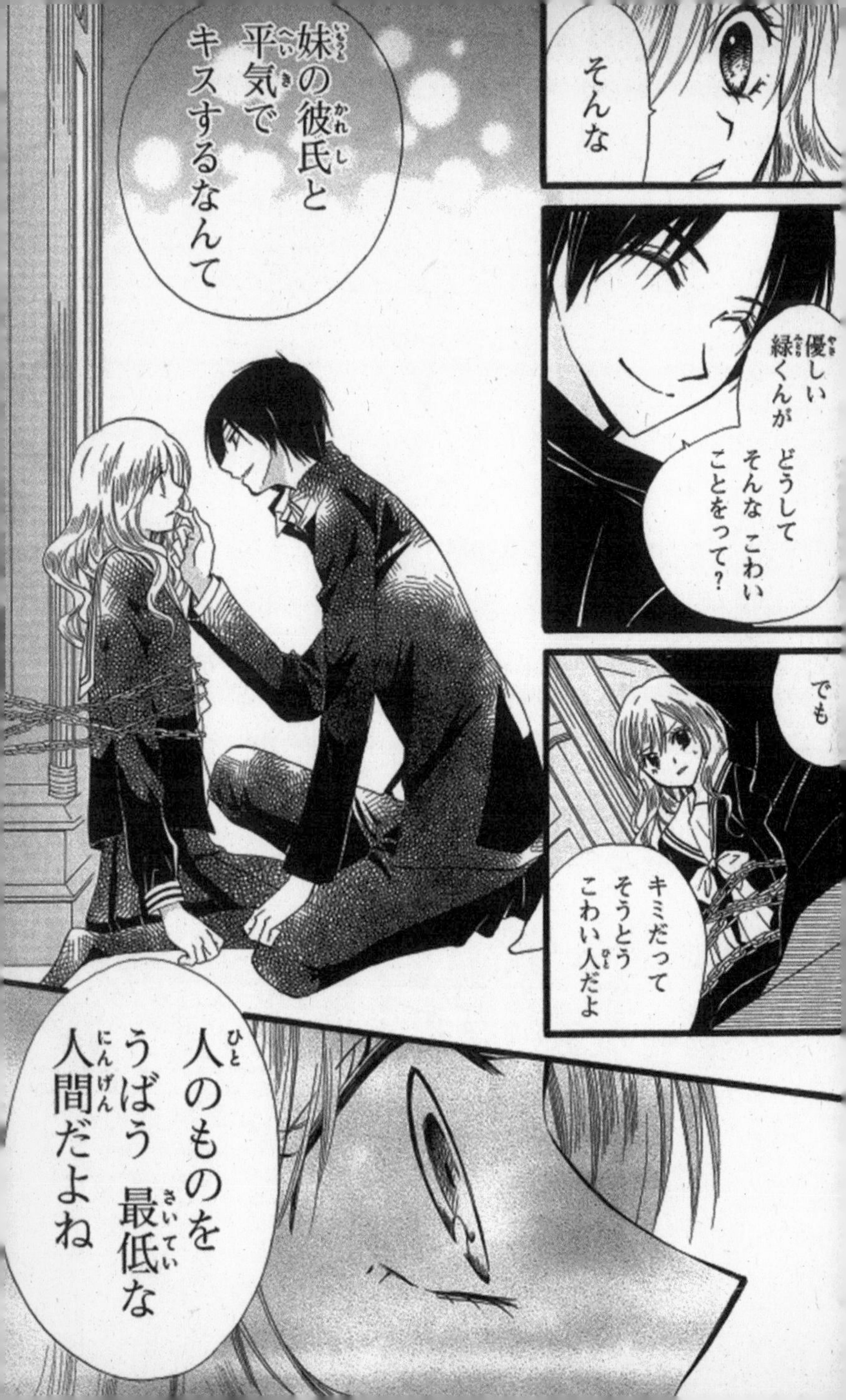
そんな
優しい緑くんが
どうしてそんなこわいことをって?
でも
キミだってそうとうこわい人だよ
妹の彼氏と平気でキスするなんて
人のものをうばう最低な人間だよね

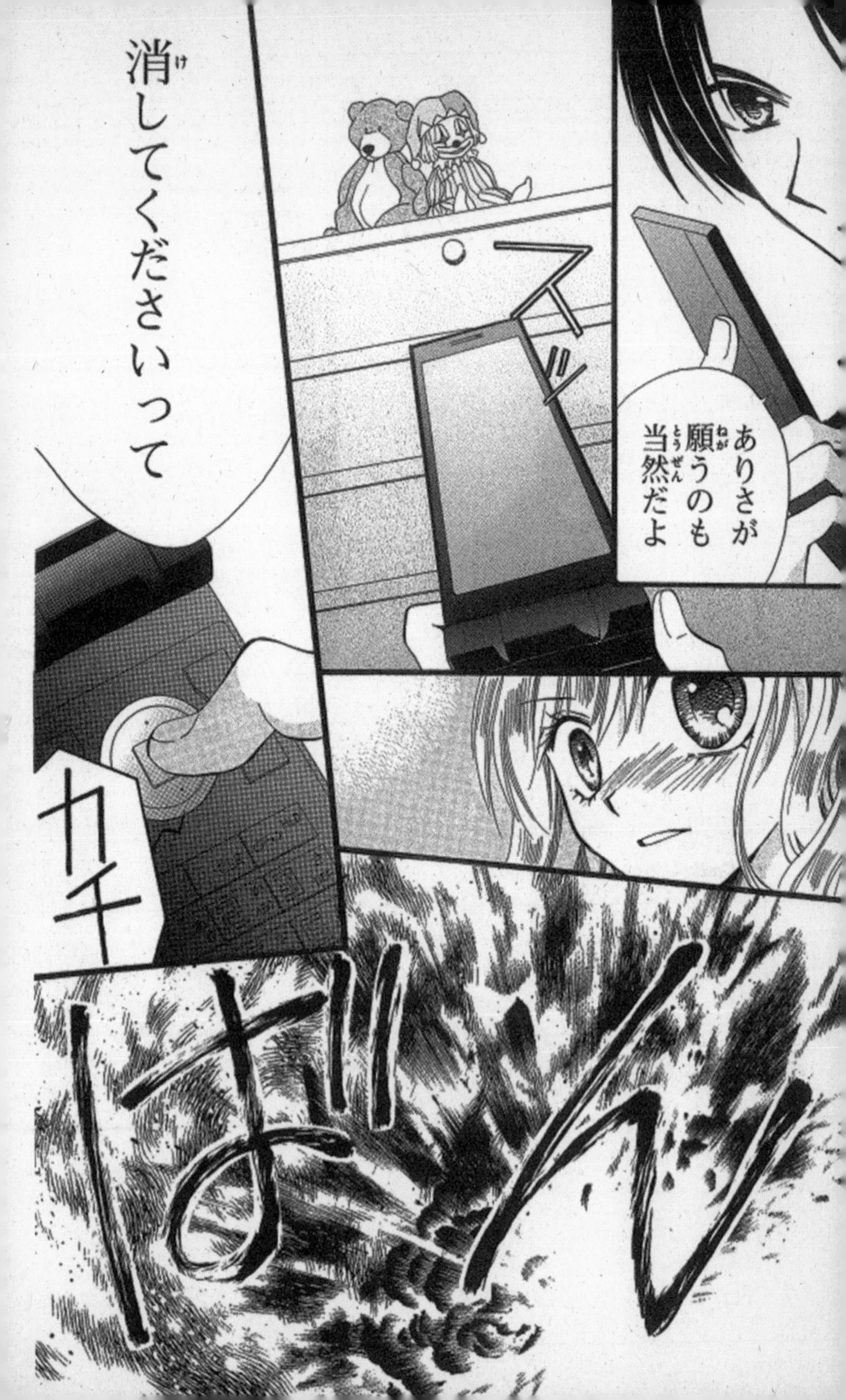
ありさが願うのも当然だよ
スッ
消してくださいって
カチ

The Pretty Guardians are back!

★

Kodansha Comics is proud to present *Sailor Moon* with all new translations.

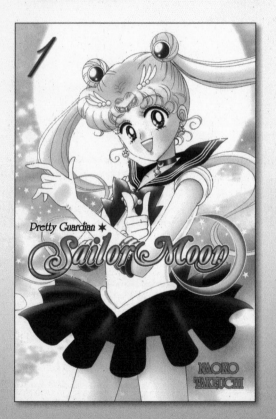

For more information, go to **www.kodanshacomics.com**

Sailor Moon © Naoko Takeuchi / KODANSHA LTD. All rights reserved.

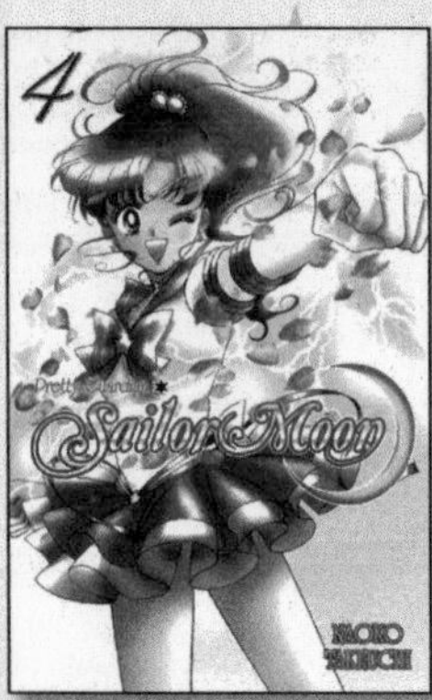
4
Pretty Guardian
Sailor Moon
NAOKO TAKEUCHI

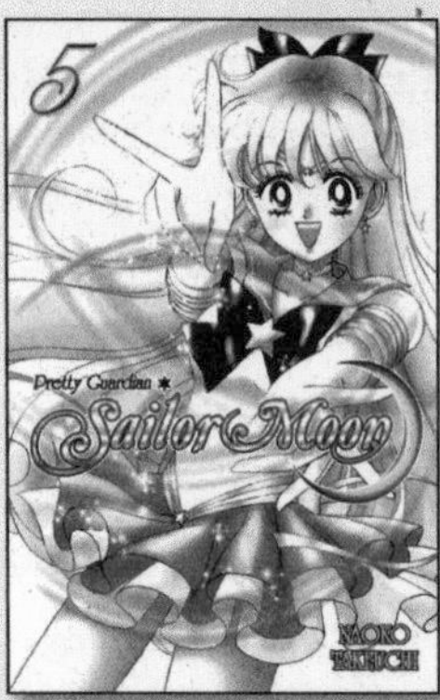
5
Pretty Guardian
Sailor Moon
NAOKO TAKEUCHI

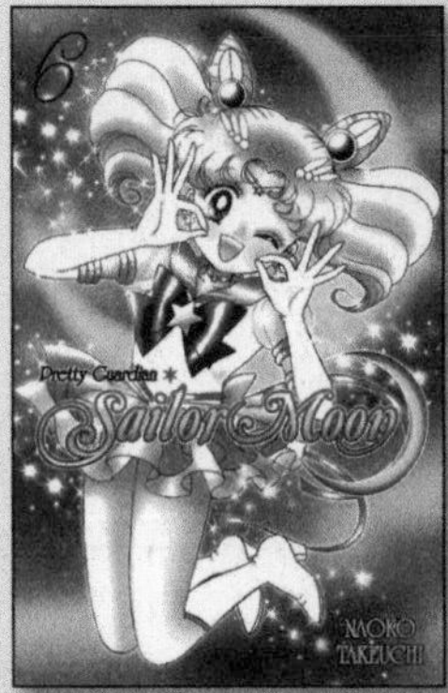
6
Pretty Guardian
Sailor Moon
NAOKO TAKEUCHI

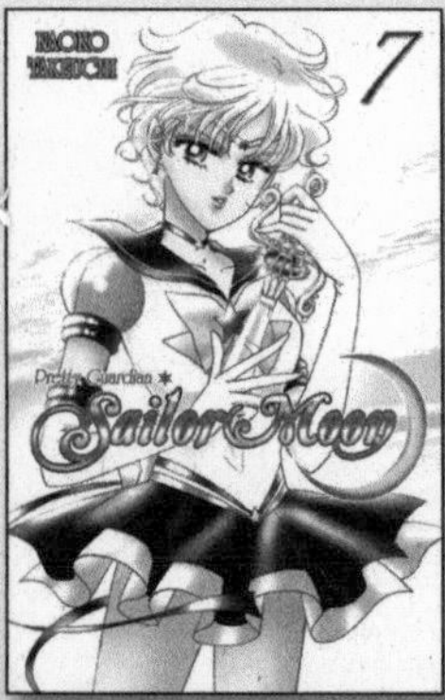
NAOKO TAKEUCHI
7
Pretty Guardian
Sailor Moon

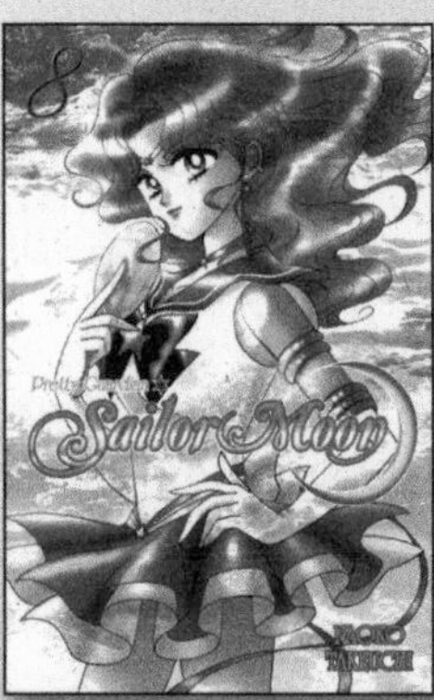
8
Sailor Moon
NAOKO TAKEUCHI

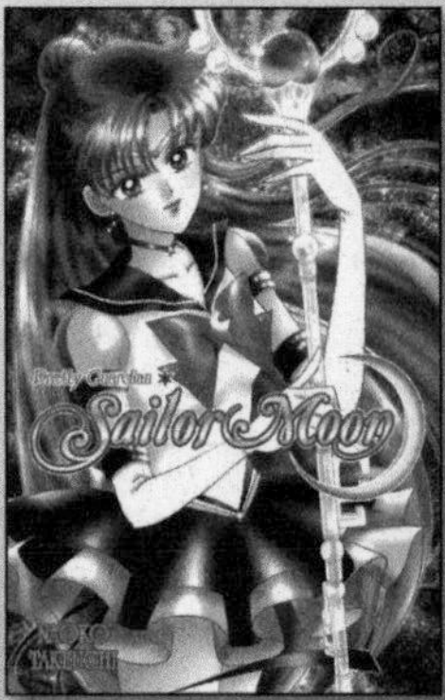
Sailor Moon
NAOKO TAKEUCHI

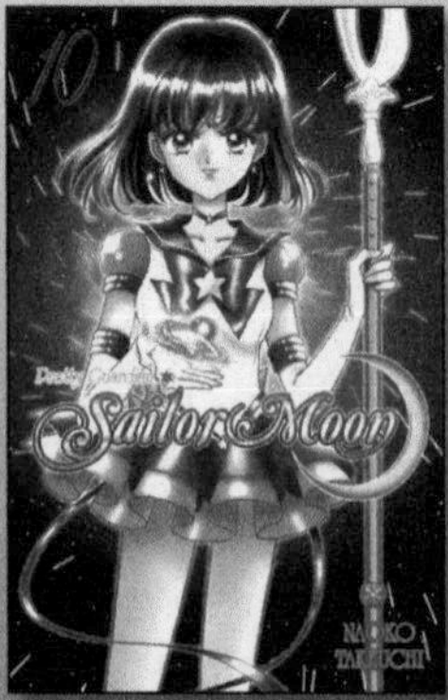
10
Sailor Moon
NAOKO TAKEUCHI

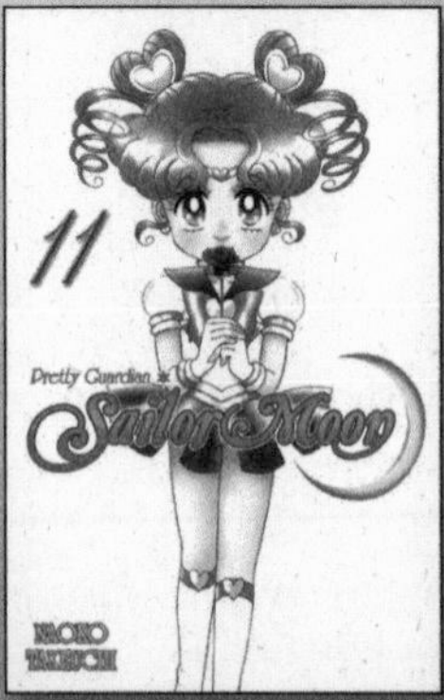
11
Pretty Guardian
Sailor Moon
NAOKO TAKEUCHI

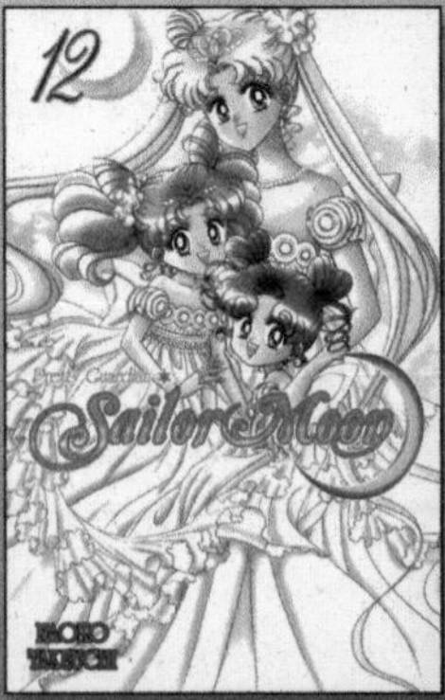
12
Sailor Moon
NAOKO TAKEUCHI

Arisa volume 9 is a work of fiction. Names, characters, places, and incidents are the products of the author's imagination or are used fictitiously. Any resemblance to actual events, locales, or persons, living or dead, is entirely coincidental.

A Kodansha Comics Trade Paperback Original

Arisa volume 9 copyright © 2011 Natsumi Ando
English translation copyright © 2012 Natsumi Ando

All rights reserved.

Published in the United States by Kodansha Comics, an imprint of Kodansha USA Publishing, LLC, New York.

Publication rights for this English edition arranged through Kodansha Ltd., Tokyo.

First published in Japan in 2011 by Kodansha Ltd., Tokyo.

ISBN 978-1-61262-240-8

Printed in the United States of America.

www.kodanshacomics.com

9 8 7 6 5 4 3 2 1

Translator/Adapter: Andria Cheng
Lettering: April Brown

TOMARE!

[STOP!]

You're going the wrong way!

Manga is a completely different type of reading experience.

To start at the *beginning*, go to the *end*!

That's right! Authentic manga is read the traditional Japanese way—from right to left. Exactly the *opposite* of how American books are read. It's easy to follow: Just go to the other end of the book, and read each page—and each panel—from the right side to the left side, starting at the top right. Now you're experiencing manga as it was meant to be!

NO LONGER PROPERTY OF ROANOKE COUNTY LIBRARY